SOCIETY FOR NEW TESTAMENT STUDIES MONOGRAPH SERIES

GENERAL EDITOR
MATTHEW BLACK, D.D., F.B.A.

ASSOCIATE EDITOR
R. McL. WILSON

23

THE GENTILES AND THE GENTILE MISSION IN LUKE-ACTS

THE GENTILES AND
THE GENTILE MISSION
IN LUKE-ACTS

STEPHEN G. WILSON

Assistant Professor of New Testament
Carleton University, Ottawa

CAMBRIDGE
AT THE UNIVERSITY PRESS
1973

CAMBRIDGE UNIVERSITY PRESS
Cambridge, New York, Melbourne, Madrid, Cape Town, Singapore, São Paulo

Cambridge University Press
The Edinburgh Building, Cambridge CB2 2RU, UK

Published in the United States of America by Cambridge University Press, New York

www.cambridge.org
Information on this title: www.cambridge.org/9780521201346

First published 1973
This digitally printed first paperback version 2005

A catalogue record for this publication is available from the British Library

Library of Congress Catalogue Card Number: 72–90489

ISBN-13 978-0-521-20134-6 hardback
ISBN-10 0-521-20134-9 hardback

ISBN-13 978-0-521-01869-2 paperback
ISBN-10 0-521-01869-2 paperback

To my Father
and in memory of my Mother

CONTENTS

ABBREVIATIONS

ARW	*Archiv für Religionswissenschaft*, Leipzig.
Bauer	W. Bauer, *A Greek–English Lexicon of the New Testament and other early Christian Literature*, Eng. trans. ed. by W. F. Arndt and F. W. Gingrich, Cambridge, 1957.
B.C.	*The Beginnings of Christianity*, vols. I–III ed. by F. J. Foakes-Jackson and K. Lake, London, 1920–6; vols. IV–V ed. K. Lake and H. J. Cadbury, London, 1933.
Bib.	*Biblica*, Rome.
BJRL	*Bulletin of the John Rylands Library*, Manchester.
Blass–Debrunner	F. Blass and A. Debrunner, *A Greek Grammar of the New Testament and other Early Christian Writings*, translated and edited by R. W. Funk, Cambridge, 1961.
BNTC	Black's New Testament Commentaries, London.
BZ	*Biblische Zeitschrift*, Freiburg.
BZNW	Beihefte zur *ZNW*, Giessen–Berlin.
CBQ	*Catholic Biblical Quarterly*, Washington.
EMZ	*Evangelische Missionszeitschrift*, Stuttgart.
ET	*Expository Times*, Edinburgh.
Ev. Th.	*Evangelische Theologie*, Munich.
Expos.	*Expositor*, London.
FRLANT	Forschungen zur Religion und Literatur des Alten und Neuen Testaments, Göttingen.
HNT	Handbuch zum Neuen Testament, Tübingen.
HTR	*Harvard Theological Review*, Cambridge, Massachusetts.
IM	*In Memoriam E. Lohmeyer*, Stuttgart, 1951.
JBL	*Journal of Biblical Literature*, Philadelphia, Pennsylvania.
JTS	*Journal of Theological Studies*, Oxford.
KEK	Kritisch-exegetische Kommentar über das Neue Testament, Göttingen.
Liddell and Scott	H. G. Liddell and R. Scott, *A Greek–English Lexicon* (rev. ed. H. S. Jones), Oxford, 1940.
Moulton and Milligan	J. H. Moulton and G. Milligan, *The Vocabulary of the Greek New Testament*, London, 1930.
Nov. Test.	*Novum Testamentum*, Leiden.
NS	*Neutestamentliche Studien für R. Bultmann*, Berlin, 1957.
NTD	Das Neue Testament Deutsch, Göttingen.
NTE	*New Testament Essays*, Studies in Memory of T. W. Manson, ed. A. J. B. Higgins, Manchester, 1959.
NTS	*New Testament Studies*, Cambridge.
RHPhR	*Revue d'Histoire et de Philosophie Religieuses*, Strasbourg–Paris.
S.B.	H. L. Strack and P. Billerbeck, *Kommentar zum Neuen Testament aus Talmud und Midrasch*, 4 vols., Munich, 1922–8.
SBU	*Symbolae Biblicae Upsalienses*, Uppsala.

SE	*Studia Evangelica*, ed. F. L. Cross (*TU*), Berlin.
SG	*Studies in the Gospels; Essays in Memory of R. H. Lightfoot*, ed. D. E. Nineham, Oxford, 1955.
SJT	*Scottish Journal of Theology*, Edinburgh.
SLA	*Studies in Luke–Acts*, Essays in Honour of P. Schubert, ed. L. E. Keck and J. L. Martyn, London, 1968.
SNTS	*Bulletin of the Studiorum Novi Testamenti Societas*, i–iii, Oxford, 1950–2.
SP	*Studia Paulina in Honorem J. de Zwaan*, Haarlem, 1953.
St. Th.	*Studia Theologica*, Lund.
Theol.	*Theology*, London.
THNT	Theologischer Handkommentar zum Neuen Testament, Göttingen.
Th. Rund.	*Theologische Rundschau*, Tübingen.
Th. Viat.	*Theologia Viatorum*, Berlin.
TLZ	*Theologische Literaturzeitung*, Leipzig–Berlin.
TU	*Texte und Untersuchungen zur Geschichte der altchristlichen Literatur*, Berlin.
TWNT	*Theological Dictionary of the New Testament*, ed. G. Kittel and G. Friedrich, vols. 1–4, London, 1964ff.; vols. 5ff., *Theologisches Wörterbuch zum Neuen Testament*, ed. G. Kittel and G. Friedrich, Stuttgart, 1955f.
TZ	*Theologische Zeitschrift*, Basle.
UNT	Untersuchungen zum Neuen Testament, ed. H. Windisch, Leipzig.
WMANT	Wissenschaftliche Monographien zum Alten und Neuen Testament, Neukirchen.
ZKG	*Zeitschrift für Kirchengeschichte*, Stuttgart.
ZNW	*Zeitschrift für die Neutestamentliche Wissenschaft*, Berlin.
ZTK	*Zeitschrift für Theologie und Kirche*, Tübingen.

PREFACE

This book is based substantially on a Ph.D. thesis which was accepted by Durham University in 1969. Some sections remain unaltered, while others have been considerably abbreviated. The footnotes have been trimmed as much as possible, which has involved referring to only a selection of the rapidly increasing flood of secondary literature.

The aim of the book is to use the results from a detailed study of Luke's treatment of the Gentile theme to assess modern approaches to the interrelated problems of the theology and historical reliability of Luke–Acts. While I have often disagreed with them, I should like to record my debt to Professors H. Conzelmann and E. Haenchen, whom I have never met in person, but whose writings have been a constant source of stimulation.

It is with the greatest pleasure that I take this opportunity to express my gratitude to Professor C. K. Barrett of Durham University, who has watched over this work at every stage. He has been an unfailing source of information, patient advice, intellectual stimulation and warm friendship. I should also like to thank the Rev. D. P. Davies of St David's College, Lampeter, and Professor R. McL. Wilson of St Andrews University, both of whom made valuable suggestions for improvement which have been incorporated into the final version. Finally, my thanks are due to my wife, whose support and encouragement have been essential for the production of this work.

S. G. WILSON

CHAPTER I

JESUS AND THE GENTILES

This brief discussion of Jesus' attitude towards the Gentiles is by way of a preliminary to the main theme of the book. It is included for two main reasons: first, it provides us with the primary attitude towards the Gentiles, with which later developments can be compared; and second, it gives us a key both to Jesus' teaching on eschatology and to the relationship between the themes of the Gentiles and eschatology. In the course of our discussion we shall be faced with two conflicting strands of evidence. This has inevitably led to strong suspicions about the authenticity of one or other strand, or even of both. We shall discuss first, therefore, the material which can reasonably be said to be authentic, to see whether it gives a uniform picture. The more controversial texts will be left till last, so that they can be discussed in relation to the overall picture gained from the other material. Further, it should be noted that two distinct questions are in mind throughout this chapter: first, what was Jesus' attitude towards the Gentiles and second, the more specific question, did he foresee a historical Gentile mission?

BACKGROUND

A complete treatment of the Gentiles in Jesus' teaching would involve a full discussion of the theme of mission in the Old Testament and Judaism. However, the majority of recent authors have reached similar and, as far as one can see, correct conclusions. A short summary of the conclusions relevant to our study, therefore, will suffice at this point.

First, one must distinguish in the Old Testament between universalism and mission. The former notion asserts that God is Lord of all the earth, including all the nations other than Israel, but it does not imply that Israel has any responsibility for evangelising other peoples. The idea that God is Lord of all creation may be an essential presupposition for universal mission, but the idea of mission is not, at least for the Old Testament, a logical implicate of universalism.

The classic expression of the Old Testament's most consistent positive approach to the nations is found in Is. 2: 2–4 (Mal. 4: 1–4. Cf. Is. 18: 7; Jer. 3: 17, 16: 19; Is. 45: 18–25, 60: 1f; Zeph. 3: 8–11; Hag. 2: 6–9; Zech. 2: 10–13, 14: 16). The idea is that of the nations' pilgrimage to Zion in the last days, when they will witness the glory of Yahweh mediated in and expressed through his relationship with Israel. In all these passages the important elements are the following: first, in all of them Israel is the centre of attention; it is Yahweh's relationship with her that the nations see and respond to. Second, none of them speak of a missionary role of Israel; rather, it is emphasised that the influx of the nations is a result solely of the intervention of Yahweh. Third, a point related to the last one, the view of history implied in these passages is centripetal rather than centrifugal; Israel does not go out to reach the nations, but the nations come to Jerusalem to witness God's dealings with Israel. Finally, it should be noted that most of these passages see these events as occurring in the End-time and not before. The two main places to which people point when they wish to prove that the Old Testament has a concept of mission, namely Jonah and Second Isaiah, in fact add nothing new in terms of mission to the picture gained from the passages already quoted.

In later Judaism the notion of the eschatological pilgrimage of the nations is retained, but it plays a less important role (Tob. 13: 13; Sib. Or. III, 716f, 772f; Test. Ben. 9: 2; I En. 10: 21, 48: 5, 53: 1, 90: 33; Ps. Sol. 17: 31; IV Ezr. 13: 12f). In apocalyptic writings and the Qumran literature there is no evidence for the idea of winning over the Gentiles; the opposite hope, namely for their destruction, is far more prominent. Even in the Rabbinic tradition, for example among the Shammaites, a negative attitude is found.

The more positive proselytising efforts of Judaism, while in some respects paving the way for the later Christian mission, are to be distinguished from the concept of mission as it developed in the early Church. The Jewish approach to the heathen was basically a matter of private enterprise undertaken by individuals; it did not spring from a belief that the community as a whole had a responsibility for all mankind. Nor was there any consciousness of a special divine commission for this task. Also, the eschatological basis of the Gentiles' conversion, which was so important for Jesus and the early Church, played no role in the efforts of Judaism. Finally, they were limited by a nationalistic approach, since for them there was an inseparable connection between religion and national custom – an attitude from which, if at first a little reluctantly, the early Church did eventually break free.[1]

THE EVIDENCE

We turn first to a passage whose authenticity is rarely doubted, namely Matt. 8: 11 (Lk. 13: 28). There are several factors which support its authenticity: the Semitic style,[2] Aramaisms,[3] and the Jewish thought-mode, namely the ideas of the Messianic banquet and of the damned seeing the blessed.[4] The πολλοί here are clearly the Gentiles, since they are contrasted with the 'sons of the kingdom', that is, the Jews (Matt. 11: 19). The time reference is, however, disputed. Some scholars make the improbable suggestion that it refers to the present reality of Jesus' ministry.[5] F. Hahn claims that the reference is not merely to 'the future, but that the future and present aspects are bound up together', and he points to Lk. 12: 8 for support.[6] But

---

[1] For further information on this subject the reader is referred to J. Jeremias, *Jesus' Promise to the Nations* (London, 1965), pp. 11–19; F. Hahn, *Mission in the New Testament* (London, 1965), pp. 18–25; D. Bosch, *Die Heidenmission in der Zukunftschau Jesu* (Zürich, 1959), pp. 17–43; J. Munck, *Paul and the Salvation of Mankind* (London, 1959), pp. 264–72; R. Martin-Achard, *A Light to the Nations* (London, 1962), pp. 8f; A. Alt, 'Die Deutung der Weltgeschichte im Alten Testament', *ZTK*, 56 (1959), 129f; R. Davidson, 'Universalism in Second Isaiah', *SJT*, 16 (1963), 166f; K. G. Kuhn, 'Das Problem der Mission in der Urchristenheit', *EMZ*, 11 (1954), 163f.

[2] Matthew has antithetic parallelism and Luke an adverbial clause and parataxis.

[3] Jeremias, *Promise*, pp. 55f. We do not assume, as Jeremias often does, that the presence of Aramaisms or Semitic structure in a saying means that we are dealing with the *ipsissima vox Jesu*. Clearly they could be the creation of the Aramaic-speaking Church. However, such arguments can be used as a tool – one of the few objective ones we have – for hinting at the reliability of a passage.   [4] IV Ezr. 7: 38; *S.B.*, II, pp. 228f.

[5] H. A. Guy, *The New Testament Doctrine of the Last Things* (London, 1948), p. 47; H. Sharman, *Son of Man and Kingdom of God* (London, 1944), p. 128.

[6] Hahn, *Mission*, p. 34 n. 2.

although it is true that there is evidence for speaking of realised eschatology in Jesus' teaching, this cannot justify Hahn's combination and confusion of present and future aspects. That they can be combined is true, but future references remain future references. The reference in this verse is clearly to a future apocalyptic event.[1] This is shown by the presence of the patriarchs, the irrevocable judgement on the sons of the kingdom, the future tenses of the verbs, and the traditional apocalyptic themes of the Messianic banquet and the outer darkness.

We note in conclusion the following points: the privileged position of Israel is challenged; the Gentiles will definitely be included in the kingdom; and the reference is unequivocally to an apocalyptic as against a historical future.

Similar ideas, with some variations, are to be found in several other passages. First, the woes on the Galilean towns (Matt. 11: 20-4, 10: 15; Lk. 10: 13-15, 10: 12). There are no convincing grounds for regarding these words as unauthentic.[2] In the milieu of first-century Palestine they are particularly striking, since in the Old Testament Tyre and Sidon were seen as the epitome of heathen sin and pride (Ezek. 26-8) and Sodom and Gomorrah as the scene of the vilest heathen practices (Gen. 13-18). The reference is explicitly to an eschatological future, the day of Judgement. The exact implication for the fate of these Gentile towns is not clear, since all that is said is that they will fare better than those who refuse Jesus, which is not saying much!

Second, there is the saying about the sign of Jonah (Mk 8: 11-12; Matt. 12: 38-42; Lk. 11: 29-32). The original form of this saying is probably to be found in Matt. 12: 39, Lk. 11: 29, and the point of comparison between Jesus and Jonah is best interpreted as referring to their preaching of repentance in the face of impending doom.[3] But whichever version and interpreta-

---

[1] Jeremias, *Promise*, p. 55; W. G. Kümmel, *Promise and Fulfilment* (London, 1961), p. 85.

[2] Despite R. Bultmann, *The History of the Synoptic Tradition* (Oxford, 1963), p. 112.

[3] Kümmel, *Promise*, p. 68; and similarly H. Tödt, *The Son of Man in the Synoptic Tradition* (London, 1965), p. 53; Hahn, *Mission*, p. 36; Jeremias, *Promise*, p. 50; V. Taylor, *The Gospel according to St Mark* (London, 1952), pp. 361-3; T. W. Manson, *The Sayings of Jesus* (London, 1950), p. 90. For other views see the discussion in Kümmel, *ibid.*; A. J. B. Higgins, *Jesus and the Son of Man* (London, 1964), pp. 134f.

tion is taken as original, there is nothing to justify the suggestion that the point of comparison between Jesus and Jonah is that they both preached to the Gentiles.[1] For even if we claim that Jesus foresaw a Gentile mission, there is no evidence that he preached to the Gentiles. Jesus as the preacher of judgement is the sign and not Jesus as the preacher to the Gentiles. The only reference to the Gentiles, therefore, is in the statement that they will judge the Jews – another startling, direct reversal of Jewish expectation.

Third, there is the parable of the sheep and the goats (Matt. 25: 31–46). Most of the objections to the authenticity of this parable,[2] even if sustained, in fact reveal no more than that there has been a certain amount of linguistic and christological recasting by Matthew; they do not affect the substance of the parable. It is the identification of πάντα τὰ ἔθνη (v. 32) and τῶν ἀδελφῶν μου τῶν ἐλαχίστων (v. 40, 45) which concerns us. The latter phrase is particularly obscure: ἀδελφός, when used figuratively, refers either to the disciples (Matt. 28: 10; Mk 3: 33 pars.) or to fellow Israelites (Matt. 5: 22f, 7: 3f, 18: 35; cf. Gen. 9: 5; Lev. 19: 15); but it is at any rate probably an addition in v. 40, since it is lacking in v. 45. No other Synoptic passage uses ἐλάχιστος to describe people, but it probably refers to all those in need rather than to a more exclusive group like the disciples.[3] The phrase πάντα τὰ ἔθνη refers either to the Gentiles,[4] or to all peoples,[5] rather than to Christians.[6] The time reference of the parable is wholly futuristic and while there is a positive hope for some Gentiles there is a negative judgement in store for some of them. According to the parable, the Gentiles will be judged on the assumption that they have not heard the gospel, since they are unaware that they are acting for or against Jesus. This suggests that Jesus did not foresee a historical Gentile mission.

[1] C. J. Cadoux, *The Historical Mission of Jesus* (London, 1943), p. 153.

[2] Bultmann, *Tradition*, p. 124.

[3] J. Jeremias, *The Parables of Jesus* (London, 1963), p. 206; F. V. Filson, *The Gospel according to St Matthew* (London, 1960), p. 267; T. Preiss, *Life in Christ* (London, 1954), p. 52.

[4] Jeremias, *Parables*, pp. 206, 209. Cf. Matt. 6: 32, 10: 5, 20: 19.

[5] G. Bornkamm, *Tradition and Interpretation in Matthew* (London, 1963), pp. 23–4. Cf. Matt. 24: 9, 14, 28: 19.

[6] Kümmel, *Promise*, p. 94.

There are other passages where a reference to the Gentiles is possible but not probable. In each case, if the reference is allowed, it is fully in accord with the material already discussed. The first of these is the parable of the lamp, a parable which the evangelists interpret differently probably because they did not know its original setting (Mk 4: 21; Matt. 5: 15; Lk. 8: 16, 11: 33f). Both T. W. Manson and J. Jeremias see a reference to the Gentiles – Manson through the use of Is. 42: 6 and Jeremias through the idea of God's eschatological light shining forth from Zion, which is a call to the nations to come.[1] However, the link with Is. 42: 6 is only through the one word 'light', and there is no evidence that λύχνος was exclusively an eschatological term for Jesus or that he would have connected it with the Gentiles. If there is a reference to the Gentiles, then it is to their inclusion in the future kingdom of God.

Manson and Jeremias also see a reference to the Gentiles in the parable of the mustard seed (Mk 4: 30–2 pars.) in the reference to birds, since in Jewish literature birds can mean Gentiles (Ps. 104: 2; I En. 90: 33) and in the eschatological term κατασκηνοῦν, which is sometimes used of Gentiles seeking refuge in the city of God (Joseph and Aseneth, 15).[2] However both of these arguments are extremely tenuous, especially the latter, and it is unlikely that Jesus would have expected his audience to pick up such obscure references. We can only say, with C. H. Dodd,[3] that 'maybe the Gentiles are included too', and note that if they are, the time reference is to the future kingdom of God.

A further parable in which a reference to the Gentiles has been seen is that of the marriage feast (Matt. 22: 1–10; Lk. 14: 16–24). F. Hahn notes that while there is no direct reference to the Gentiles, nevertheless, since all the traditional barriers are broken down, 'the Church has with good reason related the text to the mission'.[4] D. Bosch wants to go further, and he gives an analysis of the details of the parable in terms of Jesus' prediction of the exact development of mission in the early Church.[5] If one

---

[1] Manson, *Sayings*, pp. 92–3; Jeremias, *Promise*, p. 67.
[2] Manson, *Sayings*, p. 123; Jeremias, *Promise*, p. 68.
[3] C. H. Dodd, *The Parables of the Kingdom* (London, 1961, 2nd ed.), p. 191.
[4] Hahn, *Mission*, pp. 35–6.
[5] Bosch, *Heidenmission*, pp. 124f.

accepted his interpretation, however, one could only conclude that the Church's experience has so coloured the narrative that Jesus' original meaning has been lost. If, as is just possible, Jesus did refer to the Gentiles, we would suggest that it was along the lines of Matt. 8: 11–12, namely as part of his teaching about the Messianic banquet.

Another group of sayings which are relevant to this theme are those in which a universal statement is made, but without any specific mention of the Gentiles (Mk 10: 45, 12: 9, 14: 24 pars.). The authenticity of each saying has been questioned with a certain amount of plausibility, but for the sake of argument we shall use them as genuine sayings of Jesus to see what, if they are authentic, they tell us about his attitude towards the Gentiles.[1] The crucial phrase in each verse is left undefined by Mark, but appears to include a reference to the Gentiles.[2] In

[1] Mk 12: 9b is most suspect, since Jesus' answer (v. 9b) to his own question (v. 9a) is a phenomenon unparalleled in the Gospels (Dodd, *Parables*, pp. 94–5; Jeremias, *Parables*, pp. 71–2). It does not, as Dodd thinks, merely state the obvious, since the only obvious answer is that the wicked servants would be condemned. The alteration of Mk 12: 8 in Matt. 21: 39, Lk. 20: 15 (cf. Heb. 13: 12) and the reference to the 'beloved son' are secondary. But the arguments for regarding the whole parable as a creation of the early Church are not compelling: see Bultmann, *Tradition*, pp. 177, 205; Kümmel, *Promise*, p. 83; E. Lohmeyer, *Das Evangelium des Markus*, (Göttingen, 1951), p. 244. It is particularly odd that the same authors complain on the one hand that the parable is too close to the actual events (i.e. of Jesus' death), and on the other hand that it is too far from them (i.e. in the parable the wicked servants are punished for the death of the son, whereas in the Gospels the Jews are punished because they reject, and not because they murder, God's son). Mark 10: 45 is sometimes seen as a dogmatic construct of the Church (Bultmann, *Tradition*, pp. 148f; Tödt, *Son of Man*, pp. 206–8) but the reasons given are not compelling. Mark 14: 24 may well not preserve the original form of the cup saying (cf. Kümmel, *Promise*, pp. 73f, and G. Bornkamm, 'Herrenmahl und Kirche bei Paulus', *ZTK*, 53 (1956), 327f, who argue for the originality of I Cor. 11: 25), although J. Jeremias has argued in great detail for its originality (*The Eucharistic Words of Jesus* (London, 1966), pp. 160f).

[2] Since Mk 12: 2f seem to refer to the Jews as a whole (cf. Is. 5: 1–2), it is unlikely that the ἄλλοι are the poor (Jeremias, *Parables*, p. 76) or the Twelve (Dodd, *Parables*, p. 97). The reference seems to be to the Gentiles. Jeremias, *Words*, pp. 179f, has argued convincingly that πολλοί reflects a Semitism which can mean 'all' as well as 'many' and that the former meaning is intended here. If we take πολλοί to mean 'all' then it would naturally include the Gentiles. For further discussion see C. K. Barrett, 'The background of Mk 10: 45', *NTE*, pp. 2f.

each case the universal reference is linked closely with Jesus' death and will come into effect only after this event.[1]

The key, we would suggest, which best opens for us the temporal reference of these verses is Mk 14: 25, since as we have seen all these passages have a similar type of universal reference – undefined and connected with Jesus' death – and Mk 14: 25 is linked closely with one of them. Assuming that Mk 14: 25 is the original form of this logion,[2] we must try to discover the exact future reference of this vow.[3] A. Schweitzer claims that because Jesus expected the Messianic era to be forced in by his death, he also expected to eat the Messianic meal with his disciples on the first Easter Sunday.[4] W. G. Kümmel is more cautious and suggests that although the limitation of the vow implies a near End, one cannot say exactly how near.[5] Whichever of these interpretations is correct, but accepting that if any interval is expected it is to be a short one, this verse has important repercussions for the sayings concerning the πολλοί. For example, R. Liechtenhahn thinks Mk 14: 24 signifies the hour when the Gentile mission was born, in that now the proclamation to the Gentiles, in a historical sense, can begin.[6] D. Bosch, while not agreeing with Liechtenhahn, treats Jesus' death as one of the necessary presuppositions (the others are the Resurrection and Pentecost) for the apostolic proclamation to the Gentiles.[7] However, both of these views are ruled out by our

---

[1] That is, taking as original in the parable in Mk 12: 1–9 a reference to three servants, the third, who is killed, being Jesus himself.

[2] Kümmel, *Promise*, p. 30; Jeremias, *Words*, pp. 160f.

[3] Jeremias, *Words*, pp. 207f, has argued convincingly that this is a vow. He thinks that Jesus did not drink from the cup, but even if he did the saying could still be a vow.

[4] A. Schweitzer, *The Quest of the Historical Jesus* (London, 1954), pp. 377–8, 318.

[5] Kümmel, *Promise*, p. 32; Jeremias, *Words*, pp. 216f. As examples of other, less convincing interpretations see C. E. B. Cranfield, *St Mark* (Cambridge, 1959), p. 428, who sees a reference to the time between the Resurrection and the Ascension; Bosch, *Heidenmission*, pp. 178–82, who refers it to the time between the Resurrection and the Parousia, when the Apostles have the task of reaching the 'many' through common participation in the Lord's supper; and Dodd, *Parables*, p. 56, who removes the imminent reference by taking 'new' to mean 'a new sort of wine', namely the heavenly wine which Jesus will drink.

[6] R. Liechtenhahn, *Die urchristliche Mission. Voraussetzungen, Motive und Methoden* (Zürich, 1946), p. 40.   [7] Bosch, *Heidenmission*, p. 178.

interpretation and use of Mk 14: 25. Our own conclusions from Mk 10: 45, 14: 24–5, and 12: 9 can be summarised as follows:
(a) There is some form of universalistic reference in each verse, but it is undefined and inexact.
(b) This reference is connected with Jesus' understanding of his own death and is to be effected after it.[1]
(c) There is no reference to a historical proclamation to the Gentiles.
(d) The time reference we do have seems to show that Jesus expected the Parousia immediately or very soon after his death. Thus Jesus' death and its significance for the πολλοί is linked with the imminent kingdom, which rules out any notion of a universal, historical proclamation to the Gentiles.

So far we have dealt only with the sayings of Jesus, but we must now go on to consider the significance of his actions which affect the Gentiles. As representative of this class of material we shall look in detail at the story of the Syrophoenician woman (Mk 7: 24–30; Matt. 15: 21–8). We shall take the narrative basically as it stands, accepting that the interweaving of dialogue and healing is an integral part of the original.[2] Apart from Mk 7: 27a, Mark's version appears to be the more original of the two.[3] The phrase Ἄφες πρῶτον χορτασθῆναι τὰ τέκνα in Mk 7: 27a is considered by many scholars to be a later addition which softens Jesus' reply, since the πρῶτον implies a δεύτερον

---

[1] M. Kiddle, 'The death of Jesus and the admission of the Gentiles in St Mark', *JTS*, 35 (1934), 45f.

[2] Bultmann, *Tradition*, pp. 38f, and Lohmeyer, *Markus*, pp. 144f, think that the original version was a simple conversation piece which was later attached to a healing narrative. However, see Hahn, *Mission*, p. 32.

[3] Hahn, *Mission*, p. 32; J. Schniewind, *Das Evangelium nach Markus* (Göttingen, 1949), pp. 107–8. The reasons are that in Matthew's version: vv. 22–4 are an editorial insertion (cf. Matt. 9: 27, 20: 30); the request (v. 25) is transposed; v. 27 gives a subtle change of emphasis from Mk 7: 28, for even though the children take precedence, child and dog are united under one master, who is responsible for both; the answer (v. 28) is formularised; the scene is set in a street and not in a house, reflecting the fact that Gentiles were not allowed in Jewish houses; v. 24 is similar to other Matthean material (10: 5–6) and both excludes a possible misinterpretation of Mark's version and gives Matthew's own interpretation of Jesus' words; and the woman's faith is emphasised even more than in Mark, which is a common feature of Matthean miracle stories – see H. J. Held, *Tradition and Interpretation in Matthew* (London, 1963), pp. 165f.

and reflects a notion akin to Rom. 1: 16, 2: 9; Acts 3: 26.[1] The Jews' priority thus becomes a temporary rather than a permanent right. But even if it is not a later addition, it does not follow that Jesus understood it in the same way as Luke and Paul. He need not have thought of it as working out in terms of a historical mission to both Jews and Gentiles. The diminutive form κυνάριον (Mk 7: 27; Matt. 15: 26) is thought by some to refer to household rather than street dogs and is therefore considered to be a softening of Jesus' reply which either originated with Jesus or was added later by the evangelists.[2] D. Bosch thinks it is particularly important since Matthew, who is not following Mark at this point, also has it.[3] But if, as seems more likely, Matthew is following Mark here, then it may not be significant, since Mark is fond of using diminutive forms; and, as Jeremias notes, Aramaic has no diminutive form for dog.[4] Moreover, if Mark has given the correct setting for the narrative – in a house – then the diminutive form may simply have been the most natural term for him to use in describing household dogs. Nothing can therefore be built on the use of this diminutive form.[5]

How then are we to interpret this healing of a Gentile? F. Spitta thought that the fact that the woman was a Gentile played no part at all in Jesus' action. Originally, Jesus and his disciples were sitting in a house eating a meal, when along came a woman who asked for her daughter to be healed. Jesus said that first his disciples must be fed and the crumbs thrown to the dogs before they could come with her. She replies that this is not necessary – a simple word from Jesus will suffice.[6] Spitta's view scarcely needs refuting; suffice it to say that if this was to be our

[1] E. Klostermann, *Das Markusevangelium* (Tübingen, 1926), p. 82; Munck, *Paul*, p. 261; Lohmeyer, *Markus*, pp. 144f; Jeremias, *Promise*, p. 29. Cranfield, *Mark*, p. 246, agrees that Mark added it, but thinks he hit on Jesus' meaning. Bosch, *Heidenmission*, pp. 98–9, thinks Mk 7: 27a is original because Matt. 15: 24 is to be interpreted by the notion 'Jew first then Greek' and so means the same as Mk 7: 27a, and because the woman's reply is inexplicable without v. 27a. However, the former argument is based on a false interpretation of Matt. 15: 24 and the latter simply not true.
[2] Jeremias, *Promise*, p. 29; Cranfield, *Mark*, p. 248.
[3] Bosch, *Heidenmission*, p. 99.   [4] Jeremias, *Promise*, p. 29.
[5] E. Haenchen, *Der Weg Jesu* (Berlin, 1966), p. 275.
[6] F. Spitta, *Jesus und die Heidenmission* (Giessen, 1909), pp. 41–9.

exegetical method, then the prize would go to the man with the most ingenious imagination! D. Bosch suggests that Jesus referred to household dogs who have a definite, although secondary, place in God's household. Matt. 15: 24, he thinks, says no more than Mk 7: 27: the Jews are the first but not the only recipients of salvation; the Gentiles also have their share in it.[1] But Bosch builds too much on κυνάριον and gives a false interpretation of Matt. 15: 24. O. Michel similarly builds on the diminutive κυνάριον and thinks the original contrast was not between Jews and Gentiles.[2] But as we shall see below, τέκνα and κυνάριον have a definite reference, and we cannot ignore the fact that the whole passage revolves around the woman as a Gentile. F. Hahn thinks that the emphasis lies on the contrast between Jew and Gentile and on the woman's faith. Jesus speaks of the supposed boundaries and is then prepared to cross them.[3] For J. Jeremias the main point is the refusal and insult, and he notes that the woman is granted her request only when she recognises the divine division between Jews and Gentiles.[4]

What then can we conclude from these various opinions? First, the reference is undoubtedly to the contrasting status of Jews and Gentiles. Both τέκνα and κυνάριον have definite meanings; the former refers to the Jews and the latter to the Gentiles.[5] Secondly, Jesus' refusal is harsh, since the term 'dog' was an insult (Matt. 5: 47, 6: 7, 32, 18: 17). Thirdly, it is the woman's faith and not her native wit which is the cause of Jesus' eventual response. Fourthly, it is significant that the healing is done from a distance.

We are now in a position to draw together the relevant points from this passage for the Gentile question as a whole. Moreover, we can include here two other incidents in which Jesus apparently heals a Gentile, namely the Gadarene demoniac (Mk 5: 1–20 pars.)[6] and the centurion's son (Matt. 8: 5–13; Lk. 7:

[1] Bosch, *Heidenmission*, pp. 102–3.
[2] O. Michel, art. κύων, *TWNT*, III, 1104f.
[3] Hahn, *Mission*, p. 32.
[4] Jeremias, *Promise*, p. 29.
[5] *S.B.*, I, 724f.
[6] There are several hints that the Gadarene demoniac was a Gentile: the scene is set in Decapolis; the man lived among tombs which, like the swine (v. 11), were unclean for Jews; the appellation 'the Most High God' (v. 7) is used in the Old Testament mainly by non-Jews.

1–10),[1] since several of the conclusions we can draw from the story of the Syrophoenician woman apply to these incidents too.
1. Jesus is reluctant to heal and is surprised at the woman's faith.
2. In the first instance the woman comes to Jesus; he does not go out of his way to meet her.
3. The woman appears to recognise the priority of the Jews.
4. The healing of the Gentile woman's daughter is treated by Jesus as an exception to his normal practice, which is to confine himself to the Jews. This can be seen in the following facts: first, it is probably significant that the healing was done at a distance, since the only other example of this is the healing of the centurion's son. Secondly, there are only three incidents recorded in which Jesus helps a Gentile. These do not alter the basic pattern of Jesus' ministry, which was directed towards Israel. Thirdly, J. Munck notes that the commands of Jesus such as we find in Matt. 10: 5–6, 15: 24, imply that some of his hearers were inclined to think in terms of a Gentile mission.[2] Taking up Munck's hint, we can go on to suggest that these words may have been spoken to the disciples in order to prevent them from misunderstanding Jesus' exceptional dealings with the Gentiles and concluding that he intended there to be a Gentile mission.
5. We have offered several negative observations on these miracle stories in order to counteract any attempt to overrate their significance, but now we must consider their positive value.[3] F. Hahn is at pains to show, on the basis of Lk. 11: 20

---

[1] Matthew's version is probably closer to the original, since Luke has dressed the centurion up to appear as a particularly pious God-fearer and may have been influenced by his later description of Cornelius (Acts 10). Matt. 8: 7 may originally have been a question, in which case it would be another example of Jesus temporarily refusing the request of a Gentile – so Jeremias, *Promise*, p. 30, and E. Klostermann, *Das Matthäusevangelium* (Tübingen, 1927), p. 74. As with the Syrophoenician woman, it is the man's faith which is emphasised and which is the reason for the healing eventually being effected.

[2] Munck, *Paul*, pp. 255f.

[3] Three other incidents might have been included in this section on the actions of Jesus which affect the Gentiles. The first is the so-called northern journey of Jesus in Mk 7: 24 – 8: 36. However, we certainly cannot, with Spitta (*Heidenmission*, pp. 109f), make this journey the basis for calling Jesus the first Christian missionary, since Jesus clearly made no attempt to preach to the inhabitants, who were at any rate partially, if not mainly,

par., that these narratives signify a very real access to the kingdom of God for the Gentiles, for in these and in any other miracles the kingdom of God is realised. He quotes Liechtenhahn on the interrelation of Jesus' message and miracles: 'In both contexts we find people drawn into the sphere of God's rule and the gifts of the last days being offered, and the Gentiles are not excluded from either.' Hahn goes on, 'When Jesus confronts the world's hostile powers, in the form of demons, then this goes beyond any particularist boundaries'.[1] Now this is a point which is well made, but it should not be allowed to obscure the fundamental fact that Jesus limited his task to Israel and that the main thrust of his teaching is that the Gentiles will come into their own only in the future and manifest kingdom of God. That exceptional Gentiles received healing, and yet that their place in the kingdom is predominantly a future one, fits well with the notion that Jesus' teaching about the kingdom was chiefly futuristic, but that he also saw a partial realisation of the kingdom in the present. Jesus himself could have seen this and

Jews. See further A. Alt, *Kleine Schriften zur Geschichte Israels* (Munich, 1953), II, 436f; W. Marxsen, *Der Evangelist Markus* (Göttingen, 1959), p. 44. The second incident is the feeding of the four thousand in Mk 8: 1f. Cranfield, *Mark*, p. 233; Hahn, *Mission*, p. 113 n. 6; and G. H. Boobyer, 'The miracle of the loaves and the Gentiles in St Mark's Gospel', *SJT*, 6 (1953), 8of, think that a Gentile crowd is in mind. This may be so in Mark, although the evidence for it is very slight, but it almost certainly was not so in Jesus' ministry. The third incident is the cleansing of the Temple in Mk 11: 15–17 pars. The quotation from Is. 56: 7, including the phrase πᾶσιν τοῖς ἔθνεσιν, may be Mark's editorial addition, or he may have expanded Jesus' original quotation to include the phrase about the Gentiles. The setting in the Gentile court of the Temple is simply due to the fact that it was there that the money-changers set up before Passover – contrast T. W. Manson, *Jesus and the non-Jews* (London, 1955), pp. 11–12, who makes the setting in the Gentile court the basis of his interpretation. Thus the only certain reference to the Gentiles arises in connection with the Jewish belief that the Gentiles will participate in the worship of the new Temple of the Messianic era, since Jesus' action is best interpreted together with his words about the destruction and rebuilding of the Temple, and by this rebuilding he meant the appearance of the new, Messianic Temple. Thus Jesus' parabolic action includes the Gentiles only as a secondary theme, but in a way which excludes any notion of a historical Gentile mission. See B. Sundkler, 'Jésus et les Païens', *RHPhR*, 16 (1936), 491f; Hahn, *Mission*, pp. 36–8; Jeremias, *Promise*, pp. 65f; E. Lohmeyer, *Kultus und Evangelium* (Göttingen, 1942), pp. 44f.

[1] Hahn, *Mission*, p. 33; Liechtenhahn, *Mission*, p. 33.

yet still have maintained a basically futuristic hope for the Gentiles which would be fulfilled in the final, manifest in-breaking of the kingdom. When trying to discover Jesus' teaching, therefore, we cannot use the Gentile healing miracles as evidence that he either inaugurated or intended there to be a historical Gentile mission.

The passages we have discussed so far could, in terms of the distinction made at the beginning of this chapter, be described as less controversial material. Moreover, all of them speak in general terms of a hope for the Gentiles; but none of them explicitly mention anything about a Gentile mission. It is now our task to turn to the more controversial material, whose authenticity is most frequently doubted. We refer both to the commands which appear to limit the activity of Jesus and his disciples to Israel and to the sayings which appear to envisage a historical Gentile mission.

A formidable array of arguments have been given for regarding Matt. 10: 5b–6, 15: 24 as unauthentic.[1] We shall consider these in some detail, at the same time suggesting possible counter-arguments:

1. The use of the aorist ἀπεστάλην in Matt. 15: 24 both reflects the language of the later Church and treats the Jesus-event as being wholly in the past.[2] However, Jeremias has pointed out that in John's Gospel – which is Bultmann's source for late terminology – the passive is never used of Jesus being sent; rather an active verb is used. The passive in Matt. 15: 24 may be ancient and may reflect the Semitic idiom which uses a passive as a circumlocution for the divine name. Further, an Aramaic perfect need not imply a past event, but could be a present-perfect meaning 'God has sent me'.[3] Moreover, the sending could refer to the Incarnation.

2. These verses contradict Jesus' openness to the Gentiles which can be seen in authentic tradition.[4] However, there is no essential contradiction between these verses and the material we have already discussed, which includes all the material

---

[1] The assertion that these verses are the creation of Matthew or of the narrowest form of Jewish Christianity is not on its own an argument against their authenticity; rather, it is a possible explanation if for other reasons we regard them as unauthentic.

[2] Bultmann, *Tradition*, pp. 155f, 163.

[3] Jeremias, *Promise*, pp. 27–8.   [4] Hahn, *Mission*, pp. 54f.

which Hahn accepts as authentic and more. That Jesus appears to limit his own and his disciples' ministry to Israel, apart from a few exceptions, while reserving the Gentiles' inclusion for the future kingdom, fits neatly with Matt. 10: 5b–6, 15: 24.

3. The various developments in the mission of the early Church are best explained if Jesus was open to the Gentiles in principle and not so exclusive as these verses imply.[1] However, arguments back from the actual development of the Church's mission are problematic, since we know so little about it. Insofar as it can be discovered it is, as we shall see, explicable on views other than Hahn's.

4. Chapters 10 and 15 of Matthew are secondary developments of more original material in Mark; and these verses are particularly suspect since they appear only in Matthew.[2] However, the fact that Matt. 10 and 15 are Matthean compositions is not an argument against the authenticity of individual verses in them. Further, it is possible that these verses were in Q,[3] and that Luke omitted them because they would have been offensive or incomprehensible to Gentile readers, as they may have been to Luke himself.

5. These verses are incompatible with Matt. 10: 18, where it is said that the disciples will appear before Gentile kings and governors.[4] However, Matt. 10: 18 and verses like it have almost certainly been coloured by the later experience of the Church; and even if it is authentic in its present form, appearing before Gentile courts does not necessarily imply a Gentile mission.[5]

It appears, therefore, that for every argument against the authenticity of these verses there is a forceful counter-argument. Are there any factors which tip the scales one way or the other? First, Jeremias has argued that these sayings are full of Aramaisms which hint at, but do not prove, their authenticity.[6] Secondly, the strongest argument in favour of the authenticity of these verses is the fact that they fit in well with the picture we

---

[1] Hahn, *ibid.*
[2] Hahn, *ibid.*; T. F. Glasson, *The Second Advent* (London, 1947), pp. 103–4; B. Streeter, *The Four Gospels* (London, 1924), p. 225.
[3] H. Schurmann, 'Matthäus 10: 5–6', in *Neutestamentliche Aufsätze*, Essays for J. Schmid (Regensburg, 1963), pp. 270f.
[4] Higgins, *Son of Man*, p. 102; J. A. T. Robinson, *Jesus and his Coming* (London, 1957), p. 76.
[5] See below on Mk 13: 9–10.   [6] Jeremias, *Promise*, pp. 19f, 26f.

have already gained from the less disputed material concerning the Gentiles. In plain, unequivocal language Jesus limits his own and his disciples' activity to Israel. That this is not an expression of undiluted nationalism can be seen from the other material where Jesus condemns the Jews and in the same breath announces that the Gentiles will participate in the future kingdom. It appears then that Jesus expressly excluded the possibility of a full-scale historical Gentile mission.

Closely connected with these verses is the problematic verse in Matt. 10: 23b.[1] With regard to the authenticity of this verse, all except the first of the arguments discussed in relation to Matt. 10: 5–6, 15: 24 apply equally well here. In addition we note the following:

1. The saying is placed in the context of teaching about the persecution of the disciples and teaching of this kind normally had a late origin.[2] However, although in their present form the passages about persecution have been coloured by the experience of the Church, there is no reason why Jesus should not have foreseen that his disciples would encounter persecution. As a result of his own experience of opposition it would not have been a particularly difficult prediction to make.

2. It is said that Jesus made no such temporal predictions.[3] However, this assertion is based on a dubious exegesis of several other passages (e.g. Mk 9: 1, 13: 30), many of which we shall be discussing in a later chapter. It is sufficient to note at this stage that for the majority of scholars Matt. 10: 23 confirms the imminent expectation of Jesus attested elsewhere.

3. The use of the title Son of Man would make it suspect for those who claim that Jesus never used this title. However, we can note that in this saying Jesus and the Son of Man are not identified, which for some is a mark of the authentic Son of Man sayings. Even if the Son of Man title is not original, the prophecy itself may be a genuine saying of Jesus which was later recast in the form of a Son of Man saying.

---

[1] That is, treating v. 23b as an isolated logion – see Kümmel, *Promise*, pp. 61f; E. Grässer, *Das Problem der Parusieverzögerung in den synoptischen Evangelien und in der Apostelgeschichte* (Berlin, 1959), pp. 137f. Against this see Tödt, *Son of Man*, pp. 60–2.

[2] Hahn, *Mission*, pp. 56–8.

[3] A. N. Wilder, *Eschatology and Ethics in the Teaching of Jesus* (New York, 1950), pp. 129f.

In addition to this it is a fact that this verse remained doubly unfulfilled in the experience of the Church: the mission did reach out beyond the boundaries of Israel and the Son of Man did not come. Moreover the temporal limitations of this verse are so narrow that it is difficult to think that it was created, even by first-generation Christians. Finally, in favour of the authenticity of this verse we can once again quote Jeremias' arguments on the basis of Aramaisms[1] and the fact that there is no contradiction between this verse and the material we have already discussed so far. These seem good reasons for accepting the saying as authentic and we must now go on to interpret it.[2] Matthew may have found it in the same context it now has, since it fits in well with its surroundings; or he may have placed it, correctly, in a general missionary context.[3] How then are we to interpret it within this missionary context?[4] E. Grässer suggests two possible emphases: it could be a stimulus for the disciples to encourage them to hasten in their task; or it could be a word of comfort, in view of the trials and frustrations they will encounter in their missionary work.[5] Both of these suggestions are fruitful and a combination of them is possible. With this in mind we can now conclude our brief look at this verse with the following observations: first, the mission of Jesus and his disciples is once again limited to Israel; secondly, the clear implication of this verse is that this mission will not be completed because the Son of Man will appear very soon, in fact before all the towns of Israel have been covered;[6] thirdly, in a missionary

---

[1] Jeremias, *Promise*, p. 20.

[2] For interpretations which regard the saying as unauthentic see Hahn, *Mission*, pp. 56–8; Tödt, *Son of Man*, pp. 60–2; Glasson, *Advent*, pp. 103–4; Robinson, *Coming*, p. 76; Higgins, *Son of Man*, pp. 100–4; E. Schweizer, 'Der Menschensohn', *ZNW*, 50 (1959), 191f; E. Bammel, 'Matthäus 10: 23', *St. Th.*, 15 (1961), 79f.

[3] Others treat it as an authentic persecution logion: for example, A. Feuillet, 'Les Origines et la signification de Matt. 10: 23', *CBQ*, 23 (1961), 182f.

[4] Others agree that it is an authentic missionary logion, but make unconvincing attempts to avoid the plain meaning of the words. See Filson, *Matthew*, pp. 131f; W. Michaelis, *Der Herr verzieht nicht die Verheissung* (Bern, 1942), pp. 63f; J. Schniewind, *Das Evangelium nach Matthäus* (Göttingen, 1950), pp. 130–1.

[5] Grässer, *Parusieverzögerung*, pp. 137–41.

[6] τελέσητε here appears to mean 'complete' or 'fulfil', which is a possible, though not the most usual, meaning of the verb: see Bauer, p. 818.

context this verse excludes any possibility of a historical Gentile mission.

Before we turn to the final section of this chapter, this is a convenient point at which to summarise our results so far:

1. Jesus limited himself, in his earthly ministry, to Israel and commanded his disciples to do likewise. There is no evidence that he was diverted from this his main purpose, or that he preached to or even desired to preach to the Gentiles.

2. Nevertheless, according to Jesus' teaching the Gentiles have a definite place in the kingdom of God. This place is reserved almost wholly for the future, when the kingdom will be manifested in all its fullness. As subsidiary points we note that this hope for the Gentiles is frequently played off against the present disobedience and obduracy of the Jews, and that it will apparently be effected after, and as a result of, Jesus' death.

3. The link between the Gentiles and the kingdom of God is frequently made in a context where Jesus appears to have thought that this kingdom was imminent.

4. On exceptional occasions Jesus responded, though with considerable reluctance, to certain Gentiles who persistently appealed to him. Jesus' response of healing shows that at least for these Gentiles there was a participation in the kingdom of God which was, in a partial and hidden manner, in the process of realisation. This point is entirely consonant with what has been said in points 1–3.

5. There is no evidence that Jesus either foresaw or intended there to be a mission to the Gentiles such as actually took place in the early Church. In fact such a mission is indirectly excluded by Matt. 10: 23b.

Having thus summarised our results so far, we turn finally to the material which seems directly to contradict these results. In particular we shall be concerned with the straightforward prophecies of a Gentile mission in Mk 13: 10 pars., 14: 9. We shall consider the arguments for and against authenticity, interpret the verses as they stand in Mark, and then discuss the various methods by which scholars have dealt with them, at the same time propounding their own views on the Gentile question.[1] The arguments for and against the authenticity of Mk 13:

[1] Matt. 28: 16–20 is almost certainly a Matthean construction, reflecting many of the theological ideas and problems of his day. See Hahn, *Mission*,

10 (and with it 14: 9, which many see as a doublet of 13: 10) are:

1. Mk 13: 10 is clearly an editorial insertion.[1] However, the fact that it may be an insertion says nothing for or against its authenticity; it could be an isolated but genuine word of Jesus.

2. It uses the language of early Christian preaching – πάντα τὰ ἔθνη, κηρύσσειν, εὐαγγέλιον – and is therefore a *vaticinium ex eventu* from the missionary period of the Church.[2] But although it is true that the language hints at a late origin, we cannot say more. In using this language Mark was doing only what was natural for a Christian author writing in A.D. 60–5; but this does not preclude the possibility that behind this language there lies a genuine saying of Jesus. The argument that the saying is a *vaticinium ex eventu* is not, on its own, convincing; rather it is a possible explanation if for other reasons we suspect the authenticity of the saying.

3. Jesus expected the End within his own generation, which excludes the notion of a universal mission.[3] At this stage, we can merely note that it depends how one interprets Mk 13: 10, 14: 9 whether or not they contradict Jesus' imminent expectation, though as they stand in Mark Jesus could not have said them.

4. It is asked how, with such an unequivocal command, there was so much disagreement in the early Church over the Gentile mission.[4] Again, this is a point we shall be discussing later; at this stage we can say that the problems of the early Church's mission have to be more closely defined before they can be read back as arguments for or against the authenticity of these verses.

pp. 63f; G. Barth, *Tradition and Interpretation in Matthew* (London, 1963), pp. 131f; O. Michel, 'Der Abschluss des Matthäusevangeliums', *Ev. Th.*, 10 (1950–1), 16f; E. Lohmeyer, 'Mir ist gegeben alle Gewalt', *IM*, 22–49. Luke's version of the post-Resurrection commands will be dealt with in the next chapter. C. F. Evans, 'I will go before you into Galilee', *JTS*, n.s. 5 (1954), 3f, and G. H. Boobyer, 'Galilee and the Galileans in St Mark', *BJRL*, 25 (1952–3), 340f, unconvincingly interpret the enigmatic verses in Mk 14: 28, 16: 7 as prophecies of the Gentile mission. It is unlikely that Mark intended a reference to the Gentile mission, and certainly none of their evidence shows that Jesus meant this.

[1] Marxsen, *Markus*, pp. 119f; H. Conzelmann, 'Geschichte und Eschaton nach Mk 13', *ZNW*, 50 (1959), 210f.
[2] Bultmann, *Tradition*, pp. 122f; Hahn, *Mission*, pp. 71f.
[3] Kümmel, *Promise*, p. 84.   [4] Kümmel, *ibid.*

5. The omission of Mk 13: 10 in Luke is because it was not in Luke's version of Mark but was a later addition.[1] However, as we shall argue in the next chapter, there are more convincing reasons for Luke's omission of Mk 13: 10.

Once again then we find that the arguments for and against authenticity are quite well balanced. Have we anything here which will tip the scales one way or the other?[2] The linguistic argument goes against authenticity this time but, as we have seen, it is not on its own sufficient evidence on which to base a decision. More importantly, the plain meaning of these verses as they stand in Mark contradicts what we have previously found to be Jesus' view. Mark probably understood 13: 10 in the following manner: first, v. 10 is inserted here because Mark understood the phrase εἰς μαρτύριον αὐτοῖς (v. 9) to mean witness of a positive kind. Second, there was to be a historical mission to the Gentiles which would give positive significance to the time between the Resurrection and the Parousia, so that it would not simply be a time of endurance. The Gentile mission, therefore, helped to answer the problem of the delayed Parousia.[3] Third, this mission would extend to every part of the then known world before the End came.[4] It is clear how this contradicts the results we have so far obtained. But did Jesus share Mark's view? Can we resolve this contradiction? It is in their answers to this question that we find various scholars revealing their own interpretations of the Gentile question as a whole.

---

[1] Grässer, *Parusieverzögerung*, p. 158.

[2] The arguments offered by Bosch, *Heidenmission*, p. 132, are not convincing: (a) Since Matt. 16: 18 is authentic, Jesus foresaw the Church. As there cannot be a Church without mission, it is but a small step to Mk 13: 10. (b) The parables of vigilance (Mk 13: 28f; Matt. 24: 37-9) show that Jesus foresaw a *Zwischenzeit* in which the disciples would be active in the universal preaching of the gospel. The arguments of G. R. Beasley-Murray, *Jesus and the Future* (London, 1954), pp. 191f, about Jesus' universalism are too vague to be of much use. Liechtenhahn, *Mission*, pp. 31f, argues that for Jesus mission must have been a postulate of his eschatology. This may be so, but we do not agree that this mission should necessarily take a historical form.

[3] Grässer, *Parusieverzögerung*, pp. 158f; Conzelmann, *Mk 13*, pp. 218-19.

[4] In the context of Mk 13 πρῶτον must be translated 'first' and not 'above all': *contra* Marxsen, *Markus*, p. 120.

THE EXPLANATIONS

1. The most convenient way of solving the problem is simply to regard both strands of evidence as having originated in the creative activity of the early Church. This is basically the approach of R. Bultmann, to whom the two strands merely 'reveal the growing and developing ideas of mission in the early Church'.[1]

2. The next most simple solution is to deny the authenticity of one or other of the strands:

(a) A. Harnack argues that all references to the Gentiles and the Gentile mission in Jesus' teaching are not authentic. In his own words: 'The universal mission was an inevitable issue of the religion and spirit of Jesus, and its origin, not only apart from any direct word from Jesus, but in verbal contradiction to many of his sayings, is really a stronger testimony to the method, strength and spirit of his teaching than if it were the outcome of a deliberate command.'[2]

(b) F. Spitta thought that from the very beginning Jesus intended to promote the Gentile mission, an intention which clashed with the typical outlook of the Pharisees. Jesus, therefore, can be regarded as the first Christian missionary, and sayings such as those found in Matt. 10: 5–6, 23, 15: 24 cannot be attributed to him.[3]

F. Hahn, while also rejecting Mk 13: 10, 14: 9, similarly rejects the particularist sayings on the grounds that in the authentic tradition Jesus was open to the Gentiles. The promises to all nations and the acceptance of individual Gentiles are not to be torn apart. While Jesus did not perform a mission to the Gentiles, 'his message and work in Israel became a witness among the Gentiles, and still more: as the eschatological event began to be realised, salvation came within reach of the Gentiles'.[4]

Enough has already been said in the previous section to make it clear that none of these views are acceptable.

[1] Bultmann, *Tradition*, p. 145 n. 1.
[2] A. Harnack, *The Mission and Expansion of Christianity* (London, 1908), I, 36–43. Quotation from p. 37.
[3] Spitta, *Heidenmission*, pp. 72f, 83f, 109f.
[4] Hahn, *Mission*, p. 39.

3. Another approach is to accept both strands of the evidence and to argue that there is no contradiction between them. Thus G. R. Beasley-Murray argues that Matt. 10: 23 and Mk 13: 10 are not contradictory 'once the perspective of the primitive Church be adopted'.[1] It is unlikely that this is true, but even if it is, we cannot assume that Jesus shared the perspective of the primitive Church. D. Bosch, commenting on the relationship between Matt. 10: 23 and Mk 13: 10, says, 'We must therefore regard Matt. 10: 23 as an independent word of Jesus which, by analogy with the saying about the Gentile mission Mk 13: 10, expects a Jewish mission during the whole period between the Resurrection and the Parousia (*der ganzen Zwischenzeit*)'. The fact, which Bosch himself notes, that 'according to Mk 13: 10 the Gentile mission appears as an *opus perfectum*, while according to Matt. 10: 23 the Jewish mission would not yet have come to an end', only hints at one of the difficulties of his interpretation.[2] Others will be raised later under the so-called *heilsgeschichtlich* interpretation.

4. Another possible way out of the dilemma would be to divide Jesus' ministry into two periods: at first he was concerned only with the Jews – and so one could date the particularist material in this period; but after being rejected by the Jews he turns to the Gentiles – a change which gave rise to the universalistic material. However, this approach is full of loopholes: first, neither the particularist nor the universalist sayings can confidently be placed chronologically in Jesus' ministry; and second, there is no evidence to suggest that the particularist sayings were relevant for only one part of Jesus' ministry.

5. A further attempt to explain all the material in the Synoptics is found in the views of C. J. Cadoux, T. W. Manson, and J. Munck, all of whom resort to the concept of 'representative universalism'.[3] The basic notion is that Jesus' purpose in limiting his activity to Israel was 'that Israel should bring the knowledge of the true God to the Gentile peoples, and should prevail upon them to serve him aright'.[4] Jesus' task was first and

---

[1] Beasley-Murray, *Jesus*, pp. 197f.
[2] Bosch, *Heidenmission*, p. 157.
[3] Cadoux, *Mission*, pp. 160–1; Manson, *Non-Jews*, pp. 1f; Munck, *Paul*, pp. 260, 271f.
[4] Cadoux, *Mission*.

foremost to create 'such a community in Israel in the faith that it would transform the life of his own people, and that a transformed Israel would transform the world'.[1]

There are advantages to this view, since we know that Jesus did restrict his mission to Israel and that he did intend the conversion and restitution of his people, as is shown by his significant choice of the Twelve. On the other hand, we cannot ignore the fact that Jesus frequently condemns Israel for failing to repent and, more significantly, the fact that he frequently connects the Jews' obduracy with the future inclusion of the Gentiles (Mk 11: 15–17, 12: 1–9; Matt. 8: 11, 10: 15f, 11: 21–4, 12: 38–42). This is a far cry from the notion of Israel as the light of the world. Moreover, these authors assume that after the conversion of Israel a historical mission to the Gentiles would take place, whereas it seems more likely that Jesus' mission to Israel was for the purpose of converting and reconstituting her in preparation for the Messianic era, in accordance with the Jewish belief that this would be one of the events of the last days. If the conversion of the Gentiles is included incidentally in this purpose, then it would have to be understood as an apocalyptic event. Moreover, the limitations of Matt. 10: 23 militate against this interpretation.

6. G. D. Kilpatrick tries to eliminate Mk 13: 10, 14: 9 by the use of textual and linguistic criticism.[2] Briefly, his arguments are as follows:

(a) κηρύσσειν εἰς: normally the verb is used with a dative for persons addressed; therefore the accusative here means to preach 'in' or 'among' and not 'to', of which there is no clear example in the New Testament. The same argument applies to εἰς μαρτύριον αὐτοῖς (v. 9). He then interprets the verses as referring only to a mission to diaspora Jews.

(b) Some MSS have a full stop after ἔθνη (v. 10). This punctuation is supported by Matt. 10: 18. He then notes that in Mark many sentences begin with a verb, so that when the punctuation is in doubt this should be the deciding factor. Thus he connects v. 10a closely with v. 9 and v. 10b with v. 11, the result of which is to remove any idea of mission.

---

[1] Manson, *Non-Jews*, p. 18.
[2] G. D. Kilpatrick, 'The Gentiles and the Gentile mission in Mark: Mk 13: 10', *SG*, pp. 145–58.

There are, however, several objections to Kilpatrick's view. First, while his comment on κηρύσσειν εἰς has some validity, the phrase could mean preach 'unto' or 'as far as' as well as 'in' or 'among'; in either case it could still refer to a Gentile mission. Secondly, Matt. 10: 18 is probably Matthew's variation of Mk 13: 10, another of which he gives in 24: 14. The secondary reading in Mark is probably due to scribes who, being more familiar with Matthew than Mark, assimilated the latter to the former. Moreover, since the figures which Kilpatrick gives for Markan sentences are that the verb comes at the beginning of the sentence forty-eight times, sixteen times in the middle and nineteen times at the end, one can scarcely use this as the decisive criterion when the punctuation is in doubt. Finally, the connection of v. 10a with v. 9 and v. 10b with v. 11 is unconvincing, for v. 10b seems pointless in this context unless qualified by v. 10a; v. 11 does not convincingly perform this task.[1] In fact, there are good reasons for supposing that v. 10 is an insertion into vv. 9–11, which are linked by their similar content and by the catchwords παραδώσουσιν v. 9 and παραδιδόντες v. 11. Also, it is easy to imagine how the subject-matter of vv. 9–11 attracted v. 10 into this context.[2] We must conclude, therefore, that although Kilpatrick's argument is ingenious, it proves on close inspection to be weak at every point.

7. A commonly accepted thesis, first given in detail by M. Meinertz, is the so-called *heilsgeschichtlich* interpretation.[3] On this view it is possible to accept both strands of evidence by fitting them into a pattern of salvation history. Thus the particularist sayings were meant to apply only to Jesus' lifetime, for Jesus saw that after the Resurrection the Church's mission would reach out to the Gentiles and this is what he meant when he spoke Mk 13: 10, 14: 9, sayings which themselves lead on naturally to the post-Resurrection commands. What had hitherto been spoken of only occasionally and with his eyes on the future became a reality in his universal commission.

However, there are objections to this view. First, there is no evidence that Jesus saw the two sets of sayings as fitting into such

---

[1] Cranfield, *Mark*, pp. 398–9.
[2] Hahn, *Mission*, p. 39; Grässer, *Parusieverzögerung*, p. 158.
[3] M. Meinertz, *Jesus und die Heidenmission* (Münster, 1925), pp. 84f, 114f, 159f.

a pattern, even if Matthew did. Secondly, there is no evidence that Jesus intended the particularist sayings to apply only to the pre-Resurrection period; in fact, the limitations of Matt. 10: 23 would exclude such a view. Thirdly, in all the material we have discussed, apart from Mk 13: 10, 14: 9, the inclusion of the Gentiles is seen to be primarily a future event, the future, that is, seen as part of the End events. These seem good reasons for suspecting a view which otherwise makes much sense of the material.

8. The final view we shall look at is that which E. Lohmeyer hinted at and J. Jeremias has worked out more fully.[1] Their solution is to argue that Mk 13: 10, 14: 9 did not originally refer to a historical Gentile mission as they do in their present context. They are authentic words of Jesus which originally had quite another reference, namely to the apocalyptic proclamation to the Gentiles when they flock to Zion in the last days, a concept which we have already found in the Old Testament and Judaism. Jeremias, interpreting Mk 14: 9, makes the following observations:

(a) ὅπου ἐάν should be translated 'whenever' (cf. Mk 9: 18) and refers to a single event as in Mk 14: 14.

(b) εἰς μνημόσυνον is a *hapax legomenon* in the New Testament. From Old Testament examples Jeremias argues that it refers to God's remembrance of the woman's deed on the day of Judgement (Gen. 30: 32; Num. 10: 9; Ps. 25: 7).

(c) κηρυχθῇ τὸ εὐαγγέλιον has the same meaning as in Rev. 14: 6, namely the early pre-Pauline meaning of the apocalyptic proclamation of the eternal gospel.

On the basis of these observations Jeremias interprets the whole verse (and with it Matt. 24: 14, which he takes to be a more original form of Mk 13: 10) as a reference to the apocalyptic proclamation to the Gentiles in the End-time. However, Jeremias' linguistic arguments are open to doubt. First, ὅπου ἐάν could have its more usual meaning 'wherever' rather than 'whenever' in Mk 9: 18, 14: 14; this would also exclude the argument about a reference to a single event. Secondly, while

---

[1] Lohmeyer, *Markus*, pp. 272f, 295f; Jeremias, *Promise*, pp. 22–3. Since our conclusions are basically the same as Jeremias', though reached by a different method, it has been possible to keep this chapter relatively short. The aim has been merely to show how these conclusions were reached.

the idea of God remembering people does occur in the Old Testament, the Hebrew root זכר and the LXX noun μνημόσυνον are more often used of remembrance by men. In the absence of any other evidence here it should probably be given this more usual meaning.[1] Thirdly, τὸ εὐαγγέλιον is a typically Markan term that reflects the preaching of the early Church; the presumption is that it has this meaning here also. It is not at all certain that Rev. 14: 6 reflects an early pre-Pauline usage, for it may be that it is a Christian apocalyptic development of some such saying as Mk 13: 10.[2] From the point of view of the writer and readers, εὐαγγέλιον in Rev. 14: 6 probably means 'good news' in the sense that God's victory is near at hand. However, even if it is accepted that Rev. 14: 6 reflects the most primitive Christian use of εὐαγγέλιον and is to be connected with the Jewish notion of the apocalyptic proclamation to the Gentiles, the same meaning cannot be read into Mk 13: 10, 14: 9; Matt. 24: 14. In Matthew and Mark when the εὐαγγέλιον is proclaimed it is proclaimed by men and it presumably has this meaning in Matt. 24: 14; Mk 13: 10, 14: 9.

However, despite the fact that Jeremias' linguistic arguments are questionable, we would suggest that behind Mk 13: 10, 14: 9 lie genuine words of Jesus which had some such reference as Jeremias supposes, namely to the future apocalyptic proclamation to the Gentiles in the last days.[3] In all the material on

---

[1] Cranfield, *Mark*, p. 418.

[2] Jeremias has subsequently abandoned this interpretation of εὐαγγέλιον in Mk 14: 9 and now, with Hahn (*Mission*, p. 118 n. 1), sees it as a sign of Christian missionary preaching in Hellenistic circles – see *Abba* (Göttingen, 1966), pp. 115–20. P. Stuhlmacher, *Das Paulinische Evangelium. I. Vorgeschichte* (Göttingen, 1968), pp. 210–18, has argued in great detail that Rev. 14: 6 (cf. 10: 7) is not a piece of late Christian apocalyptic, but is directly linked to the Jewish notion of the proclamation to the nations in the End-time. Thus he thinks that from a tradition-historical viewpoint it gives the most primitive Christian usage of εὐαγγέλιον. He also argues that εὐαγγέλιον, like its equivalent בשורה, is neutral in meaning; that is, it refers to the 'proclamation' of the coming of God in judgement, but not necessarily in a positive sense. But while Stuhlmacher has unquestionably shown how close Rev. 14: 6 is to the Jewish notion of the apocalyptic proclamation to the nations, he has not proved that this connection is not accidental, a result of Christian development of sayings like Mk 13: 10 in an apocalyptic context.

[3] It is improbable that Jesus made an indirect allusion to a Gentile mission in the phrase εἰς μαρτύριον αὐτοῖς (Mk 13: 9). These texts about persecu-

Jesus' teaching about the Gentiles they are the odd men out, and since all attempts to reconcile them with the other material have failed, we can either simply reject them as unauthentic or we can interpret them differently from Mark, since as they stand in Mark they cannot be Jesus' words. Taking the second alternative, we could then understand Mark's versions as a conscious recasting or a genuine misunderstanding of Jesus' words, a process which probably took place long before Mark wrote. This process can then be considered as part of the Church's historicising of material in order to accommodate it to the unexpectedly delayed Parousia, since there is evidence for this process in other apocalyptic material.

The advantages of this view of Mk 13: 10, 14: 9 are that it is based on a well documented Old Testament and Jewish expectation which we know, from other sayings, Jesus shared; that it accords well with Jesus' teaching elsewhere, where the hope for the Gentiles is orientated towards the future kingdom of God and where there is no hint that he foresaw or expected there to be a historical Gentile mission; and that it goes a long way towards explaining the reluctance of the early Church to embark on a Gentile mission. For if Jesus gave no command for the Gentile mission and if his followers held the same apocalyptic view of this mission that he had, it becomes clear why the Gentile mission was so slow to get off the ground and why it encountered so much hostility. It is often said that the real problem in the early Church was not the Gentile mission as such, but merely the terms on which the Gentiles could become members of a predominantly Jewish Church. However, it is peculiar that there was a considerable time-lapse between the Resurrection and the beginning of the Gentile mission, a fact for which some explanation must be given. Further, almost all the preaching to the Gentiles was done not by those who were supposed to have received the direct command of Jesus, but by the Hellenists, Paul and Barnabas. Also, although it appears that sometimes the disputes in the early Church were over the terms of the Gentiles' entry into the Christian community, we

tion have been edited by the Church in the light of her experiences; and further, it is possible that, if he spoke these words, Jesus meant them negatively, i.e. 'as a witness against them'. Cf. Mk 1: 44, 6: 11, and see H. Strathmann, art. μάρτυς, *TWNT*, IV, 508f.

can go on to ask what lay behind this strict line. Was it merely Jewish scruples, or was it a more fundamental conviction, namely that the Gentiles would not participate in salvation until the final inbreaking of the kingdom of God? It is to these murky, obscure corners of the actual developments and disputes in the mission of the early Church that we shall turn in our attempt to unravel the narrative of Acts.

In concluding this chapter we shall draw out the implications of our results on Jesus' attitude towards the Gentiles for his teaching on eschatology. The relation between the two themes has come to light at several points in our discussion. In fact it is fair to say that scarcely any of the material concerned with the Gentiles stands in isolation; almost all of it is connected in one way or another with the theme of eschatology. We have found that Jesus did not expect there to be a historical Gentile mission and that his teaching on the Gentiles is inseparably linked with his teaching on eschatology. The answer to the question why Jesus did not expect such a mission is implied in the second observation, that is, his eschatological expectations logically disallowed it. Jesus believed that the Parousia was imminent, so that there was no room for a historical Gentile mission. He maintained a positive hope for the Gentiles, but believed that this hope would be fulfilled in the apocalyptic events of the End-time; then and only then would the Gentiles enter the kingdom of God. Thus our study of Jesus' attitude towards the Gentiles has become a key to the understanding of his eschatology.

CHAPTER 2

THE GENTILES IN LUKE'S GOSPEL

THE MARKAN VIEW

The previous chapter has, by implication, dealt with the Markan view of the Gentiles and the Gentile mission. However, before embarking on a study of the Gentiles in Luke's Gospel it is necessary to draw this material together and to summarise Mark's view. This will serve to clarify what has happened to the tradition from Jesus up to and including Mark, with which Luke's presentation can be compared to see if and how it differs.

Four passages are especially worthy of note. We shall state only our conclusions, since the arguments have already been given.

1. In Mk. 12: 1–9 we noted that Mark has probably added the reference to the 'others' in v. 9, although this is not certain. If he did add it then he has made a clear reference to the Gentiles which would otherwise be lacking in the parable. We noted also that it is almost certain that Mark has added the reference to the 'beloved son', recalling Mk 1: 11, 9: 7. This addition enhances the connection which Mark sees between the death of Jesus and the admission of the Gentiles. The original parable spoke of three servants, the last of whom was killed; by adding a reference to the son, Mark has made the meaning of the parable unambiguous, for there is no longer any doubt that a reference to Jesus' death is intended.

2. In Mk. 11: 15–17 we argued that Mark probably added the quotation from Is. 56: 7, drawing out – quite correctly – the implications of Jesus' action, namely that in the new, Messianic Temple the Gentiles would have their rightful place. The whole action is best understood in the light of the sayings about the destruction of the Temple, showing that the inclusion of the Gentiles is to be connected with the End events.

3. More significant for our purposes is that Mark has added the phrase 'Let the children first be fed' in Mk 7: 27a. The πρῶτον implies a δεύτερον and probably reflects the notion

'Jew first and then Greek' as it is found in Rom. 1: 16, 2: 9; Acts 3: 26, 13: 46. Israel's priority becomes a passing right of only temporary significance, for as a result of her refusal the Gospel goes to the Gentiles. For Jesus, the healing of the Gentile's daughter was an exception to his normal practice. It was the exception which proved the rule, the rule being that his own ministry was directed almost exclusively towards Israel. Whereas for Jesus this incident was a proleptic sign of the future participation of the Gentiles in the kingdom of God, for Mark it has become part of the justification for the Church's Gentile mission.

4. Mk 13: 10, 14: 9 show that Mark clearly envisaged a historical Gentile mission which would give positive significance to the period of time caused by the delay of the Parousia. This mission would extend to every part of the then known world before the End. It is not clear whether Mark means literally the whole world or whether he thought in terms of representative cities or areas. The temporal limitations of the whole chapter perhaps suggest the latter.

The results of these few observations can be summarised as follows:

(a) Mark firmly connects the inclusion of the Gentiles with Jesus' death. In all the passages, 10: 45, 14: 24 and 12: 1–9, it is made clear that this will occur after Jesus' death. Apart from this temporal connection between the two events, 12: 1–9 suggests a direct causal relationship between them. The other two sayings express not so much a causal relationship, but rather are statements of the universal implications of Jesus' death.

(b) Mark does not introduce the Gentile mission anachronistically into Jesus' ministry; rather, he adopts what we have called the *heilsgeschichtlich* view. The Gentile mission is not considered by Jesus to be part of his own vocation, but he nevertheless foresees that it will take place after his death and Resurrection. Jesus himself is not a Gentile missionary, but he does command his followers to fulfil that role.

(c) For Mark, the Gentile mission is to be seen in an eschatological context. By this is meant that although not in itself one of the supernatural, apocalyptic events of the End, it is a necessary prelude to them. Thus Mark's view is at one remove from that of Jesus. Whereas for Jesus the proclamation to the Gentiles was an apocalyptic event, for Mark it is a historical event. But since it is a necessary prelude to the End, it also has eschatological significance.

THE LUKAN VIEW

We can now turn to the material in Luke's gospel. The purpose of this section is to discover what, if anything, is distinctive in Luke's presentation of Jesus' attitude to and teaching about the Gentiles. Since this is the case, we can briefly dispense with four passages which merely repeat, without significant alteration, the tradition which Luke received. These are: the oracle on Tyre and Sidon Lk. 10: 12–16; the oracle against the Galilean towns Lk. 11: 29–32; the parable of the mustard seed Lk. 13: 18–21; and the parable of the wicked husbandmen Lk. 20: 9–19. For the first three passages we merely refer to the chapter on Jesus and the Gentiles, and for the last passage to the comments in our summary of Mark's view.

We turn now to passages in Luke's Gospel which have direct parallels in the other Gospels but which differ, according to some scholars, in significant details.

Lk. 7: 1–10

The parallel versions of Matthew and Luke agree at this point only in the description of the man as a centurion and in the dialogue. The framework of the narrative is given separately by each Evangelist. Ellis thinks that Luke's is the more original version and that Matthew's is a telescoping of it 'which corporately identifies the representatives with the centurion'.[1] It is more probable, however, that Luke has added these details both to bring into focus the personality of the centurion and his faith, and to enhance the parallel with the narrative of Cornelius, the first Gentile Christian (Acts 10–11).

For Luke, the man was clearly a God-fearer[2] or, less probably, a proselyte.[3] King argues that this implies a damping down of Luke's universalism because 'the only reason that can be given

---

[1] E. Earle Ellis, *St Luke* (London, 1966), p. 118.
[2] A. R. C. Leaney, *The Gospel according to St Luke* (London, 1958), p. 97; Manson, *Sayings*, p. 64; K. H. Rengstorf, *Das Evangelium nach Lukas* (Göttingen, 1966), p. 97.
[3] Bosch, *Heidenmission*, p. 95; G. B. Caird, *St Luke* (London, 1963), p. 108.

for helping a Gentile is that he loves the Jewish race and built them a synagogue'.[1] But it should be noted that:

(a) According to Luke, Jesus heals the boy because of the centurion's faith. The fundamental significance of the narrative is to be found in the climax in v. 9 – 'I tell you, not even in Israel have I found such faith.' It is quite probable, too, that although in this case the healing is effected by Jesus' word from a distance, Luke saw it as prophetic of the reception of the Gentiles in Acts.

(b) This narrative as a whole is closely parallel to the Cornelius narrative in Acts. Luke's knowledge of the Cornelius episode may well have influenced his description of the centurion here. If this is so, then it is improbable that the description of the centurion's piety and partial commitment to Judaism is an anti-universalist device, for this is patently not the case in Acts 10–11.

(c) We would suggest that the motivation for Luke's portrait of the centurion is quite different, namely, what we shall call his pragmatic approach to the Jew–Gentile problem. By emphasising the piety of this Gentile, Luke seems to imply that on the whole the Gentiles are just as good as the Jews; they are not necessarily any better, but neither are they any worse. Gentiles can be as dedicated to and respectful of God as the Jews, and therefore there is no good reason why the Church should not accept them. We shall find this pragmatic approach again in Acts where we shall discuss it further. Thus Luke has one eye on the problems of the Church of his day, in particular, the right of the Gentile mission.

We conclude, therefore, that Luke's alterations to this passage do not weaken the universalistic element as understood by both Jesus and Matthew; rather, they enhance it. Insofar as Luke has altered the narrative, it is with the purpose of emphasising rather than toning down the implicit universalism. Apart from the pragmatic element which has influenced Luke's description of the centurion, there is nothing significantly new for his presentation of Jesus' attitude to the Gentiles.

[1] N. Q. King, 'Universalism in the Third Gospel', *TU*, 73 (1959), 199f.

Lk. 11: 33

T. W. Manson argues that the Matthean version of this saying –
'and it gives light to all that are in the house' (Matt. 5: 15b)
– refers to a reform within Judaism, whereas the Lukan form –
'that those who enter may see the light' – looks forward to the
influx of the Gentiles.[1] But as Dodd notes, Luke's version reflects a house of the Graeco-Roman style with a lamp in the
vestibule, whereas Matthew's reflects the simpler Galilean
house with one living-room.[2] That is, Luke's reference to a lamp
which guides the visitor arriving in the dark merely reflects the
type of house most familiar to him; it is not the result of a desire
to make a veiled reference to the influx of the Gentiles.

Lk. 13: 28; Matt. 8: 11

N. Q. King argues that since Lk. 13: 28 echoes Ps. 107: 3,
where the reference is to Diaspora Jews, Luke's reference is to
the same group of people.[3] Thus Luke gives a neutral interpretation to a potentially universalistic saying. Certainly, Luke
omits the words 'sons of the Kingdom' and 'many' from
Matthew and reverses the order of Matthew's vv. 11 and 12.
But it is doubtful whether this materially affects the basic sense
of the saying as we interpreted it in the previous chapter.
Although Luke lacks the phrase 'sons of the Kingdom', the
general context implies that he is referring to the same group of
people, that is, the Jews. And the reference in Lk. 13: 29 is, in
contrast to the group mentioned in v. 28, presumably to the
Gentiles. Thus the divergences in Luke's version of this text are
not sufficient to justify the statement that he has neutralised or
altered the original meaning.[4] The same can be said with regard
to the setting of the saying in Luke and Matthew. Whereas
Matthew's setting makes the meaning of the saying unambiguous,
by connecting it with the story of the centurion, it could be
argued that Luke's setting does not make the meaning so
obvious. However, it is probably Luke rather than Matthew

---

[1] Manson, *Sayings*, pp. 92–3.   [2] Dodd, *Parables*, p. 106 n. 32.
[3] King, 'Universalism', pp. 202–3; Leaney, *Luke*, p. 209.
[4] Rengstorf, *Lukas*, p. 276; Caird, *Luke*, p. 173; and N. Geldenhuys, *Commentary on the Gospel of St Luke* (London, 1950), p. 380 assume this without
discussing it.

who retains the original setting, so that it is a case of Matthew emphasising rather than Luke toning down the meaning by means of the context.

Lk. 14: 16–24; Matt. 22: 1–10

We have already seen that it is not easy to use either version of this parable for Jesus' view of the Gentiles; but what of Luke's view? Almost all the commentators think that the double invitation to those who were originally uninvited includes, in the second group, the Gentiles.[1] It is possible that Luke preserves the original point of the parable here,[2] but much more likely that he has added the second invitation to those originally uninvited, thereby reflecting what to him was already a historical fact, namely the inclusion of the Gentiles. If this is Luke's addition and if it refers to the Gentiles, then he must have understood it as a reference to the Church's Gentile mission. And although it is no more than an unspecified allusion, it is perhaps significant that whereas Jesus sees the Messianic banquet wholly as an apocalyptic event, Luke sees it as being prepared for on a historical plane. For while Luke probably does not think of the Messianic banquet itself as taking place in the present, he does see the calling of the Jews and Gentiles in preparation for the Messianic banquet of the future as occurring in history.

So far we have found that apart from the description of the centurion in ch. 7 and the veiled allusion in ch. 14, when Luke transmits material which we can compare with Mark or Matthew or both, the evidence suggests that he neither minimises, nor in any obtrusive manner expands, the references to the Gentiles in Jesus' teaching. We turn next to those passages which are peculiar to Luke to see how far they either confirm or alter the impression we have gained so far.

Lk. 2: 10

The proclamation of the angel to the shepherds includes the phrase παντὶ τῷ λαῷ. Some take this to be a reference to the

---

[1] Hahn, *Mission*, p. 130; Jeremias, *Promise*, p. 24; Manson, *Sayings*, p. 130; W. Manson, *The Gospel of Luke* (London, 1930), p. 174.

[2] The original parable was probably parallel to Matt. 8: 11–12, having two calls, one to the invited and one to those originally uninvited. Both Matthew and Luke have added an extra call at different points in the narrative.

Gentile nations,[1] while others think the reference is to all the people of Israel.[2] Rengstorf thinks that the two terms Σωτήρ and εὐαγγελίζομαι, which can be interpreted against a pagan background, are used deliberately with Gentile readers in mind.[3] This could perhaps then be said to support the interpretation of those who see a reference to the Gentiles.

The main criterion is, of course, Luke's other uses of λαός in the singular. Oliver argues that λαῷ here can include the Gentiles because elsewhere the reference is to the Jews only because they are Jesus' or the Apostles' audience, and where there is a question of identity the word 'Israel' is usually added (Acts 4: 10, 13: 24).[4] But while these last two observations may be correct, they are no basis for assuming that the Gentiles are included in Lk. 2: 10. The only positive support for such an interpretation is the use of λαός in Acts 15: 14, 18: 10, where the context makes it clear that the Gentiles are included in the new people of God.[5] But apart from these two examples, the singular λαός always refers to the Jews. Moreover, the normal reference of the phrase πᾶς ὁ λαός is to the Jews (Lk. 3: 21, 7: 29, 8: 47, 18: 43, 19: 48, 21: 38, 24: 19), and although the context and emphasis are not always the same as in 2: 10, it does show that Luke can use the phrase without any emphasis on πᾶς in a universalistic sense. Thus while admitting that a reference to the new people of God, both Jews and Gentiles, is possible in 2: 10, we conclude that it is unlikely. Also, while it is true that the words Σωτήρ and εὐαγγελίζομαι both have Hellenistic connotations and that Luke may be using them with an eye on Gentile readers, both words also have a distinctive Old Testament background and they do not necessarily affect the meaning of the word λαός.

---

1 Rengstorf, *Lukas*, p. 41; Geldenhuys, *Luke*, p. 119; H. H. Oliver, 'The Lukan birth-stories and the purpose of Luke–Acts', *NTS*, 10 (1963–4), 202–26, here 221.
2 H. Sahlin, *Der Messias und das Gottesvolk* (Uppsala, 1945), p. 213.
3 Rengstorf, *Lukas*, p. 41.
4 Oliver, 'Birth-stories', p. 221.
5 J. Dupont, 'ΛΑΟΙ 'ΕΞ 'ΕΘΝΩΝ Acts 15: 14', *NTS*, 3 (1956–7), 47f; N. A. Dahl, 'A People for his Name', *NTS*, 4 (1957–8), 319f.

Lk. 2: 30–2

The three crucial phrases to be considered in Simeon's prophecy are, πάντων τῶν λαῶν, φῶς εἰς ἀποκάλυψιν and ἐθνῶν.

1. G. D. Kilpatrick argues that the plural form λαῶν is, like the only other examples in Luke–Acts (Acts 4: 25–7), a reference to the Jews.[1] He also notes that if Luke is echoing Is. 52: 10 then he has substituted λαῶν for the ἐθνῶν in the LXX, which may be more than Luke simply avoiding repetition – a thing to which he is normally insensitive. However, this last point loses some of its weight when we consider how elusive some of Luke's references to Isaiah are. Is. 42: 6, 49: 6, 40: 5, and 52: 10 are all alluded to, but never exactly quoted.

Kilpatrick is probably correct in his interpretation of Acts 4: 25–7, because the phrase ἔθνεσιν καὶ λαοῖς Ἰσραηλ v. 27, which gives Luke's own interpretation of the previous two verses, excludes the possibility of taking ἔθνη and λαοί as synonymous.[2] However, we may be dealing with a different case in Lk. 2: 30, because here πάντων is added to the plural λαῶν.[3] It may be that by this phrase Luke wishes to incorporate both Jews and Gentiles under a common designation.[4] If so, then it is quite logical for him to make a reference to each group separately in the following two phrases: the Jews as λαοῦ σου Ἰσραηλ and the Gentiles as ἐθνῶν.[5] But even if this interpretation is illegitimate, we still have other references to the Gentiles, and to these we now turn.

2. Two attempts have been made to avoid seeing a reference to the Gentiles in the word ἐθνῶν:[6]

(a) By taking ἐθνῶν as a synonym for Ἰσραηλ.

(b) H. Sahlin argues that the phrase φῶς εἰς ἀποκάλυψιν

---

[1] G. D. Kilpatrick, 'ΛΑΟΙ at Lk. 2: 31 and Acts 4: 25, 27', *JTS*, n.s. 16, (1965), 127.

[2] Luke apparently treats it as the same as his more usual contrast between the ἔθνη (plural) and the λαός (singular), cf. Acts 26: 17, 23.

[3] We have already seen that πᾶς ὁ λαός means the Jews.

[4] The phrase πάντα τὰ ἔθνη (Lk. 24: 47) may include the Jews, whereas ἔθνη standing alone in the plural refers to the Gentiles alone.

[5] Oliver, 'Birth-stories', p. 221; Caird, *Luke*, p. 62; J. Dupont, 'Le salut des Gentils et le livre des Actes', *NTS*, 6 (1959–60), 142f.

[6] The omission of ἐθνῶν in D is not to be taken seriously, since it spoils the parallelism. It may be due to the grammatical difficulty, since we might have expected ἔθνεσι.

ἐθνῶν is a mistranslation of a proto-Lukan φῶς τῇ αἰχμαλωσίᾳ (διασπορᾷ) τῶν ἐθνῶν.[1] That is, the phrase originally referred to Diaspora Jews.

Sahlin's argument is not strictly related to our theme, since we are not concerned with the task of searching out proto-Lukan theology, but with what Luke actually wrote, whether he transmitted, created or mistranslated it. It would be significant if we could show that Luke had altered his source, but unless we are dealing with Markan or Matthean parallels the contents of Luke's source are a matter of sheer conjecture. Moreover, this phrase as a whole probably alludes to Is. 49: 6, which Luke certainly understood in a universalistic way.

There is no justification for taking ἐθνῶν as a synonym for 'Israel'. In Lukan usage the plural of ἔθνος, when it stands alone, always refers to non-Jewish peoples. Combined with πᾶς in the plural it might include the Jews, but never refers to them exclusively.

3. Kilpatrick interprets the phrase φῶς εἰς ἀποκάλυψιν ἐθνῶν to mean 'a light that the Gentiles may see', that is, something they can observe but which does not affect them.[2] One might go on to argue that the word φῶς is ambiguous, since it could refer to a light which brings judgement rather than salvation.

With regard to the first argument, we should note that while such an interpretation may be suitable for Is. 42: 6, 49: 6, it cannot automatically be transferred to Luke, since he gives his own interpretation of these prophecies when he recalls them in Acts 13: 47 and 26: 22–3, where they clearly mean that salvation has come to the Gentiles.

The term φῶς in the LXX is ambiguous. It is normally a symbol of salvation and is compared to the natural darkness in which men live (Ex. 10: 23; Job 12: 22; Ps. 4: 6, 36: 9, 56: 13, 119: 105; Is. 2: 5, 9: 2, 60: 1), but it can also have strong connotations of judgement (Job 28: 11; Ps. 37: 6, 90: 8; Is. 10: 17, 51: 4; Hos. 6: 5). In Luke too, we find that it can be used as a symbol of judgement (Lk. 8: 17, 12: 2–3) as well as a sign of salvation (Lk. 16: 8; Acts 9: 3, 22: 6, 9, 26: 18). With regard to the verse we are discussing, it is the usage in Acts 13: 47, 26: 22–3 which reveals the primary reference at this point; Luke is thinking of the salvation that would be offered to the Gentiles.

[1] Sahlin, *Gottesvolk*, p. 256.   [2] Kilpatrick, 'ΛΑΟΙ', p. 127.

It would be false, however, to think in terms of an antithesis between salvation and judgement as the function of φῶς, since both functions spring from the same source and are in reality inextricable. Salvation inevitably brings judgement with it; and judgement, if it is the judgement of God, is a prelude to the offer of salvation.

We can therefore conclude that the attempts that have been made to prove that Luke did not intend a universalistic reference in 2: 30–2 are unsuccessful. Luke has placed in Simeon's mouth a prophecy, the fulfilment of which he describes in his second volume. It is significant that Luke picks up this prophecy only at the end of the Gospel and in Acts; he does not anachronistically place its fulfilment in Jesus' earthly ministry.

Lk. 3: 1, 6

In 3: 1 Luke synchronises salvation history with general world history.[1] Luke is not so much describing two lines of history, the sacred and the secular, which meet at a certain point, as placing a set of events in the context of world history and thereby hinting at their universal significance. It is probably part of Luke's attempt to convince educated Gentiles that Christianity is not a narrow sect, but has world-wide significance.

In 3: 6 Luke alone of the Evangelists extends the quotation of Is. 40: 3f to include the phrase 'and all flesh shall see the salvation of God'. He has substituted τὸ σωτήριον τοῦ θεοῦ for ἡ δόξα κυρίου in the LXX, probably because the word σωτήριον is one of his favourite terms.

Two authors doubt whether Luke is particularly concerned to make a universal reference here:

(a) H. J. Cadbury thinks that it is more likely that the phrase Luke was interested in when he extended the quotation was 'the salvation of God' rather than 'all flesh'.[2] In support of this he notes how in Lk. 19: 46 Luke omits the phrase 'for all nations' from Mark's sentence 'My house shall be called the house of prayer for all nations' (Mk 11: 17).

We shall note later that there are other, more convincing reasons why Luke should have omitted the phrase in 19: 46,

---

[1] Caird, *Luke*, p. 69; H. Flender, *Heil und Geschichte in der Theologie des Lukas* (Munich, 1965), p. 105.
[2] H. J. Cadbury, *The Making of Luke–Acts* (London, 1961), p. 254.

rather than mere indifference to its universalist implications. Further, we cannot assume that Luke was interested in one rather than the other half of this phrase. While it is true that Luke does use Old Testament passages with his eye on only one part of the quotation,[1] the way in which he connects the concept of salvation with the universal proclamation of the gospel at other points in his narrative (Lk. 2: 30–2; Acts 28: 28) suggests that in Lk. 3: 6 the whole quotation was important to him.

(b) N. Q. King remarks that πᾶσα σάρξ could be equivalent to כָּל־בָּשָׂר which can mean 'everyone' and, therefore, 'does not imply any conscious universal intent'.[2] This is a curious form of argument, for one would have thought that 'everyone' was as universalistic a word as one could use. One certainly cannot avoid the universal implications of πᾶσα σάρξ by referring back to Hebrew equivalents. Moreover, such an interpretation ignores both the way in which this theme is taken up in the whole narrative of Acts, where a universal intent is indisputable, and Luke's interest in and interpretation of the universal prophecies from Isaiah (Lk. 2: 30–2; Acts 26: 22–3).

We can conclude, therefore, with J. Dupont and many others, that we are dealing here with a conscious addition by Luke, which therefore points to a theme which was of prime importance to him.[3] This is enhanced by the fact that this verse, picking up 2: 32, stands at the head of Luke's narrative of Jesus' ministry. Since it is a prophecy, it is perhaps as important to see how Luke thought it was fulfilled as it is to note that he has it. Clearly, it is a further expression of what Luke has already hinted at in 3: 1, namely the universal significance of Jesus. To discover how and when this universality becomes operative, we must turn to the other material in Luke's Gospel.

Lk. 3: 23

It is common among commentators to assume that by taking Jesus' genealogy back to 'Adam, the son of God', Luke wished to show 'the organic relation of Christ to all humanity'[4] and

---

[1] See later on Acts 3: 25 and 15: 16.   [2] King, 'Universalism', p. 200.
[3] Dupont, 'Gentils', pp. 138–9; Hahn, *Mission*, p. 129; Rengstorf, *Lukas*, p. 56; H. Conzelmann, *The Theology of St Luke* (London, 1961), p. 161.
[4] W. Manson, *Luke*, p. 35.

that 'his mission was ultimately to all mankind'.[1] This, it is said, is the main point of including the genealogy.[2] However, others have argued that the mention of Adam, the son of God, is from Messianic rather than universalistic motives. Luke places the narrative 'among a series of narratives attesting Jesus' Messiahship',[3] and it is a possibility, though a remote one, that his alteration of the numbers of the descendants to eleven groups of seven reflects the tradition that the Messiah would come at the end of the eleventh week.[4]

It is not easy to decide between these two alternatives; maybe Luke intended both. Suffice it to say that if there is a universalistic reference here, it is probably a secondary motif, which is obscure and undeveloped.

Lk. 4: 16f

The mention in 4: 25–7 of the actions of Elijah and Elisha is correctly taken by most commentators to contain an allusion to the future inclusion of the Gentiles.[5] The whole section 4: 16–30, which is basically a Lukan construction, gives a programmatic statement of the rest of Luke's account of Jesus' ministry. It is significantly placed at the very beginning of Jesus' public ministry and differs considerably from the parallel openings in Matthew and Mark. Several of Luke's most important themes, among them universalism, are previewed here: the Holy Spirit, the Jews' rejection of the gospel, prophecy and fulfilment, eschatology, Elijah typology, and the poor and needy. The numerous problems of interpretation do not, on the whole, concern us directly.[6] We merely note the following points:

(a) The prime motif of this section is the rejection of Jesus by the Jews, which is a recurrent theme of Luke–Acts.

---

[1] Caird, *Luke*, p. 77.
[2] Geldenhuys, *Luke*, p. 153.
[3] Ellis, *Luke*, p. 93.
[4] Rengstorf, *Lukas*, pp. 62–4. As evidence he quotes only the Latin text of IV Ezr. 14: 11. The more usual expectation was that the Messiah would come after the ninth week.
[5] King, 'Universalism', p. 200; Conzelmann, *Luke*, p. 38; Flender, *Lukas*, p. 132.
[6] See Jeremias, *Promise*, pp. 44–5; Ellis, *Luke*, pp. 95–7; Flender, *Lukas*, pp. 132–8; Conzelmann, *Luke*, pp. 35–8.

(b) The main reason, in the immediate context, for the inclusion of vv. 25–7 is that they give Old Testament precedents for performing miracles among strangers. Jesus' fellow countrymen are jealous of the works he has performed in Capernaum and he defends himself by reference to the Old Testament.

(c) The deeper meaning of vv. 25–7, however, is that they are prophetic of the one positive result of the Jews' rejection, namely the inclusion of the Gentiles. However, we should note that the reference to the Gentiles is not made explicit. For Luke, who was to write a second volume, and for us who read both Luke and Acts, the deeper significance of the rejection narrative is apparent, but in its immediate context it is allusive and unspecified.

Lk. 9: 51–18: 14

The central section of St Luke's Gospel poses many problems for the interpreter, since exactly what Luke is trying to relate and his purpose in doing so are obscure. It is relevant to our theme because it may bear on Luke's presentation of the Samaritan mission in Acts, which he sees as the stepping-stone between the Jewish and Gentile missions.

The first and most basic problem is whether or not Luke intended to describe a journey at all. An affirmative answer is given by several scholars and especially by Conzelmann,[1] who thinks that it is the journey motif above all which Luke wishes to convey. Others consider the journey motif to be subsidiary, if not absent altogether; they interpret this section of Luke thematically rather than chronologically.[2] There is the additional problem of whether the journey, if there was one, went through Samaria, and if it did, what significance this had for Luke. To help sort our way through these problems we note the following points:

1. The traditional interpretation which takes the whole of 9: 51f as a journey through Samaria is based on taking v. 56 as

---

[1] Conzelmann, *Luke*, pp. 60–5; Bosch, *Heidenmission*, pp. 103f; Flender, *Lukas*, pp. 35f; W. Gasse, 'Zum Reisebericht des Lukas', *ZNW*, 34 (1935), 293f.

[2] Ellis, *Luke*, pp. 146f; A. Schlatter, *Das Evangelium des Lukas* (Stuttgart, 1960), pp. 331f; W. Grundmann, *Das Evangelium nach Lukas* (Berlin, 1966), pp. 198–200; J. Blinzler, 'Die literarische Eigenart des sog. Reiseberichtes im Lukas-Evangelium', in *Synoptische Studien*, Festschrift for A. Wikenhauser (Munich, 1953), pp. 45f.

a reference to a Samaritan village.[1] But several scholars have noted that this verse could as well refer to a Jewish as to a Samaritan village, thereby affording something of a parallel to 4: 16f.[2] We merely note that Luke leaves the matter open, and that to build on it either way is a precarious undertaking. Moreover, if Luke intended to convey something significant by a specifically Samaritan journey, it is perhaps odd that he has left the reference so vague.

2. The notices which signify the movement of a journey are exceedingly sparse:

9: 51f Jesus determines to go towards Jerusalem.

9: 52 Jesus is in a Samaritan village.

17: 11 The debated phrase[3] καὶ αὐτὸς διήρχετο διὰ μέσον Σαμαρίας καὶ Γαλιλαίας.

18: 35 Jesus comes to Jericho.

Other than these we have a handful of vague phrases like 'as they went on their way' (10: 38, 13: 22, 14: 25), which sometimes refer to unspecificed towns and villages. While these verses leave an impression of movement, they do not follow any exact chronological or geographical pattern. It is pertinent to note that Jesus is no nearer Jerusalem in 17: 11 than in 9: 51, so that it is difficult to imagine that the journey motif as such was of supreme importance to Luke.

3. Support for the above contention is found in the fact that much of the material in 9: 51f demands a setting which makes havoc of any notion of a neat chronological account. In 13: 31 Jesus appears to be in Galilee, and several passages are set in Judea (10: 1f, 25-7, 11: 37f, 13: 1-9, 14: 1-6, 18: 1-10). It can scarcely be argued that Luke has arranged his material carefully; his method is either haphazard or based on something

---

[1] Caird, *Luke*, p. 139; E. Lohse, 'Missionarisches Handeln Jesu nach dem Evangelium des Lukas', *TZ*, 10 (1954), 1 f.

[2] Bosch, *Heidenmission*, p. 104; Conzelmann, *Luke*, pp. 65-6; Manson, *Sayings*, p. 256.

[3] Bosch, *Heidenmission*, p. 106, says that Luke wants 'merely to emphasise that Jesus finds himself to be on the journey to Jerusalem and that this journey has something to do with Samaritans. It is not said that this journey went through Samaria.' Together with the observation that this topographical notice is probably attached only to the following pericope, this seems the best explanation. For other views see Conzelmann, *Luke*, p. 71; Lohse, 'Handeln', p. 7; Gasse, 'Reisebericht', p. 295.

other than a travelogue. Luke can hardly have been unaware of this fact, and we must either admit the tension between his framework (if it is meant to be a Samaritan journey) and its contents, or argue with Lohse that Luke 'has subordinated the individual pericopes to the salvation-historical aspect of his theology and has, accordingly, arranged the whole of the second main part of the activity of Jesus under the theme of the journey to Jerusalem through Samaria'.[1] It may be simpler and, in view of points 1 and 2 above, more faithful to the facts to abandon the notion of a journey through Samaria altogether.

4. Some have argued that the Samaritan material in 10: 30f, 17: 11 supports the notion that 9: 51f is a portrayal of a journey through Samaria.[2] However, when we consider that both narratives gain their point by being directed at Jews and only have meaning in this context,[3] and when we note that there is no hint (apart from 17: 11) that they are local Samaritan traditions,[4] this argument loses much of its weight.

5. Lohse believes that 9: 51f is intended to be a Samaritan journey of Jesus, which was constructed by Luke primarily as a precedent for the Church's Samaritan mission (and in Lk. 10: 1f, the Gentile mission): 'the earthly Jesus – he wishes to show – therefore took pains to announce the arrival of the kingdom of God also to the alien Samaritans. The Samaritans stand as clear representatives of the Gentiles, who are also invited to participate in the time of Salvation.'[5]

However, we have already seen reason to doubt the validity of the words 'Samaritan' and 'journey' as a description of 9: 51f. Besides, one cannot overlook the Samaritans' brusque rejection of Jesus in 9: 51f, which offsets 10: 30f and 17: 11 more than Lohse is prepared to admit. Further, there is no warrant for the statement that Jesus preached the inbreaking of the kingdom of God to the Samaritans. Even so, we might still ask whether despite the fact that we cannot speak of a Samaritan journey or of Jesus preaching to the Samaritans these pericopes have any significance. Treated as individual narratives, they

---

[1] Lohse, 'Handeln', p. 9. [2] Rengstorf, Lukas, p. 132.
[3] Bosch, Heidenmission, p. 106.
[4] Conzelmann, Luke, pp. 71–2.
[5] Lohse, 'Handeln', p. 11. Cf. Conzelmann, Luke, p. 72, who sees 17: 11f as Luke's attempt to justify the Samaritan mission in the early Church.

probably do.[1] They are one of the examples of Jesus breaking down traditional barriers by meeting with and healing non-Jews.[2] Since Luke wrote the story of the Samaritan mission in Acts, he can scarcely have been unaware of the precedent set by Jesus' healing of a Samaritan. But apart from the fact that he relates the narrative in 17: 11f and is the only evangelist to do so, Luke does not use it specifically as a justification of the later Samaritan mission.

6. What then are we to make of 9: 51f? B. Reicke has pertinently observed that the bulk of this central section of Luke is concerned with the teaching of Jesus, alternating between instruction for the disciples and controversies with opponents – both of which were important for leaders and missionaries in the early Church.[3] Ellis, developing this point, correctly describes Luke's picture as one of Jesus the teacher rather than Jesus the traveller.[4] References to the latter theme, while present, are subordinate to the former; they help to keep the teaching in perspective, since they are seen as the teachings of a Messiah who is rejected by the Jews and who is appointed by God to suffer in Jerusalem (9: 51, 12: 50, 13: 33, 18: 31).[5] This links well with Conzelmann's comment that according to 13: 33f the journey (we would add, such as it is) is an expression of Jesus' awareness that he must suffer: 'He does not travel in a different area from before, but he travels in a different manner.'[6] To which one can add the comment of Flender that: 'The journey towards Jerusalem is to be seen not only from the viewpoint of a way to suffering but at the same time as a triumphal procession of Jesus to his heavenly exaltation.'[7]

---

[1] Bosch, *Heidenmission*, p. 107, thinks the Samaritan stories are placed here because Jesus is on his way to Jerusalem and death, since there is a clear connection between the Samaritans, the Gentiles and Jesus' death.

[2] See ch. 1 above.

[3] B. Reicke, 'Instruction and discussion in the travel narrative', *S.E.*, 1 (1959), 216.   [4] Ellis, *Luke*, pp. 146f.

[5] W. Grundmann, 'Fragen der Komposition des luk. Reiseberichtes', *ZNW*, 50 (1959), 252f, and C. F. Evans, 'The central section of St Luke's Gospel', *SG*, pp. 37f, also interpret Lk. 9: 51f thematically and emphasise Jesus as the teacher.

[6] Conzelmann, *Luke*, pp. 64–5; Grundmann, *Lukas*, p. 198; J. Schneider, 'Zur Analyse des luk. Reiseberichtes', in *Synoptische Studien*, Festschrift for A. Wikenhauser (Munich, 1953), pp. 207–29.

[7] Flender, *Lukas*, pp. 36, 85–6.

We conclude that the whole section 9: 51f has no direct or exceptional significance for Luke's view of mission.

The mission of the Seventy. Lk. 10: 1f

There are two problems which concern us in 10: 1: first, is the correct reading 'seventy' or 'seventy-two' and second, is the number symbolic, and if so to what does it refer?

Many commentators think that the basic reference is to Gen. 10, where it is said that there are seventy nations in the world.[1] The LXX at this point has seventy-two and this is thought to account for the textual variant in Lk. 10: 1. The reference is then frequently assumed to be to a Gentile mission of the Seventy, seen as a parallel to the mission of the Twelve to Israel (Lk. 9). Thus Lk. 10: 1f foreshadows the Gentile mission in Acts.

Others think that the primary reference is to Num. 11: 16–17, 24–5, where seventy elders are appointed by Moses to help him bear the burden of his task.[2] Leaney thinks that as in Num. 11 Eldad and Medad are added, it may mean that the number of elders was seventy-two and that this explains the variant reading in Lk. 10: 1.[3]

B. Metzger has dealt thoroughly with the problems which face the interpreter of Lk. 10: 1.[4] He has made it clear that the problem of the variant reading cannot be decided by the normal logic of textual criticism. Both readings have good manuscript support, and every argument in favour of one or the other reading can be countered or reversed. He goes on to list all the possible references in the Old Testament and Judaism for the numbers seventy and seventy-two; once again the result is negative, since there are various feasible allusions for both numbers.[5] To aid us in our decision we note the following points:

---

[1] Rengstorf, *Lukas*, p. 135; Jeremias, *Promise*, p. 24; W. Manson, *Luke*, p. 123; Flender, *Lukas*, p. 26.

[2] Caird, *Luke*, p. 143; King, 'Universalism', p. 201; Leaney, *Luke*, p. 176; Manson, *Sayings*, p. 257.

[3] Leaney, *Luke*.

[4] B. Metzger, 'Seventy or seventy-two disciples?', *NTS*, 5 (1958–9), 299f.

[5] Nevertheless, many of the allusions listed as possible by Metzger are highly improbable. To take as a possibility any reference with the number 70 or 72, whether it is to books, angels or bullocks, is to go beyond the bounds of credibility. After all, Luke is thinking of men whose task is to preach. This also makes improbable a reference to the Letter of Aristeas, where the 72

(a) As a preliminary point we note that to assert with any certainty one or the other reading or reference is impossible. There is no single interpretation which is indisputable.

(b) The attempt by Bosch to include a double reference to both Num. 11 and Gen. 10 probably asks too much of the text.[1]

(c) We must allow for the possibility that the number is merely a convenient round number which has no symbolic significance.

(d) The chief argument in favour of a reference to Gen. 10 is that we know that Luke wrote the story of the Gentile mission in Acts. It is perhaps also true that the number seventy as a reference to the nations of the world is the most obvious of the possible allusions. That the Pentecost narrative (Acts 2) can be read as a reversal of the story of the tower of Babel (Gen. 11) might add a little support to this interpretation of Lk. 10: 1f. Moreover, the seventy-two nations enumerated by the LXX of Gen. 10 is probably the simplest explanation of the textual variant in Lk. 10: 1. But this last point does not necessarily support the claim that Luke intended a reference to Gen. 10. He may have alluded to Num. 11 and a later editor altered it to a reference to the LXX of Gen. 10.

(e) There are several factors which support a reference to Num. 11. First, the parallelism with the mission of the Twelve. Secondly, whatever Lk. 10: 1 symbolises, if it symbolises anything at all, according to the rest of the chapter the mission of the Seventy was to Israel. Thirdly, Luke is fond of using Old Testament figures, especially Moses and Elijah, typologically of Jesus' person and work.[2] Finally, the process of reading back our knowledge of Acts into Luke's Gospel, while often legitimate, has to be treated with considerable care. We can easily see references which Luke may not have intended. Further, the Lukan material we have already considered shows that Luke does not anachronistically place the Gentile mission in Jesus' pre-Resurrection ministry.

are translators of the Hebrew Old Testament – cf. S. Jellicoe, 'St Luke and the Letter of Aristeas', *NTS*, 6 (1959–60), 319–21. Gen. 10 and Num. 11, or the Rabbinic variations on the latter passage given by Metzger, are still the most likely references.

[1] Bosch, *Heidenmission*, p. 109; cf. Ellis, *Luke*, p. 153.
[2] G. W. H. Lampe, 'The Lucan portrait of Christ', *NTS*, 2 (1955–6), 160f.

Taking these points together, it seems that if a symbolic reference is intended, it is to Num. 11 rather than to Gen. 10. In recounting the mission of the Seventy, Luke may well have had one eye on the later mission of the Church, but in the immediate context the mission of the Seventy is clearly to Israel.

Lk. 24: 46f

The last passage for our consideration contains the first open and direct command for, as distinct from prophetic hints of, the Gentile mission.[1] The importance of this section can be seen in the following observations:

1. Lk. 24: 47 is Luke's equivalent to Mk 13: 10. Various reasons have been suggested for Luke's omission of Mk 13: 10. E. Grässer suggests that it may have been because Luke's version of Mark did not contain Mk 13: 10, the verse having been added by a later editor.[2] G. Harder thinks that it was because the universal mission had not begun by the time Luke wrote his Gospel.[3] Conzelmann makes a far more convincing suggestion when he says that Luke omits Mk 13: 10 because he wants to sever the connection between the mission and the End.[4] Luke's equivalent to Mk 13: 10 is lifted out of the apocalyptic context it has in Mark and, as a result, loses the temporal limitations implicit in the whole of Mk 13. For Luke the End comes after, but in no way determines, the Gentile mission. The way is thus cleared for Luke to give a historical account of the progress of this mission in his second volume. But while Conzelmann has explained the significance of Luke's omission of Mk 13: 10, he does not emphasise the equally important equivalent to this verse in Lk. 24: 47.[5]

2. The command for the Gentile mission is closely connected with several other important Lukan themes: witness, the Holy

[1] Some would include Lk. 15: 11–32. Ellis, *Luke*, p. 198, thinks that Luke's readers would have seen the prodigal as a symbol of the Gentiles. But Luke gives no hint that this is so. The contrast is probably between the Jewish leaders (elder son) and the 'poor of the land' (prodigal).

[2] Grässer, *Parusieverzögerung*, p. 160.

[3] G. Harder, 'Das eschatologische Geschichtsbild der sogenannten kleinen Apokalypse Mk 13', *Th. Viat.*, 4 (1952), 78f.

[4] Conzelmann, *Luke*, p. 214 n. 1.

[5] Hahn, *Mission*, pp. 130–1, draws out the parallels between Lk. 24: 47 and Mk 13: 10

Spirit, prophecy and fulfilment, Jerusalem, the Ascension and eschatology. Later, we shall look more closely at these themes. There is also a close parallelism between Lk. 24: 46f and Acts 1: 1f. The command for the Gentile mission and its related themes are inseparably linked with the account of the development of this mission in Acts.

3. The phrase οὕτως γέγραπται in v. 46 is of immense significance in this context. It introduces a new line of thought, namely that the mission is based not only on Jesus' command but also on Old Testament prophecy. The reference is probably intentionally dual, both to the Old Testament prophecies themselves[1] and to Luke's versions of them in 2: 10, 2: 30–2, 3: 6. Luke picks up a prophetic theme of the earlier part of his work and re-presents it in the form of a direct command of the Risen Lord. A comparison with Mk 13: 10 is also instructive. In place of Mark's δεῖ, which is both set in and to be interpreted by its eschatological context, we have Luke's οὕτως γέγραπται, which alters the setting to that of prophecy and fulfilment. The Gentile mission is thus firmly embedded in the scheme of prophecy and fulfilment.

4. In the phrase μετάνοιαν εἰς ἄφεσιν ἁμαρτιῶν Luke introduces concepts which are especially significant for him. The term μετάνοια is connected with Jesus' preaching and, above all, with the missionary preaching in Acts (Lk. 5: 32; Acts 2: 38, 5: 31, 17: 30). When connected with ἄφεσις τῶν ἁμαρτιῶν (Lk. 3: 3; Acts 2: 38, 5: 31) or πίστις / πιστεύειν (Acts 11: 17–18, 17: 30f, 20: 31f, 26: 18–20), it becomes *the* term for conversion in Luke–Acts.[2] The phrase ἐπὶ τῷ ὀνόματι αὐτοῦ expresses for Luke, in a special way, the presence of Christ.[3] This terminology betrays the influence of the preaching of the early Church and of the Church in Luke's day, in particular, the concept of conversion and the exaltation christology which is so predominant in Acts.

---

[1] Old Testament prophecies for Jesus' death and resurrection were found in Is. 53: 4, 11; Hos. 6: 2. The exact reference for 'the preaching of repentance for the forgiveness of sins to all nations' is not clear. No Old Testament passage gives a precise parallel to this commission (cf. Is. 42: 6, 49: 6; Joel 2: 1; Wisd. 3: 14).

[2] Conzelmann, *Luke*, pp. 99f, 225f; U. Wilckens, *Die Missionsreden in der Apostelgeschichte* (Neukirchen, 1963), p. 178.

[3] Conzelmann, *Luke*, p. 177.

THE LUKAN OMISSIONS

Before turning to a final summary of the results of this chapter we must consider several significant omissions which directly relate to the Gentile question. For example, the omission of Mk 7: 24–30, 10: 45, 11: 17 'all nations', 14: 9, all of which make either direct or indirect references to the Gentiles, could be taken to betray a deliberate attempt by Luke to damp down the universalism of Mark. On the other hand, the omission of verses such as Matt. 10: 5b, 6, 15: 24, reveals exactly the opposite tendency, which in turn should make us wary of assuming that the other omissions are significant for Luke's overall picture of the Gentiles:

1. The omission of Mk 7: 24–30 could be explained by saying that Luke is writing for Gentile readers, to whom the equation 'dogs equals Gentiles' would have been offensive. However, since the end of the story is definitely pro-Gentile, and since Luke could have rewritten the incident omitting the reference to dogs, this explanation is not convincing. This omission is part of the so-called 'great omission' from Mark (Mk 6: 47 – 8: 26), which has puzzled scholars for many years. It may well be that the explanation for this is a purely mechanical one, namely, Luke did not have this part of Mark, since all of Mk 7 is the sort of material which Luke could well have used. That he has the story of Jesus' healing of the centurion's servant shows that his omission of the story of the Syrophoenician woman is not because he wants to reduce Mark's universalism.

2. The omission of Mk 10: 45 is very difficult to explain. If it was the ἀντὶ πολλῶν which worried Luke, then presumably he could have omitted this phrase and included the rest of Mk 10: 45. Therefore, the omission cannot be described as anti-universalist. It might be argued that the sacrificial interpretation of Christ's death was uncongenial to Luke and that this accounts for the omission. It may be true that Luke has no distinctive *theologia crucis*, but it is also apparent from Acts 20: 38 and Lk. 19b–20, if we can include the latter text,[1] that where

---

[1] On this complex textual problem see H. Chadwick, 'The shorter text of Lk. 22: 15–20', *HTR*, 50 (1957), 249f; Jeremias, *Words*, pp. 138f; H. Schurmann, 'Lu. 22: 19–20 als ursprüngliche Textüberlieferung', *Bib.*, 32 (1951), 364f, 522f.

Luke finds such material in his tradition, he does not see any need to suppress it. Presumably, therefore, he did not find it objectionable. It could be that Luke's rearranged setting of Mk 10: 42–5 explains the omission. That is, he has transposed Mk 10: 42–5 to the setting of the Last Supper Lk. 22: 24–7, so that if we take 22: 19b–20 as genuine, it could be argued that, having already included a saying on the redemptive significance of Jesus' death, he does not repeat himself in vv. 24–7. If this explanation is unsatisfactory, then the purpose of Luke's omission remains a mystery.

3. The omission of the phrase 'all the nations' from Mk 11: 17 is understandable on the presupposition that Luke wrote his Gospel after A.D. 70, when the Temple had been destroyed and was manifestly not a house of prayer for all nations. One can compare Luke's account of the destructive work of the Gentiles in the Temple and its surroundings in Lk. 21: 20–4.

4. The omission of Mk 14: 9 could also be explained on the assumption that Luke is correcting sayings which in his time were either manifestly unfulfilled or even contradicted. Luke, who wrote the story of the preaching of the Gospel in all the world, could find no trace of the fulfilment of this prophecy; the woman was not mentioned in every place that the gospel was preached. More likely, however, is that Luke preferred to follow a separate version of the story of the sinner woman (Lk. 7: 36–50) which did not contain an equivalent to Mk 12: 9.

5. Assuming that Lk. 22: 19b–20 was originally in Luke, it is noticeable that Mark's ὑπὲρ πολλῶν Mk 14: 24 is altered to Luke's ὑπὲρ ὑμῶν, thus obliterating one more universal reference. But since Luke is probably quoting a liturgical formula at this point the alteration cannot automatically be ascribed to him. It probably arose as a result of a tendency to personalise the reference in liturgical usage, a process which had affected the tradition before it reached Luke.

6. The omission of Matt. 10: 5b–6, 15: 24, is difficult to assess, since we cannot be sure that these verses were in the common source used by Matthew and Luke; they may have been known to Matthew alone. If we assume, for the sake of argument, that they were in Q and that Luke knew of them, then their omission is understandable. Matt. 10: 23 remained unfulfilled, and Matt. 10: 5b–6, 15: 24 express a particularism

which is uncongenial to Luke's own understanding of Jesus' attitude to the Gentiles. Matthew can incorporate them by re-interpreting them in a special way. He neutralises their particularism by understanding it to be confined to one period of a *heilsgeschichtlich* scheme. That is, Jesus' particularism applied only to his pre-Resurrection ministry. Matthew's understanding of the temporal limitations of 10: 23 is not so easy to explain. Perhaps he took it to mean that the Son of Man would come to the villages before the disciples could get there, that is, he would move faster than they; or perhaps he recorded the saying without fully realising its implications. Luke omits these sayings because he, unlike Matthew, did not see the possibilities of reinterpretation.

We can conclude from the above points that for each of the Lukan omissions a convincing explanation can be found without assuming that they have any particular relevance for the Gentile question, except to say that Luke was keen to avoid both unfulfilled prophecies and expressly particularist sayings. Certainly, none of them can be said to prove that Luke was anxious to tone down the universalism which he found in Mark.

CONCLUSIONS

1. It has frequently been assumed that of all the Evangelists it is Luke, above all, who is the universalist. In the past it has been the habit of commentators to accept this uncritically and pass it on to the next generation. Cadbury was the first to challenge the notion, though with a certain amount of moderation.[1] More recently King has spoken of 'partial krypsis of his universalism while he is writing his Gospel',[2] and in the course of proving this he has reinterpreted almost every universalist reference in Luke in a non-universalist manner.

Our results lead us to maintain both of these viewpoints with some modification. The addition of 2: 10, 30–2, 3: 6, 4: 25–7, and 24: 47 to the gospel narrative by Luke encourages the notion of Luke as a universalist. And while we have seen reason to disagree with almost all of King's detailed exegesis, he is nevertheless right in speaking of a partial krypsis. We note, for

[1] Cadbury, *Making*, pp. 254f.
[2] King, 'Universalism', p. 205; Hahn, *Mission*, p. 128.

example, that the distinctively Lukan material we have just mentioned occurs in the chapters which either precede or programmatically outline the ministry of Jesus, or, as with 24: 47, is limited to Jesus' post-Resurrection activity. But we cannot agree with King that this krypsis is a result of a deliberate damping down by Luke of the universalism which he found in Mark. Rather, he is basically following the tradition he received, and where he does not follow it, as for example in his omissions, it is normally for a very good reason. Luke does not anachronistically place the Gentile mission within the earthly ministry of Jesus. His additions at the beginning of the Gospel are always prophetic and forward-looking; they are only picked up in the form of a command in 24: 47, a passage which points forward to the unfolding universal mission which Luke relates in Acts.

2. We have already led ourselves into our second conclusion, namely that Luke is almost always a faithful recorder of tradition which speaks about the Gentiles. He relates material which gives both what we have found to be Jesus' attitude to the Gentiles (Lk. 7: 1–10, 10: 12, 13–16, 11: 29–32, 33, 13: 18–21, 28) and what we have considered to be a Markan development of this theme (Lk. 20: 9–19). In these passages Luke gives no hint of his own view, but simply passes on the tradition which he received.

3. In two cases, 14: 16–24, 24: 47, we have discovered material which is distinctively Lukan. The latter verse, especially, is fundamental for discovering Luke's own viewpoint. Cadbury, in his discussion of Luke's universalism, merely noted that it exists without offering any explanation of it or attempting to relate it to Luke's overall plan.[1] King attributes Luke's special material, including this verse, to Luke's artistic genius: 'The theme which he played over earlier and had repeated now and then, has to wait until the second part of the work for its crescendo.'[2] But apart from this general comment, King does not consider 24: 47 in any detail or try to relate it to the total framework of Luke's thought. Hahn comes closest to understanding Luke's own viewpoint, both because he sees the importance of 24: 47 and because he relates it to other themes in Luke. He speaks of 'the fact that the preaching of the gospel among the Gentiles belongs neither to Jesus' earthly activities

---

[1] Cadbury, *Making*, pp. 254f.   [2] King, 'Universalism', p. 205.

nor to the eschatological events, but has its place in the period of the Church. Luke, therefore, logically connects the first saying about it with an appearance of the Risen Lord, and does not develop his own view of mission until he comes to Acts.'[1] Thus Hahn has begun, but not fully developed, a study of the distinctiveness of Luke's viewpoint and its relation to the rest of his ideas. Two of these, in particular, are of fundamental importance for understanding Luke's attitude to the Gentiles; others can wait for fuller treatment when we delve into Acts.[2]

The first of these is the notion of proof from prophecy – or, perhaps better, promise and fulfilment – which has slowly come to light as a central theme of the Lukan writings.[3] Again, Cadbury gave it its embryonic form, and since then it has received increasing attention.[4] In connection with the Gentiles we noted the use of or allusion to prophecy in Lk. 2: 30–2, 3: 6, 4: 21, 25–7 and, above all, in 24: 45–6. In this manner Luke makes it clear that the inclusion of the Gentiles is not the result of a mere quirk of history or a whim of God; rather, it is grounded in the eternal will of God and is an integral part of his promises to Israel.

The theme of promise and fulfilment is closely connected with Luke's conception of *Heilsgeschichte*. As will be seen in the next chapter, we do not use the term *Heilsgeschichte* pejoratively, nor do we necessarily imply, *pace* Conzelmann, that Luke saw this *Heilsgeschichte* as divided into three distinct epochs. It is the twofold structure of promise and fulfilment which dominates Luke's understanding of salvation history. In fact, because of the

---

[1] Hahn, *Mission*, p. 129.

[2] These are the connections with Jerusalem (24: 47), the Apostles as witnesses (24: 48), salvation (2: 10, 32, 3: 6), and the connection between the acceptance of the Gentiles and the rejection of the Jews (4: 25–7, 7: 9, 13: 28, 14: 16–24).

[3] Oliver, 'Birth-stories', p. 255, doubts its importance as a theme: 'Against it is the consideration that it has played no part in recent *redaktionsgeschichtliche* study of Luke–Acts.' To which it has been aptly replied: 'All the worse for *Redaktionsgeschichte* if that is the case' – N. A. Dahl, 'The story of Abraham in Luke–Acts', *SLA*, pp. 139f, quotation from p. 157 n. 54.

[4] Cadbury, *Making*, pp. 303f; Conzelmann, *Luke*, pp. 157–63; Dahl, 'Abraham', pp. 139f; P. Schubert, 'The structure and significance of Lk. 24', *NS*, 165f; E. Lohse, 'Lukas als Theologe der Heilsgeschichte', *Ev. Th.*, 14 (1954), 256f; Ph. Vielhauer, 'On the "Paulinism" of Acts', *SLA*, pp. 33f; P. S. Minear, 'Luke's use of the birth-stories', *SLA*, pp. 111f.

various connotations which have attached themselves to the term *Heilsgeschichte* in recent Lukan studies, the theme of promise and fulfilment is probably a better framework in which to place Luke's ideas. It is also important to note that the theme of promise and fulfilment is not automatically to be seen as a substitute for imminent eschatology;[1] this pattern can as easily be present in a scheme dominated by imminent expectation, or where this expectation is present in one form or another. Nevertheless, it is a fact that the theme of promise and fulfilment is one of the fundamental themes which characterise Luke's account of Jesus' ministry and the history of the Church, an account which in turn has moved away, at least in part, from imminent expectation.[2] As Vielhauer says: 'The old and the new (aeons) are related to each other as are promise and fulfilment, that is as historical processes. The expectation of the imminent End has disappeared and the failure of the Parousia is no longer a problem; Luke replaces the apocalyptic expectation of the earliest congregation and the christological eschatology of Paul by a redemptive historical pattern of promise and fulfilment in which eschatology also receives its appropriate place.'[3]

The importance of this theme for Luke's understanding of the Gentile mission now becomes clear. It confirms what we have already concluded from 14: 16–24 and 24: 46–7. Luke has lifted the Gentile mission out of its Markan eschatological context and placed it in his scheme of *Heilsgeschichte*. Thus in the promise–fulfilment theme we can claim added support for our contention that Luke's handling of the Gentile mission is deliberate rather than accidental. How far this can be called a Lukan 'theology' of the Gentiles and the Gentile mission is not

[1] As Vielhauer and sometimes Conzelmann appear to do.

[2] Cf. the comments on 24: 47. The importance of this theme for Luke may be indicated in Lk. 1: 1f, if 'those things which have been accomplished among us' can be taken as a reference to the fulfilment of Old Testament prophecies. Moreover, as Dahl, 'Abraham', p. 153, notes, this theme is found especially where there may seem to be a break in historical continuity: the beginning of the gospel story, Jesus' passion and resurrection, the transition to the time of the Church and the conversion of Cornelius.

[3] This does not mean that we subscribe fully to all the statements in this quotation or to the whole of Vielhauer's reconstruction of Lukan and Pauline theology.

easy to say, for in many respects Luke is simply reflecting what were for him two indisputable historical facts: the delay of the Parousia and the Gentile mission of the Church. However, we shall return to this theme when we have studied the material in Acts.

The second theme which we shall discuss at this point in connection with the Gentile mission is that of the Holy Spirit, which has long been recognised as one of the major theological ideas in Luke's writings.[1] There is much that can be said, but for our purposes it is sufficient to consider the relationship between the Holy Spirit, the Gentiles and eschatology. The connections between the Gentiles and the Holy Spirit are not so abundant in Luke's Gospel as they are in Acts. However, we can note that the prophecy of Simeon in 2: 30–2 was spoken 'in the Spirit' (2: 27) and that the mention of the Gentiles in 4: 25–7 is made by one who claims that 'the Spirit of the Lord is upon me' (4: 18a, 21). In fact, all of Jesus' sayings or activities concerning the Gentiles are, in Luke's view, the words and deeds of one who was conceived (1: 35) and anointed (3: 21f) by the Spirit, and whose possession of it, while in some ways similar to that of the pious men and women in Lk. 1–2 and Acts, was in other ways unique.[2] In Acts, the link between the Spirit and the Gentiles is firmly forged, but it is prepared for in Lk. 24: 47f. The disciples are commanded to go on a universal mission, but not before they have received the 'power from on high' (v. 49), and in Acts 1: 4–8 the two themes are inseparably linked. This is confirmed throughout the rest of Acts, where the Spirit guides and prompts every vital stage of the Church's mission (Acts 8: 29, 10: 19f, 13: 2, 16: 6 etc.).[3]

How then is the Spirit related to Luke's eschatology? For Conzelmann and Schweizer the Spirit is no longer the eschato-

[1] C. K. Barrett, *The Holy Spirit in the Gospel Tradition* (London, 1954); pp. 101f; Cadbury, *Making*, pp. 286–8; Conzelmann, *Luke*, pp. 173–84, Flender, *Lukas*, pp. 122–31; A. Ehrhardt, *The Framework of the New Testament Stories* (Manchester, 1964), pp. 64f; G. W. H. Lampe, 'The Holy Spirit in the Lukan writings', *SG*, pp. 159f; E. Schweizer, art. πνεῦμα, *TWNT*, VI, 399f; E. Lohse, 'Die Bedeutung des Pfingstberichtes im Rahmen des luk. Geschichtswerkes', *Ev. Th.*, 13 (1953), 422f; H. von Baer, *Der Heilige Geist in den Lukasschriften* (Stuttgart, 1926), pp. 1f.

[2] Barrett, *Spirit*, p. 101; Conzelmann, *Luke*, pp. 180f.

[3] We shall return to this theme in later chapters.

55

logical gift,[1] but is a theme which Luke uses to deal with the delay of the Parousia: 'Luke is the first to make this deliberate appeal to the phenomenon of the Spirit as a solution to the delay of the Parousia.'[2] It is probable that Conzelmann overestimates both the originality and the extent of Luke's 'theological' thinking about the Spirit, but there is some truth in what he says.[3] Three observations make it clear how Luke understood the relationship between the Spirit and eschatology:

1. In Mk 9: 1, 13: 26, the word δύναμις is used in one of its characteristic Markan contexts, namely that of eschatology. In Lk. 4: 14, 24: 49, Acts 1: 8 the concepts δύναμις and πνεῦμα are linked. Only Luke connects δύναμις with the Spirit; that is, 'the third Evangelist seems to have regarded "power" as the energy of the Spirit, whereas the characteristic connotation of δύναμις in Mark is eschatological'.[4] Conzelmann comments, 'thus in Luke the concept δύναμις is linked with the historical ministry of Jesus and the present life of the Church'.[5]

2. In Acts 1: 8 the gift of the Spirit and the universal mission – the one being, in Luke's view, the implicate of the other – are seen as the substitutes (see especially ἀλλά v. 8a) for the knowledge of the End. This does not, of course, cancel out hope for the End (Acts 1: 11), but it does correct the expectation that it was imminent.[6]

3. If we take the longer reading in Acts 2: 17, then we have another clear example of the meaning of the Spirit for Luke.[7] The Old Testament prophecy from Joel is expanded by Luke to include the phrase 'in the last days'. For Luke, as well as for Joel, the Spirit is a sign of the End, but for Luke the emphasis is on 'days' and not 'last', since the phrase refers to an extended period of history in which the Spirit is active.

---

[1] Conzelmann, *Luke*, pp. 95f, 136; Schweizer, *TWNT*, vi, 404f. Cf. Lohse, 'Pfingstberichtes', pp. 422f, who sees Pentecost both as an eschatological event and as inaugurating a new period of salvation history, the last stage before the Parousia.　　　[2] Conzelmann, *Luke*, p. 136.

[3] Conzelmann underestimates the extent to which Paul has thought out the relationship between the Spirit and eschatology (Rom. 8: 23; II Cor. 1: 22, 4: 5). In fact, if anything it is Paul rather than Luke who has 'thought it out theologically'.

[4] Barrett, *Spirit*, p. 77.　　　[5] Conzelmann, *Luke*, p. 183.

[6] Conzelmann, *Luke*, p. 136; Grässer, *Parusieverzögerung*, pp. 204f.

[7] For further discussion of Pentecost see chapter 4.

These examples are sufficient to show that for Luke the Spirit is the power at work in salvation history. He is no longer the gift of the last days, in the original sense, but is the gift to the Church in the period between the Resurrection and the Parousia. It would be misleading to call this a 'theology' of the Holy Spirit, if by this we mean something that has been carefully and methodically thought out. Luke does not appear to have done this; rather, he simply tries to reconstruct and make intelligible the experience of the early Church, at the same time reflecting the experience of the Church of his day. The evidence we have adduced, therefore, is best described as a number of uncoordinated hints of how Luke understood the gift of the Spirit to the Church.

Both of the themes with which Luke links the Gentile mission, promise and fulfilment and the Holy Spirit, express his awareness of the continuation of history; they both allow for and to some extent explain the delay of the Parousia. Thus Luke makes it clear that the Gentile mission is no longer to be seen as an apocalyptic or even as an eschatological event; it is a part of ongoing history. How far this is a result of systematic theological thinking by Luke, and how far simply a reflection of the historical facts as he knew them, is a question to which we shall return.

We can now draw together some of the results we have gained so far. For Jesus, the proclamation to the Gentiles was strictly an apocalyptic event. He neither promised, foresaw, nor commanded a historical mission to the Gentiles. When we turn to Mark, we find that a significant change has taken place. Now the Gentile mission is seen to be a historical process which must be completed before the End comes. For Mark, the Gentile mission still stands in an eschatological context, but it is no longer an apocalyptic event. Luke makes the final and perhaps inevitable break, by severing even the eschatological connections. Both in the verses 14: 16–24, 24: 47 and in the way he consistently links the Gentile mission with the Holy Spirit and the fulfilment of prophecy, Luke betrays his own viewpoint. The Gentile mission, planned for in God's eternal purpose, takes place in ongoing history, the salvation history of the Church. It is neither determined by nor determines the End. In this manner, Luke, in his Gospel, prepares for the narrative which he relates in Acts.

In the previous chapter we noted the firm interconnection in Jesus' teaching between the Gentiles and eschatology. The fact that Jesus expected the End to come soon or even immediately after his death had as one of its logical implicates an apocalyptic view of the Gentile mission. The explanation of Jesus' attitude to the Gentiles lay in his eschatology. The same is true of Luke, to the extent that his view of the Gentile mission fits in with his understanding of history and eschatology. His presentation of Jesus' attitude towards the Gentile mission should logically lead him to tone down Jesus' imminent expectations. To this extent, Luke's view is the opposite of Jesus', in that it is the Gentile mission as a historical phenomenon which is one of the factors which explain Luke's eschatology rather than vice-versa. We know, therefore, what Luke should have done with the eschatology of Jesus. It is now our task to discover how far he did it.

CHAPTER 3

LUKAN ESCHATOLOGY

Our chief concern in this chapter is to discover how far Luke betrays his own views in his portrayal of Jesus' eschatology. Frequent reference will be made to H. Conzelmann,[1] since his is the view which is most influential and widely held today. Since the advent of his book *The Theology of St Luke* it has become a byword of New Testament studies that Luke is a man with a theological axe to grind. He is pictured as one who has systematically manipulated and recast his sources down to the smallest detail, in order to squeeze them into his overall theological framework. A brief outline of Conzelmann's view will suffice at this stage: Jesus and the early Christians expected the Parousia to occur very soon, at least within their lifetimes. This hope was disappointed and it led to a series of crises. By the time Luke came to write, stop-gap answers had worn thin; it was no longer sufficient to postpone the date of the End bit by bit; a final, lasting solution was needed. This Luke provides. He consistently eradicates expectation of an imminent End from his texts; in its place he propounds a theory of *Heilsgeschichte* in which the Parousia loses its dominant position by being relegated to the far-distant and indefinite future. This *Heilsgeschichte* is divided into three distinct epochs: the first is the Old Testament epoch, up to and including John the Baptist; the second is the period of Jesus' earthly ministry, characterised in the German title of Conzelmann's book as 'The Middle of Time'; the third epoch is that of the Church. These three eras are, for Conzelmann, more significant for their differences than for their continuity, and he sees this scheme as the key to the whole of Luke's theology. The details of Conzelmann's theory will be elucidated in the discussion of individual texts.

[1] For similar views see also Lohse, *Lukas*, pp. 300f; Grässer, *Parusieverzögerung*, pp. 180f; Cadbury, *Making*, pp. 282f; E. Käsemann, *Essays on New Testament Themes* (London, 1964), pp. 41f; Ph. Vielhauer, 'Paulinism', pp. 33–50.

JOHN THE BAPTIST AND THE THREE EPOCHS

Luke's portrait of John is basic to Conzelmann's theory.[1] The spheres of activity of John and Jesus are said to be precisely demarcated: the phrase ὀπίσω μου (Mk 1: 7) is omitted in Lk. 3: 16, and Jesus' baptism is related (Lk. 3: 21–2) without reference to John, whose imprisonment is described in the preceding verse. Further, in Matthew and Mark, John is an eschatological forerunner equated with Elijah (Mk 9: 9–12, Matt. 11: 3) and in Matt. 3: 2 he preaches the kingdom of God. In Luke this connection is severed and consequently these verses are absent. John is firmly embedded in the Old Testament era, preaching a timeless ethic (Lk. 3: 8–20) which is no longer motivated by an expectation of an imminent end. U. Wilckens has argued that the same pattern is followed in Acts 10: 37, 13: 27.[2] The use of the preposition πρό in προκηρύξαντος and πρὸ προσώπου is Luke's way of emphasising that John belongs to the Old Testament epoch. To all of this we can say the following:

    1. In Lk. 1: 17 it is said that John will act in 'the spirit and power of Elijah'. There is no good reason why we should disregard this verse which, while not identifying John and Elijah, does draw a close parallel between the two figures. Moreover, in Lk. 7: 27 the passage from Mal. 3: 1 – 'Behold I send my messenger before your face' – is used of John, which makes the omission of ὀπίσω μου in Lk. 3: 16 of less significance. In Jewish tradition, the messenger of Mal. 3: 1 is, by way of the explanatory addition in Mal. 4: 5, identified with the figure of Elijah, who in turn is seen as the eschatological forerunner of the Messiah.[3] Luke may, of course, have been unaware of this tradition, but we cannot simply assume this.

    2. The claim that in John's preaching 'the eschatological call to repentance is transposed into timeless ethical exhortation'[4] is scarcely a fair exegesis of Lk. 3: 8–20. The use of ἤδη in 3: 9 and the tenses of the verbs in 3: 17 show that John's teaching was

---

[1] Conzelmann, *Luke*, pp. 18f, 101–2; Grässer, *Parusieverzögerung*, pp. 197f.
[2] Wilckens, *Missionsreden*, pp. 101f.
[3] *S.B.*, IV, 748f; J. Jeremias, 'Elijah', *TWNT*, II, 928f; C. H. Dodd, *According to the Scriptures* (London, 1934), p. 21.
[4] Conzelmann, *Luke*, p. 102.

motivated by the threat of an imminent judgement; and the substance of 3: 17 makes it clear that Conzelmann's attempt to differentiate between the coming of the Messiah and the coming of judgement is misleading. Further, the use of εὐηγγελίζετο in 3: 18 does not, as Conzelmann thinks, merely mean that John exhorted the people with moral homilies. It has strong overtones of eschatological proclamation, as the twenty-five occurrences of the verb in Lk.–Acts show.[1] Also, the fact that Luke has no equivalent to Matt. 3: 2, where John proclaims the kingdom, is significant only if the verse was in Q and Luke omitted it, which we have no means of telling.

3. More convincing reasons can be given for the way in which Luke places the account of John's imprisonment immediately before Jesus' baptism. For example, it could be a result of Luke's desire to round off one narrative before starting another;[2] one could compare Acts 11: 27–30, where the fulfilment of Agabus' prophecy of famine is related immediately, though it actually occurred years later in Claudius' reign. More probably, it may reflect an attempt to damp down excessive veneration of John by the Baptist sect – a motive we shall consider later. Or again, perhaps Matthew has left us the clue in 3: 13ff, where he makes it clear that the Church felt considerable embarrassment over Jesus' baptism by John, and this may well be why Luke removed John from the scene. The reason why one of these latter motives seems more likely is twofold:

(a) If Luke had only wanted to separate the ministries of the two men he could have related John's imprisonment between Lk. 3: 22 and 23, that is, after Jesus' baptism (as Mark does in 1: 14). By placing it where he does, it seems to be the connection with Jesus' baptism which Luke is specifically trying to avoid.[3]

---

[1] The associations of the word are predominantly eschatological: Lk. 1: 19, 2: 10, 3: 18, 4: 10, 43, 7: 22, 8: 1, 9: 6, 16: 16, 20: 1; Acts 5: 42, 8: 4, 12, 24, 35, 40, 10: 36, 11: 20, 13: 32, 14: 7, 15, 21, 15: 35, 16: 10, 17: 18. Cf. Flender, *Lukas*, p. 26; G. Friedrich, art. εὐαγγελίζομαι, *TWNT*, II, 707f.

[2] Caird, *Luke*, p. 75.

[3] W. C. Robinson Jnr., *Der Weg des Herrn* (Hamburg, 1964), p. 12. This book also has a thorough discussion of Conzelmann's interpretation of the geography of the third Gospel. For a full discussion of John the Baptist in Luke see W. Wink, *John the Baptist in the Gospel Tradition* (Cambridge, 1968), pp. 42–86, which unfortunately escaped our notice until after this chapter was written.

(b) At several points, including chs. 1–2,[1] Luke seems concerned to interweave the chronology and significance of John and Jesus. For example, Lk. 3: 1, the synchronism of the ministries of both John and Jesus with contemporary history;[2] also Lk. 7: 29–30, and Lk. 20: 1–8 on which Caird comments, 'John and Jesus belong together. A person's attitude to John is a decision about Jesus.'[3]

4. The implication of the above points is that:

(a) John is not denied eschatological significance as forerunner of the Messiah.

(b) Where there is a demarcation of Jesus' and John's activity it is not for eschatological reasons. This is not to say that Luke does not distinguish the two men; this he does – a distinction which H. H. Oliver has conveniently summarised under the titles 'prophet of the Highest' and 'Son of the Highest'[4] – but this does not stop him from interweaving their activity and significance.

Yet although one may not agree with many of the details of Conzelmann's view of Luke's understanding of the relationship between John and Elijah, one must find some explanation for the lack of any direct identification such as is evident in Mk 9: 9–13. H. J. Cadbury suggests that it is in deference to his Gentile readers that Luke omits this obscure detail of Jewish Apocalyptic.[5] Yet Luke retains 'Son of Man' and 'Kingdom of God' language which is just as Jewish and, for a Gentile, just as obscure. It might be argued that the latter concepts are too fundamental to omit whereas Elijah is not; but why then does Luke use the phrase 'the spirit and power of Elijah' in 1: 17? Conzelmann's explanation has much to recommend it, since if J. Jeremias is correct in thinking that Mk 9: 9–13 shows that Jesus expected an imminent End, Elijah *redivivus* being its herald,[6] then it would fit in with Luke's other attempts to tone

---

[1] Conzelmann has rightly been challenged for his refusal to take account of Lk. 1–2. See Oliver, 'Birth-stories', pp. 202f; Minear, 'Birth-stories', pp. 111f.

[2] Cf. Flender, *Lukas*, p. 111: 'If Luke has in view a clear division between the time of John and the time of Jesus, then he cannot see the beginning of their activities as simultaneous.'

[3] Caird, *Luke*, p. 75.

[4] Oliver, 'Birth-stories', pp. 205f.   [5] Cadbury, *Making*, p. 290.

[6] Jeremias, *Elijah*, p. 938.

down imminent expectation. Yet we have seen that Luke sees John as the herald of an imminent judgement, the very thing that the omission of the Elijah motif is supposed to avoid. It could be argued that the reason for the omission is to combat excessive adulation of John in the Baptist sect.[1] If E. Käsemann is correct in thinking that Luke is dealing with the problem of the *Una Sancta Catholica* in Acts 18: 24ff,[2] then one might expect him to prepare for this in his Gospel. But although this might explain the tendency to play down John's importance, it does not explain the omission of the identification with Elijah, since such an identification would once and for all put John firmly in his place – as Elijah and not the Messiah – thereby denying any Messianic pretensions of the Baptist sect.

The explanation is probably simpler. One of the surprising facts about Luke's Gospel is that whereas he omits Elijah material found in Mark, he preserves traditions that we do not find elsewhere. More significantly, most of these traditions are applied to Jesus and not to John: Lk. 4: 21 (I Kings 17: 1); Lk. 7: 11 (I Kings 17: 17–24); Lk. 24: 43 (I Kings 19: 5); and certain words which may recall the Elijah tradition – ἀναλήμ-ψεως in Lk. 9: 51 and ἀποκατάστασις in Acts 3: 21.[3] It may be that we have here a relatively simple answer to our problem. For Luke, Elijah was a model of the godly man, and he wants to use him typologically of both John and Jesus, more especially of Jesus. For this reason Luke avoids directly identifying Elijah with either John or Jesus. Thus Luke's immediate motive was typo-logical, or perhaps christological, rather than eschatological.

We turn our attention now to the verse which Conzelmann sees as the key to Luke's eschatology, Lk. 16: 16. John, he says, is placed firmly in the Old Testament epoch, which is quite separate from the second epoch – that characterised by the kingdom of God.[4] His use of the verse has earned a timely, if somewhat sharp, rebuke from P. S. Minear: 'It must be said that rarely has a scholar placed so much weight on so dubious

---

[1] For the denial of the existence of such a sect see J. A. T. Robinson, 'Elijah, John and Jesus', *NTS*, 4 (1957–8), pp. 263f.

[2] Käsemann, *Essays*, pp. 136–48.

[3] Flender, *Lukas*, p. 48 n. 6; Jeremias, *Elijah*, pp. 935f.

[4] He mentions it on numerous occasions: pp. 16, 20, 25, 40, 101, 112, 160, 185, 220.

an interpretation of so difficult a logion.'[1] Conzelmann's interpretation seems to be based on two main suppositions: first, that in both context and content Luke's is a secondary version of the Q saying in Matt. 11: 12–13; second, that Matthew's ἀπὸ δὲ τῶν ἡμερῶν 'Ιωάννου includes John, whereas Luke's ἀπὸ τότε excludes him from standing on the same side of the 'change of aeons' as Jesus.

However, we can note:

(a) It is probable that this saying reached Matthew and Luke as an isolated logion; but if we were going to argue that either Matthew or Luke has retained the original context, then Luke's is probably more original since it gives the *connexio difficilior*.[2] Verses 16, 17 and 18 are joined by the link-word νόμος but have no apparent logic, and their position between 17: 1ff and 17: 19ff bears no obvious relation to these parables. The very obscurity of its position should warn us not to place too much weight on it in any reconstruction of Lukan theology.[3]

(b) It is quite probable that v. 16a is better preserved in Luke than in the Matthew parallel. E. Jüngel, for example, reconstructs the original saying as follows: ὁ νόμος καὶ οἱ προφῆται μέχρι 'Ιωάννου· ἀπὸ τότε ἡ βασιλεία βιάζεται καὶ βιασταὶ ἁρπάζουσιν αὐτήν.[4] While all such reconstructions are somewhat arbitrary, there is much to be said for Jüngel's version. The motive Jüngel suggests for Matthew's alteration of the logion is that he wants to place John on the same side of the 'change of aeons' as Jesus, 'because of anti-Jewish polemic', a motive he does not further define and which, as it stands, does not mean much. G. Barth gives a more convincing reason: Matthew was, in part, combating antinomians who denied the validity of the law (cf. Matt. 5: 17–18, 7: 12–27, 24: 10, and the use of πᾶς in connection with the law: 3: 15, 5: 18, 23: 3, 28: 20).

---

[1] Minear, 'Birth-stories', p. 122.

[2] D. Daube, *The New Testament and Rabbinic Judaism* (London, 1956), pp. 294f. Daube makes a subtle but unconvincing attempt to find a connection of thought in vv. 16f.

[3] Noted by Wilckens, *Missionsreden*, p. 104 n. 4.

[4] E. Jüngel, *Paulus und Jesus* (Tübingen, 1964), p. 191. He is arguing against Käsemann's view that the original version placed John on the same side of the 'change of aeons' as Jesus. Jüngel therefore takes the phrase ἀπὸ τότε to exclude John.

Luke's version, that is Q, implied that the law was valid only up until John, and Matthew was therefore forced to alter it.[1]
(c) It could be argued that Matthew's phrase ἀπὸ δὲ τῶν ἡμερῶν is exclusive of John, and Luke's ἀπὸ τότε inclusive.[2] The word 'from' (ἀπό) is ambiguous, and it is unwise to build on it either way.

These three points are enough to challenge Conzelmann's use of v. 16a and to show that in all probability Luke was at this point merely reporting Q. When we turn to v. 16b things are somewhat different, for here Matthew's version seems more original since it is more obscure, whereas Luke's is a simplified, 'Christianised' version. The original seems to have referred to a violation of the kingdom by its enemies, who are left undefined.[3] Luke appears to have replaced it with a reference to men who violently push to get into the kingdom.[4] We should notice, however, that the 'preaching' of the kingdom is something that John does (Lk. 3: 18), Jesus and his disciples do (Lk. 4: 43, 8: 1, 9: 11, 60ff), and is also a characteristic of the early Church in Acts (Acts 8: 12, 20: 25, 28: 23, 31). This reveals a very real connection between John, Jesus and the Church which runs across Conzelmann's strict three-epochal notion, suggesting that such a threefold pattern is unnatural for Luke.

Before leaving this section we must first take a brief look at another verse which Conzelmann thinks proves his threefold division – Lk. 22: 36: 'But now, let him who has a purse take it, and likewise a bag. And let him who has no sword sell his mantle and buy one.' In contrast to the time of Jesus' ministry, Satan is now back at work, the time of persecution is at hand. Thus Conzelmann takes the phrase ἀλλὰ νῦν to refer to the time

---

[1] G. Barth, *Tradition and Interpretation in Matthew* (London, 1963), pp. 63–4.
[2] So Daube, *Judaism*, p. 235; Grundmann, *Lukas*, p. 323. The phrases ἕως 'Ιωάννου (Matt.) and μέχρι 'Ιωάννου (Lk.) are equally ambiguous.
[3] For a summary of the main views on the interpretation of the word βιάζεται see Kümmel, *Promise*, pp. 121f. Cf. Jüngel, *Paulus*, pp. 190f; and Daube, *Judaism*, pp. 285–300, who offers some fascinating sidelights on the problems.
[4] It is possible to give Luke a similar meaning to Matthew by taking εἰς to mean 'against' – a possible, though rare, meaning of the word – or by taking εἰς as the equivalent of an Aramaic preposition not needed in the Greek, but included because a direct translation was being made. For the latter see M. Black, *An Aramaic Approach to the Gospels and Acts* (3rd ed. Oxford, 1967), p. 116.

of the Church.[1] However, while this is a fair interpretation of this notoriously obscure passage, it seems that P. S. Minear has offered a more convincing exegesis of the verse when it is interpreted in connection with the following verses.[2] Minear takes the phrase ἀλλὰ νῦν to refer to the immediate future, that is, to the story of the disciple who cut off the ear of the High Priest's slave (Lk. 22: 50–1). The 'transgressors' of v. 37 (Is. 53: 12) are the disciples and the odd phrase 'it is enough' (v. 38) then means 'it is enough to fulfil the prophecy'. Jesus' command is then partially an artificial literary device to set the stage for the Scripture's fulfilment and partially a means of disclosing that the disciples had already secretly, disobediently, secured swords, thereby nullifying Jesus' previous teaching and practice. The incident of the cutting off of the slave's ear is thus seen as fulfilment of prophecy, it being probable that such a forced use of the Old Testament was far less foreign to Luke than it would be to us.

If our interpretation of Lk. 16: 16 and 22: 36 is correct then it must be said that Conzelmann's attempt to straitjacket Luke into a strict threefold pattern has failed. This is not the key to Luke's eschatology. Luke was not concerned to draw hard and fast lines between John, Jesus and the Church. This is not to say that Conzelmann has not hit on some important distinctions in Luke's work, more especially the division of his work into two volumes – an account of Jesus and an account of the Church. But even here it could be shown that Luke was far more concerned to show how these two epochs were decisively linked than how they were separated (see, for example, Luke's concept of apostleship and, more important still, his double account of the Ascension). If we have to find a scheme for Luke then a far more congenial one would be that of 'prophecy and fulfilment':[3] the period of prophecy covers the Old Testament era up to, but not including, John; the period of fulfilment from and including John. There are differences between the activity of John and Jesus, as there are between various parts of Jesus' ministry, but they are all linked by being part of the era of fulfilment. It is this scheme rather than a threefold pattern which takes over from the

---

[1] Conzelmann, *Luke*, pp. 16, 81, 107.
[2] P. S. Minear, 'A note on Lk. 22: 35f', *Nov. Test.*, 7 (1964), 128f.
[3] To this extent the analysis of Lohse, *Lukas*, is more satisfactory. Cf. also Dahl, 'Abraham', pp. 54f.

traditional eschatological outline (cf. Mk 1: 15 'The kingdom of God is at hand' with Lk. 4: 21 'Today this scripture is fulfilled in your ears'; and see Lk. 21: 22 where Luke sees the destruction of Jerusalem as a fulfilment of prophecy, whereas for Mark it is a mysterious apocalyptic event).

THE TWO STRANDS IN LUKE'S ESCHATOLOGY

In this section, it will be shown that there are two strands in Luke's eschatology, one which quite definitely allows for a delay in the Parousia and one which, with equal firmness, asserts that the End will come soon.

The delay strand

After Conzelmann's work, it would seem impossible to deny that parts of Luke–Acts are intended to allow for a delay in the Parousia. To show this, it is necessary to look at only a few of the many texts which reveal this tendency:

Luke 22: 69; Mark 14: 62. Despite several attempts to argue the contrary,[1] the most natural meaning of Mark's version is that Jesus is prophesying an imminent Parousia which would occur in the lifetime of the members of the Sanhedrin. What then has Luke done with this saying?

(1) He has added the phrase ἀπὸ τοῦ νῦν. The use of this phrase is significant in that its other occurrences in Luke show that it marks a decisive time-change.[2] Here and in 22: 18 it seems to refer to the period after Jesus' death, though one should not make too much of this, since in 12: 52 the same phrase is used, where its position in the Gospel implies that the future reference is to both the time of Jesus' ministry and the time of the Church.[3]

---

[1] J. A. T. Robinson, *Coming*, pp. 54f, argues that the two halves of Mk 14: 62 are, synonymously parallel, both referring to Jesus' exaltation. However, Tödt, *Son of Man*, pp. 36f, has collected conclusive evidence against Robinson's view. Equally improbable is the view of Cranfield, *Mark*, pp. 444–5, that the Sanhedrin will see the Son of Man coming, but probably after they have died, at the Last Judgement.

[2] G. Stählin, art. νῦν, *TWNT*, IV, 1112f. See Lk. 1: 48, 5: 10, 12: 52, 22: 18; Acts 18: 6.

[3] A different view is found in G. Klein, 'Die Prüfung der Zeit. Lk. 12: 54–6', *ZTK*, 61(1964), 374–5.

(2) Luke significantly alters Mark's 'You will see' to 'He will be'; that is, it is no longer a case of men seeing but of the Son of Man being. Luke also omits the phrase 'coming with the clouds of heaven', and consequently all weight is placed on the *sessio ad dexteram Dei*. This is partly motivated by a desire to avoid imminent expectation, but not only by this. If he had only wanted to avoid this imminent expectation he could simply have omitted the phrase about the Sanhedrin seeing. The reason why 'coming with the clouds of heaven' is omitted is that he wants to place considerable weight on the Ascension, which for Luke bears much of the weight that in Matthew and Mark is placed on the Parousia.[1] Luke's motivation is pastoral; he wants to strengthen the Church of his day. Jesus' exaltation is the basis of their faith; his commission in Acts 1 : 8 is unthinkable without it. The End has not come, but the Church must go on living and expanding.

Luke 19: 11. 'As they heard these things he proceeded to tell a parable, because he was near to Jerusalem, and because they supposed that the kingdom of God was to appear immediately.' This verse is probably a creation of Luke's,[2] serving as an introduction to the parable which follows. It gives the parable a new meaning, which is basically that 'Jesus is not coming, He's going'.[3] The disciples have the idea that the kingdom is earthly – a political Messianic kingdom – and that it is coming soon. The parable tells of a king who goes away for a certain period and then returns. This is apparently to teach the disciples not to expect the End immediately; the kingdom will not break in when Jesus arrives in Jerusalem; before the kingdom comes, Jesus must go. This situation is closely paralleled in Acts 1 : 6–8, where a similar misunderstanding is corrected.

It is even more significant if v. 11 reflects, as some think, a view which Jesus himself held, that is, that his entry into Jerusalem was connected with the coming of the Parousia. Grässer has argued this in some detail, chiefly on the basis of Mk 11 : 10, but though an attractive view, it is impossible to prove.[4] If it is true, then Luke is directly contradicting it. His

---

[1] Tödt, *Son of Man*, pp. 102–3; Flender, *Lukas*, p. 94.
[2] Jeremias, *Parables*, pp. 99f; Ellis, *Luke*, pp. 224–5.
[3] Manson, *Sayings*, p. 212.
[4] Grässer, *Parusieverzögerung*, pp. 24–8.

contradiction has, however, more than a mere negative value, since positively it makes way for a theology of the Ascension, which is of central importance for Luke. 'Jesus' entry into Jerusalem has been seen by the early Christian tradition in association with his Parousia. In Luke, on the other hand, the "type of Parousia" becomes a type of the lordship of Jesus in heaven.'[1]

Luke 9: 27; Mark 9: 1. Mark's version of this saying appears to reflect his overall view, namely that though there may be a delay in the Parousia, the End will come soon.[2] G. Bornkamm has argued that the original purpose of the saying was to explain the delay and make it more palatable, since it reflects an acute problem in the early Church, namely that some Christians were dying before the Parousia had come (I Thess. 4: 15; I Cor. 15: 51; II Cor. 5: 1–4).[3] Thus there is a subtle change of emphasis from saying that the End will come soon, to saying that some will survive until the Parousia. The logion may, therefore, be a community creation,[4] though it could also be a saying of Jesus that has been touched up by the Church in response to a pastoral crisis.

Luke's omission of the phrase ἐληλυθυῖαν ἐν δυνάμει opens his version to an interpretation which is independent of any temporal limitation. Conzelmann argues that the verb ἴδωσιν in Luke means 'perceive' and that the phrase τινες τῶν αὐτοῦ ἑστηκότων refers to mankind in general, rather than to any specific group of people.[5] He thus takes it to mean that some of mankind will, before they die, perceive the kingdom – thought of as some transcendent reality. It is doubtful, however, if this interpretation of τινες τῶν αὐτοῦ ἑστηκότων is feasible, and it should not be overlooked that while Luke can use the verb 'see' in connection with the *heilsgeschichtlich* significance of Jesus'

---

[1] Flender, *Lukas*, p. 85.

[2] For a discussion of the various attempts to give this verse some other meaning see Kümmel, *Promise*, pp. 27f; Beasley-Murray, *Future*, pp. 150f; A. L. Moore, *The Parousia in the New Testament* (Leiden, 1966), pp. 125f.

[3] G. Bornkamm, 'Die Verzögerung der Parusie', *IM*, pp. 116f.

[4] It is no argument against this to say that the early community would not create an obviously unfulfilled saying (Kümmel, *Promise*) since for the first generation of Christians hope for an early Parousia was still possible (Grässer, *Parusieverzögerung*, pp. 131f.).

[5] Conzelmann, *Luke*, pp. 104–5.

ministry (Lk. 2: 20, 10: 35, 13: 35), he can also use it with a clear reference to future eschatological events (Lk. 13: 28, 21: 27). Nevertheless, the use of ἴδωσιν to mean 'perceive' does seem to give the best interpretation of Luke's version at this point, though we should take it as a reference to Jesus' contemporaries. It has been argued against this (and similarly against our interpretation of Lk. 22: 69) that if Mk 9: 1 was an embarrassment to Luke and his contemporaries, he would have omitted it altogether, thus solving all the problems in one simple but effective move.[1] Certainly Luke is not immune to this practice; but he retains the verse because, in its revised form, it gives a new slant on the kingdom. Simple omission would not solve any problems, whereas retention in a revised form could dispel difficulties.[2]

Another way of interpreting this verse is to take the verb 'see' in the same way as in Mark,[3] and assume either that Luke has simply handed on an unfulfilled saying without fitting it in to the rest of his material which allows for a delay, or that when Luke was writing there were still some alive who had been alive during Jesus' ministry and who might yet see the coming of the kingdom at the End. We shall meet this problem again when we consider Lk. 21: 32 and discuss it further there.

Luke 19: 41f, 21: 20–4. The origin of these oracles has been much disputed and their interpretation even more so. Dodd suggests that at this point in Luke we have a section independent

[1] Moore, *Parousia*, pp. 130f.
[2] Conzelmann gives an analysis of Luke's presentation of the kingdom in *Luke*, pp. 113f. Two points are worth noting: (a) He is correct when he says that language of the 'coming' of the kingdom is usually avoided in Luke, and when it is used (17: 20, 19: 11, 21: 7) Luke often criticises it. In contrast language of 'seeing' or 'preaching' the kingdom is more frequent. We should note, however, that Luke has no monopoly of this kind of language (cf. Mk 1: 14, 9: 1; Matt. 4: 23, 9: 35, 16: 28; and in Mk 4: 11 we have a close parallel to Luke's use of 'see' to mean 'perceive'). (b) Conzelmann thinks that Luke only speaks of the kingdom as future, never as present. It is the 'message' or 'image' of the kingdom that is present, not the kingdom itself. This is surely a false distinction, for Lk. 11: 20, 16: 16 imply that the kingdom itself is present and not just its image or message.
[3] On ἴδωσιν in Mk 9: 1 see Kümmel, *Promise*, p. 27 *contra* Dodd, *Parables*, pp. 42, 53f. Luke gives no hint that he saw this saying fulfilled either in the Transfiguration or in Pentecost.

of Mark; both oracles, he says, were composed from Old Testament prophecies before A.D. 70.[1] It is, however, an improbable explanation of their origin, mainly because one has to imagine a hotchpotch oracle being composed with one word from one Old Testament verse and two from another, etc. – a scarcely conceivable process. Luke appears to be dependent on Mark at this point. What then did Mark mean in 13: 12ff? It appears that he saw the destruction of Jerusalem as connected in some way with the End. This is not to say that it is the End itself or that it precludes other signs meanwhile. Those who experience the destruction are not experiencing the End, but the End will follow very soon; they are the community of the 'End-time'.[2] Already in Mark there is a separation of the two events. Luke, it is argued, has taken the final step of divorcing the End from the destruction of Jerusalem completely. We no longer have the cryptic, apocalyptic references of Mark, but a cool, objective description of an event which has already occurred. The destruction is seen as a purely historical event with no apocalyptic significance.[3]

Now it is clear that Lk. 19: 41ff and 21: 20ff were written after A.D. 70 and it is, therefore, inevitable that Luke should distinguish this event more clearly from the End. Flender argues, however, that if the connection between the destruction and the End was embarrassing for Luke, he would have omitted these passages or at least made do with the allusive references in 19: 41ff.[4] Again it must be said that this is not a very convincing form of argument, since it was very much to the point for Luke to include it in his Gospel and to interpret it in what he considered to be the correct fashion. Omission would not solve any problems, whereas inclusion in a revised form could dispel misunderstandings.[5] However, we would be doing Luke an

---

[1] C. H. Dodd, 'The Fall of Jerusalem and the "Abomination of Desolation"', *Journal of Roman Studies*, 37 (1947), 47f.

[2] Conzelmann, *Mk 13*, pp. 219f; Marxsen, *Markus*, pp. 128f.

[3] Conzelmann, *Luke*, pp. 134f. According to Marxsen, *Markus*, Luke has produced a complete 'elimination of expectation for the Parousia from the context of the destruction of Jerusalem'.

[4] Flender, *Lukas*, p. 103.

[5] Even so too much has been made of the division between v. 24b and v. 25. The former, which refers either to the Gentile mission or to the military occupation of Jerusalem after its destruction, certainly suggests a hiatus,

injustice if we pictured him sitting down to rethink carefully and radically what he found in Mark. To a large extent he is merely reflecting the fact that he was writing after A.D. 70 and it was natural for him to separate the events of A.D. 70 from the End, since one was inescapably a fact of past history and the other as yet unfulfilled. Furthermore, in Mark the seeds had already been sown for making such a distinction. If we are to ascribe to Luke anything other than this purely pragmatic motive, then it may be that we should see his alterations as inspired in part by a practical, pastoral problem in the church of his day, namely the disappointment caused by the failure of the End to come with the events of A.D. 70.

These verses are, we hope, sufficient to show that there is a very distinct delay strand in Luke's eschatology. The same teaching is to be found, though not always so clearly, in Lk. 11: 2, 12: 49–50, 16: 1–13, 21: 7, 8, 12, 19.[1]

The imminent expectation strand

Luke 18: 8. 'I tell you he will vindicate them speedily...' This verse will be taken first since it seems to give the best clue

but as to its length nothing is said. The καί in v. 25 gives some form of a link between v. 24 and vv. 25f, though to go on from here and argue that the whole of vv. 25f refers to politico-historical events, albeit in cosmic-eschatological language, is unwarranted (cf. Caird, *Luke*, p. 232; Leaney, *Luke*, pp. 262f). It may be that vv. 20–4 are symbolic of the events described in vv. 25f (Flender, *Lukas*, p. 104) but this does not mean that they are not also temporally linked.

1 See Conzelmann and Grässer on these verses. Also on 11: 2f see Leaney, *Luke*, pp. 6of, and W. Ott, *Gebet und Heil* (Munich, 1965), pp. 112f. On 12: 49–50 see G. Delling, 'βάπτισμα, βαπτισθῆναι', *Nov. Test.*, 2 (1958), 92f. On 16: 1–13 see Jüngel, *Paulus*, pp. 157f, and G. Bornkamm, *Jesus of Nazareth* (London, 1960), p. 88. Lengthy discussion of Lk. 17: 22–37 has not been attempted, since all the basic teaching is paralleled in Mk 13: false prophets and Messiahs (vv. 5–7), the incalculable nature of the End (v. 32), and the suddenness of the End and the need to watch at all times (vv. 33f). Thus none of the basic teaching is specifically Lukan; rather, it is material he received from his tradition. Conzelmann, *Luke*, pp. 120f, thinks that the emphasis on the idea of the suddenness of the End marks a significant shift away from the primitive imminent expectation. However, this theme of suddenness also occurs in Mark, and was also probably part of Jesus' original teaching, so that it may be that we are dealing here with one of the strands of Jesus' teaching rather than with a new emphasis imposed on it by Luke.

to Luke's eschatology. The problem for our purposes is to balance v. 7b and v. 8a. The phrase καὶ μακροθυμεῖ ἐπ' αὐτοῖς in 7b is obscure, but whichever translation we take, a delay in God's activity of vindication seems to be envisaged.[1] Then 8a, in contrast, gives the assurance that God will act speedily on behalf of his elect. To avoid this conclusion some have suggested that ἐν τάχει v. 8a should be translated 'suddenly' rather than 'soon'.[2] This is, they say, because otherwise it contradicts Luke's avoidance of imminent expectation. But on linguistic grounds the translation 'suddenly' is impossible and must be rejected.[3] Thus in v. 7b we have a recognition of the delay of the Parousia, while in v. 8a we have an assurance that this delay will be short.

This reaffirmation of an imminent hope is of the greatest significance for Luke's eschatology, even more so if, as some suggest, this particular element is a Lukan insertion into the original parable. In its Lukan form the parable seems to have been motivated by a desperate pastoral situation. The Church, like the widow, suffered frequent injustices and persecution and, as a result of the delay in God's intervention to vindicate the elect, many of its members lost their faith. Luke's response to this situation is twofold: first, their expectation of immediate vindication is taken seriously, and v. 8a reaffirms that God will intervene in the very near future; secondly, their questioning of God's reliability is turned back on them as a question of their own reliability (v. 8a).

Luke 10: 9, 11. In both of these verses there is a reference to the kingdom coming soon. Some avoid this conclusion by

---

[1] On the various attempts to make sense of this phrase see the excellent articles by C. E. B. Cranfield, 'The Parable of the Unjust Judge and the Eschatology of Luke–Acts', *SJT*, 16 (1963), 297f, and G. Delling, 'Das Gleichnis vom gottlosen Richter', *ZNW*, 53 (1962), 1–25, especially 17f.

[2] Jeremias, *Parables*, p. 116; Grässer, *Parusieverzögerung*, p. 38; Ellis, *Luke*, p. 214; Ott, *Gebet*, pp. 63–5.

[3] The evidence offered is the LXX of Dt. 11: 17; Ps. 2: 12; Josh. 8: 18. But (a) the Hebrew for Ps. 2: 2 is כְּמְעַט and for the other two verses מְהֵרָה – and for neither of these words do the main lexicons give the meaning 'suddenly'. (b) None of the main Greek lexicons give 'suddenly' as a possible meaning for ταχέως or adverbial phrases which use the noun τάχος. (c) In the context of 18: 1f a reassurance that the End will come suddenly – though not necessarily soon – is scarcely a promise that would bring comfort to the oppressed. See Cranfield, 'Parable', and Delling, 'Gleichnis'.

translating ἤγγικεν 'has come',[1] or by interpreting the coming of the kingdom as something other than the Parousia. On the first point, Kümmel has shown the linguistic improbability of translating ἤγγικεν in this way;[2] and secondly, it is highly improbable that when he speaks of a future coming of the kingdom Luke means anything other than the Parousia (Lk. 21: 32). The kind of challenge that the preaching of Jesus and his disciples brought to men may be reflected in Lk. 9: 60. Although Conzelmann says that these words now refer to the importance of missionary preaching, whereas originally they referred to the nearness of the kingdom, yet Luke still seems to retain a note of urgency, which is a result of the kingdom being near.

Luke 12: 38–40 and 41–8. This parable is found in essentially the same form in Matt. 24: 42ff. It is thought by many scholars, probably correctly, that the original version referred to an imminent crisis, probably the Parousia.[3] As we have it in Luke, however, the parable makes provision for a delay, in the same way that the Markan parallel does (Mk 13: 34). This is not, however, the point that Luke is most concerned to emphasise. In v. 41, by means of Peter's question, Luke 'contemporises' his material; the answer given to Peter is used by Luke as a warning to all the Church leaders of his time. In the period between the Resurrection and the Parousia the οἰκονόμοι have special responsibilities and, owing to the nature of their position, special dangers (vv. 44, 46, 47).[4] The main point, however, is the warning that despite something of a delay, the man who says χρονίζει ὁ κύριός μου ἔρχεσθαι (v. 45), blithely supposing that he can do as he wishes, is likely to be caught unawares. Luke is apparently addressing his contemporaries here who, owing to a delay, were apt to be lax and complacent. By warning them of the need for watchfulness lest the Parousia should catch them

---

[1] Dodd, *Parables*, pp. 44f; M. Black, 'The Kingdom of God has come', *ET*, 63 (1951), 289f.

[2] Kümmel, *Promise*, pp. 19f; K. Clark, 'Realised eschatology', *JBL*, 59 (1940), 367f. The addition of ἐφ' ὑμᾶς in Lk. 10: 9 could possibly be construed to mean that Luke understood it to mean that the kingdom was 'here' and not 'near' (Ellis, *Luke*, p. 155); but it could also mean that the kingdom is chronologically near (Rengstorf, *Lukas*, p. 135).

[3] Jeremias, *Parables*, pp. 93f; Dodd, *Parables*, p. 167; Conzelmann, *Luke*, p. 109; Robinson, *Coming*, p. 113.

[4] Ellis, *Luke*, p. 180; Caird, *Luke*, p. 164; Dodd, *Parables*, pp. 160f.

out, Luke makes it clear that the hope of an imminent End was not a lost cause, to be abandoned by the Church. Once again we can see how Luke's reaffirmation of an imminent End springs from a practical, pastoral situation.

What we have said above is confirmed by an observation of H. Tödt in his book on the Son of Man,[1] namely that in Luke's Gospel the Son of Man motif tends to be used for the purpose of exhortation to watchfulness. Tödt, like Grässer, seems to think that the motif of watchfulness itself implies that men must reckon with a delay in the Parousia.[2] This is similar to Conzelmann's point that in Luke the kingdom is thought of as coming suddenly rather than soon, an emphasis which he thinks originated in the early communities as a result of a disappointed hope in an imminent Parousia.[3] But there is no good reason to suppose that Jesus did not warn men of the possibility of a sudden End which, if they were not watchful, would catch them unawares. Further, though in Lk. 21: 36, for example, the Son of Man motif is used as an exhortation to watchfulness, the point is not that the Church cannot be sure of an early return of Jesus, but that they cannot bank on an indefinite delay.

Luke 12: 54 – 13: 9. Conzelmann interprets vv. 54–9 as meaning that 'one must not be misled by the delay',[4] which may be Luke's meaning, though the delay is not in fact mentioned. Verses 57–9 depend for their point on the nearness of the judgement which men will meet and, in connection with them, vv. 54–6 probably also have a note of urgency.[5] The important point for our purposes is to decide what Luke meant by this impending judgement. To help us here we can turn to 13: 1–9, the message of which seems to be that there is an impending judgement on Israel, and the parable in vv. 6–9, in particular, emphasises the imminence of this judgement.[6] How then does Luke understand this judgement?

---

1 Tödt, *Son of Man*, pp. 96f.
2 Grässer, *Parusieverzögerung*, pp. 84f.
3 Conzelmann, *Luke*, pp. 113f.   4 Conzelmann, *Luke*, p. 109.
5 Kümmel, *Promise*, p. 22; Ellis, *Luke*, pp. 182–3.
6 Manson, *Sayings*, pp. 272f; Jeremias, *Parables*, pp. 170f. Cadbury, *Making*, p. 292, is scarcely correct when he sees the main point of Lk. 13: 6–9 as being that there will be a delay in the judgement. It is worth noting that if Lk. 13: 6–9 is Luke's equivalent of Mk 11: 12f, then Luke places more emphasis on the imminence of the End.

(a) He could have meant the destruction of Jerusalem, which is prophesied elsewhere. This was probably Jesus' meaning, since for him the destruction was an integral part of the End events. But as we have seen, Luke did not view the destruction in the same light. If this were so, then although there is a note of imminence, it refers to the events of A.D. 70 and not to the End.

(b) It could be that the whole section refers to the Final Judgement, and we would then have yet one more example of Luke's imminent expectation.

Both of these interpretations are feasible and it is difficult to decide between them. It may well be that Luke knew of their original reference, but used these verses in a more general way as a warning of the nearness of judgement.

Luke 21: 32. There is no space to go into the myriad interpretations of this verse, and a very short summary must suffice. Conzelmann thinks that Luke's omission of Mark's word ταῦτα is significant, since πάντα now refers to the End itself and the preceding signs, that is 'the whole plan of God'.[1] Luke's alteration may, however, simply be stylistic, since in place of Mark's ταῦτα in 13: 29 and ταῦτα πάντα in 13: 30 Luke has ταῦτα in 21: 31 and πάντα in 21: 32.[2] More important is Conzelmann's interpretation of ἡ γενεά, which he takes to mean 'the whole human race, mankind'. But of all the other uses of this word in Luke–Acts, only two could be cited as possible parallels to this meaning,[3] and neither this nor any other attempt to give ἡ γενεά a meaning other than Jesus' contemporaries carries any conviction.[4] The most recent commentator, Ellis, offers two objections to this view:[5] first, Luke must have understood it to mean something other than Jesus' contemporaries, since he was writing too late to take it in this way; yet such a presupposition should not be allowed to influence our exegesis too far, since a different exegesis may alter our presupposition. Secondly, he tries to draw on a phrase in 1 QpHab 2: 7 and 7: 2 – 'the last generation' – which apparently includes several lifetimes. This

---

[1] Conzelmann, *Luke*, p. 131.
[2] Matthew also smooths out Mark's version by using πάντα ταῦτα in both 24: 33 and 24: 34.   [3] Lk. 1: 48, 50.
[4] Such as those who take it to refer to the Jewish race or to Christians. See further Kümmel, *Promise*, pp. 61f.
[5] Ellis, *Luke*, p. 246.

phrase is not, however, sufficiently close to the phrase ἡ γενεὰ αὕτη to suggest that they mean the same and that Luke meant more than one generation when he wrote 'this generation'. This verse is, therefore, unique in Luke (unless we interpret 9: 27 similarly) in delimiting the End in a precise manner. The other verses which betray an imminent expectation never limit themselves to one generation. Apart from saying that Luke has thoughtlessly taken this verse over from Mark without realising that it was so limiting, we can only assume that he stretched the meaning of 'this generation' to its fullest extent and took it as referring to the contemporaries of Jesus who were, at the time Luke wrote, still alive. This carries with it the implication that although he made ample room for the delay of the Parousia Luke still thought it a possibility, and a real one, that the End would come soon.

THE ESCHATOLOGY OF ACTS

In the next chapter we shall look at Acts 1–2 in considerable detail, but to round off our study of Lukan eschatology it is necessary to take a brief look at the relevant material in Acts. Three points in particular call for comment:

1. The very fact that Luke thought of writing Acts reveals a significant shift away from primitive eschatology. That Luke saw the need for some form of Church history is significant because it shows a Church which is standing back to reflect on its own past rather than single-mindedly looking forward to an imminent End.[1]

2. In Acts 7: 56 we have a verse in which Luke seems to be trying to answer one of the problems caused by a delayed Parousia, namely the death of some believers before the End. The two peculiar features of this verse – the use of ἵστημι and the title Son of Man – are most satisfactorily explained by seeing the verse as a reference to a personal, private Parousia which Stephen experiences at the moment of death.[2] Luke knew

[1] Grässer, *Parusieverzögerung*, p. 204; E. Haenchen, *Die Apostelgeschichte* (rev. ed. Göttingen, 1965), p. 87.

[2] C. K. Barrett, 'Stephen and the Son of Man', in *Apophoreta*, Festschrift for E. Haenchen (Berlin, 1964), pp. 32f. This article also gives a convenient summary and critique of most modern interpretations of this verse. See also Higgins, *Son of Man*, pp. 144f; Tödt, *Son of Man*, pp. 304f.

that the delay of the Parousia would mean that some Christians would die beforehand, so he introduces this concept of an individual's 'eschaton', which he speaks of in eschatological terms: 'Thus the death of each Christian would be marked by what we may term a private, personal Parousia of the Son of Man. That which was to happen in a universal sense at the last day, happened in individual terms when a Christian came to the last day of his life.'[1] As well as explaining the two exegetical problems this interpretation fits in well with Luke's development of the Son of Man concept (Lk. 22: 69) and with previous references to the idea of individual resurrection (Lk. 14: 12–14, 16: 9, 31. Cf. also 23: 43) – which is in turn a development of the more primitive theme of a general Resurrection associated with expectation of an imminent End.[2]

3. One of the most striking characteristics of Acts is the complete absence of imminent expectation. Four features of this are worth noting. First, it may be that the command to stay in Jerusalem (Acts 1: 4f) was originally for the purpose of awaiting the Parousia.[3] If this were true – and it cannot be proved – and if Luke was aware of it, then it is significant that he has substituted the event of Pentecost for that of the Parousia as the purpose of this command.

Secondly, one of the most characteristic features of Acts 1–2 is the schematic, objective approach that Luke has to eschatological events.[4] Thus it is only in Luke that we have an account of the Ascension as a distinct event, separate from both the Resurrection and Pentecost. Likewise, Luke has rationalised and schematised the account of Pentecost, reshaping an originally obscure tradition into what was for him a relatively intelligible narrative.

Thirdly, the kingdom of God is mentioned in Acts but it is never said that is it imminent. As in his Gospel, Luke normally speaks of the kingdom being 'preached' or 'proclaimed' (Acts 8: 12, 20: 25, 28: 30–1, cf. 19: 8, 28: 23); nothing is said, except critically in Acts 1: 6–8, of its coming. Apart from 1:

---

[1] Barrett, 'Stephen', pp. 35–6.   [2] Conzelmann, *Luke*, pp. 111–12.
[3] Haenchen, *Apg.*, p. 112 n. 4. Cf. *S.B.*, III, 300f, 588f; Test. Zeb. 9: 8.
[4] H. J. Cadbury, 'The Eschatology of Acts', in *The Background of the New Testament and its Eschatology*, in honour of C. H. Dodd (Cambridge, 1956), pp. 300f.

6–8 the only clear reference to the future kingdom is 14: 22, and there it is a question of men coming into the kingdom rather than the kingdom itself coming.[1]

Fourthly, the motivation given for repentance in Acts is never the imminence of the kingdom. In 10: 42 judgement is a motive, but nothing is said about its nearness; and similarly it is the certainty rather than the imminence of the Resurrection which is a motive elsewhere (24: 14f; cf. 4: 2, 23, 17: 18, 23: 6). Kümmel has argued that in 3: 20f and 17: 31 imminent expectation is a motive for repentance.[2] However, 17: 31 speaks only of the certainty and not of the imminence of judgement, and the obscure verses in 3: 20–1, if they do refer to the Parousia, do not suggest that this event is near.[3]

How then are we to explain this surprising silence of Acts on the topic of imminent expectation? J. A. T. Robinson thinks it is because the Parousia was not originally part of Jesus' or the Church's belief.[4] He thinks two factors warrant this assumption. First, the Parousia is not a regular part of the speeches in Acts. They do not give the impression that the last section has been lopped off, for they have their own climax – the Ascension (cf. Acts 2: 32–6). Secondly, the earliest traceable, irreducible element of the Church's confessions is the phrase 'Jesus is Lord' (Rom. 10: 9, I Cor. 12: 3), which emphasises the present lordship of Christ and not his Parousia. However, apart from much dubious exegesis, the basic objection to Robinson's view

[1] Haenchen, *Apg.*, p. 254, takes the 'preaching of the kingdom' to mean the proclamation of the coming kingdom. But in all cases except 1: 6–8, 14: 22, the kingdom in Acts seems to be a vague way of characterising the content of Christian preaching without any specific reference to the future (e.g. 19: 8, 20: 25 and the phrases which are parallel to 'kingdom of God'). In fact, Luke's use of the phrase in Acts appears to be somewhat loose and haphazard.

[2] W. G. Kümmel, 'Das Urchristentum', *Th. Rund.*, 22 (1954), 208–10.

[3] Contrasted with Kümmel is H. Conzelmann, *Die Apostelgeschichte* (Tübingen, 1963), p. 35, who asserts that Acts 3: 19f envisages a long gap between the Resurrection and the Parousia. However, the passage speaks neither of the imminence nor of the delay of the Parousia, but only of its certainty. Flender, *Lukas*, pp. 89f, and A. Wikenhauser, *Die Apostelgeschichte* (Regensburg, 1961), think the reference is to something already realised, namely the meeting of a repentant man with the Risen Lord which brings 'seasons of refreshing'.

[4] Robinson, *Coming*, pp. 144–54.

is that he gives no convincing reason why belief in a Parousia should have developed. A crisis caused by a delay in the Parousia gives a cogent reason why imminent expectation should have been toned down, but Robinson's idea of a crisis of christology, which he finds in Acts 2–3, is scarcely a convincing explanation for the growth of belief in a Parousia. Moreover, while belief in an exalted Lord may have been the dominant conviction of the early Church, it could happily co-exist with belief in a Parousia.

Cadbury thinks that the silence of Acts about the Parousia is because it is being assumed rather than denied.[1] We would not expect many references in a mainly narrative work. He notes that we should be wary of thinking of the kerygma as a fixed entity and must allow for a certain elasticity. For example, not all the clauses are coeval, and both before and after the kerygma as we have it in Acts there were processes of development. Taking the speeches as mutually supplementary, we could argue that the references to the Parousia in 3: 19f can be assumed in all the other speeches. However, while many of these comments are illuminating, they are not sufficient to explain the overall silence of Acts about the Parousia or why the references we do have to the 'End' never imply its imminence.

The correct explanation seems to be that in Acts we have a further development of one of the strands we found in Luke's Gospel to the exclusion of the other. Luke has moved away from belief in an imminent end. One of his methods of doing this is to schematise and objectify the eschatological timetable. Another is to substitute Ascension theology, the present activity of the exalted Lord in his Church, for belief in an imminent end. This is done not so much by dogmatic statement as by the concentration on this element in Acts. The time-scheme of Acts allows for a hiatus between the Resurrection and the Parousia in which the Church can exist and grow. His readers are exhorted not to yearn wistfully for the end, but to receive the spirit and fulfil their missionary task.

---

[1] Cadbury, *Eschatology*, pp. 300f.

CONCLUSIONS

The task before us now is to explain our findings and draw conclusions both on the problem of Luke's eschatology in general and on its relationship to the Gentile mission. Before drawing our conclusions two preliminary points need to be made. First, Luke is not the first or the last to deal with the problem of the delayed Parousia. We have already seen how quite often the first steps were taken by Mark (Mk 9: 1, 13: 10, 13: 14f). To have shown this is the chief value of Grässer's book. Thus Luke's recognition of and attempt to deal with this problem is not distinctive. Often he is merely drawing out the implications of the tradition he received. A related point is that the tendency to place more soteriological weight on Jesus' earthly ministry is an early factor in the gospel tradition, a tradition which Luke received at a relatively late stage (Lk. 1: 1–4). U. Wilckens puts it well: 'To overstate the matter for emphasis: an essential fact about the Jesus-tradition was that it had already basically solved the problem of the delayed Parousia by concentrating salvation in Jesus himself and by affirming that his followers participate in salvation now. Only when we recognise that the Lukan theology of *Heilsgeschichte* fits into the history of the Jesus-tradition in this manner, can we properly evaluate Luke's personal theological achievement.'[1]

Second, as we have noted, the very fact that Acts was written shows how uneschatologically Luke thinks. Certainly, the fact that Luke can reflect on the origins of the Church and its significance for his contemporaries presupposes a delay, but it does not imply that he has abandoned End-expectation altogether. One could equally well point to the existence of Mark's Gospel. A contributory if not the underlying cause of its composition was the fact that it began to dawn on the Church that the End was not coming as soon as they had expected and that the continued existence of the Church meant that her various needs – whether they were liturgical, doctrinal or practical – had to be met.

Bearing in mind these preliminary points, it appears that Luke is not such a unique man after all. Much of his teaching

---

[1] U. Wilckens, 'Interpreting Luke–Acts in a period of existentialist theology', *SLA*, p. 67.

on eschatology he holds in common with his sources and it is false to imagine that, receiving a tradition wholly orientated towards an imminent expectation, he went through it meticulously pruning the pieces that did not appeal to him, replacing them with his own theory of *Heilsgeschichte*.

How then are we to explain Luke's eschatology, particularly that of the Gospel? We have found that he has two apparently contradictory strands of teaching, both of which he asserts with equal firmness. On the one hand he moves away from imminent expectation, claiming that Jesus foresaw the time of the Church and his own exaltation (Lk. 9: 27, 19: 11, 21: 20–4, 22: 69; Acts 1: 6–8) and answering the problem of Christians dying before the Parousia by speaking of individual Resurrection and a personal, private Parousia (Lk. 14: 12–14, 16: 9, 31, 24: 43; Acts 7: 56). On the other hand, Luke firmly maintains the possibility of an imminent End (Lk. 10: 9, 11, 12: 38–48, 12: 54 – 13: 9, 18: 8, 21: 32). How are we to explain these two strands?

1. The explanation given by Conzelmann and many others is that the material which betrays an imminent expectation is a hangover from the tradition Luke received and does not represent his own view. He records it only because he was faithful to his sources and not because he agreed with it. One meets this form of argument frequently in books on Luke and it is often used for the purpose of ignoring one strand of evidence in the interests of a neat, logical scheme. If one were to accept this explanation, then it has a corollary which is not often recognised, namely that Luke is not the theologian he is often made out to be. His scheme is not neat and tidy; it has many loose ends, if not contradictions. However, although it may help to explain some of the evidence (e.g. 21: 32), there are good reasons for thinking that this explanation is insufficient:

(a) There is too much evidence for both strands in Luke's eschatology for one to be eliminated in this convenient manner. Moreover, who is to say that because Luke merely transmits some material unchanged this does not represent his own view? Surely, the very fact that he transmits material shows, at the least, that he did not find it objectionable; if it had been, then presumably he would have omitted or altered it. According to Conzelmann, Luke has no scruples on this score; he is a dab hand at manipulating his sources to fit his theories. If at some points Luke eliminates imminent expectation by fiddling the books, why, on Conzelmann's logic, does he not go the whole way?

(b) It is at least probable that some of the texts which show an imminent expectation are Luke's creation and not from his tradition (Lk. 18: 8 and possibly 12: 38f). Here the argument from tradition falls down, for we have Luke's own hand at work.

2. A second explanation would be to date Luke very early (say, A.D. 65–70) and argue that he wrote soon after Mark. We could then think of him as allowing for a delay long enough to include the Ascension, Pentecost and the Gentile mission, but a delay which would come to an end with the destruction of Jerusalem. We could then interpret the oracles on Jerusalem as prophecies before rather than descriptions after the event. The difficulty of this view is that it involves dating Luke before A.D. 70, which is not the impression one gets from Lk. 19: 41–4, 21: 20–4, nor is it the impression one gets from the way Luke handles Mark's material. Why, for instance, were all the alterations necessary if he was writing so soon after Mark?

A variation on this view which dates Luke after A.D. 70 but not long after (say, 75–85) is a valuable alternative. It would explain why Luke saw the need to alter some of Mark – because of the upheavals of A.D. 70 – and why he left other parts intact. Taken together with our next point this helps to explain what Luke has done, but on its own it does not get to the heart of Luke's teaching.

3. The fundamental explanation of the two strands in Luke's eschatology is to be found in the pastoral situations with which he was faced. A Church faced with a delayed Parousia could easily lapse into one of two false extremes. The first is a fervent renewal of apocalypticism, which included false Messiahs who claimed that the End was near or already here. If sometimes their hopes were dashed they were not destroyed, but were renewed all the more fervently. Disappointment only served to fan the flame of their fanaticism. Not satisfied with the promise of God, they wished to force the kingdom in by their own efforts or, at least, to be able to calculate exactly when it would come. This reaction J. Pieper called *praesumptio* – 'a premature, self-willed anticipation of the fulfilment of what we hope for from

God'.[1] Such views Luke was combating in Lk. 17: 20f, 21: 7, 8, 20–4; Acts 1: 6–8. This does not explain all of what we have called the delay strand, since some of these passages seem to be no more than the inevitable reflection of the fact that Luke was writing some forty or more years after Jesus' death. Passages like 19: 11 and 22: 69 are simply due to the realisation that after Jesus' death it was not the kingdom but the time of the Church with its exalted Lord which came. Nevertheless, false apocalypticism is one, if not the most important explanation of why Luke emphasises the delay of the Parousia and makes it clear that when the End comes it will be sudden and universally manifest.

But yet another problem can arise from a situation where an expected Parousia fails to materialise, namely a denial that the Parousia would come at all. For some, when their expectations were not fulfilled, simply abandoned them altogether. Disappointment did not serve to feed but to destroy their hope. This situation may have been aggravated by intense persecution.[2] Those undergoing it would look to their Lord to vindicate them, and when this did not take place they would be tempted to abandon their faith altogether. This reaction J. Pieper would

[1] J. Pieper, *Über die Hoffnung* (1949), quoted by J. Moltmann, *Theology of Hope* (London, 1967), p. 23.

[2] G. Braumann, 'Das Mittel der Zeit', *ZNW*, 54 (1963), 117–45, thinks Luke was dealing with practical problems, especially persecution. However, he thinks that Luke's response was not to reaffirm an imminent End, but to show the Church that she stood on the side of God and to assert that the End, though a long way off, was certain. H. W. Bartsch, *Wachet aber zu jeder Zeit. Entwurf einer Auslegung des Lukasevangeliums* (Hamburg-Bergstedt, 1963), arrived too late for full consideration in this section. He argues that Luke was in no way concerned with the problem of excessive imminent expectation. On the contrary, he was chiefly concerned to correct the primitive Christian belief that Jesus' Resurrection and Parousia were one and the same event (II Tim. 2: 18). At the same time, by exhortation to constant watchfulness, he tried to revive imminent expectation amongst those who had lost interest in eschatology. The latter point overlaps with our own interpretation, but evidence for the view expressed in II Tim. 2: 18 being widespread in primitive Christianity is entirely lacking, since the only other place where this view may be alluded to is in I Cor. 4: 8f, 15: 12. Luke shows no awareness of this view and, moreover, it seems to have arisen in connection with 'gnostic' beliefs and there is no other evidence that Luke was concerned with the problem of Gnosticism. See C. K. Barrett, *Luke the Historian in Recent Study* (London, 1961), pp. 62–3. For a different view see C. H. Talbert, *Luke and the Gnostics* (New York, 1966).

call *desperatio* – 'a premature, arbitrary anticipation of the non-fulfilment of what we hope for from God'.[1] Such a situation appears to lie behind Lk. 18: 1–8 where, faced with an urgent crisis in which men are denying their faith, Luke encourages them with the promise that the Lord will come soon. It is noticeable that most of the other passages which reaffirm imminent expectation spring from pastoral situations. Lk. 12: 38f which addresses Church leaders in particular, and Lk. 21: 36 which speaks to all Christians, refer to a situation in which, as a result of either projecting the Parousia into the far-distant future or of abandoning hope for it altogether, Christians were becoming morally lax. Similarly, Lk. 12: 54 – 13: 9 is addressed to those who live under the false impression that since judgement is a long way off, there is no need for immediate repentance. Nor would it be too fanciful to see 10: 9, 11 as pastorally motivated because, as has often been noted, the mission of the Seventy in Lk. 10 is described with at least one eye on the later mission of the Church.

To summarise, both strands in Luke's eschatology are well attested and neither can legitimately be ignored; more especially, neither one should be overrated at the expense of the other. Both strands are motivated essentially by practical, pastoral problems which faced Luke in the Church of his day. It is this which explains their apparent contradiction, since it was both necessary and possible for Luke on the one hand to allow for a delayed Parousia and on the other to insist that the Lord would come soon. Thus Luke was fighting not merely on one but on two fronts. By treading a deliberate *via media* he both avoided and corrected the two false extremes which some of his contemporaries had fallen into. Exactly how we are to translate this into chronological terms is not easy to say. At a guess we can say that Luke was writing around the period A.D. 75–85, sufficiently close to Mark to account for both their similarities and differences. For Luke the date of the End is not tied up with the events of A.D. 70, nor is it limited to 30–40 years after Jesus' death. On the other hand, he did not expect the Church to continue existing for some 2,000 years. For him the End was a sure hope, which he expected to be fulfilled in the near future. To define it any further would be to go beyond what the facts warrant.

[1] Pieper, *Hoffnung*.

A few important conclusions emerge from this study of Luke's eschatology:

1. This emphasis on the pastoral, practical motivation of Luke's eschatology has an important corollary, namely that Luke was not concerned with the delay *qua* delay. It was for him not a theoretical but a practical problem. It was the pastoral effects of the delay of the Parousia which led him to write as he did and not a desire to find a semi-philosophical and lasting solution for the Christian Church. Primarily Luke was a pastor and not a theologian. This is not meant to imply that a theologian cannot be a pastor and vice-versa. In putting it in this way we are simply trying to show where the centre of gravity of Luke's thought lies.

2. Because Luke was writing in this way, we have to be wary of talking about Luke writing with set plans in mind, of Luke the theologian who sets out to fit all the material before him into a neat outline. We may for our own convenience find a *heilsgeschichtlich* or a prophecy-fulfilment pattern in Luke's writings as an aid to sorting out his ideas, but it is false to imply that such a pattern was in Luke's mind when he wrote. It is to put the cart before the horse.

3. Luke's eschatology is not the same in the Gospel and Acts. In the Gospel there is a tension between imminent expectation and the allowance which is made for a delay in the Parousia; in Acts there is no imminent expectation. This can best be shown by putting Lk. 18: 1–8 and Acts 1: 6–11 side by side. In both the delay is presupposed, and in both the hope for a Parousia is explicitly reaffirmed. The difference is that in the Gospel Luke speaks of an imminent Parousia, whereas in Acts he avoids any such temporal limitation (v. 11). This, like other differences between the two books, should make us wary of expecting the same teaching in both – an assumption which is common in recent studies of Luke. It might also suggest that Acts was written a considerable time after the Gospel and that it is not improbable that Luke's views had developed in this time or perhaps, in the case of eschatology, the problems he faced had altered.

4. It is a common practice to compare Luke unfavourably with Paul. Luke, it is said, with his notion of *Heilsgeschichte*, has lost the Pauline existential dialectic, the moment of crisis and

decision which all men face in the eschatological 'now'. Thus Conzelmann contrasts Lk. 4: 21 'Today this scripture is fulfilled in your ears' with II Cor. 6: 2 'Behold, now is the acceptable time', and he says that whereas for Paul the 'now' expresses an eschatological present, for Luke salvation is a thing of the past.[1] This is, however, a false analogy. Paul is writing in the present about the present, whereas Luke is writing in the present about the past. Paul is speaking of present realities and Luke of historical facts. Moreover, Luke's 'today' does not exclude Paul's 'now' if it had been Luke's purpose to express it. More generally, it is probably as false to interpret Paul exclusively in existential terms and to deny him a concept of *Heilsgeschichte* as it is to do the opposite with Luke.

5. We set out in this study to see how far Luke is logical in his presentation of Jesus' eschatology as it related to his teaching about the Gentile mission. The immediate answer to our question has become abundantly clear. When he portrayed Jesus as both foreseeing and commanding the Gentile mission, Luke altered Jesus' eschatological expectations to allow for this. Jesus' eschatological predictions leave ample room for the Gentile mission. Some of Luke's alterations which allow for a delay of the Parousia seem to be a direct result of his awareness that it was the Church with its mission and not the Kingdom which came after Jesus' death. In doing this Luke was not an innovator; he merely extends a process already begun by Mark. Yet while Luke has removed the Gentile mission from the apocalyptic context of Mk 13, with its temporal restrictions, he does not abandon imminent expectation altogether. He has not produced a neat theory of *Heilsgeschichte* in which the Parousia has been relegated to the far-distant and indefinite future. The End had been delayed, but Luke still thought it was near. For, while one of the motivations of Luke's eschatology was the need to make allowance for indisputable historical facts, such as the existence of the Church and the Gentile mission, it was the practical problems of the Church of his day, above all, which were his main inspiration. The former motive he shared with his predecessors; it was the latter which called forth his distinctive eschatological teaching.

---

[1] Conzelmann, *Luke*, p. 103; Grässer, *Parusieverzögerung*, pp. 187–8.

CHAPTER 4

THE EARLY CHAPTERS OF ACTS

Our aim in this chapter is to discuss four separate sections of Acts 1–2: Acts 1: 6–8; Acts 1: 9–11; Acts 1: 15f; Acts 2: 1f. Some of these have either a direct or an indirect bearing on the Gentile mission and the reason for our discussion of them is obvious. The story of Matthias' election is relevant because it gives us an insight into the problems of the title 'Apostle', which for Luke is closely connected with the Gentile mission. The Ascension is important for Luke's eschatology in Acts and as a background to Jesus' command for the universal mission. Moreover, all of these topics are very important for giving us a clue to the beliefs and practices of the earliest Christians, which may in turn shed light on their attitudes towards the Gentile mission.

THE COMMISSION (ACTS 1: 6–8)

As the following study will show, these three verses bristle with problems. As usual in Luke–Acts, the problems are easier to state than to answer, but we shall attempt to do both.

v. 6

We must first ask who is included in οἱ συνελθόντες. Haenchen thinks the reference is intentially inexact, since 1: 21 implies that at least two more than the Eleven were present.[1] But the most obvious reference for v. 6 is not a vague but an exact one, namely to the Eleven (τοῖς ἀποστόλοις v. 2). At first sight this contradicts vv. 21–2, but this depends somewhat on our interpretation of these verses. The qualification of an Apostle is that he should have been a member (συνελθόντων v. 21 = 'to accompany') of the larger group of disciples who existed from

---

[1] Haenchen, *Apg.*, p. 111; G. Schille, 'Die Himmelfahrt', *ZNW*, 57 (1966), 183–99, here p. 186. Lk. 24: 33 implies that more than the Eleven were present at the subsequent departure of Jesus, since it is the last notice in ch. 24 of who was present. However, as the dating of the Ascension shows, we cannot expect complete harmony between Lk. 24 and Acts 1.

the beginning of Jesus' ministry until the Ascension.[1] This does not mean that such men have experienced all that the Twelve have. This is precluded by the unique position of the Twelve in the Gospel narratives. 'To accompany' is a vague term which does not imply that this wider coterie impinged on the special privileges of the Twelve.

'Lord, will you at this time restore the Kingdom to Israel?' It is certain that this question reflects a nationalistic Jewish expectation. Less clear is the extent to which it implies an imminent expectation and how an apparently gross misunderstanding on the part of the disciples could still exist after forty days of teaching on the subject (Acts 1 : 3). To take the last point first: Haenchen argues that we cannot take Acts 1 : 1f as a genuine historical record, for if the disciples retained this misunderstanding after forty days of teaching then we must assume either that they were exceptionally stupid or that Jesus was a singularly incompetent teacher.[2] Rejecting both of these possibilities, he argues that v. 3 is to be explained on literary-stylistic grounds as the preparation for vv. 6f where Luke intends to give his own view of the relationship between End events, the Spirit and the mission. This may be the correct explanation, or it may be that the reference to teaching in v. 3 is no more than an artificial filling-up for the forty days, where the kingdom of God, as often in Acts, is a non-specific term equivalent to 'the whole Christian message' (cf. Acts 19: 8, 20: 25 and 8: 12, 28: 23, 28).

Most commentators assume correctly that v. 6 expresses an imminent expectation. Although χρόνος is a general word for time, its use in v. 6 and in the whole context of vv. 1f implies a reference to an imminent End. The phrase 'at this time' v. 6 refers back to the phrase 'before many days' in v. 5: when told that the Holy Spirit was coming, the disciples naturally connected this with the End events; therefore they ask Jesus whether when the Spirit comes the End would come also.[3]

[1] In Lk. 6: 13 the Twelve apostles are chosen from a wider group of disciples (cf. Lk. 10: 1f, 24: 33). In Acts 1: 17, 21–2, ἡμῖν is ambiguous: in v. 22b it appears to refer to the Twelve (cf. v. 17), but in vv. 21–22a it could refer to the 120 brethren (v. 15).

[2] E. Haenchen, 'Judentum und Christentum in der Apostelgeschichte', *ZNW*, 54 (1963), 155–87, here p. 160.

[3] Since the Spirit was connected with the End events in Jewish expectation Joel 2: 28f; *S.B.*, ΙΙ, 128f). Some think that behind Acts 1: 4 there is a

v. 7

Jesus' answer is both negative and positive, but in neither case is it straightforward. This verse is the negative response which picks up a logion found in a different form in Mk 13: 32, Matt. 24: 36 (cf. I Thess. 5: 1). Luke has done two things with the original: first he has omitted the reference to the son's ignorance, so that his version is open to the assumption that the son does know the times and the seasons; secondly, he has removed it from the apocalyptic discourse and placed it in this post-Resurrection context. In itself this verse is not a denial of imminent expectation.[1] It corrects the disciples' concern to know exactly when the End will come, but it does not say whether the End will be delayed or not. At this point Jesus does not say that the End will not come with the Spirit, but that what will occur is God's concern and not theirs.

v. 8

This verse contains the positive element in Jesus' reply. He will not say when the End will come, but he does say that when the Spirit comes they will receive the power to perform miracles (δύναμις) and will be his universal witnesses.[2] Luke has left unclear the exact relation between the Spirit, the mission and the question in v. 6. It could be that the Spirit is the substitution for or elimination of imminent expectation and the mission is the correction of the nationalistic hope; that is, the Spirit and the mission are two promises which correct the double misunderstanding of v. 6.[3] Yet the actual sequence of thought suggests that the Spirit is not the substitute for but the cause of *Naherwartung* and that this part of the disciples' question is answered in

primitive tradition that the disciples went to Jerusalem to await the Parousia (Test. Zeb. 9: 8; *S.B.*, II, 300f). See A. Loisy, *Les Actes des Apôtres* (Paris, 1920), p. 152; J. Wellhausen, *Kritische Analyse der Apostelgeschichte* (Berlin, 1914), p. 2.

[1] *Contra* Grässer, *Parusieverzögerung*, p. 205.

[2] δύναμις is used of the miracles of Jesus (Acts 2: 22, 10: 38) and the early Church (Acts 3: 12, 4: 7, 8: 10, 13, 9: 11). It is again connected with μάρτυρες in 4: 33. 'Witness' in Acts is mainly witness to the Resurrection (Acts 1: 22, 2: 32, 3: 15, 4: 33 etc.).

[3] Haenchen, *Apg.*, p. 112; Conzelmann, *Apg.*, p. 22; Wikenhauser, *Apg.*, p. 27; G. Stählin, *Die Apostelgeschichte* (Göttingen, 1966), pp. 17–18.

v. 7, which leaves the date of the End open. If anything it is the mission which is the substitute for imminent expectation, since a world mission such as is envisaged in v. 8 will necessarily postpone the End. At the same time this universal mission corrects the nationalistic hope of the disciples. Whatever the exact details of interpretation, it is generally agreed that in vv. 6–8 Luke is saying in effect that the End will be delayed. The coming of the Spirit is not the herald of the End but of the universal mission of the Church. It is also probable that Luke is not concerned here merely with giving a historical record but is also addressing the Church of his day, some of whose members not only believed in an imminent End but also tried to calculate the exact date of its arrival.

The second half of the verse – 'you shall be my witnesses in Jerusalem and in all Judea and Samaria and to the end of the earth' – is equally problematic. We shall ask a series of questions and, in our answers, attempt to clarify and answer some of the problems.

1. Is it deliberately ambiguous? K. H. Rengstorf suggests that Luke intentionally left v. 8b open to two interpretations. As well as a reference to the world-wide mission which would include the Gentiles, it could also be understood as a command only for a Jewish Diaspora mission.[1] Thus he explains the odd fact that according to Acts it required a special vision to convince Peter that preaching to the Gentiles was part of God's will, when in 1 : 8 Jesus had already commanded such preaching. It is true that v. 8b could be interpreted in this way, but it is improbable that Luke understood it so. He never uses it as an excuse for the Jerusalem leaders' reluctance to embark on a Gentile mission; on the contrary, the same phrase as in v. 8b, ἕως ἐσχάτου τῆς γῆς (Is. 49: 6 LXX), is used in Acts 13: 47 as Paul's justification for his missionary work among the Gentiles. Further, v. 8 is parallel to πάντα τὰ ἔθνη – ἀρξάμενοι ἀπὸ Ἱερουσαλημ in Lk. 24: 47, where the reference to the Gentile mission is unequivocal. The contradiction between Acts 1: 8 and Acts 10 is best seen as a tension between Luke's own view,

---

[1] K. H. Rengstorf, 'The Election of Matthias', in *Current Issues in New Testament Interpretation*, essays in honour of O. Piper (London, 1962), pp. 186–7; Haenchen, 'Judentum', p. 160. The future ἔσεσθε is probably to be taken as an imperative (cf. v. 2).

namely that Jesus authorised a Gentile mission, and the actual course of events, namely the Church's reluctance officially to endorse this mission, partially because Jesus had not in fact commanded it.

2. Does v. 8b give the plan of Acts? This question is answered in the affirmative by most scholars: v. 8 is the δέ-clause, the apodosis which is otherwise lacking in vv. 1f. While it may not be possible to divide up Acts exactly according to this plan, v. 8b certainly corresponds to the fundamental movement of the Church's mission in Acts.[1] It foretells the decisive moments when the mission will take a new direction and is rightly understood to give the narrative of Acts in a nutshell.

3. How is v. 8b related to Luke's concept of apostleship? This question is inspired by one of the most curious facts about v. 8, namely that it is addressed to the Apostles. As Stählin says, 'It is certainly extraordinary that even after Pentecost the Twelve do not think of making a start on the world mission and that they were rather first brought, half unwillingly, to the point of affirming a mission beyond Judaism partly through express guidance from God (10: 9f) and partly through the enterprises of others (8: 5f, 11: 19f, 15: 12f).'[2] The remarkable fact is that the Twelve, apart from Peter, are not only non-participants in this mission, but seem reluctant for it to occur at all. Even within Judea their fundamental role is that of guiding and leading the Christian community and not one of active missionary enterprise. According to Acts, even when the whole community scatters under persecution the Twelve remain firmly entrenched in Jerusalem.[3] We saw above that Rengstorf's explanation of this as a result of the disciples' misinterpretation of Jesus' command in 1: 8 is improbable. Equally improbable is E. Trocmé's view that 1: 8 finds its fulfilment in the Pentecost narrative.[4]

[1] E.g. Haenchen, *Apg.*, p. 112; Conzelmann, *Apg.*, p. 22; Dupont, 'Gentils', pp. 140f. Contrast E. Trocmé, *Le 'Livre des Actes' et l'Histoire* (Paris, 1957), and G. Klein, *Die Zwölf Apostel* (Göttingen, 1961), p. 209. Haenchen uses the rough divisions: 1–7 Jerusalem–Judea; 8–9 Samaria; 10–28 all the world.

[2] Stählin, *Apg.*, p. 18.

[3] This accords with Paul's view that the apostles were normally to be found in Jerusalem (Gal. 1). Paul speaks only of Peter as a missionary (Gal. 2: 1f).

[4] Trocmé, *Actes*, p. 206.

Apart from the fact that the details of 1: 8 and 2: 1f do not coincide, a more fundamental objection is that the basic directions of the two are diametrically opposed: 1: 8 speaks of a centrifugal movement of the mission out from Jerusalem, while 2: 9–11 portrays a centripetal influx of Diaspora Jews from all nations into Jerusalem.

G. Klein argues that v. 8 expresses the characteristically Lukan concept of apostolic succession. One of the Twelve, Peter, clears the basic hurdle and the way is then open for others like Paul and Barnabas to do the bulk of the missionary work. It is not the Twelve in person who will go to the ends of the earth, but their representatives. Klein thinks that 'the principle of the apostolicity of tradition and succession cannot be formulated more pregnantly'. In the context of 1: 6–8 this means that 'Apostolic tradition and succession are established next to the Spirit as substitutes for an eschatology which has been relegated to the *locus de novissimis*'.[1] However, although Klein may have hit on a partial explanation of v. 8, one cannot draw such far-reaching conclusions about a Lukan principle of apostolic succession which is inserted between the Ascension and the unexpectedly delayed Parousia. Where he may be correct is that Luke, if he was aware of the anomaly of v. 8, may have understood Peter's initial step as a sufficient fulfilment of 1: 8. But even so, the Apostles can scarcely be said to have preached widely in Judea and Samaria either. It may be that Luke's view of the Apostles as the founder-members of the Church means that what the Church did through its individual members, the Twelve, as the basis of this Church, also did. But while this takes account of the importance of the Twelve for Luke, it does not explain their curious disappearance half-way through Acts, at a time when the Gentile mission was really getting under way. One might say that as the impetus for the Gentile mission increases so, in inverse proportion, the significance of the Twelve decreases.

It seems that we must understand v. 8, in its relationship to the Twelve, as an anomaly of which Luke may well have been unaware. It is best understood as a Lukan creation, which does not accord with some of the more traditional material he relates

---

[1] Klein, *Apostel*, p. 210. He sees it as the dominating theme of Acts. Even if this were true, it would be difficult to read all this into Acts 1: 8.

elsewhere. In this he may have been influenced by the early Patristic picture of the Twelve as active missionaries (cf. *I Clem.* 42: 3f; Just. *Apol.*, I. 39. 3f).

4. Is v. 8b to be understood representatively? This is a question which must be put with regard to all the early texts which authorise a Gentile mission. Mk 13: 10, for example, can scarcely be interpreted to mean that the gospel must be preached to every single Gentile or even to every town or village in each nation, in view of the temporal limitations of Mk 13 as a whole. Therefore it must be understood representatively, namely that all the main cities of each nation should be evangelised before the End. Paul's statements in Rom. 15: 19–20 have been interpreted in the same way. With Luke there could be a difference, because he has removed Jesus' prophecy of the Gentile mission from the apocalyptic context it has in Mark. In the Lukan post-Resurrection context it lacks any specific temporal limitations. Even so, it is probable that Luke understood v. 8b basically in a representative sense; at least that is the impression he gives in the narrative of Acts. The ending of this narrative in Rome may, therefore, be significant, because in a sense Rome represented the end of the earth.[1]

5. What is the purpose of v. 8 in the context of Acts? The answer to this question is complex, since we have to consider all the possible views which Luke was trying to combat or encourage in the Church of his day. We shall mention several possibilities in order of preference, while acknowledging that the preference is arbitrary and that Luke may have been concerned with only one or with a combination of these motives:

(a) Fundamental to v. 8 is that the mission of the Church, and in particular the Gentile mission, is rooted in a command of Jesus. Jesus foresees the development of the Church after his death and gives it his divine seal. We have already suggested several times that this verse and others like it are constructions of the early Church or, at least, a misunderstanding of Jesus'

---

[1] The exact meaning of Acts 1: 8b is obscure. The first three areas are clear enough, but the last phrase – 'the end of the earth' – if it denotes Rome, is strange, since for Luke and his readers Rome was scarcely the end of the earth. However, Acts 13: 46–7 show that the expression can have a meaning that is not strictly geographical, namely as a reference to the Gentile mission.

prophecies of an apocalyptic Gentile mission.[1] This is confirmed by the material we find later in Acts which, as we have seen, makes it difficult to suppose that Jesus commanded a Gentile mission, still less a mission to be performed by the Twelve. This process is similar to Luke's use of Old Testament prophecies of the Gentile mission. Both are intended to show that this universal outreach was not a chance occurrence, a mere trick of Fate, but was from the beginning an integral part of the eternal will of God.

(b) The central significance of Jerusalem as the base camp for the Church's mission is drawn out here and in Lk. 24: 47f. In a similar way to the Ascension, Jerusalem plays an important role in Luke–Acts.[2] It is one of the central bearings on which the double work swivels: it is the goal towards which Jesus' ministry moves and the base from which the Church's mission expands. The basic pattern of v. 8 is that found elsewhere in the New Testament (cf. Rom. 1: 16), namely 'Jew first and then Greek'. The narrative of Acts follows this pattern throughout and even Paul, the Gentile missionary *par excellence*, begins his preaching in each new area with an appeal to the Jews. The continual obduracy of the Jews opens the way for a Gentile mission, but this does not mean that the Jews are excluded. The Jewish mission does not end with Jesus' ministry.

(c) It is implied in vv. 6–8 that the essence of the Church is its mission. Church and mission are inseparably interrelated. On Luke's definition, a Church with no missionary activity is not a true Church. It may be that Luke's contemporaries were lacking in missionary zeal and that by his account of the mission of the early Church he is trying to show that missionary endeavour is of the essence of a true Church.

(d) By giving an exact, detailed plan of the progress of the Church's mission, v. 8b differs significantly from any other word on the Gentile mission attributed to Jesus. The other, probably earlier versions (Lk. 24: 47; Mk 13: 10; Matt. 28: 19) are simple commands, promises or statements to the effect that

---

[1] Cf. *B.C.*, iv, 6: 'the disciples came to this [the Gentile mission] reluctantly, and only in the light of their experience, but once they had done so their conclusion was justified by being thrown back into the mouth of Jesus in the form of Matt. 28: 19; Lk. 24: 47f and Acts 1: 8.'

[2] Conzelmann, *Luke*, pp. 132f; J. C. O'Neill, *The Theology of Acts in its Historical Setting* (London, 1961), pp. 54f.

there will be a Gentile mission. Luke's version in Acts 1: 8 may be no more than an expansion which reflects his own view of the course of the mission and which at the same time gives a rough outline of Acts. It may, however, partially be an explanation, if not an apology, for the fact that the Gentile mission was so slow to get off the ground. Once the mission was rooted in the words of Jesus, it must have seemed odd that it was only slowly and reluctantly accepted by the early leaders. By showing that it was not simply an immediate outward rush to the Gentiles, but a gradual, planned development that Jesus envisaged, Luke may be explaining why the mission took the form it did.

THE ASCENSION (ACTS 1: 9–11)

Fully to understand Luke's account of the Ascension in Acts, that is, to discover the purpose and meaning of it, we have to view it together with his earlier version in Lk. 24: 50f and against the background of the New Testament as a whole.

To take the latter point first: in other parts of the New Testament the Ascension is spoken of as distinct from the Resurrection (Jn 20: 17; Eph. 4: 8–10; I Tim. 3: 16; I Pet. 3: 22; Heb. 4: 14, 6: 19, 9: 24).[1] These passages show that there was a widespread theological distinction between the Ascension and the Resurrection, but that Luke is alone in giving a concrete description of them as separate events in a logical sequence. This is particularly true of the Acts narrative where Luke attempts to give a logical rationale of the immediate post-Easter events,[2] while at the same time his concrete bent of mind encourages him to give a firm historical foundation to some of the cardinal beliefs of the Church in his day. Luke's earlier account betrays what appears to be a more primitive view, namely that the Ascension was part of the events of the first Easter day.[3] Thus the Ascension has a distinct place in Luke's scheme, which comes out particularly clearly in Acts.[4] It is distinct from the Resurrection on the one hand and Pentecost on the other. It is

---

[1] A. M. Ramsey, 'The Ascension', *SNTS*, 2 (1952), 49f; Wikenhauser, *Apg.*, pp. 27f.   [2] Cadbury, *Eschatology*, pp. 300f.

[3] A. N. Wilder, 'Variant traditions of the Resurrection in Luke–Acts', *JBL*, 62 (1943), 307f.

[4] Conzelmann, *Luke*, p. 203 n. 4; C. K. Barrett, *Luke*, p. 57.

separated from the Resurrection by a forty-day interval and it is the necessary presupposition for the sending of the Spirit (Acts 2 : 33). Yet we should not make too much of this. Although the narrative of the Ascension in Acts is unique, its uniqueness is to some extent inevitable, since Luke is the only New Testament author who attempts to give a historical account of the early years of the Church.

He alone tries to unravel the complex and obscure chronology of the first few years after the Resurrection, and at the same time provide the historical origins of the Church's belief in her exalted Lord and the Holy Spirit. Luke's distinctive approach to the Ascension is therefore to a large extent a part of his unique position in the New Testament as the first and only Church historian.

We turn now to a comparison of Luke's two versions of this event. To ease some of the difficulties in harmonising them it has been suggested that the shorter text of Lk. 24: 50f, which omits the phrase καὶ ἀνεφέρετο εἰς τὸν οὐρανόν, is the more original.[1] However, there are good reasons for thinking that the longer text is the one which Luke wrote,[2] and even with the shorter text there is still a reference to the Ascension in Lk. 24, since Acts 1 : 2, in particular the word ἀνελήμφθη,[3] refers back to and interprets the phrase διέστη ἀπ' αὐτῶν in Lk. 24: 51. Despite the difficulties, therefore, we must accept that Luke wrote two accounts of the Ascension.

Before noting the difference between the two narratives it is instructive to observe their basic similarities. Both narratives are compact and precise; in neither is there any excessive legendary embellishment. The account of the actual Ascension is in both cases remarkably brief. Yet despite this there are striking differences:

[1] Conzelmann, *Luke*, p. 94; A. W. Argyle, 'The Ascension', *ET*, 66 (1955), 240–2.

[2] Haenchen, *Apg.*, p. 116; Wilder, 'Resurrection', p. 311; Grundmann, *Lukas*, p. 454. The arguments are most comprehensively set out by P. A. van Stempvoort, 'The interpretation of the Ascension in Luke–Acts', *NTS*, 5 (1958–9), 30f.

[3] Van Stempvoort, 'Ascension', p. 32, thinks that ἀνελήμφθη in Acts 1 : 2 should be interpreted like Lk. 9: 51, i.e. in a general, non-technical way, which refers to the whole process of passing away and being taken up. But in Acts 1 : 2 the singular ἡμέρας defines the word ἀνελήμφθη and implies that it refers to a specific event, namely the Ascension.

(a) Most obvious and problematic are the two different dates. The whole of Lk. 24, including the Ascension vv. 50f, is presumably dated on Easter day, since Lk. 24: 1 is the last time reference which Luke gives in his Gospel. Acts 1: 3 assumes a forty-day interval between the Resurrection and the Ascension.

(b) According to Lk. 24: 33 there were more than the Eleven at the Ascension, whereas the implication of Acts 1: 2 is that only the Apostles were present.

(c) In Lk. 24: 50 the Ascension takes place in Bethany and in Acts 1: 2 on the Mount of Olives. This may not have been a discrepancy for Luke, since he may have thought of the latter as situated within the former.

(d) There are several further details which are different in each account: the picture of Jesus departing as he blesses the disciples is missing in Acts;[1] the reference to the two angels in Acts 1: 10–11, which forms the bulk of this narrative, is lacking in the Gospel; finally, Lk. 24: 52–3 tells of the disciples' great joy and continual praising of God in the Temple, whereas Acts makes no mention of their joy and says that they went back to the upper room.

Why did Luke write two such different accounts? If he had written two similar accounts, one at the end of the Gospel and one at the beginning of Acts, our question would be relatively easy to answer. It is the divergence of the two accounts which complicates matters. Above all, the new dating in Acts needs some explanation, since it is the most serious discrepancy.

The forty days of Acts 1: 3 has attracted many explanations. It is almost certain that the choice of this round number is based on Biblical and Jewish parables.[2] It is probably not meant to be chronologically exact,[3] though neither is it grossly inaccurate. Schille is probably correct when he says that Luke was not motivated by the same reasons as the Gnostics who later extended the period to 545 days or more in order to accommodate their claim to possess secret traditions of Jesus' post-Resurrection

---

[1] Daube, *Judaism*, p. 231, and van Stempvoort, 'Ascension', pp. 34–5, interpret Lk. 24: 50 as the blessing of a priest, since 'lifting up the hands' means 'to bless' (Cf. Sir. 50: 20).

[2] Apart from being a favourite round number (Ex. 34: 28; I Kings 19: 8; Mk 1: 13 pars.), it may be significant that both Ezra and Baruch waited forty days before they ascended (IV Ezr. 16: 23, 49; Apoc. Bar. 76: 4).

[3] Cf. the vague parallel phrase in Acts 13: 31 – 'for many days'.

teaching (Iren. *Haer*. I. 30. 14, 32 etc.).[1] The period of forty days is too short for this and Luke gives the content of the teaching in 1 : 3; moreover, teaching about the kingdom of God was not confined to the post-Resurrection period. Haenchen thinks the significant fact is that Jesus and his disciples drank and ate together after as well as before the Resurrection (Lk. 24: 42; Acts 1 : 4, 10: 41): 'they were in a position to testify that the earthly Jesus and the Risen One were one and the same person'.[2] But while this probably gives the correct explanation of the references to eating and drinking in Lk. 24 and Acts 1, it does not explain why Luke extended the period from one to forty days, since one day of eating and drinking would be as convincing as forty days. It may simply be that after completing his Gospel Luke received new traditions about the post-Resurrection appearances;[3] but then one would have expected him to have given a few more details. He gives no new accounts not already in Lk. 24; the only new thing is the forty days dating.

The explanation of the forty days is probably quite simple and is the result of two main factors. The first is that in Lk. 24 Luke could afford to be vague in his chronology, since he was not writing an account of the Church's origins but an account of the triumphant climax to Jesus' ministry.[4] When faced with the problems of a Church history, as he was in Acts, Luke is forced to think more about the timing and order of the post-Resurrection events. This leads us to the second factor, namely the dating of Pentecost. Luke wanted to date the coming of the Spirit at Pentecost as this was one, if not the only date which he had for the first year of the Church in what little tradition he received. This left him with the task of filling in the fifty-day hiatus

---

[1] Schille, 'Himmelfahrt', pp. 184–5.   [2] Haenchen, *Apg.*, p. 159.

[3] It is improbable that Luke was intentionally allowing for Galilean appearances. *Contra* C. F. D. Moule, 'The Ascension', *ET*, 68 (1957), 207.

[4] Stählin, *Apg.*, p. 13, comments: 'Lk. 24 displays one of the frequent instances when Luke, in recounting events which are definitely, temporally separated, omits all the dates, so that the impression is given that they occurred simultaneously.' It is probable that Luke was not too concerned to date the Ascension exactly: in Lk. 24 the chronology is vague, and although Acts is more precise, the purpose of the forty days is not so much to give an exact date for the Ascension as to fill in the gap between Easter and Pentecost. We must also allow for the possibility that by the time he came to write Acts Luke had quite simply forgotten what he had written in Lk. 24.

between Easter and Pentecost, which he does by means of the forty days. By mentioning the forty days in Acts 1 : 3, which he vaguely characterises as a time of teaching about the kingdom of God, and by use of the inexact notice in Acts 1 : 15, Luke manages to bring the narrative in Acts 1 more or less up to the date at the beginning of Acts 2. Thus it is not the forty days which forces Luke to date the coming of the Spirit at Pentecost, but the date of Pentecost which forces him to use the forty days.

The problem of the forty days is, however, only one of the differences we have to explain. We have yet to look at the various attempts to explain why Luke wrote two accounts and why they came out so differently:

1. P. H. Menoud argued that both Luke and Acts were expanded after the original single book containing these two parts was divided.[1] Lk. 24: 50–3 and Acts 1 : 1–5 were added in order to tidy up the loose ends left by the separation of the two books. However, Haenchen has argued decisively against this view and Menoud has retracted it in favour of another.[2]

2. A. Wikenhauser thinks that Acts 1 : 9–11 is not to be understood as an account of the Ascension, but as a description of Jesus' final departure after the Resurrection appearances. The Ascension took place on Easter day (Lk. 24: 50f) when Jesus was exalted to the right hand of power; from there Jesus appeared to his disciples for forty days until his final departure (Acts 1 : 9–11): 'The account in Acts of the ascension of Christ forty days after Easter does not stand in contradiction to Lk. 24. For the ascension from the Mount of Olives before the eyes of his disciples is only the conclusion of the final time of fellowship with them.'[3] There is, however, no warrant for this view in Lk. 24 and Acts 1. The end of Luke and the beginning of Acts are not to be read as chronologically successive. Lk. 24 is as much a farewell scene as Acts 1 : 9f. Both follow immediately on teaching about the Holy Spirit and the Gentile mission and presumably, therefore, describe the same event. A. N. Wilder makes a similar point when he argues that Acts 1: 3 should be read parenthetically,

---

[1] P. H. Menoud, 'Remarques sur les textes de l'ascension dans Luc–Actes', in *NS*, pp. 148f.

[2] Haenchen, *Apg.*, pp. 107, 113–15. P. H. Menoud, 'Pendant quarante jours (Actes 1: 3)', in *Neotestamentica et Patristica*, Festschrift for O. Cullmann (Leiden, 1962), p. 148 n. 1.

[3] Wikenhauser, *Apg.*, p. 28.

and that this forty-day period of appearances occurred after the Ascension.[1] Certainly, Acts 1:3 does not connect naturally with Acts 1: 1–2 because, after a review of the previous work, we would expect a preview of the present work and not a return to events which occurred before the terminus given in v. 2. In this case, however, we should have to read the whole of vv. 3–11 in parenthesis and not just v. 3.

3. One scholar, G. Schille, has recently made a serious attempt to show that the bulk of vv. 9–11 is not Lukan but comes from an early liturgical tradition. He thinks that 'the account of the ascension (Acts 1: 9–11) would have been a cult-aetiology for a gathering of the Jerusalem community on the Mount of Olives on the fortieth day after the Passover, by which one reflected on the ascension of Christ'.[2] However, there are several reasons for supposing that Schille's attempt to find a liturgical *Sitz im Leben* for Acts 1: 9–11 is unconvincing:

(a) While he gives a detailed analysis of vv. 9–11, Schille omits the observation that the language and style of these verses are predominantly Lukan, which makes it highly probable that the narrative is his own construction rather than a unit of tradition which he received. If it reflects pre-Lukan tradition, then we must assume that Luke has rewritten it to an extent which makes it impossible to distinguish Lukan and pre-Lukan elements. Admittedly, a mere word-count is not always easy to assess, because Luke–Acts forms such a large part of the New Testament that some words inevitably occur more frequently here than in other parts of the New Testament. However, the statistics are reasonably conclusive: the 'conjugatio periphrastica' – ἀτενίζοντες ἦσαν – is a construction particularly common in Luke–Acts, revealing an author fond of describing concrete situations;[3] καὶ ἰδού is a LXX phrase frequent in Luke (24 times) and Acts (8 times) cf. καὶ νῦν ἰδού in Acts 13: 11, 20: 22, 25; ἀτενίζω occurs twelve times in Luke–Acts, otherwise only in II Cor. 3: 7, 13; the singular νεφέλη is often seen as a parallel to Luke's use of Dan. 7: 13 in Lk. 21: 37; ἄνδρες δύο is parallel to Lk. 24: 4 (cf. Jn 20: 12), but not to Mk 16 or Matt. 28; ὑπολαμβάνω occurs four times in Luke–Acts, otherwise only

[1] Wilder, 'Resurrection', p. 312.
[2] Schille, 'Himmelfahrt', p. 193. The points discussed are on pp. 185f.
[3] Haenchen, *Apg.*, p. 116 n. 7.

in III John 8; ἐσθής occurs five times in Luke–Acts, otherwise only in James 2: 2; Luke has ten out of fifteen uses of ἀναλαμβάνω in the New Testament, and five out of the seven of those which refer to the Ascension.

(b) Schille thinks that the forty days of v. 3 is to be explained by analogy with the fifty days of Acts 2: 1. The dating of Pentecost is based on the Jewish calendar and is, he says, therefore a result of a liturgical concern rather than of the inner logic of the Church's Easter faith. Similarly, the dating of the Ascension on the fortieth day after the Passover is a piece of pre-Lukan tradition which is liturgically motivated. We have already given our own explanation of the forty days and when we turn to the Pentecost narrative we shall discover that when Luke dates the first outpouring of the Spirit at this time he was not motivated by liturgical concerns or by any desire to draw analogies with the Jewish Pentecost festival. For Luke, the dating of Pentecost had neither theological nor liturgical significance; it was simply a date.

(c) Schille suggests that the use of συνελθόντες in Acts 1: 6 may reflect the notion of Christians coming together to worship. Otherwise, he thinks, the phrase οἱ συνελθόντες is redundant, since according to Acts 1: 3f they are already together. However, there is no linguistic evidence to support this interpretation. Two of the three parallels he points to in Acts (Acts 10: 27, 28: 17) appear from their context to have the neutral, non-technical meaning 'come together'. The third (Acts 16: 13) does refer to women who come together to pray, but only as a result of its context and not because any such meaning is inherent in the word itself. From this one example we cannot say that this word sometimes has a neutral and sometimes a semi-technical meaning. Its other uses in Acts (5: 16, 19: 32, 21: 22, 22: 30) are neutral and, unless otherwise defined (as in 16: 13), we must always assume this neutral meaning. An occasional usage in a technical way in Paul (I Cor. 11: 18, 20, 14: 23, 26) cannot be used to interpret a passage in Acts. Further, although 'when they had come together' v. 6 is repetitive it is not redundant, since it presumably marks the change of scene from wherever they were in vv. 2f to the Mount of Olives in vv. 6f.

(d) Schille notes that vv. 9–11 are quite distinct from their context. There is a sudden change of scene from eating together

(v. 4) to the Mount of Olives (v. 6), combined with an equally sudden change from dialogue to description (vv. 4–8 and vv. 9f). This, he thinks, can only be explained on tradition-historical grounds: in vv. 9–11 Luke is using a source. Certainly, the change of scene in v. 6 is odd, but not more so than most of the first two chapters of Acts, where the exact time and place are often obscure, probably a result of Luke's lack of any detailed knowledge of these first few weeks of the Christian Church. Moreover, the switch from dialogue to narrative in v. 9 is a natural result of the change of subject matter from Jesus' final command to the Ascension itself; after all, Luke could scarcely have recounted the Ascension in the form of a dialogue.

(e) The actual description of the Ascension is, as Schille notes, brief and concise. The lack of legendary embellishments together with some almost hymnic elements (e.g. οὗτος ὁ v. 11) are explicable, he thinks, only on liturgical grounds, a result of their *Sitz im Leben* in early Church worship. The only element which spoils the rhythmic structure is the phrase 'while they were gazing into heaven as he went' v. 10, and he therefore takes this to be a Lukan addition which reinforces the point of the narrative. However, this last point is clearly arbitrary, for why should Luke have been so heavy-handed as to ruin the rhythmic structure of this unit of tradition simply to labour a point that was already clearly and emphatically made in the tradition itself by the threefold repetition of the phrase 'into heaven'? Apart from this, the brevity of the narrative would be explained if we could place it in a liturgical context where 'the celebration itself is the exposition of its central pericope'.[1] But there is also another explanation of why Luke, if we take him to be the author of it, should deliberately have kept his description of the actual Ascension brief. Although the Ascension itself was important for Luke as an event separate from the Resurrection, it was equally important for him to emphasise men's correct response to it. Thus it is that the description of the event itself is brief, while far more weight is placed on the disciples' response to it. This is a point we shall return to later.

(f) Finally, Schille suggests that the phrase 'a sabbath's day's journey away' v. 12 reflects a take-over of Jewish sabbath laws by Jewish Christians, who then applied them to their own

---

[1] Schille, 'Himmelfahrt', p. 193.

festivals. They could overlook the discrepancy in distance for the sake of celebrating their Ascension feast in the desired place, namely the Mount of Olives.[1] However, we have no evidence that the early Christians took over Jewish laws for their own festivals. Certainly it seems that, if not in belief, then at least in practice they remained within Judaism. This may have involved them in keeping the Jewish sabbath laws on the Jewish sabbath, but not on their own festivals. This verse is probably no more than Luke's way of giving a rough estimate of the distance between the Mount of Olives and Jerusalem; and, after all, his estimate is not too far out.

The sum total of the above points is that there is good reason to suppose that Acts 1:9–11 is not a unit of pre-Lukan tradition whose original *Sitz im Leben* was the worship of the early Church, but an expression of Lukan theology. Much of the evidence points to a Lukan origin and certainly none of it is irreconcilable with this view. To argue that Acts 1:9–11 is a piece of Luke's handiwork is not a particularly unusual conclusion; but it needed to be shown that, despite Schille's view, this is still the most likely hypothesis.[2]

4. P. A. van Stempvoort has provided the basic clue for understanding Luke's double account of the Ascension, namely that the two versions differ because they were written for different theological purposes: 'The first was a doxology in the refined style of worship, the second hard and realistic, leading to the future, but at the same time into the history of the Church "beginning from Jerusalem".'[3]

Taking this as his starting-point Flender goes on to give a

[1] Schille, 'Himmelfahrt', pp. 190f. He gives the distances as follows: a Sabbath day's journey 880m (*S.B.*, II, 590f) and the distance between the Mount of Olives and Jerusalem just over 900 m.

[2] Various parallels may have influenced Luke: J. G. Davies, 'The prefiguration of the Ascension in the Third Gospel', *JTS*, n.s. 6 (1955), 229–31, suggests the Transfiguration Lk. 9:1f. Some parallels he draws are clear, but most of them are irrelevant or unconvincing. Haenchen, *Apg.*, p. 118, suggests the story of the empty tomb (Lk. 24:4f), but apart from a few details there is no real parallelism. G. Kretschmar, 'Himmelfahrt und Pfingsten', *ZKG*, 66 (1954–5), 217f, suggests, perhaps more plausibly, the Jewish tradition of the ascension of Moses.

[3] Van Stempvoort, 'Ascension', p. 39; Barrett, *Luke*, p. 57; R. P. C. Hanson, *The Acts of the Apostles* (Oxford, 1967), pp. 57–8. In many ways Lk. 24:50f has a more 'liturgical' atmosphere than Acts 1.

different account from van Stempvoort of the purpose of the two narratives. Lk. 24: 50f, he says, is basically a farewell scene which says that 'such a view of Jesus is not promised for all time and for all believers, but comes to an end also for the disciples'.[1] This is the Ascension as seen from an earthly viewpoint. Acts 1: 9–11 sees the Ascension from a heavenly viewpoint, in the light of the destiny of the Lord of heaven. The language of these verses is eschatological, implying that Jesus is now the Lord of heaven, who will one day assume his dominion visibly. However, although Flender is right to find different purposes for the two versions, his analysis is unconvincing. In particular, the narrative in Acts does not seem so concerned with the heavenly viewpoint of the Ascension as with the reaction of the disciples to this event on earth. The bulk of the narrative is concerned with the communication between the angels and the disciples and not with the Ascension itself.

Lk. 24: 50f is, as van Stempvoort says, basically a doxological interpretation of the Ascension. The departing Christ, like a priest, blesses his disciples, who in turn respond with worship. The Ascension brings them joy and not sadness. It is the end of Jesus' ministry, but it is a triumphant end. The Gospel is concluded on the same triumphant note which permeates Luke's passion narrative.[2] This is the Ascension as seen from the viewpoint of Jesus' ministry of which it is the glorious climax: 'It is a glorious but limited interpretation, for history goes on and the Church cannot remain in the attitude of the προσκύνησις and the εὐλογία.'[3] But as well as being the climax of Jesus' ministry it is also the beginning and presupposition of the Church: 'the Ascension is not one event but two; or, rather, it is one event which bears different appearances when looked at from different angles'.[4] Thus while it marks a division between the story of Jesus and the history of the Church, much more significant is the way in which it firmly links these two epochs.[5]

---

[1] Flender, *Lukas*, p. 17, quoting Schlatter, *Lukas*, p. 457.
[2] Apart from Lk. 22: 43–4, a curious and dubious reading, there is no hint of the heart-rending struggle that we find in Mark (Mk 15: 34 is omitted). In Luke, Jesus approaches and undergoes the Passion with complete control and calmness.   [3] Van Stempvoort, 'Ascension', p. 37.
[4] Barrett, *Luke*, p. 57.
[5] Thus Conzelmann is wrong when he says that 'the Ascension does not form the conclusion of the first, but the beginning of the second volume of

Yet we have still not explained the details of Luke's second version. Van Stempvoort is right insofar as he calls it an ecclesiastical-historical interpretation, but he does not apply this in any exact manner to the text: 'it is clear that the second interpretation and the surrounding text are an answer to the questions of the old Church: Why did the Christophanies end? Why did the End not come? Why hang on in Jerusalem where the prophets were killed?'[1] But which of these in particular, if any, was Luke concerned with? We have noticed several times in passing that the most striking feature of the narrative in Acts is that two-thirds of it are concerned not with the event itself, but with the disciples' response to it. This suggests that Luke was motivated primarily by practical, pastoral problems in the Church of his day. He is concerned to teach his contemporaries by way of using the disciples as examples: 'Luke takes the disciples here, as in 1:6, so to speak as the model of a definite attitude that still prevails in many Christian communities in his time also: the expectation of an imminent End.'[2] Now insofar as he sees that Luke is writing for his contemporaries Haenchen is correct, but when he defines the problem being dealt with simply as 'imminent expectation' he fails to go far enough. The phrase καὶ ὡς ἀτενίζοντες ἦσαν εἰς τὸν οὐρανόν (v. 10) does not imply that the disciples were waiting for an immediate Parousia; it is merely descriptive.[3] Further, the words οὕτως ἐλεύσεται ὃν τρόπον (v. 11) are scarcely an answer to men who are expecting an imminent End. Rather, they are an answer to those who were inclined to deny that there would be any Parousia at all. Luke is not dealing with the problem of imminent expectation as such. He is dealing with a problem that arose as a result of a disappointed imminent expectation, namely a denial that the End would come at all. In the face of this denial Luke firmly reasserts that the End will come (v. 11). The delay of the Parousia is guaranteed not nullified by the Ascension. Christ will return in the same way that he has gone.

Thus within the short compass of Acts 1:6–11 Luke deals

Luke's historical work' (*Luke*, p. 203 n. 4). As his double account of the Ascension and his concept of apostleship show, Luke was far more concerned to show how these two epochs were linked than how they were separated.

[1] Van Stempvoort, 'Ascension', p. 39.   [2] Haenchen, *Apg.*, p. 118.
[3] *Contra* Haenchen, *Apg.*; Conzelmann, *Apg.*, p. 23.

with two practical problems in the Church of his day: false apocalypticism and loss of faith. They are the same two problems which we found to underlie Luke's teaching on eschatology in general. The difference is that here, unlike in the Gospel, Luke does not say that the End will come soon. Thus our study of the Ascension confirms our findings in the chapter on the eschatology of Luke. It also forces us to conclude that the narrative in Acts 1: 9–11 tells us nothing about the experiences and beliefs of the earliest Christians. If Schille's hypothesis was correct, we would be able to speak a little more confidently about the beliefs of the earliest Christians; but as it stands in Acts, Luke's account of the Ascension gives us an insight only into the problems of the Church of his day. This is not to say that there was no such thing as the Ascension, for presumably the Resurrection appearances came to an end at some time. But exactly what happened and how the Church reacted to it cannot be discovered from Luke's accounts.

THE ELECTION OF MATTHIAS (ACTS 1: 15F)

The overall impression which Acts 1: 15f leaves is of a complex amalgam of old tradition and Lukan innovation. The language Luke uses is reminiscent of the Old Testament. Some have claimed the influence of Jewish traditions at this point, especially those from the Qumran scrolls; but the parallels are often imprecise and unconvincing.[1] Certain parts of the narrative

---

[1] B. Reicke, 'Die Verfassung der Urgemeinde im Lichte jüdischen Dokumente', *TZ*, 10 (1954), 95–112; E. Stauffer, 'Jüdisches Erbe im urchristlichen Kirchenrecht', *TLZ*, 77 (1952), 210f. The number 120 in v. 15 is said to reflect the Jewish rule that 120 people were needed before a synod could be elected; thus the 120 are equivalent to the local Sanhedrin. However, the equation is uncertain since, as Conzelmann notes (*Apg.*, p. 23), in vv. 13–14 women are included. Reicke's attempt to find a parallel between the Apostles and the twelve men and three priests of Qumran – by assuming that the three priests are part of the group of twelve – is unconvincing (he admits that it is only a possibility). Apart from the inexactness of the parallel, owing to the arbitrary inclusion of the priests in the twelve, the overall role of the two groups differs considerably. See Haenchen, *Apg.*, p. 130: 'One may not compare the individual details with those of Qumran, but must take into account the overall context. Only then does one see both that which connects the early Church with the phenomena of the world around it and that which particularly makes it stand out.'

seem to reflect reliable tradition. Matthias' election is a case in point. The fact that Matthias rose from and, after a brief moment under the spotlights, returned to obscurity, and that he had no known significance in the later development of the Church is *a priori* in favour of its reliability. The use and interpretation of the two Old Testament verses in v. 20 probably reflect a pre-Lukan usage, though how far back it goes is difficult to say.[1] The casting of lots (v. 26) may reflect old tradition. The same procedure is found in the Old Testament (Num. 26: 55f; I Sam. 10: 20f), but it played a relatively small part in post-exilic Jewish tradition.[2] As a procedure it was more common in the Graeco-Hellenistic world (cf. Hom. *Il.* VII. 170f). More important in Jewish tradition is the theological use of the metaphor to describe the sovereign purpose of God (Ps. 16: 5; Is. 34: 17), a usage which recurs in Apocalyptic and Qumran literature (I En. 37: 4, 48: 7; Dan. 12: 13; Jub. 5: 13; IQs 1: 9f, 2: 2, 4; IQm 13: 5, 9; IQh 3: 22–3). The way in which Luke probably handles this tradition is well expressed by W. A. Beardslee: 'Luke's sources told of a decision of the community, using the metaphorical language which is evidenced from Qumran. Luke understood its theological meaning, that this was God's choice not men's; and in shaping his story he objectified the mechanism of the divine choice in a literal casting of lots, a practice particularly familiar for the choice of responsible officials in the tradition of the Gentile world.'[3]

At the same time Acts 1: 15f has a number of elements which are Lukan and which reflect a later date. The account of Judas' death vv. 18–19 is probably secondary to Matthew's version (Matt. 27: 3–10, though this version may also be legendary), as it reflects a common literary motif (II Macc. 9: 7–12; Jos. *Ant.* XVII. 168f; Acts 12: 23). The translation of the Aramaic *Akeldama* (v. 19) shows that Luke is writing for Greek readers, as does the use of the LXX in v. 20. The term καρδιογνώστης (v. 24) is a favourite with post-apostolic writers (*Ap. Const.* II. 24, 6; III. 8; IV. 6, 8 etc.). The way in which Luke brings the

---

[1] Haenchen, *Apg.*, p. 128; E. Schweizer, 'Zu Apg. 1: 16–20', *TZ*, 14 (1958), p. 46. Both verses reflect the LXX and the original meaning has been lost in the Church's reapplication of them.

[2] W. A. Beardslee, 'The casting of lots at Qumran and in the Book of Acts', *St. Th.*, 4 (1960), 245–52. Much of the above paragraph is indebted to this excellent article.   [3] Beardslee, 'Lots', p. 35.

casting of lots up to date has already been mentioned. Klein has argued that the whole of vv. 21–2 are Lukan, whereas Flender considers only the phrase ἐν παντὶ χρόνῳ . . . ἀνελήμφθη ἀφ᾽ ἡμῶν to be Lukan.[1] It is almost impossible to decide what is Lukan and what is tradition. The only certain thing is that the verses *in toto* express, whether in his own or traditional terms, Luke's view of apostleship. The qualification of having been with Jesus from his baptism onwards is almost certainly late and probably Lukan. It is never elsewhere mentioned as a qualification for apostleship and even some of the Twelve did not fulfil these requirements since, according to the Gospel accounts, they were called after Jesus' baptism. The verse also contradicts Acts 1 : 2 unless v. 21 refers in a general way to members of the wider circle of disciples.

If it is accepted that, despite frequent Lukan impositions and alterations, there is an old tradition underlying the present narrative, we have to ask what the original significance of Matthias' election was. Why was the circle of Twelve reconstituted after the Resurrection?[2] One might argue that it was for the purpose of making them the leaders of the new community, but this does not explain the need for twelve rather than eleven. Rengstorf suggests that the position of Peter and his fellow Apostles, as described by Luke, accurately reflects the

---

[1] Klein, *Apostel*, p. 205; Flender, *Lukas*, p. 110.

[2] This assumes that the Twelve disciples were chosen by Jesus during his ministry. The suggestion of Klein, *Apostel*, pp. 34–8, and W. Schmithals, *Das kirchliche Apostelamt* (Göttingen, 1961), pp. 59–61, that the Twelve were a post-Resurrection synod elected to rule the Church is incredible. The assertion that all the places where οἱ δώδεκα occurs in Mark are late is unfounded. This view also necessitates taking Lk. 22: 30 as a community creation, a possible but unlikely view, since it fits in well with what we know from elsewhere about Jesus' eschatological expectations. The unimportance of the Twelve in the early Church and the confusion over their names is taken not as an argument in favour of Jesus' having chosen them, but as proof that this synod was quickly disbanded after the Church's eschatological hopes were dashed. Most difficult of all is their explanation of the figure of Judas and the use of the title 'eleven' in the Gospels. This is explained by the fantastic thesis that Judas, who was originally a member of the synod, became an apostate and was condemned and executed by the others, and that this apostasy was projected back in the form of an actual betrayal into Jesus' ministry. In fact, the betrayal of Judas is much rather an argument in favour of Jesus' having chosen the Twelve during his ministry.

historical situation between the Ascension and Pentecost. That is, the Apostles faced a twofold situation. On the one hand, they had to reconstitute to group of Twelve to give 'public acknowledgement of the continuation of their Lord's mission to the chosen people'. On the other hand, their scope was 'bounded by the commission which Jesus had given them when he first made them his Apostles, expressly limiting their witness for him to Israel'.[1] Rengstorf's suggestions are valuable as long as they are not taken to imply missionary activity of the Twelve, since all evidence shows that under normal circumstances they resided in Jerusalem (Acts 8: 1; Gal. 1: 17).[2] He is right to emphasise that the reconstitution of the Twelve was directed at the hoped for reconstitution of Israel. But one must enquire further to find the reason for this hope. The clue to the action of the early community is in Lk. 22: 30 par.: 'that you may...sit on thrones judging the twelve tribes of Israel'. The election of Matthias was a result of the fervent eschatological expectations of the earliest community.[3] Jesus had led them to expect that when the End came they would rule and judge the reconstituted Israel which was expected in the End-time. Thus the number twelve was essential for the fulfilment of the eschatological programme which they believed to be imminent. The reference to the casting of lots agrees with this,[4] and it also explains why no successor was chosen for James (Acts 12: 2).[5] By this time, twelve to fourteen years after Matthias' election, eschatological expectations had become less fervent and the need for a continuation of the institution of the Twelve on a historical plane no longer felt. If this was the original significance of the Matthias narrative then it is clear that Luke was either

---

[1] Rengstorf, *Matthias*, pp. 185–6.
[2] Schmithals, *Apostelamt*, p. 57: 'The early tradition knows nothing of missionary journeys of the Twelve disciples.'
[3] Wikenhauser, *Apg.*, p. 33; Rengstorf, *Matthias*, p. 184; Beardslee, *Lots*, p. 252; E. Schweizer, *Church Order in the New Testament* (London, 1961), p. 48 n. 155.
[4] Beardslee, 'Lots'; Stauffer, 'Kirchenrecht', pp. 201f. Cf. the view that the title 'pillar' (Gal. 2: 9) may have had an eschatological meaning in connection with the hope for a new Temple – C. K. Barrett, 'Paul and the "Pillar" Apostles', *SP*, pp. 16, 19.
[5] Also, Judas died dishonourably and James after faithful service to Jesus. Klein, *Apostel*, p. 206, thinks it was because by the time James died the principle of apostolic succession had been firmly established.

ignorant of or has overlooked it. Nothing in his version suggests that the purpose of Matthias' election was to prepare the Twelve for the End. To discover Luke's purpose we must look further.

An important point is that the context of the narrative appears to enhance its significance. It is said that Luke must have had other traditions of events which occurred between the Ascension and Pentecost.[1] That he chose to relate only Matthias' election signifies that it was particularly significant for him. But this form of argument has to be treated with care, for we do not know what traditions Luke had at his disposal and it is quite probable that this was the only section he had which could reasonably be fitted in between the Ascension and Pentecost. More important is its inclusion in the first two chapters of Acts where Luke sets out many of the themes which are to be important in the later narrative. One assumes that the Twelve are to play an important role in the rest of Acts and to some extent this is the case: the Twelve are mentioned only in 6: 2 and by implication in 1: 26, 2: 14, but wherever the word 'Apostle' is used (apart from 14: 4, 14) it means the Twelve; they organise the Jerusalem community (chs. 1–5), appoint assistants (6: 1f), control other communities (11: 22f, 15: 22f) and dispense the Holy Spirit (8: 17–19). In contrast to this it is odd that most of their activities are the work of one man, Peter (2: 14f, 3: 1f, 5: 1f, 8: 14f, 9: 32f; cf. Jn 3: 1f, 8: 14f, 12: 2f), that the control of the Jerusalem Church is mysteriously taken over by Jesus' brother James who was not an Apostle (chs. 15, 21) and that after ch. 15 the Apostles disappear altogether. These paradoxical facts must be accommodated in any attempt to assess Luke's purpose in recounting the Matthias narrative.

Before speculating on possible theological motives we must first recognise that the primary reason for Luke's recounting of this narrative is that he received a tradition which led him to believe that this event actually took place at this time. In the course of writing it up, however, Luke has naturally 'not produced a tedious historical report, but has created a living scene out of it'.[2] Various motives may have been at work. Rengstorf thinks Luke used the narrative gladly, as a confirmation of

---

[1] Stählin, *Apg.*, pp. 28–9; Flender, *Lukas*, pp. 111f.
[2] Haenchen, *Apg.*, p. 128.

God's plan for a continuing mission to Israel. Luke uses it 'to help his readers recognise that any feeling in the Church against Jewish evangelism is wrong – it is not in accordance with the will of God'.[1] This finds support in Acts 1 : 8 where the Apostles are commanded to perform a universal mission. It may also help to explain why Luke, after restricting the title 'Apostle' in 1 : 21f, can also call Paul and Barnabas Apostles (14 : 4, 14), for these two were, above all, missionaries. The pattern of Paul's missionary work is also 'Jews first, then Greeks', which shows that the Jewish mission was not unimportant. But there are problems: although the Apostles' call to mission is confirmed by 1 : 8, which includes a Jewish mission, this verse also speaks of a world mission as the ultimate goal, which in a sense contradicts the re-establishment of the Twelve; further, if this was Luke's motive, we would expect to find its fulfilment in the rest of Acts, which is not the case. Apart from Peter, Acts relates no missionary activity of the Twelve; nor does it suggest that lack of enthusiasm for the Jewish mission was a problem with which Luke was concerned. It is the problems of the Gentile mission which, if anything, Luke faces. Similarly, Rengstorf's view that, as a result of 'a wide experience of human obstinacy' and a 'long experience of the Holy Spirit and his activity', 'Luke relates before the Pentecost story the by-election of Matthias, with its almost too pompous air, and then afterwards lets the Twelve disappear so suddenly and so completely into the background',[2] spiritualises and makes too much of the legitimate observation that the relative sobriety of the Apostles in 1 : 15f contrasts with their ecstasy in 2 : 1f. Again, we saw above that the Twelve had a certain juristic function in chs. 1–15,[3] but this is not of the essence of an Apostle in 1 : 21f.

Luke sees one basic qualification and one basic function of an Apostle in 1 : 21–2: the qualification is to have been with Jesus throughout his ministry; the function is to be a witness of the Resurrection. Qualification and function are closely interrelated. 'Witness to the Resurrection' sums up one, if not the, basic theme of Christian preaching in Acts;[4] and the qualification for

---

[1] Rengstorf, *Matthias*, p. 189. [2] Rengstorf, *Matthias*, pp. 191–2.

[3] *B.C.*, v, 52f; Reicke, 'Verfassung', p. 94.

[4] Haenchen, *Apg.*, p. 128: 'The centre of gravity of his theology is the Resurrection.'

this role is important because it acted as a guarantee that it was the same Jesus who had led his disciples during his ministry that now led the Church as her exalted Lord. Thus a link was forged between the epochs of Jesus and the Church; this link was the Apostles.[1] They stood astride the two eras, a foot planted firmly in each. For Luke, the number twelve is not significant as such; it occurs because it was in his tradition. He was much more concerned to show the historical link between Jesus and the Church.[2]

We must finally consider the thorny problem of the origin of Luke's concept of apostleship and its relation to Paul's view. For our purposes the essential question is whether Luke's view is his own creation or part of the tradition he received. It divides into two parts: how did the Twelve get the title Apostle, and why in some circles of the Church was it limited to them? These questions revolve mainly around the relationship between the Lukan and Pauline views, since of the seventy-nine occurrences of the word in the New Testament, thirty-four are in Luke and twenty-five in Paul. We cannot hope to review fully the background, origin and usage of the word 'Apostle', for this is a complex task and at every point there is disagreement.[3] Our task is to concentrate on Luke and pass quickly over the other important areas of study. We would be wise at the start to take note of H. von Campenhausen's conclusion that, with regard to the origin and development of the idea, 'only conjectures are possible which, through a lack of primary sources, can probably never advance to real certainty'.[4]

The background to both the form and content of the Christian

---

[1] Flender, *Lukas*, pp. 110f; Barrett, *Luke*, pp. 52f.

[2] This, like the Ascension, cuts across Conzelmann's threefold division.

[3] The main studies used here are Klein, *Apostel*; Schmithals, *Apostelamt*; H. von Campenhausen, 'Der urchristliche Apostelbegriff', *St. Th.*, 1 (1948), 96–130; H. Mosbech, '"Apostolos" in the New Testament', *St. Th.*, 2 (1949–50), 166–200; K. H. Rengstorf, art. ἀπόστολος, *TWNT*, 1, 407–47; K. Lake, *B.C.*, v, 37–59; E. Lohse, 'Ursprung und Prägung des christlichen Apostolates', *TZ*, 9 (1953), 259–75; W. G. Kümmel, 'Kirchenbegriffe und Geschichtsbewusstsein in der Urgemeinde und bei Jesus', SBU, 1 (1943), 1–52; J. Munck, 'Paul, the Apostles and the Twelve', *St. Th.*, 3 (1950–1), 96–110; E. Käsemann, 'Die Legitimität des Apostels', *ZNW*, 41 (1942), 33f; A. Fridrichsen, *The Apostle and his Message* (Uppsala, 1955).

[4] Von Campenhausen, 'Apostelbegriff', p. 127.

use of 'Apostle' is obscure. The LXX, Philo and Josephus only rarely give relevant parallels.[1] The Cynic–Stoic concept of κατάσκοπος is the closest parallel which classical Greek affords to the common technical usage of ἀπόστολος in the New Testament, but it cannot be considered a direct influence on the growth of the Christian use of 'Apostle'.[2] Rengstorf appeals to the Jewish שָׁלִיחַ concept of a fully empowered representative who is 'as good as oneself' (Bar. 5: 5).[3] But this does not explain much of the content of the Christian usage, and there is no evidence that ἀπόστολος was ever used to translate שָׁלִיחַ before A.D. 70, since there were other more common and natural equivalents (ἄγγελος, πρεσβευτής).[4] W. Schmithals tries to prove Gnostic influence on the Christian usage, but he never really proves that it was not the Gnostics who borrowed from the Church rather than vice versa.[5] To date, therefore, the background of the Christian use of 'Apostle' is obscure.

Who originally used the word 'Apostle' and where are equally difficult to decide. It is unlikely that the originator was Jesus, since the word is used only once in the Gospels where we can be sure that he spoke it, or rather its Aramaic equivalent.[6] The most likely guess is that the word was first used, probably quite fortuitously, in some early Christian centre, possibly Antioch.[7] It may well be that the word was first used without any specific background in mind, as a description of those who had a special commission from Jesus or his Church.

Paul's use of the word has frequently been seen as the key to its development. It is universally recognised that Paul thinks of the Apostles as a relatively wide circle: Junias and Andronicus

---

[1] I Sam. 14: 6 LXX is the only example of the noun.
[2] Rengstorf, *TWNT*, I, 409f; Schmithals, *Apostelamt*, p. 103, says that 'it is just as unlikely that the early Christian apostolate derives from κατάσκοπος as that the opposite is true'.
[3] Rengstorf, *TWNT*, I, 407f; von Campenhausen, 'Apostelbegriff', pp. 98–100; Lohse, 'Apostolates', pp. 260–2.
[4] Schmithals, *Apostelamt*, pp. 87–9; Klein, *Apostel*, pp. 22–9; A. Ehrhardt, *The Apostolic Succession* (London, 1953), pp. 15f.
[5] Schmithals, *Apostelamt*, pp. 103–216.
[6] Mk 6: 30, and even here it is probably not used technically. If 'Apostle' is read in Matt. 10: 2, it probably reflects later usage. The uses in Luke's Gospel reflect his own and not Jesus' ideas.
[7] Mosbech, 'Apostolos', pp. 193f; Lake, *B.C.*, v, 50f; Schmithals, *Apostelamt*, pp. 78–84.

(Rom. 16: 7),[1] Paul himself (Gal. 1: 1; I Cor. 1: 1, 9: 1f; Rom. 1: 1), and maybe Barnabas (I Cor. 9: 6; Gal. 2: 9)[2] and James (I Cor. 15: 5; Gal. 1: 19)[3] are all Apostles. Paul only mentions the 'Twelve' in I Cor. 15: 5 and if he means v. 7 to refer back to v. 5 then he also saw this group as Apostles. Gal. 1: 17 is also ambiguous: it probably refers to a ruling college of Apostles resident in Jerusalem, since Paul's opponents seem to have assumed that when in Jerusalem Paul saw the Apostles, and it is quite probable that the Twelve were at least a part, if not the dominating element, of it.[4] Thus it seems that for Paul the Twelve, as well as many others, were legitimately called Apostles.

The distinctive mark of an Apostle is not easy to define. After a careful survey Schmithals concludes that any closely defined answer is impossible.[5] Apostles perform miracles (II Cor. 12: 2) and live off Churches (I Cor. 9: 5f), but so do others (Rom. 15: 19; Gal. 6: 6). Apostles were often missionaries, but not all missionaries were Apostles.[6] Many Apostles witnessed a Resurrection appearance, but not all (I Cor. 15: 6).[7] Munck thinks that the distinctive element in Paul's apostleship is his unique sense of calling to a special place in the eschatological plan of God, namely as Apostle to the Gentiles (Rom. 9–11; Gal. 2: 7–9; Rom. 15: 15–16).[8] This certainly appears to be a clue to Paul's self-understanding, but it does not advance our attempt to discover the meaning of apostleship for the other Apostles. In fact, we are left with the situation where it is impossible to define

---

[1] ἐν τοῖς ἀποστόλοις is ambiguous, but ἐν probably means 'among' rather than 'by' and includes them in the rank of Apostles (Schmithals, *Apostelamt*, p. 51).

[2] Kümmel, 'Kirchenbegriffe', p. 45; Schmithals, *Apostelamt*, p. 53.

[3] Both passages are ambiguous. I Cor. 15: 7 may refer to the Twelve and James or may simply refer to all the Apostles up till that time. Gal. 1: 19 may not refer to James as an Apostle (Klein, *Apostel*, p. 46), and Paul may be stating his independence from both the Apostles and the non-apostolic leader James. However, the mention of James in this context can only mean that he is equivalent to (and probably therefore in fact) an Apostle (Schmithals, *Apostelamt*, p. 54).

[4] Cf. Käsemann's view that in II Cor. 11: 5f Paul is addressing the self-styled emissaries of the Twelve.

[5] Schmithals, *Apostelamt*, pp. 14–46.

[6] The Twelve were not missionaries and Timothy and Titus were missionaries but not Apostles.

[7] Rengstorf, *TWNT*, 1, 431f, thinks this was the distinguishing mark.

[8] Munck, 'Apostles', pp. 97–9; Fridrichsen, *Apostle*, pp 1f.

the distinctive mark of an Apostle more closely than to say that it involved a special commissioning either from Jesus or his Church.

We must now define Luke's view of apostleship and attempt to trace its origin. Luke normally restricts the title Apostle to the Twelve. Only twice is it used of anybody else (14: 4, 14). Taking this as a clue, some scholars have noted the emphasis which Luke places on Paul's conversion, when he met the Risen Lord, and have concluded that he also saw Paul as an Apostle. Moreover, Paul is equal to Peter when it comes to miracles, is called God's 'chosen vessel' (Acts 9: 15), and is distinguished by his sufferings.[1] Clearly there is a tension here which needs some explanation. The majority of scholars either ignore or explain away 14: 4, 14 and argue that all the other factors, although important, do not qualify Paul for apostleship. However, all attempts to explain away 14: 4, 14 are unsatisfactory:

1. Haenchen treats 14: 1f as a piece of old tradition which Luke has unwittingly included and which does not represent his own view.[2] It may be that the material is traditional, but this does not mean that one can assume that the passage has no significance for Luke. Its inclusion by him means, at the very least, that the significance attached by many scholars to Luke's apparent restriction of the title 'Apostle' to the Twelve is dubious. For if it was imperative for Luke to restrict the title to the Twelve, it is difficult to understand why he did not omit 14: 1f or at least erase the word 'Apostle'.

2. It is possible to omit the word 'Apostle' from v. 14 with the Western text, but one cannot go on to say that v. 4 is then 'no longer unequivocally to be taken to refer to Paul and Barnabas'.[3]

3. It is difficult to take seriously the suggestions of Klein and Schmithals as a means of explaining these two verses. Klein thinks Luke includes them as a deliberate decoy, in order that his readers should not realise that it was he who had restricted

---

[1] Flender, *Lukas*, pp. 110f. Klein, *Apostel*, p. 148, notes that while Luke normally uses πάσχειν of Jesus' sufferings, in Acts 9: 15–16 it is used of Paul's.

[2] Haenchen, *Apg.*, pp. 360f; Lake, *B.C.*, v, 51.

[3] G. Sass, 'Die Apostel in der Didache', *IM*, p. 235. Klein, *Apostel*, p. 213, thinks this is also a possible explanation.

the title to the Twelve and excluded Paul![1] This explanation is desperate in the extreme and is clearly inspired by the necessity of explaining away these verses if Klein is to maintain his thesis that Luke was the first to restrict the title to the Twelve. Schmithals is completely illogical when he says that 'He [Paul] is so self-evidently not considered to be an Apostle in the Lukan sense, that he can be called an Apostle without hesitation in Acts 14: 4, 14'.[2] This amounts to saying that Luke calls Paul an Apostle because he is not one, the logic of which is not easy to follow.

It appears that we must accept that for Luke, Paul and Barnabas also were Apostles,[3] in many ways equal to the Twelve but unable, of course, to usurp their unique historical position. This might also imply that the title 'Apostle' as such was not important to Luke. He uses it so frequently in the first part of Acts because it was a convenient designation for some or all of the Twelve and meant that he did not have to list all their names each time they appeared. He can call Paul and Barnabas apostles, but does not do so frequently because it was easy enough to give their names. This is not a very exciting or theological explanation of Luke's use of the word, but it may be the correct one. It is similar to our earlier point that the number twelve was not in itself important for Luke; it occurs because it was in his sources.

The source of Luke's ideas is not easy to surmise. Klein has argued in considerable detail that the restriction of the title to the Twelve is a Lukan construction deliberately aimed at the exclusion of Paul. Luke was motivated by the claims of ex-Christian Gnostics who used Paul as their authority. Luke reclaimed Paul for the Church by subordinating him to the Twelve and thereby placing him in the line of true apostolic succession reaching back to the earthly Jesus. Klein's thesis has been subjected to damaging criticism by Schmithals, from which it can no longer emerge as the answer to Luke's usage and the

[1] Klein, *Apostel*, pp. 212–13.
[2] Schmithals, *Apostelamt*, p. 236.
[3] And not simply 'Apostles of the Church' as contrasted with the 'Apostles of Christ' (*contra* von Campenhausen, 'Apostelbegriff', p. 115; Lohse, 'Apostolates', p. 273 n. 46). The relation between these two groups in Paul is not clear; it is difficult to know whether he equates or distinguishes them.

development of the apostolic idea.[1] Apart from all the details of Klein's argument, one is left at the end of his book with the uneasy feeling that he has totally misunderstood Luke. This is not easy to define, but the best example is his treatment of Acts 14: 4, 14, which belie Klein's attempt to prove that Luke was the first to restrict the title to the Twelve. His interpretation of these verses credits Luke with a subtlety which is difficult to accept, for as a rule Luke gives the impression of being theologically naive. He does not come across as a fully-fledged, systematic theologian. However, this is a theme to which we shall return.

If the origin of the 'Twelve Apostles' idea is not Lukan then it is presumably pre-Lukan. Exactly where and why it originated is difficult to say. Some date it early, either contemporary with or before Paul.[2] Others date it later, supposing it to be a result

[1] Schmithals, *Apostelamt*, pp. 244–7, 266–72. Stated briefly his points are: (a) Not all writers with the Twelve Apostles idea are later than Luke, and even if they were it does not prove that Luke was the originator of this view. (b) Paul's theology is in many ways anti-Gnostic; it is unlikely that the Church would abandon the instrument of Paul's letters in the struggle with Gnosticism. (c) Many of the early anti-Gnostic writers used Paul (e.g. Polycarp and Clement of Rome). Conversely, some Gnostics used the Twelve or individuals from them (Epiph. *Haer.* 30. 13. 23) while others expressly reject Paul (Epiph. *Haer.* 28. 5). (d) If one works out the logic of Klein's position on his own presuppositions some curious results emerge. If Luke was writing for Gnostics, then his picture of Paul in Acts would play right into their hands, by showing that when they call on Paul they are also calling on Jesus *via* the Twelve. One would have to assume therefore that Luke was writing for Gnostics for whom the Lukan portrait of the historical Jesus was a scandal. But even so Luke could not have imagined that his picture of Paul would arouse anything but derision from Gnostics who knew the true Paul, since they could disprove it by a few sentences from Galatians. If Luke was writing for the Church, one has to show that there were communities where Paul's position was in doubt owing to Gnostic use of him; it is difficult to find positive evidence for such communities. Further, one must ask, 'Which Paul is Luke preserving?' On Klein's presuppositions Luke's is a false picture of Paul, ignoring the true man.

[2] Mosbech, 'Apostolos', pp. 191f, thinks the source of the restriction to the Twelve was the controversy between Paul and the Judaisers. Lohse, 'Apostolates', pp. 266–9, thinks it was a result of Paul's unique self-consciousness, which in turn derived from the controversies with his opponents. Rengstorf, *TWNT*, I, 407f, thinks that the Twelve were chosen as Apostles by Jesus and that the idea was later expanded to include such as Paul.

of Paul's unique sense of vocation.[1] Schmithals dates it later still and does not see any necessary connection with Pauline thought.[2] It is not easy to assess these views, since there is a lot to be said for almost all of them. We would suggest, very tentatively, that the development of the word 'Apostle' was something like the following:

(a) As we saw earlier, the origins of the word are obscure. Its original use by Christians was probably fortuitous and, with regard to the content of the word, they had no particular background in mind. It was used to describe those who had received a special commission from Christ or his Church. This commission was probably for missionary work amongst both Jews and Gentiles. The title was probably also given to the Twelve early on in its development, on account of their missionary work during Jesus' ministry; for in a sense they were, if not in name then in practice, the first 'Apostles'. Thus originally the word described a function rather than an office and it was not restricted to any one group like the Twelve. However, once the Twelve had been called Apostles, the word would gain extra weight, since their connection with the historical Jesus probably meant that they were specially revered. The vogue for this word must have been pre-Pauline, since Paul does not appear to be the innovator of its use, and he also seems to know that the Twelve were called Apostles.

(b) During the Judaising controversies there may have been an early attempt to limit the title to the Twelve, which was aimed at denying Paul's authority.[3] Paul's reaction is to claim equality with the Twelve, which may be the source of his frequent use of the phrase 'Apostle of Christ' – the highest

[1] Munck, 'Apostles', pp. 96f; Fridrichsen, *Apostle*, pp. 1f.

[2] Schmithals, *Apostelamt*, pp. 247–54, divides Hellenistic Christianity into two strands, the 'Pauline' and the 'Synoptic'. In the latter stream, as the memory of the Twelve diminished their significance grew, particularly with regard to their missionary activity. Since 'Apostle' originally meant a missionary, it was natural for it to be given to the Twelve. This process took place late in the first century A.D. and was probably helped by the fact that Peter was an Apostle in earlier days. For criticism see Klein, *Apostel*, pp. 64–5.

[3] Probably one, or a combination, of the following accusations was made: (a) that Paul had no knowledge of the earthly Jesus; (b) that Paul did not experience a Resurrection appearance – hence I Cor. 9: 1, 15: 8; (c) that Paul was dependent on Jerusalem for his authority – hence Gal. 1–2.

Christian appellation, which Paul believed he, too, could claim.

(c) If there was such an early attempt to limit the title to the Twelve, this opinion may have lingered on in certain circles and formed the basis of later views. At any rate these controversies were soon forgotten, which left the tradition open to various lines of development. The title 'Apostle' could be used of the Twelve alone, of Paul or of both together – a process which was probably influenced as much by geographical as theological factors. In some areas the notion of the Twelve as the only Apostles arose, maybe for a second time. The causes of this development were probably similar to those suggested by Schmithals: the excessive veneration of the Twelve and their missionary activity; and the struggle with Gnosticism, where an appeal back to the historical Jesus was of paramount importance.[1]

Whatever may have been the origin of the idea of the 'Twelve Apostles', Luke stands at the end of the process; if it developed out of a Judaising or Gnostic context all this is lost on him. Although he normally uses the title of the Twelve, the casual references in 14: 4, 14 show that the word has no polemic significance for him. He is quite content to have two apparently contradictory strands standing side by side – a phenomenon which we shall come across frequently in Acts. This may show that the title as such was of little importance to him, other than as a convenient designation of the Twelve. For Luke it was the unique position of the Twelve and the unique activity of Paul which were important. Thus in a way, the so-called qualifications for apostleship (1: 21–2) are perhaps better called the qualifications for belonging to that unique circle of first-generation Christians who stood astride the two eras of Jesus' earthly and heavenly existence. The original missionary connotations of the word are lost on Luke, for while the Twelve do receive the commission in 1: 8, the ensuing narrative shows that, with the exception of Peter's preaching to the Jews and initial step towards the Gentiles, they never fulfil it. The missionary work of the Church is carried on in the main by Paul and Barnabas, and they are only twice called Apostles.

[1] Schmithals, *Apostelamt*, pp. 253f; von Campenhausen, 'Apostelbegriff', p. 119.

PENTECOST (ACTS 2: 1f)

Of all the narratives in Acts, the description of Pentecost is exceptionally obscure.[1] The first question to ask is, 'Did Luke intend to relate a speaking or a hearing miracle?' If the former, did he think in terms of foreign languages or glossolalia? The linguistic evidence is ambiguous: ἕτερος can mean 'different' or 'foreign';[2] γλῶσσα could refer to foreign languages or to a mysterious Spirit-language;[3] διάλεκτος can refer to both national languages and to local dialects.[4] Various combinations of the different translations lead to different interpretations.

Some think that the Apostles spoke a mysterious Spirit-language, which the crowd heard as their own language or dialect.[5] The evidence for this view is threefold. First, the other references in Acts (10: 46, 19: 6) to speaking in tongues say nothing about foreign languages, so Luke presumably did not mean that in 2: 4. Secondly, apart from v. 4, which is ambiguous, it is never said that the Apostles spoke in foreign languages but that the crowd heard them speak in foreign languages. The repetitive use of ἀκούω (vv. 6, 8, 11) may be a simple reporting of speech. But if the Apostles spoke in tongues, this may be Luke's way of emphasising the hearing miracle; and one might argue that it means, in effect, they heard them as if they were speaking in foreign languages, though in fact they were speaking a Spirit-language. Thirdly, if Judea is included in the list of nations vv. 9–11, as it probably should be,[6] it might be argued

---

[1] As well as the commentaries see K. Lake, *B.C.*, v, 112–21; Lohse, 'Pfingstberichtes', pp. 422f, and art. Πεντηκοστή, *TWNT*, vi, 44–53; Kretschmar, *Himmelfahrt*, pp. 217f; E. Schweizer, *The Spirit of God* (London, 1961), pp. 40f; Flender, *Lukas*, pp. 140f; W. L. Knox, *The Acts of the Apostles* (Cambridge, 1948), pp. 80f.

[2] Bauer, p. 315. Cf. Is. 28: 11 LXX; Sir. Prol. 1: 22.

[3] Bauer, p. 161; Moulton and Milligan, p. 128, show how it could also mean 'local peculiarities of speech' or 'sub-dialects'.

[4] Bauer, p. 184; Moulton and Milligan, p. 150.

[5] πάντες in 2: 1 is ambiguous: it could refer to the 120 brethren (v. 15) or to the Twelve. In support of the latter are 1: 4f, where it is only the Apostles who receive the promise of Jesus (cf. 10: 41), and 2: 14.

[6] *Contra* Haenchen, *Apg.*, p. 134; A. Harnack, *The Acts of the Apostles* (London, 1909), p. 65. There is very little MS evidence for omitting it and the variations are best explained as attempts to resolve the tension with v. 5. The inclusion of Judea is best explained as a rough way of saying that all nations were present.

that this is more natural if the Twelve spoke a Spirit-language, since this would be as unintelligible to Judeans as to any others.[1]

However, the above interpretation places too much weight on the use of ἀκούω, and it is more likely that Luke intended to describe a speaking miracle involving either foreign languages or local dialects.[2] The usual argument for this view is that since διάλεκτος normally means 'language', the ambiguous phrase ἑτέραις γλώσσαις v. 4 must mean the same. This would explain the amazement of the crowd in v. 7[3] and if, as is likely, the original tradition described some form of glossolalia,[4] it would not be out of character for Luke to rationalise this by interpreting it as speaking in foreign languages. The inclusion of Judea in v. 9 is odd; but if Luke thought the miracle involved speaking in dialects,[5] the inclusion of Judea can be justified on the grounds that they may have spoken a dialect different from the Galilean dialect of the Twelve. However, it is probably best explained, in the context of vv. 9–11, as part of Luke's rather loose way of saying that all nations were present. It is quite probable, therefore, that the original event of Pentecost was concerned with a miracle of glossolalia, a phenomenon which Luke's concrete mind has transposed into a miracle concerned with the speaking of foreign languages.

Some authors have claimed that the crowd consisted mainly

---

[1] Since the Judeans spoke the same language as the Twelve and a speaking miracle, therefore, would in their case be unnecessary.

[2] Haenchen, *Apg.*, pp. 132f; Conzelmann, *Apg.*, pp. 25–6; Lohse, *TWNT*, VI, 44–53; Knox, *Acts*, p. 83; C. S. C. Williams, *A Commentary on the Acts of the Apostles* (London, 1964), pp. 62–3.

[3] Haenchen, *Apg.*, p. 133: 'That shows: the audience do not believe that they are hearing a Spirit-language, since a Galilean could speak such a language as well as any other.' The accusation of drunkenness (v. 13) can be used to argue either way: glossolalia might seem like drunken gibberish, but so also might foreign languages when spoken fervently – especially if all the Twelve spoke at the same time.

[4] It is unlikely that it referred to the speaking of foreign languages, since Diaspora Jews probably did not know the language of the countries they lived in, and they would all have known Aramaic and/or Greek, so that two languages would have been sufficient at Pentecost. See Haenchen, *Apg.*, pp. 134f; Knox, *Acts*, p. 83.

[5] F. F. Bruce, *The Acts of the Apostles* (London, 1962), p. 83, thinks the miracle was that the Twelve were freed from their rough Galilean dialect.

of Gentiles.[1] The evidence for this view is as follows: some verses in the surrounding narrative are universalistic – πᾶσαν σάρκα (v. 17, cf. Lk. 3: 6), πᾶς ὃς ἐὰν ἐπικαλέσηται (v. 21), and καὶ πᾶσιν τοῖς εἰς μακράν (v. 39); vv. 9–11 are parallel to the universal outreach of the Church's mission as described in Acts; v. 9 mentions Judeans, so that the others are presumably Gentiles; and finally, this interpretation would give a partial fulfilment of Acts 1: 8.

However, vv. 17, 21, and 39, if they refer to Gentiles,[2] are not descriptions of what has happened but proleptic hints of what will happen. The only parallel between vv. 9–11 and the rest of Acts is that they both end with a mention of Rome and, as we have seen, the mention of Judea in v. 9 does not imply that the rest of those present were Gentiles, but is simply part of Luke's way of saying that Jews from all nations were present. Moreover, 2: 1f could at the most be only a partial fulfilment of 1: 8, for the latter speaks of a centrifugal movement out from Jerusalem not a centripetal influx to it. Also, if we include 'Ιουδαῖοι in v. 5[3] and interpret 'Jews and proselytes' v. 11 as a description of all the aforementioned groups,[4] as we probably should do, a reference to the Gentiles is excluded. We can add that the references in Peter's speech are mainly to Jews (vv. 22, 36, 39) and that according to Acts 10: 45 the Spirit is indisputably given to the Gentiles, apparently for the first time.

Thus we conclude that the crowd were Jews. They may have been visitors who had come in for the festival of Pentecost,[5] or they may have been former Diaspora Jews who were now

---

[1] Lake, B.C., v, 114; C. Sleeper, 'Pentecost and Resurrection', JBL, 84 (1965), 390.

[2] Verse 39, for example, may refer to Diaspora Jews.

[3] Many authors omit 'Ιουδαῖοι with ℵ and Vulg. (Harnack, Acts, p. 65; Sleeper, 'Pentecost', p. 391; Lake, B.C., v, 113; Bruce, Acts, p. 83), often in order to interpret vv. 9–11 as a reference to the Gentiles. However, it is best to retain it, because the MS evidence for its omission is slight and probably arose because of the apparent contradiction with 'Judea' (v. 9).

[4] In view of 'Judea' (v. 9) it is unlikely that this phrase describes a separate group. It could qualify 'those dwelling in Rome', but probably describes all the aforementioned nations. 'Cretes and Arabians' does not add two new groups, but describes all the previous groups as belonging to the east or west (O. Eissfeldt, 'Kreter und Araber', TLZ, 12 (1947), 207–12).

[5] Bruce, Acts, pp. 82–3; Hanson, Acts, pp. 62–3.

permanently residing in Jerusalem.[1] If the former is intended, as is most probable, Luke has presumably overlooked the fact that these men would probably begin to preach when they returned to their own countries, since he does not utilise this in his account of the progress of the Gentile mission. It may be, however, that although this does not fit Luke's pattern of events, it hints at what actually happened; that is, the gospel first reached the Gentiles not as a result of a planned, centralised mission of the Church, but through the intermittent preaching of travelling believers.

While Acts 2: 1f is not directly concerned with the Gentiles, Luke probably intended it to be prophetic of the future universal extension of the Church's mission, for he could not have been blind to the implications of vv. 17 and 21. The experience of the Spirit given to the Jews of all nations is a proleptic hint that the Spirit will eventually be given to the Gentiles. In this limited sense these Diaspora Jews can be called the representatives of all nations. However, the universal implications of Pentecost are best described as 'proleptic' rather than 'symbolic', for whereas the movement of Acts 2 is centripetal, the movement of the Church's mission, as commanded in Acts 1: 8 and as it actually developed, is centrifugal.

Lohse has shown how the Pentecost narrative fits neatly into Luke's concept of *Heilsgeschichte*.[2] It is part of his account of a logical sequence of events following the Resurrection. The Ascension was a necessary prelude to the outpouring of the Spirit (Acts 2: 33), an event which itself signifies the beginning of a new era characterised by the inspiration and guidance of the Spirit in every aspect of the Church's life. Thus the event of Pentecost, which is the fulfilment of the promises of the Old Testament (Joel 2: 28f), John (Lk. 3: 16) and Jesus (Lk. 24: 47f; Acts 1: 4f) fits well into the overall framework of Luke–Acts.

For Lohse, as well as fitting into the pattern of *Heilsgeschichte*, Pentecost is also an eschatological event.[3] For Conzelmann and Schweizer eschatology and *Heilsgeschichte* are, as far as Luke is

---

[1] Haenchen, *Apg.*, p. 132; Conzelmann, *Apg.*, pp. 25–6. The distinction between κατοικοῦντες as 'habitual dwellers' and ἐπιδημοῦντες as 'temporary dwellers' was not always made (*B.C.*, IV, 19).

[2] Lohse, 'Pfingstberichtes', pp. 422f.

[3] Lohse, 'Pfingstberichtes', p. 432.

concerned, mutually exclusive.[1] But this is in fact only a terminological difference, since in essentials these authors agree. We must ask, however, how far Luke saw Pentecost as an eschatological event. The coming of the Spirit to the Church is clearly not for Luke equivalent to the End itself. This view is expressly rejected in Acts 1: 6–8, and elsewhere Luke speaks of an End which is still to come (Acts 1: 11, 3: 19f, 17: 30–1). It is eschatological insofar as it marks the inauguration of the last period before the End, namely the period of the Church, and insofar as the Spirit is a gift of the last days. But in Acts 2: 17 Luke's emphasis is on 'days' rather than 'last', for he goes on to describe a lengthy period of Church history.[2] The significance of the several End-time themes which appear to hover in the background of Acts 2: 1f is lost on Luke. For him, the coming of the Spirit is the realisation of one of the promises of the last days, but there are still many other phenomena which must occur (Acts 2: 19–21) before the realisation of the End itself.

Finally, we turn to the question of whether Luke used sources in Acts 2: 1f and how far he was influenced by Old Testament and Jewish parallels. It is frequently asserted that the Pentecost narrative can be divided into two sources, one of which spoke of glossolalia (vv. 1–4, 13) and the other of speaking in foreign languages (vv. 5–12). Luke, it is said, has either imposed the latter on the former or vice versa.[3] But these and other source theories[4] are both unprovable and unnecessary.[5] It is more likely

---

[1] Conzelmann, *Luke*, p. 183; Schweizer, *Spirit*, p. 48.

[2] Haenchen, *Apg.*, p. 142, argues that the μετὰ ταῦτα of B and the LXX is the original text here because 'according to Lukan theology the End-time does not break in with the pouring out of the Spirit'. However, the Western text is probably correct at this point, since in the context of Acts it is the more difficult reading and since it differs from the LXX, and later scribes were more likely to harmonise with than vary from the LXX.

[3] Lohse, *TWNT*, VI, 50; Sleeper, 'Pentecost', p. 391; Conzelmann, *Apg.*, pp. 26–7.

[4] Williams, *Acts*, p. 62, thinks that Luke's source told of the Twelve apostles going to twelve different parts of the world. Luke altered this to fit the plan of Acts given in 1: 8, namely the gradual extension of the gospel throughout the world. But if Luke did have such a source it is inconceivable that he would have changed it for material which did not fulfil Acts 1: 8 with anything like the same exactness.

[5] The variation between γλῶσσα and διάλεκτος is probably stylistic and does not necessarily betray the use of sources. The accusation of drunken-

that Luke received a vague and confused tradition, which he then attempted to unravel and present as an intelligible narrative.[1] The confusion of his source probably reflects the fact that the early Church itself did not fully understand this experience. The actual event was probably one of mass ecstasy or glossolalia, which Luke has interpreted as speaking in foreign languages. This does not mean that Luke has deliberately substituted his own interpretation for another, but simply that he did his best to make intelligible a confused and vague tradition.

There are various possible traditions which may lie behind Luke's account of Pentecost. The LXX of Isaiah 28: 11 – διὰ φαυλισμὸν χειλέων διὰ γλώσσης ἑτέρας ὅτι λαλήσουσιν τῷ λαῷ τούτῳ – may be a source of some of the ideas in Acts 2, but it is unlikely that reflection on this verse alone has produced the whole narrative. A reversal of the story of the tower of Babel (Gen. 11) hovers somewhere in the background of Acts 2: 1f.[2] It may have been more prominent in Luke's tradition than it is in his own version, for whereas the original story told of speaking in a single Spirit-language, Luke tells about speaking in several foreign languages.

It was usual a few years ago to assume that the Jewish tradition which connects Pentecost with the giving of the Law was later than Luke and could not, therefore, have influenced him, since he would have known Pentecost only as a harvest festival (Lev. 25: 15f; Dt. 16: 9).[3] However, new evidence for a pre-Christian dating of this connection has been found, it is said, in the Qumran texts, and it may therefore have influenced Luke.[4] The Qumran sectarians are said to have celebrated Pentecost as a feast of the renewal of the Covenant. Conzelmann, however, is wisely more cautious and shows how difficult it is to draw such far-reaching conclusions. He notes that at Qumran Pentecost was celebrated more as a 'sign' than as a 'renewal' of the Covenant: 'A renewal of the covenant certainly cannot be proved, and the *argumentum e silentio* is, in view of the regulation for the festival in IQs 1f, resolved.'[5]

ness (v. 13) is often said to be appropriate only to glossolalia, but we have seen that it is also appropriate to the fervent speaking of foreign languages.
[1] Haenchen, *Apg.*, pp. 135f.   [2] Haenchen, *Apg.*, pp. 137f.
[3] Lohse, *TWNT*, VI, 47–9; Lake, *B.C.*, V, 114–15. Cf. *S.B.*, II, 604f; Philo, *Dec.*, 32, 33.
[4] Dupont, 'Gentils', p. 144.   [5] Conzelmann, *Apg.*, p. 27.

Many would agree that this complex of traditions has had some influence on Luke or his tradition, but none of it is exact enough to be pinned down as a direct source. For example, Luke does not appear to be interested in the Philonic notion of the Torah being given to the seventy nations in seventy languages. Nor does he give any hint that the Torah tradition was in any way relevant or meaningful for him, certainly not enough to warrant the statement of Williams that 'All that the Torah was to a Jew, Jesus was to Paul and the Holy Spirit to Luke, and more'.[1]

Thus when Luke dates the first outpouring of the Spirit at Pentecost, it does not appear to have any special theological significance. It may have been his way of giving an air of realism to the narrative, since at that time there would probably be representatives from most areas of the Diaspora in Jerusalem for the festival. More probable is that Luke merely repeats what is in fact good tradition, namely that the Church first received the Spirit on the first Pentecost after Easter. For Luke and, as far as we can see, for his tradition it had neither theological nor liturgical significance. It was simply a date. This is in accord with what we suggested earlier, namely that it was the dating of Pentecost which forced Luke to use the forty days of Acts 1 : 3 rather than vice-versa.

There is one more area of Old Testament and Jewish background which is rarely exploited as a possible source for the main ideas of Acts 2 : 1f, namely the notion that in the End-time the nations would flock to Jerusalem and there hear a proclamation from God.[2] The presence of all nations, at least in a representative sense, and the setting in Jerusalem are not the only End-time themes in Acts 2;[3] the concept of a single language,[4] which was probably an original element in the tradition, and the gift of the Spirit[5] are also themes which are connected with the End. Behind the narrative in Acts 2, therefore, it would seem that we have an ancient picture of an apocalyptic event, where the nations flock to Jerusalem and, through the agency of the Spirit, are reached by a Divine Spirit-language which leaps the bounds of nationality and communicates with all those

[1] Williams, *Acts*, p. 62. [2] Hanson, *Acts*, pp. 62–3.
[3] Is. 66: 18f; Test. Zeb. 9: 8; *S.B.*, II, 300f.
[4] Test. Jud. 25: 3. [5] Joel 2: 28f; *S.B.*, II, 128f.

present, thereby reversing Gen. 11. It is probable that Luke did not deliberately alter, but simply failed to understand this tradition. When he utilises it he reshapes it to fit his own understanding of the course of the Church's mission. For him, Pentecost is concerned with Jews alone; the Gentiles will be reached later, according to a definite plan (1: 8). Thus by historicising the narrative and by understanding it as concerned with Jews alone, he can utilise a tradition which is orientated in the opposite direction to his own narrative, that is, centripetally rather than centrifugally.

Thus this early tradition which we can detect behind Acts 2 reflects the same apocalyptic view of the Gentile mission which Jesus held. If we can attribute this view to the earliest community, we may have discovered one of the major reasons why the Gentile mission was only slowly and reluctantly begun, namely that the early Church, like her Master, expected only an apocalyptic and not a historical proclamation to the Gentiles. And since they believed it was God's concern and not theirs, they needed a considerable amount of prompting before they would embark on a Gentile mission.

CHAPTER 5

STEPHEN AND THE HELLENISTS

In an attempt to find a path through the maze of problems associated with this section our summary will be divided into two distinct sections. The first will deal with Luke's use of this episode and its relation to the total structure of Acts. The second will consider criticisms of Luke's presentation and consequent attempts to reconstruct the course of events.

THE NARRATIVE ACCORDING TO LUKE

The sudden, unexpected appearance of two groups within the Jerusalem Church in Acts 6: 1 probably means that Luke is drawing on a source at this point.[1] We are not told the difference between the two groups apart from their names. It is clear that for Luke the Hellenists are Jews and not Gentiles, since according to Acts 10 Cornelius is the first Gentile convert.[2] That Luke saw the Seven as Hellenists is probable though not certain. If he did, then the fact that Nicolaus is called a proselyte[3] and that the speech attributed to Stephen begins, 'Brethren and fathers, hear me, The God of glory appeared to our father Abraham...' confirms that Luke saw the Hellenists as Jews.

---

[1] Since previous to this stress had been laid on the unity of the Church (1: 14, 2: 46, 4: 32, 5: 12). Also, several new words appear: 'Hebrews', 'Hellenists', 'disciple', and the first reference to 'the people' as opponents of the Church (6: 12; contrast 2: 37, 5: 13, 26). For views on the 'Antioch source' see J. Dupont, *The Sources of Acts* (London, 1964), pp. 62–72. There appear to be no good reasons for denying the connection between 8: 4 and 11: 19f in a pre-Lukan source – the important point for us at this stage – but how far this source extends and whether it is correctly called the 'Antioch source' is difficult to say.

[2] Contrast H. J. Cadbury, *B.C.*, v, 59–74: see below.

[3] This is not meant to call attention to his place of origin – so B. Reicke, *Glaube und Leben der Urgemeinde* (Zürich, 1957), p. 117, and W. Grundmann, 'Die Apostel zwischen Jerusalem und Antiochia', *ZNW*, 38 (1939), 57; nor is it meant to imply that the others were Jews – so G. P. Wetter, 'Das älteste hellenistische Christentum nach der Apostelgeschichte', *ARW*, 21 (1922), 412; rather, it means that the others were Jews by birth.

5   129   WGG

The distinctive mark of the Hellenists is less clear: they may have been Greek-speaking,[1] of Diaspora origin, 'hellenisers', that is, those who aped and propagated the Greek way of life, or any combination of these three.

The dispute between the Hebrews and Hellenists and the consequent institution of the Seven is not related because Luke has a particular interest in 'offices' or 'ranks' in the Church. He is not concerned to give the historical origins of the diaconate[2] or presbytery,[3] though the practices of his own day may have coloured his presentation.[4] Luke includes 6: 1–7 mainly in order to introduce Stephen and Philip and to show how they rose from a position of obscurity to one of prominence in the early community. This is already clear in 6: 5 where Stephen is singled out as a man 'full of faith and the Holy Spirit'. Accordingly, Stephen is presented both as an individual rather than as a representative of typical Hellenist views, and more as a representative of the whole Church than as a leader of a breakaway faction over against the Twelve and the Hebrews.

Stephen's trial and death are closely parallel to those of Jesus in Luke's Gospel. Stephen is rejected by his own countrymen (Acts 6: 9; cf. Lk. 4: 16f); his vision of the Son of Man is parallel to Jesus' words at his trial (Acts 7: 56; cf. Lk. 22: 69), as are his final prayers (Acts 7: 59–60; cf. Lk. 23: 34, 46). But there are also significant differences: the charges against

[1] E. C. Blackmann, 'The Hellenists of Acts 6: 1', *ET*, 48 (1937), 524f, thinks that all the Hellenists were proselytes; but if this were so, why did Luke not simply call them proselytes? C. F. D. Moule, 'Once more, who were the Hellenists?', *ET*, 70 (1959), 100f, thinks the Hellenists spoke only Greek and the Hebrews a Semitic language and Greek, and thus harmonises Paul's use of 'Hebrew' in Phil. 3: 5 with Luke's. This may be true, but cannot be proved.

[2] C. Gore, *The Church and the Ministry* (London, 1921), pp. 8f. Luke uses διακονία (vv. 1, 4) and διακονέω (v. 2), in a non-technical sense. He does not use διάκονος, though his readers may have understood a reference to the diaconate of their day.

[3] A. Farrer, *The Apostolic Church*, ed. K. E. Kirk (London, 1946), pp. 138f. Luke knew of the office of elders and would have mentioned it if this had been its historical beginnings.

[4] There are Jewish parallels to the Seven (*S.B.*, II, 641f) and to the laying on of hands, whether done by the people or the Twelve (Daube, *Judaism*, pp. 229f), so that Conzelmann (*Apg.*, p. 44) may be wrong when he insists that Acts 6: 1f is a witness only to the practices of Luke's day and not to those of the early Church.

Stephen (Acts 6: 11–13, 14; cf. Mk 14: 58, 15: 29, Matt. 26: 61, 27: 40) and the words about false witnesses (Acts 7: 13; cf. Mk 14: 56 pars.) use elements which are missing from Luke's account of Jesus' trial. It is unlikely that Luke transfers this material because it did not accord with his own and the early Church's attitude towards the Temple,[1] since if this were so he could as easily have omitted it from Stephen's as from Jesus' trial. J. C. O'Neill is correct when he suggests that Luke was concerned with what he considered to be a genuinely false charge. He thinks that the charge was that Jesus, Stephen and Paul prophesied only the destruction of the Temple and not its rebuilding. In this way he explains the omission of the second half of Mark's version – 'in three days I shall build another not made with hands' (Mk 14: 58). At the same time, O'Neill thinks that Luke may be answering a charge levelled at Christianity in general.[2]

It is significant, however, that the only version of the Temple logion in Luke's Gospel (21: 5–6) is not cast in the first person singular such as we find in Mk 14: 58, 15: 29; Matt. 26: 61, 27: 40. In Lk. 21: 5–6 the destruction of the Temple is prophesied, but it is not said that Jesus will either destroy or rebuild it.[3] It is foreseen as a historical event of the future, divorced from the End events. Thus by the reference to false witnesses Luke is not asserting that in fact Jesus claimed that he would rebuild as well as destroy the Temple; on the contrary, he is denying that Jesus claimed any connection at all with this event.[4] According

---

[1] M. Simon, *St Stephen and the Hellenists* (London, 1956), pp. 23–6; W. L. Knox, *St Paul and the Church of Jerusalem* (Cambridge, 1925), p. 50 n. 10. Haenchen, *Apg.* p. 227, and Conzelmann, *Apg.*, p. 45, suggest that it was because it would have been dangerous to use this material in Jesus' trial; but why was it less dangerous in Acts than in the Gospel? Stählin, *Apg.*, p. 102, thinks Luke is avoiding doublets; but this explains neither the close parallels between Jesus and Stephen nor the use of this material here rather than in the Gospel.   [2] O'Neill, *Acts*, pp. 73–4.

[3] On the original form of the Temple logion see Bultmann, *Tradition*, pp. 120f; Hahn, *Mission*, p. 37 n. 1; Lohmeyer, *Markus*, pp. 326f.

[4] Other suggestions for what the false witnesses refer to are that Stephen did not disobey or disregard the Law (Conzelmann, *Apg.*, p. 45), that what he said was not blasphemy (Wikenhauser, *Apg.*, p. 83), or that he did not continually speak against the Law and Temple (Stählin, *Apg.*, p. 102). As a Christian writer Luke probably saw all accusations against the Church or its leaders as false.

to Luke, Jesus merely prophesied the destruction of the Temple; he did not claim to be the instrument of that destruction or that the Temple would later be rebuilt. Clearly, Luke is exercising hindsight: writing after A.D. 70, he knew that the Temple had been destroyed without any personal intervention by Jesus and that it had not been rebuilt, so he adjusted his material accordingly. Thus we can see this as part of Luke's reinterpretation of the significance of the destruction of Jerusalem (cf. Lk. 19: 41–4, 21: 20–4).

The second part of the accusation against Stephen, that he said that Jesus 'will change the customs which Moses delivered to us', is obscure. It may refer to the introduction of a new interpretation of the Torah or to a rejection of circumcision.[1] Whatever it was, Luke makes it clear in ch. 7 that it was a false charge and that it was the Jews and not the Christians who were disobedient to the Law.

Stephen's speech poses two major problems. The first is that there is no obvious connection between the charges against him and his speech,[2] and the second is that when the speech finally does touch upon the accusations (vv. 35f) it appears to confirm rather than to deny them.[3] We shall discuss the latter point first, at the same time assuming that at least part of the speech is related in some way to the charges in 6: 11.

The apocalyptic view in 6: 14 is neither mentioned nor refuted in the speech. On the contrary, the whole speech is concerned with Israel's past and not with apocalyptic predictions of the future. The speech is clearly, therefore, not a direct rebuttal of the charges. Yet it is difficult to think that the charges, whether Luke created or received them,[4] bear no relation to the speech. As we shall see, there is a connection, though only a loose one.

---

[1] Hanson, *Acts*, p. 93, and Haenchen, *Apg.*, p. 227, respectively.

[2] M. Dibelius, *Studies in the Acts of the Apostles* (London, 1956), p. 167: 'The irrelevance of most of this speech has for long been the problem of exegesis.'

[3] G. B. Caird, *The Apostolic Age* (London, 1955), p. 85: Luke calls them false witnesses 'but at once contradicts himself by putting into the mouth of Stephen a speech that goes far to substantiate the charge on which he was indicted'.

[4] W. Schmithals, *Paul and James* (London, 1965), p. 20, thinks the charge against Stephen is pre-Lukan in essentials. Contrast O'Neill, *Acts*, p. 73: 'Since Luke formulated the charge he must have believed that the speech answered it.'

The sections most directly related to the question of the Law are vv. 35–40 and 50–3. They do not pick up the question of 'changing the customs of Moses' (6: 12), but do deny that Stephen and the Church were disobedient to the Law. This is done both subtly by the amount of space devoted to a veneration of Moses and more bluntly by turning the charges back on the Jews themselves, showing that from the beginning they received the Law and did not keep it. Their disobedience culminated in the rejection and execution of Jesus (v. 52). Thus the characteristic disobedience of the Jews, from Moses until the present, puts them in no position to sit in judgement on Stephen; and 'there is no suggestion in the speech that the Jewish charge of antinomianism is justified'.[1]

Opinions vary on how we are to interpret the section on the Temple and its cult in vv. 41–50. It is unlikely that Stephen is radically rejecting the sacrificial cult as idolatrous in vv. 41–3.[2] Luke probably took this section to be a condemnation not of the cult *per se*, but of a wayward people who preferred the worship of the creature to the Creator. The point is not so much that God did not require sacrifice, but that the sacrifice he desired was offered to other gods.[3] In vv. 45–50 M. Simon finds an 'absolute and unrestricted opposition to the Temple'.[4] Although this statement is a little extreme, there is nevertheless a direct contrast in these verses between the tabernacle which is of divine origin and the Temple which is made with hands.[5] This amounts to a denial of the validity of the Temple as the

[1] O'Neill, *Acts*, p. 77, and similarly most commentators.

[2] As, for example, Simon thinks (*Stephen*, pp. 45f). His view is based mainly on a radically anti-cultic interpretation of the quotation from Amos 5: 25–7 LXX, namely that sacrifice and the Temple had their origin not in the will of God but in the wilful disobedience of man. However, as Conzelman notes (*Apg.*, p. 49), this interpretation does not fit well with either v. 42a or v. 44.

[3] Stählin, *Apg.*, pp. 111–12; Haenchen, *Apg.*, p. 236. This may not, of course, have been the original meaning of the prophecy.

[4] Simon, *Stephen*, p. 53. He thinks there is a direct contrast between David and Solomon and the buildings each represents. However, to get this he has to fill out the few verses in Acts with Nathan's prophecy in II Sam. 7, and he also fails to notice that Solomon is not condemned directly in vv. 46–7, but only implicitly in vv. 48–9 (the quotation from Is. 66: 1 LXX).

[5] It is apparently overlooked that the tabernacle was also made with hands.

exclusive confine of God's presence and activity. In other words it is an attack on the fundamental position of the Temple in the Judaism of that time. This being so, we must conclude that the charge that Stephen spoke 'against this holy place' (6: 13) is justified, while the charge that he had said that 'Jesus of Nazareth will destroy this place' (6: 14) has no foundation. His attack on the Temple is based not on apocalyptic predictions, but on an analysis and reinterpretation of its historical origins, supported by quotations from the Old Testament itself. Perhaps Luke, writing after A.D. 70, is saying that even if the Temple is destroyed it is of no matter, since from the beginning God has never shared Israel's excessive veneration for it. Since it has no great value, its destruction is no tragedy. This kind of view is probably, therefore, a *post eventum* rationale of the events of A.D. 70.

We can conclude, therefore, that there is at least a general thematic connection between the charges brought against Stephen and his speech in vv. 35f. Both charges are indirectly denied, but that concerning the Temple is seen to be partially justified. But what of vv. 2–34? How are they related to Stephen's situation? There is much justification for Dibelius' remark that 'from 7: 2–34 the point of the speech is not obvious at all; we are simply given an account of the history of Israel'.[1] This same fact has inspired commentators to any number of ingenious interpretations. For some, the clue lies in typological exegesis, for in this way the speech can be seen to be packed with allusions to Christ;[2] but this kind of approach is as unconvincing as it is ingenious. The only reference to Christ, apart from 7: 52, is 7: 37; other than this, typology is present only in the sense that the treatment of Jesus was typical of the way Israel had always treated its leaders and prophets.

In an original and interesting piece of exegesis, Dahl has argued that 7: 2–34 'contains a philosophy or rather a "theology of history", dominated by the motif of prophecy and fulfilment'. Dahl is right in emphasising the prophecy-fulfilment theme as the key to this section: he notes the prominence given to the quotation of Gen. 15: 13–14 in Acts 7: 6–7, and points out how

[1] Dibelius, *Acts*, p. 167.
[2] Hanson, *Acts*, pp. 94–102; Williams, *Acts*, pp. 104–10. Contrast Conzelmann, *Apg.*, p. 51.

the fulfilment of this promise is related to the stories of Joseph (7: 9–16), Moses (7: 20–36) and finally Joshua (7: 45). But his exegesis of 7: 46–50, though attractive, breaks down on a vital point and destroys his case for a unified theme throughout the speech.[1]

When it becomes difficult to view this section as relevant to the charges, one may simply admit with Haenchen that 'here simply sacred history is related without any other theme than this history', and conclude that it is irrelevant to the situation of Stephen.[2] One might argue that it is a sort of *captatio benevolentiae*, but it is difficult to avoid the impression that had this really beeen Stephen's speech he would soon have been interrupted and told to keep to the point!

Consequently, many commentators have tried to interpret this section from the situation of Luke rather than that of Stephen. For some it is a prefigurement of the Gentile mission: the speech is 'a theoretical justification in advance for Christianity's turning away from the Jews to the Gentiles, made in terms of the stubbornness of the Jews. This is, from the point of view of the author of Acts, the main purpose of the speech.'[3] One might argue that this is a natural conclusion to draw since, according to Luke, one of the main results of Stephen's death and the ensuing persecution was the start of the Gentile mission. But in fact the speech gives no hint of a turning to the Gentiles.[4] It may be implied, but it is not stated. Certainly, the condemnation of the Jews in 7: 51–3 is parallel to the key passages in Acts 13: 46, 18: 6 and 28: 28. But in each of these it is expressly concluded that the Jews' rebellion leads to the Gentile mission, while in Acts 7 this is not the case. Nor is the theme of God's revelation to his people outside the promised land a prefigurement of his intention to turn to the Gentiles,[5] since the promise

---

[1] Dahl, 'Abraham', pp. 142–8, quotation from p. 147. The problem with his exegesis of Acts 7: 46–50 is the use of Heb. 4: 3–11 as an analogy, since the former passage cannot, without considerable reading between the lines, be interpreted by analogy with the latter.

[2] Haenchen, *Apg.*, p. 239; Dibelius, *Acts*, pp. 167–8.

[3] O'Neill, *Acts*, p. 83, quoting F. Overbeck.

[4] Hanson, *Acts*, p. 101, suggests that Acts 7: 45 should be translated, 'when he [Jesus/Joshua] gained possession of the Gentiles', thus giving a definite reference to the Gentiles in the speech.

[5] Munck, *Paul*, pp. 222–4.

(and fulfilment) of possession of the Holy Land is taken for granted in Acts 7. Here we should distinguish between the content of the speech itself and its position, together with the Stephen-episode as a whole, within the total structure of Acts. Thus Dibelius is correct when he says that the speech 'inaugurates that section of Acts (chs. 6–12) which portrays the progress of the gospel to the Gentile world', for this is its function within the framework of Acts.[1] But Hanson, when speaking about the content of the speech, is also correct when he notes 'that the speech does not so much prepare us for the movement of the Church's mission towards the Gentiles as for its movement away from the Jews'.[2] It is to this last point that some refer for the main theme of vv. 2–34,[3] and if we were to look for a unified theme for the whole of the speech it would be here, since this theme most naturally includes vv. 2–34. Even so, it is better to speak of a unified complex of interrelated themes than of a single theme. These are: the faithfulness of God in keeping his promises; the constant disobedience of the Jews, who have rejected his Law, prophets and leaders; and the steady stream of individuals who, over against the mass of Jews, remain righteous – Joseph, Moses, the prophets, Jesus and Stephen.[4] This theme of the Jews 'who always rebel against the Holy Spirit' (v. 51) has as its corollary later in Acts a turning to the Gentiles. But this corollary is not specifically drawn out here.

Despite the views attributed to Stephen in his speech, it does not appear that even these were sufficient to ensure his condemnation and death. The climax is reached in 7: 56, when he claims to see the Son of Man, so that like his Master before him he provides the final provocation which leads to his death. In the end it is not his attitude to the Law and the Temple, but his confession of Christ which, in Luke's view, is the final cause of his death.[5]

How Stephen died is not clear. There seems to be some con-

---

[1] Dibelius, *Acts*, p. 169.

[2] Hanson, *Acts*, p. 102.

[3] O. Bauernfeind, *Die Apostelgeschichte* (Leipzig, 1939), p. 110.

[4] Haenchen, *Apg.*, pp. 240–1, emphasises how Luke sees Stephen's death within the wider context of the rejection and murder of the prophets (which is itself partially a late Jewish legend, cf. *B.C.*, IV, 82f).

[5] Haenchen, *Apg.*, p. 246, thinks the vision in 7: 56 shows that 'the Christians are, in God's view, in the right and the council is at enmity with God'.

fusion between a legal trial before the Sanhedrin and a public lynching. This has led some to suppose that Luke is combining two sources,[1] and others to think either that Luke's source had an account of a public lynching which he has reshaped as a formal trial or vice versa.[2] If the original version told of a trial by the Sanhedrin, there remains the problem of whether they had the power of capital punishment.[3] Also, many of the details of Stephen's death do not fit the usual Jewish process of legal stoning.[4] However, there may not be any need to speak in terms of sources, for the confusion may have arisen out of the event itself. It is not inconceivable that Stephen was forced into defending himself before the Sanhedrin. They may have indicted him, possibly with a view to securing a judgement on him from the procurator, when the frenzied crowds took matters into their own hands, dragged Stephen out and publicly lynched him – an action which the Sanhedrin had no good reason to halt, as long as it did not cause too much of a public disturbance. It is possible, therefore, that we need not think of two sources, or of Luke imposing his own view on a source with another view; the confusion may reflect the actual course of events.

The immediate result of Stephen's death is a persecution of the whole Church. Acts 8: 1 says the whole Church was scattered, except the Apostles. Luke makes it clear by his use of πάντες in 8: 1 that Stephen was a representative of the whole Church and not just of a Hellenist faction. This does not mean that Luke thought that the whole Church agreed with Stephen's views; this would not have been necessary for them to become victims of the persecution. The instigator of this persecution was Paul, who develops quickly from a bystander at Stephen's death to the leader of the opposition to the Church.[5]

Finally, we must note how brilliantly Luke has woven this episode into the total structure of his work. First, it forms a climax to chs. 1–5: in 4: 17, 21 the Christians receive a mere

---

[1] B.C., II, 148f.
[2] For the former see Haenchen, Apg., pp. 225–6, and for the latter A. Loisy, Actes, p. 308.
[3] This difficulty is often avoided either by claiming that these events occurred during an interregnum between two procurators or by assuming that the Sanhedrin had some special arrangement with the Romans with regard to the persecution of Christians.
[4] Haenchen, Apg., pp. 242–50.   [5] Klein, Apostel, pp. 114–20.

warning, in 5: 40 a flogging and, finally, in chs. 6–8 one of them is put to death. Ch. 7 is also the climax to a progressive condemnation of the Jews: 2: 23 merely mentions their guilt and 3: 23 excuses it as ignorance; in 4: 12 Jesus' claim is formulated more exclusively, and in 5: 29 the Apostles claim that they obey God rather than men (the Jews); finally, ch. 7 – in a long and pessimistic survey of Israel's history – shows how the Jews' rebellion and disobedience has been a constant factor in their relations with God. Secondly, a connection is made forwards, for the persecution becomes the immediate cause of the Church extending its frontiers to Samaria (8: 4 referring back to 8: 1) and to the ends of the earth (11: 19 referring back to 8: 1). The Church's mission grows from the persecution which tried to destroy it. Moreover, Luke takes the opportunity to introduce Paul, whose conversion and central role in the Gentile mission he will later relate. His role as a violent persecutor contrasts vividly with his later role as the Church's chief missionary. Thirdly, by the phrase 'except the Apostles' in 8: 1 Luke maintains one of his most consistent themes in the early chapters of Acts, namely the role of Jerusalem as the headquarters of Christianity from which all its various developments emanate. Thus he prepared not only for the expansion of the Church to include Samaritans and Gentiles, but also for the apostolic sanction which makes this expansion valid (8: 14, 11: 22). Thus we can say that Luke's handling of this episode is masterly. He has seen and utilised to the full all the possibilities of this episode in its relation to the events which both precede and follow it. Luke the artist has been highly successful, but has he neglected the role of Luke the historian?

INCONSISTENCIES AND RECONSTRUCTION

The first and most pressing problem is to define the terms Ἑλληνιστής and Ἑβραῖος. In a celebrated essay H. J. Cadbury argued that on linguistic grounds we must understand Ἑλληνιστής as a synonym for Ἕλλην, that is, it refers to Gentiles and not, as Luke thought, to Jews.[1] In contrast to this, the majority of modern scholars maintain that the reference is to Jews,

---

[1] Cadbury, *B.C.*, v, 59f; H. Windisch, art. Ἕλλην, *TWNT*, ii, 511–12. Cadbury thinks that Luke also saw them as Gentiles.

though they are not always agreed on the exact distinction between the Hellenists and Hebrews. Some consider the distinction to be basically linguistic,[1] while others add to this a distinction in origin: the Hebrews were Palestinian and the Hellenists Diaspora Jews.[2] Others argue that while differences of language and origin may be incidentally included, the basic meaning of 'Hellenist' is one who is committed to the Greek way of life as a whole, a word which could be applied to Jew and Greek alike, depending on the word with which it is contrasted.[3]

How are we to assess these views? Cadbury starts from Acts 11: 20, arguing that only here do we find a decisive definition of Ἑλληνιστής. He takes Ἑλληνιστάς as the original reading and argues that in contrast to Ἰουδαίοις (v. 19) it must mean 'Gentiles'. Thus for Luke Ἑλληνιστάς is synonymous with Ἕλληνας and Ἑβραῖοι with Ἰουδαῖοι. A glance through the lexicons shows that, such as it is, the evidence is in favour of Cadbury's view.[4] Apart from Acts, the other occurrences of Ἑλληνιστής are late, but none of them support a purely linguistic interpretation and most of them could be said to support Cadbury's view.[5] The same can be said for Ἑβραῖος; very little evidence supports a purely linguistic interpretation, its normal usage showing it to be synonymous with Ἰουδαῖος.[6] It is possible that Luke was either unaware of the significance of the distinction or deliberately covered it up, since it did not fit in with his view of the progression of the Gentile mission.[7]

---

[1] Munck, *Paul*, pp. 218–21.

[2] Haenchen, *Apg.*, p. 214; Conzelmann, *Apg.*, p. 43; Stählin, *Apg.*, p. 97; Wikenhauser, *Apg.*, p. 78; Hanson, *Acts*, p. 89.

[3] Simon, *Stephen*, pp. 9–15; Schmithals, *James*, pp. 26–7; Wetter, 'Christentum', pp. 410f.

[4] Philo, *Con. Ling.*, 129, is ambiguous; Chrys. *Hom.* 14 (on Acts 6: 1) is no more than an inspired guess; and Test. Sal. 6: 8 is confused by a textual variation similar to Acts 11: 20.

[5] Philostorgius, *H.E.*, 7. 1; Sozomenos, *H.E.*, 3. 17, 5. 16, 7. 15. The variant reading in Acts 11: 20 may reveal that its perpetrator was unaware of any distinction between the two words; but there are other explanations of this (see below). The Greek names of the Seven are possible support, although Jews also had Greek names. Luke speaks of other Greek-speaking Jews without calling them Hellenists, but one could argue that this name was restricted to Jerusalem.

[6] II Cor. 11: 22; Phil. 3: 5; Eus. *H.E.*, II. 4. 2.; *Praep. Ev.*, XIII. 11. 2.

[7] Cadbury argues against this by introducing Gentiles as early on as Pentecost (see above).

However, despite this evidence – and it must be said that Cadbury makes the most of the evidence for his view – there remain both linguistic and historical problems. Acts 11: 20 is ambiguous: if Ἑλληνιστάς is taken as the original reading, on the grounds of it being the *lectio difficilior*, we would then have to assume that for Luke at least, who is our earliest witness to its usage, the word referred variously to Jews and Greeks according to the context. For we saw that in 6: 1f Luke sees the Hellenists as Jews, whereas in view of Ἰουδαίοις (11: 19) the reference in 11: 20 must be to Gentiles. It is difficult, therefore, to think that Luke originally wrote Ἑλληνιστάς in 11: 20 and it is probable that Ἕλληνας is the original reading.[1] The reading Ἑλληνιστάς may be an attempt to avoid the harsh juxtaposition of vv. 19 and 20 or possibly to avoid diminishing the importance of Peter as the inaugurator of the Gentile mission.[2] In 6: 1 and 9: 29 alone there is nothing to suggest that the reference is to Gentiles. Both references are explicable as being to Jews – Christian Jews in 6: 1f and non-Christian Jews in 9: 29. It is historically improbable that there was a separate Gentile Church in Jerusalem at this time, or even that there were sufficient Gentiles there for some of their number to form such an important faction in the Christian community.[3] Further, it involves taking two words as synonymous whose linguistic roots are, strictly speaking, separate:[4] Ἑλληνιστής is based on the verb ἑλληνίζω, which means to live like a Greek, to simulate his customs and culture.[5] Moreover, if the reference to Nicolaus in 6: 5 as a proselyte is taken to imply that the rest of the Seven were Gentiles, it is difficult to understand why he is associated with them, and not with the Hebrew faction in the Church. Further, if the Hellenists were Gentiles, it is odd that

---

[1] Haenchen, *Apg.*, p. 309; Conzelmann, *Apg.*, p. 67.
[2] Since the reference of 11: 19–20 is to a time before the events of chs. 8–10. Cf. Moule, 'Hellenists', p. 100.
[3] Schmithals, *James*, pp. 20–1; J. Jeremias, *Jerusalem zur Zeit Jesu* (Göttingen, 1937), I, 66f.
[4] Cadbury, *B.C.*, v, 70, draws a parallel with Luke's use of both the Greek and the Semitic spellings of 'Jerusalem' and 'God-fearer'. But these are not true parallels to Ἕλληνας and Ἑλληνιστάς, neither of which is Semitic.
[5] The linguistic arguments are further confused by the fact that the opposite of Ἑλληνιστής should be Ἑβραϊστής and not Ἑβραῖος.

when driven out of Jerusalem they preached at first only to Jews (11: 19).

Thus almost all the snippets of evidence we can glean from Acts suggest that the Hellenists in Jerusalem were Jews, which in turn may seem to produce a tension with the later linguistic evidence which uses the word of Gentiles. However, if we resort to the root form ἑλληνίζω, most of the evidence can be explained. Given the basic meaning 'to live like a Greek', we can argue that the reference of the word Ἑλληνιστής is only further defined by its context. If we read Ἑλληνιστάς in 11: 20 then Luke is our first witness of this variable usage. For in 9: 29 it probably refers to Diaspora Jews as opposed to Palestinian Jews, whereas in 11: 20 the reference is to Greeks as opposed to Jews. Thus it is that some later writers call Greeks, who remain pagan and refuse Christianity, 'Hellenists' as opposed to 'Christians'.[1] In contrast, Ἑβραῖος 'is the name of the genuine Jew who is aware of his intimate bond with the traditions of his fathers, his national and Palestinian home, even though he speaks the Greek language'.[2] Therefore, neither word is connected essentially with either place of origin or language, but with an attitude to and way of life.

When we turn to the rest of the narrative we find several alleged inconsistencies. The dispute over the widows' charity is in itself understandable. Although Luke may be exaggerating when he gives the numbers by which the Church increased (2: 41, 47, 4: 4, 5: 14, 6: 1), it is quite feasible that a sizeable increase in membership occurred and it put considerable strain on the primitive economy of the Church.

The Seven who are chosen to deal with this problem all have Greek names, and this has led to the assumption that they were all members, if not leaders, of the Hellenist section of the Church. If this is so, then it is argued that it is inconceivable that the Twelve and the rest of the Hebrews would have allowed seven members, and still less leaders, of the disgruntled faction to take over the administration of charity for the whole community.[3] This depends, however, on the size of the Hellenist

---

[1] This would also explain the evidence from Philostorgius and Sozomenos.
[2] Schmithals, *James*, p. 26.
[3] Stählin, *Apg.*, p. 99; Haenchen, *Apg.*, p. 219; Conzelmann, *Apg.*, pp. 43–4; Simon, *Stephen*, p. 6; Schmithals, *James*, p. 7.

faction, for if they were in the majority and it was the community who made the decision, the result may have been quite natural. Besides it would be a shrewd tactical move by the Hebrews to make such an appointment, for it would channel the energies of the Hellenists' leaders into an area where they would be well out of harm's way.[1]

A further peculiarity is that after Luke has specifically said that the Seven were appointed to 'serve tables', in order that the Twelve can be free to devote themselves 'to prayer and to the ministry of the word', he immediately goes on to describe Stephen as a preacher (6: 9, 11, 13–14) and a miracle worker (6: 8). One could argue that once they had been given a prominent position as leaders, the Seven developed other latent gifts,[2] but it is more likely that we should take this as a hint that the Seven were already leaders of the Hellenists before their appointment by the Twelve. The fact that they were already recognised leaders helps to explain why only members of one section were chosen to act on behalf of the whole community.

We turn now to the difficult verse in 8: 1, the rewriting of which is the basis of most attempts to rconstruct the actual events behind Acts 6: 1 – 8: 4. Luke says that the whole of the Jerusalem Church was persecuted as a result of Stephen's death and that they all dispersed into Judea and Samaria, apart from the Apostles. This account is clearly suspect, for if a Church is persecuted one expects the leaders to be attacked first, and it is difficult to think that they alone remained inviolable.[3] Further, the hints that we have later in Acts seem to contradict this picture: in 9: 26 it is said that there were disciples in Jerusalem; according to 9: 31 the Church in Judea and Samaria is happily united and living peacefully; and in 11: 1–2 it is implied that more than the Twelve were in Jerusalem. Then in 11: 19–20 we read that those who were scattered by the persecution were preaching far and wide in the Diaspora! Moreover, those who are specifically mentioned as preaching are Hellenists: Philip

---

[1] Moule, 'Hellenists', p. 101, thinks it was either a generous gesture by the Church or that it was assumed that care for the Hebrew widows would continue smoothly as before.

[2] W. L. Knox, *Jerusalem*, p. 39.

[3] Bruce, *Acts*, p. 181, and Caird, *Apostolic Age*, p. 187, think the Twelve remained out of a sense of duty. But one might argue that their duty was with their community, which was scattered.

(8: 4f) and 'the men of Cyprus and Cyrene' (11: 20). This has led to the almost universal assumption that 8: 1b is no more than a 'redactional expedient' of Luke to preserve the continuity of the Mother Church at Jerusalem.[1] If this is so, there are various possibilities open to us.

One might argue that in fact there was no persecution in Jerusalem immediately after Stephen's death or, if there was, that Paul had no part in it. However, it is not clear that Galatians does conflict with Acts at this point to the extent which Haenchen, for example, supposes.[2] Certainly, there is no warrant for G. B. Caird's view that the phrase τὴν ἐκκλησίαν τοῦ θεοῦ (Gal. 1: 13) means the Church at Jerusalem,[3] but it could nevertheless be a reference to the events described in Acts 8: 1f, 9: 1f. It is argued against this that Gal. 1: 22 excludes persecution activity by Paul in Jerusalem. However, it may be that we should distinguish between Jerusalem and Judea, or that we should distinguish between Paul's pre- and post-conversion activity.[4] Even if we include Jerusalem in Gal. 1: 22, it is not certain that Paul's persecution activity brought him face to face with the Churches.[5] Thus while there are ambiguities, Gal. 1: 22 is not incompatible with persecution activity of Paul in Jerusalem. And even if Paul was not involved, there is no good reason to doubt that the Church was persecuted at this time.

Alternatively, we could suppose that not only the Church but also most, if not all, of the Apostles fled at this time. Certainly, we have no evidence for a mass exodus from Jerusalem, but it might explain, for example, how it was that not so long after the leadership of the Jerusalem community passed into the

---

[1] J. Weiss, *Earliest Christianity* (New York, 1959), 1, 170 – and similarly most scholars.

[2] Haenchen, *Apg.*, pp. 248–9.

[3] Caird, *Apostolic Age*, p. 87.

[4] For the first point see J. B. Lightfoot, *The Epistle to the Galatians* (London, 1892), p. 86; H. Schlier, *Der Brief an die Galater* (Göttingen, 1962, rev. ed.), p. 63. For the second point see P. Althaus, *Die kleineren Briefe des Apostels Paulus* (Göttingen, 1955), p. 14.

[5] E. D. Burton, *The Epistle to the Galatians* (Edinburgh, 1921), pp. 63–4. If τῷ προσώπῳ means 'personally' rather than 'by sight' (Schlier, *Galater*, p. 63) and if we recognise that Paul must have had a gang of helpers for the activity described in Acts 8: 1f, then Burton's suggestion has some force.

hands of James. If all or most of the Apostles had gone and James had remained, he could easily have usurped the position of Peter. It might also explain why, when Paul went to Jerusalem a few years after his conversion, he saw only Peter and James.[1] But this solution is improbable, for if we can take Gal. 1: 11f as to some extent parallel to Acts, then Gal. 1: 17 implies that immediately after Paul's conversion the Apostles were still in Jerusalem.[2]

The only other solution, which is taken by the majority of scholars, is to assume that it was only the Hellenists and their leaders who were persecuted and subsequently scattered,[3] whereas the Twelve and the Hebrews remained in Jerusalem.[4] The fact that it is one of the Hellenists, Stephen, who is killed – whereas earlier the Apostles had escaped with warnings and floggings – and the fact that the preaching that is a result of the persecution is apparently done by Hellenists (8: 4f, 11: 19f), supports this view.

However, if we take this view, we cannot stop there, for we are then led to suspect that behind Acts 6–8 there lies a deeper rift between the Hellenists and Hebrews than a mere dissatisfaction over the administration of the widows' charity.[5] Otherwise it is difficult to explain why one group incensed the Jews sufficiently

[1] Gal. 1: 18–19 does not necessarily imply that of the Twelve only Peter was in Jerusalem; but it is difficult to understand why, if they were there, Paul did not see them.

[2] This view would also involve either dating the Stephen-episode much later than Luke does, or drastically readjusting the chronology of Acts, neither of which is justified.

[3] We could, of course, abandon the notion of a persecution altogether and simply assume that the Hellenists scattered because they feared that they would suffer the same fate as Stephen if they stayed in Jerusalem.

[4] We cannot exclude the possibility that some Hebrews were caught up in the general mêlée, fled into Judea and Samaria, and either returned to Jerusalem soon after or settled elsewhere. The Hellenists on the other hand went further afield into Diaspora Judaism and eventually to the Gentiles. We need not assume, as Schmithals does (*James*, pp. 32f), that Luke was aware of a deep rift in the Church, but preferred to cover it up. We have to distinguish carefully between a deliberate attempt to hide unpleasant facts and an honest attempt to unravel what went on in the early Church. Luke seems more concerned with the latter than the former.

[5] The dispute in 6: 1f may, therefore, be symptomatic of the deeper rift, which may have led to a cooling off of relations between the two groups and a subsequent neglect of the Hellenist widows.

for them to react with murder and persecution, while the other group, both before and after this episode, melted into their Jewish background and remained relatively undisturbed. What was the distinctive viewpoint of the Hellenists and where did it and they originate?

Traditionally, one has looked to Luke's account to provide an answer to these questions. Clearly, we are looking for something which was both distinctive to the Hellenists and abhorrent to the Jews. Haenchen, in the first edition of his commentary,[1] suggested that Luke was basically correct to see the peculiarity of the Hellenists' teaching in their attitude to the Temple and the Law. What Luke ascribes to false witnesses is probably what the Hellenists actually taught,[2] namely that Jesus would destroy the Temple and change the Mosaic customs.[3] This view has been disputed and Haenchen himself has abandoned it in favour of another.[4] The objections to it are set out by Schmithals:[5] first, any Jew could announce the abolition of the Temple at the End-time. Moreover, it was not uncommon in Judaism lightly to regard the Temple and its cult. Schmithals refers to the Old Testament (I Kings 8: 27; Ps. 40: 6, 50: 8f, 51: 7; Is. 1: 11, 66: 1f; Jer. 7: 21f; Hos. 6: 6; Mic. 6: 6–8), to the attitude of Qumran and the Samaritans, to a passage from Justin (*Dial.* 117. 2) and to the fact that even though the early Christian community gathered in the Temple, Luke does not say that they joined in the sacrificial worship. Secondly, it was not uncommon to ignore or dispute individual regulations of the Mosaic Law. The 'poor of the land' and Diaspora Jews were not strictly obedient to the Law,[6] but they were not persecuted or killed on that account: 'If a certain laxity in observing or esteeming the Law had brought Stephen to his death, it would have been consistent to depopulate half Palestine.'[7]

---

[1] Haenchen, *Apg.* (10th ed. Meyer commentary, 1956), p. 226.

[2] Luke's view that it was a confession of Christ which caused Stephen's death is unlikely to be correct. It may have been a contributory cause, but on its own it would not have caused his death.

[3] Schmithals, *James*, p. 20, thinks that in 6: 14 Luke has given a more concrete form to the general accusation that Stephen spoke against the Temple and Law.

[4] By G. Klein in his review of Haenchen in *ZKG*, 68 (1957), p. 368.

[5] Schmithals, *James*, pp. 21–2.   [6] *S.B.*, I, 106f, 362f; II, 495; III, 79f.

[7] Schmithals, *James*, p. 22.

It is true that 6: 14, whteher we take it at its face value as an apocalyptic prophecy or whether we see in it a hint that Stephen himself disputed individual regulations of the Law, would not in itself be sufficiently unorthodox to excite violent opposition. If it was a dispute over the Law which led to Stephen's death, we must assume that the disagreement was greater than a mere squabbling over details. Stephen and the Hellenists must have challenged orthodox Judaism on a sensitive and fundamental point. When we turn to Stephen's speech we are disppointed, for there is no hint of an unorthodox or radical critique of the Law in it. The summary of Israel's past, though concluding on an unusually pessimistic note, is not unparalleled. Such summaries were frequently made, though as a rule they concluded with a call to repentance and an emphasis on God's continuing love.[1]

Klein suggests, therefore, that we must read back into chs. 6–8 the situation of 11 : 19f. The scattered Hellenists preached to the Gentiles in Antioch and we must assume that this approach to the Gentiles was not hampered by demanding their submission to the Law. Accordingly, Klein sees 'in their avowal of a mission to the Gentiles unfettered by the Law their fundamental heresy in Jewish and "Hebrew Christian" eyes'.[2] The difficulty with this view is that the problem of the Gentile mission, while at home in the Diaspora, is unlikely to have arisen at this stage in Jerusalem. Moreover, we know from Gal. 2: 1f that Paul's Law-free Gentile mission was recognised by the Church in Jerusalem.[3] Further, unless we regard the whole of the speech in ch. 7 as Lukan, we can note that there is no hint here of a mission to the Gentiles. Schmithals, having rejected Klein's view, goes on to suggest an even more radical viewpoint for Stephen and the Hellenists. It was not simply a question of a Law-free Gentile mission, but that they 'declared the Law as a whole, including circumcision, to be abolished both for Jews and for Jewish

---

[1] I Sam. 12: 6–15; Pss. 78, 106; Jer. 2; Ez. 20; Neh. 9; IQS 1 : 21–3.

[2] Klein, *ZKG* (1957), p. 362, quoted in Schmithals, *James*, p. 25.

[3] Schmithals, *James*, adds a further criticism of Klein: Why should a Jew be concerned when the Jewish Law was not imposed on a Gentile who became a Christian? But the force of this point is considerably diminished when we consider that at this stage Christianity in Jerusalem, in practice if not in belief, was still intimately bound up with Judaism, so that joining the Church involved becoming a part of Judaism.

Christians, as Paul also did'.[1] If this were true, it would certainly explain the violent reaction of both the Jews and the Jewish Christians! But apart from the dubious nature of the last phrase in Schmithals' assertion, he can give no convincing explanation of either where and why such radical antinomianism originated or how it came to be propounded in Jerusalem.[2]

This being so, can we find any other source for what seems to have been 'a considerable freedom over against the Law'?[3] Haenchen suggests that the source of the Hellenists' view was the teaching and practice of Jesus, and that the Hellenists remained more faithful to Jesus' view than the Hebrews. The problem with this view, if we assume that the Hellenists had interpreted Jesus correctly and had not perverted his teaching, is that while Jesus claimed an authority which at times appears to usurp the position of the Law (cf. Mk 3: 1-6, 10: 21, 2: 1-12; Matt. 5: 21f), as a rule his interpretation of the Law, though radical, remains within the scope of the scribal discussion of it.[4] Even so, it does seem that it is here, if anywhere, that we shall find the source of the Hellenists' views. Perhaps they overemphasised one side of the delicate balance in Jesus' teaching between obedience to and criticism of the Law. But what this

[1] Schmithals, *James*, p. 25. He notes that such views would provoke violent political as well as religious reaction, since the Law was the basis of Jewish national existence.

[2] Schmithals suggests that early on the gospel was spread widely and quickly by the nucleus of disciples who had remained in Galilee after the Crucifixion. They soon reached Antioch, among other places, and it was here that the antinomianism arose, possibly in connection with a Gentile mission. This involves a reversal of Luke's account in Acts 11: 19f, i.e. the Hellenists came from and did not found the Church in Antioch. He suggests that they came to Jerusalem to await the Parousia. However, most of this is pure speculation, without a shred of supporting evidence. He does not explain how it was that some Jews permanently abandoned the Law and demanded the same for all others. We have no other evidence of any Jewish Christian, not even Paul, who unambiguously and permanently abandoned their Jewish heritage, or who propagated such a radical form of antinomianism, because they had become Christians – though this did not, of course, mean that Paul could not defend the Gentiles' right to freedom from the Law and deny that the Law was efficacious for salvation.

[3] Haenchen, *Apg.*, p. 221.

[4] R. Bultmann, *Theology of the New Testament* (London, 1952), I, 34f; P. Winter, *On the Trial of Jesus* (Berlin, 1961), pp. 132f.

freedom involved and how radical their antinomianism was is impossible to say.

Can we find any additional clues in their attitude to the Temple? Here we meet with a further difficulty, for if the views imputed to Stephen in Acts 7 are those which he and the Hellenists really held, as Simon thinks, then it could be argued that most of the evidence which Schmithals produces is irrelevant. The Old Testament passages he quotes have frequently been interpreted not as attacks on the cult itself, but as a polemic against the abuses and corruptions which have become associated with it.[1] But either way, it is still true to say that 'important though it is for an explanation of Stephen's thought, even the prophetic tradition is not sufficient, for he goes a good length further than the prophets'.[2] The same can be said for the Qumran sectarians' attitude to the Temple:[3] they were opposed to what they considered to be a false priesthood and invalid cult, but they were not opposed to the Temple as such. Likewise the Samaritan critique of the Temple was not a rejection of the notion of a Temple in principle, but a claim that their Temple on Mt Gerizim and not the one in Jerusalem was God's real dwelling place. Moreover, because Luke does not specifically say that the early Christians were involved in the sacrificial cult, we cannot conclude that they were not; Matt. 5: 23 may suggest the opposite.[4] Further, groups like the Qumran sectarians and the Samaritans probably escaped persecution largely because, unlike the Hellenists, they did not make a habit of preaching their beliefs in Jerusalem – the very nerve centre of Judaism. Also, while it may not have been uncommon to announce the abolition of the Temple in the End-times,[5] it is understandable

---

[1] B. Gärtner, *The Areopagus Speech and Natural Revelation* (Uppsala, 1955), pp. 205f.

[2] Simon, *Stephen*, p. 84.

[3] The Qumran critique of the Temple is found mainly in IQS 9: 3, IQM 2: 5, but there is no parallel to Stephen's radical position; it is more in line with the Old Testament prophecies. For a detailed and decisive critique of Cullmann's view that the Hellenists were syncretists who formed the link between Qumran and the early Church, and that they had close affinities with the Samaritans, see Haenchen, *Apg.*, p. 214 n. 1.

[4] Schmithals, *James*, p. 21, thinks this verse shows only that the early Church did not abandon the sacrificial cult on principle.

[5] I En. 90: 28; Tobit 16: 5; IV Ezr. 7: 26, 13: 26.

that Sadducean orthodoxy, for whom the Temple was a symbol of personal and national prestige, when brought face to face with this belief through the preaching of the Hellenists, would have been aroused to violent opposition. Finally, the passage from Justin, like many similar examples from Hellenistic Judaism which show a light regard for the Temple and cult, reflects a view which arose only after A.D. 70.[1] With the destruction of Jerusalem and the movement of the centre of orthodox Judaism to Jamnia, a re-evaluation of the cult became essential. All the close parallels we have to Stephen's view in Acts 7: 40f come from sources later than A.D. 70 (Sib. Or. 4. 8–12; *Barn.* 16: 1–2; Ps. Clem. I. 38, II. 44; Acts 17: 24).

Yet it is just this fact which raises a problem, namely how far we can attribute the views of Acts 7 to Stephen and how far they are the views of a later generation, or even of Luke himself. In other words, what is tradition and what is Lukan in Acts 7? This is not an easy question to answer. For example, much of the speech, especially vv. 2–34, is quite conceivable on the lips of Stephen, though whether it is relevant to his trial is another question.[2] On the other hand, because all the parallels to Acts 7: 41–50 are later than A.D. 70, it is probable that we have here not the words of Stephen,[3] but the sort of thing which Luke, writing towards the end of the first century, thought a Hellenistic Jew would say in Stephen's situation. They are the views of a later Hellenistic Judaism and may have been shared by Luke himself. This would not exclude the possibility that these views were to be found in embryonic form among Stephen and the Hellenists. Their views must have been more radical than those normally held by the Diaspora Jews of that time, because it was apparently they who first took exception to them (6: 9).[4]

---

[1] O'Neill, *Acts*, pp. 84f; Gärtner, *Areopagus*, pp. 205–6; Conzelmann, *Apg.*, p. 50.

[2] Also, what is understandable on the lips of Stephen is not necessarily what he said.

[3] Simon, *Stephen*, pp. 100, 115, thinks that Stephen formed his radical views under the influence of Hellenistic Judaism before becoming a Christian.

[4] On the number of synagogues implied by 6: 9 see commentaries *ad loc.* The members were Diaspora Jews and were probably also called Hellenists (Acts 9: 29). It is peculiar that they and not the Palestinian Jews first object to Stephen's views, unless we can assume that they were not so influenced by the freer attitude of Hellenistic Judaism or that when in Jerusalem they maintained a strict line.

Can we glean anything else which may help us to locate the origin of Stephen's distinctive views? As with the Law, Jesus' teaching is as likely a source as any.[1] It is possible that the Hellenists, already perhaps inclined by their background to be critical of the Temple, picked up and used Jesus' sayings about the destruction of the Temple. They may have received or propagated a perverted form of them, but it may also be that 6: 14 is nearer the truth than is often supposed. Luke may unwittingly have given the real teaching of Stephen about the Temple. For while it was certainly not just Messianic claims which caused the uproar, since the early preaching of the Apostles did not provoke a similar reaction, nor was it caused by a simple announcement of the abolition of the Temple at the End, it may be that the fusion of these two notions was the last straw. An announcement that it was Jesus – a Jew whom his countrymen had only just put to death as a Messianic pretender – who would destroy the Temple, may have been precisely the sort of fusion which would spark off a violent reaction.

If this kind of view about the Temple was combined with a certain antinomianism, we can understand why it was that Stephen and the Hellenists were persecuted. They shared a certain laxity in both respects with other Diaspora Jews, but it was the addition to this of distinctively Christian elements which caused even their fellow countrymen to take offence. How far they perverted Jesus' own views and exactly what they taught is unclear. If Acts 7: 50–3 is not simply a Lukan construction, then such an abusive condemnation of the Jews may well have been the last straw which led to Stephen's lynching, in the wake of which the opportunity was taken to winkle out all those who had been associated with Stephen, even though they may not have shared his extreme views. This group of Hellenists probably came from the Hellenist synagogues in Jerusalem (9: 29; cf. 2: 9–11), who probably attracted this name to themselves because they were more open to influence by Greek ways. The members of this group who became Christians probably brought the name Hellenists with them,[2] as well as a tendency to be somewhat off-

---

[1] L. Goppelt, *Die apostolische und nachapostolische Zeit* (Göttingen, 1962), pp. 36–7. Contrast O'Neill, *Acts*, p. 88.

[2] Thus it was not originally a nickname for a faction in the Church (Wetter, 'Christentum', p. 410; Cadbury, *B.C.*, v, 70).

hand with regard to the Temple and Law. With this tendency they fused elements of Jesus' teaching and produced an amalgam that was even more radical and, for the more orthodox Jews, more offensive.[1]

Finally, we must consider the results of our investigation as they bear on the history of the beginnings of the Christian mission. For Luke it was clear that the Gentile mission had always been an integral part of God's will; even so, its beginning is marked as a decisive turning point in the development of the early Church. Above all, it is given divine sanction through a miraculous intervention by God and apostolic sanction by the decisive role which Peter plays in the conversion of Cornelius. Luke follows the plan of Acts 1: 8 almost exactly – a straight line of development from Jerusalem out to the Gentiles. This is clearly an idealised and simplified picture, but how close is it to the events? Schmithals considers it to be a long way off the truth. He thinks that the Christian mission was initiated in Galilee, from whence it spread quickly to other centres, including the places in Acts where Christian communities are taken for granted (Antioch, Damascus etc.). It is in Antioch that he places the beginnings of the Christian mission to the Gentiles, which was either inspired by or the inspiration of the antinomianism of the Hellenists, who eventually came to Jerusalem to form the Hellenist faction of the Church.[2] But this reconstruction is extremely speculative, for we do not know that there was a Galilean Christian community at all, and there is no good reason totally to reverse the implications of the connection between Acts 8: 4 and 11: 19f and to assume that Luke has got things completely back to front. Rather, with Simon, we can guess that Luke has got things basically correct.[3] Certainly, there is a tension between Acts 11: 19f and chs. 8–10 of Acts. Luke appears artificially to have separated 8: 4 and 11: 19, in order to insert the accounts of the Samaritan mission (8: 4f), Paul's conversion (9: 1f) and the conversion of Cornelius (10–11). Thus we should probably assume that 11: 19f refers to a time

---

[1] Thus although Luke has overdone the parallelism between the deaths of Jesus and Stephen, there may have been a close similarity between the charges on which they were indicted.

[2] Schmithals, *James*, pp. 20f.

[3] Simon, *Stephen*, pp. 34–6.

prior to chs. 10–11 at least, at the same time giving Luke full credit for an artistically persuasive account – since in 8: 1–4 those who were scattered are located carefully in Judea and Samaria alone, whereas in 11: 19 they are much further abroad.

Thus it appears that the earliest missionary work among Gentiles was haphazard; it was not organised or authorised and it was effected by unknown disciples. This contrasts with Luke's account of a simple and straightforward development, which was initiated and authorised by a major apostolic figure. Moreover, these early Gentile missionaries seem to have gone about their task unaware of the principle behind the Cornelius narrative. There was no decisive theological step; rather, the Gentiles were accepted freely into the Church. They were not asked to become Jews before they could become Christians; it was taken for granted that this was not necessary. If the Gentiles accepted the gospel they were accepted into the Church, since there was no good reason for excluding them. Moreover, it is significant that the first steps out to the Gentiles came not as a result of conscious intention to fulfil a command of Jesus, but as a result of persecution by the Jews.[1] If Luke is correct in supposing that the scattered Hellenists preached only to Jews and Samaritans at first,[2] why was it that they eventually turned to the Gentiles? Presumably it was partially a natural result of the geographical circumstances, since beyond Judea Jews would become more scarce and Gentiles more numerous. But there may have been more to it than this. Our study of the Gospels and Acts 1–2 led us to think that the early Church, like Jesus, expected the influx of the Gentiles to be effected only by an apocalyptic act of God and not by a historical Gentile mission. Moreover, they believed that these End events were near at hand. Thus the way in which they centred their life around the Temple and Jerusalem was not the result of blind obedience to the Jewish cult, nor was it simply a missionary tactic; rather, it was because they fully expected the arrival of the End in a short while. Perhaps it was the continual disappointment of this expectation over a matter

---

[1] This confirms our earlier conclusion that Jesus did not command a Gentile mission, cf. Goppelt, *Apostolische*, p. 38.

[2] Since the Hellenists were Jews they would naturally approach other Jews. They may have approached Samaritans because they shared similar views about the Jerusalem Temple (Simon, *Stephen*, p. 34).

of months and even years – the last straw being when they were driven out of Jerusalem – which led those who were scattered to abandon their apocalyptic hopes. It had become manifestly clear that there was going to be no mass conversion of the Jews, which would have been the prelude to God's apocalyptic proclamation to the Gentiles, so that this new turn of events may have been the factor which first convinced the Church that God was pushing them out into the Gentile world, with the ultimate purpose of carrying out a mission among its inhabitants.

CHAPTER 6

PAUL'S CONVERSION

THE PRE-CHRISTIAN PAUL

The pre-Christian history of Paul has been probed often enough, but without much success. Psychological analyses of Paul, which usually result in his being portrayed as the victim of a divided mind or as thoroughly discontented with the Law and Pharisaism, have been justly discredited. There is no positive evidence for such views, unless one reads Rom. 7 as a thinly disguised autobiography of Paul's pre-Christian existence,[1] or overloads with significance the proverb which Luke uses in Acts 26: 14.[2] Moreover, they are contradicted by the significant remark of Paul in Phil. 3: 6 – 'as to righteousness under the Law blameless' – which reveals a man who had not the slightest qualms about the value of the Law or of his own ability completely to fulfil its demands. As Dibelius says, 'Paul was not converted from a life of sin to a life of righteousness; one might rather say that he turned from a religion of righteousness to a religion of the sinner'.[3] This is not to say that psychological analyses are inherently false. An analysis which took account of all the facts might be correct, but it might just as easily be false. Since the evidence is so sparse, speculation is endlessly possible, but ultimately fruitless. Besides, this kind of speculation is basically anthropocentric, whereas the overriding impression

[1] So A. Deissmann, *Paul* (London, 1926), p. 130. Both the use of the present tense in Rom. 7: 14–18, 25b and the fact that if 7: 7–25 is autobiographical it contradicts all other records (especially Phil. 3: 6), make it improbable that Rom. 7 can be used to describe Paul's pre-Christian existence.

[2] Much has been read into this verse to the effect that Paul's persecution activity shows an inward pull towards the truth of Christianity – so A. D. Nock, *St Paul* (Oxford, 1955), p. 73. Munck, *Paul*, pp. 11f, who has done much to discredit the misuse of this proverb, refers it unconvincingly to Paul's future as an Apostle of Christ. He fails to see that it is merely a literary device of Luke, whose readers would give it its general proverbial meaning, namely that it is impossible and stupid to struggle against one's destiny (cf. Euripides, *Bacc.* 795).

[3] M. Dibelius, *Paul* (rev. by W. G. Kümmel, London, 1962), p. 46.

conveyed by the narratives of both Luke and Paul is theocentric.[1] It shifts the centre of gravity from God to man. Neither Luke nor Paul was concerned with psychological explanations, but with an act of God and its palpable results.

U. Wilckens tackles the problem of Paul's pre-Christian existence in a novel and interesting way.[2] He tries to discover a structural continuity between Paul's pre- and post-Christian thought. On the basis of I Cor. 15: 8, Gal. 1: 11f and Phil. 3: 4f he argues that in his calling as an apostle to the Gentiles Paul sees a special fulfilment of the *heilsgeschichtlich* plan of God, in which the gospel is open to both Jews and Gentiles. For Paul the gospel to the Gentiles is equivalent to the gospel of Christ which is, in turn, antinomian, since 'faith in Christ and service of the Law are mutually contradictory'.[3] The bone of contention between Paul and his opponents was his new understanding of the role of the Gentiles in the *Heilsgeschichte*. For whereas Paul claimed that the Gentiles had an independent and distinctive place in the *Heilsgeschichte* together with the Jews (Rom. 9–11), the Judaisers demanded circumcision of the Gentiles in order that they might become part of the salvation-community, whose position was based on the gift, recognition and preservation of the Law. Thus the puzzle of Paul's conversion resolves into the question of his radical change from the Law to Christ, the latter usurping the role of the former. The only explanation for this, Wilckens argues, is to conclude that Paul's view of the Law was not 'Pharisaic-Rabbinic' but 'apocalyptic'. Here, he is using a distinction made by D. Rössler: in apocalyptic literature the Law is seen as a unity and not as a bundle of individual precepts; and the language used is that of 'keeping the Law as a whole' or 'preserving it' and not that of 'doing' any particular command. The Law has a specific function in line with the distinctive apocalyptic view of history, namely to show in 'this Age' that those who preserve the Law will participate in the 'Age to come'.[4] It is this *heilsgeschichtlich* function which is usurped, in Paul's thought, by Christ, thus revealing a structural continuity between the two phrases of Paul's existence.

[1] Goppelt, *Apostolische*, p. 49.
[2] U. Wilckens, 'Die Bekehrung des Paulus als religionsgeschichtliches Problem', ZTK, 56 (1959), 273–93.   [3] Wilckens, 'Bekehrung', p. 276.
[4] D. Rössler, *Gesetz und Geschichte* (Neukirchen, 1960).

Wilckens' view is interesting if only because it is the best modern example of a scholar who, aware of all the dangers, attempts to probe into Paul's pre-Christian existence without shirking the difficulties. But there are problems, not the least of which is his reliance on Rössler's results. It is questionable how far Rössler is making a real distinction between Rabbinic and apocalyptic thought; and, even if we could accept his conclusions, how does it accord with Paul's description of himself as a Pharisee in Phil. 3: 4f? If we are to take Paul seriously in Phil. 3, and yet accept that the so-called 'apocalyptic' view of the Law is at least an, if not the, element in Paul's thought, we must conclude that Rössler has made too rigid a distinction between the 'Rabbinic-Pharisaic' and 'apocalyptic' strands of Judaism, since here is one man, at least, in whom they are combined. Also, Wilckens' reliance on the simple contrast between Law and gospel in Paul rests too heavily on Rom. 10: 4 (and on one interpretation of this verse); he never defines, for example, in what sense Paul was antinomian – a problem which is far more complex and problematic than he would have us think. Nor does he make clear the precise relationship between the Law and the Gentiles: that is, did Paul's insight into the usurpation of the Law by Christ lead to his attitude to the Gentiles, or was his call to and experience of the Gentile mission a decisive factor in his final attitude to the Law? Wilckens inclines towards the former view without seriously considering the latter. Finally, he does not allow sufficiently for any element of originality in Paul's thought. He argues, for example, that if Paul held the 'Rabbinic-Pharisaic' view of the Law and then saw fit to throw it overboard, this leaves unexplained why his Christian predecessors had not done this before him.[1] This assumes, however, that Paul never had an insight which others before him had missed – a palpably false assumption. It is distinctly probable that Paul possessed a unique perception of the essentials of both Judaism and Christianity. It may well be that he was the first man really to understand how Judaism was radically undermined by the Christian faith. Possibly this was a result of belief in a crucified Messiah (Dt. 21: 23)[2] and Paul, precisely because of

[1] Wilckens, 'Bekehrung', pp. 278f.
[2] H. G. Wood, 'The conversion of Paul; its nature, antecedents and consequences', *NTS*, 1 (1954–5), 176–89, here p. 178. Dibelius, *Paul*, pp. 51f,

his Pharisaic scrupulosity over individual regulations, was quick to see how this undermined the Jewish attitude to the Law. In Paul's writings and Acts we are given only two facts about Paul's pre-Christian existence, namely that he was a Jew and that he persecuted the Church. In considering these we must turn immediately to the views of G. Klein, who has given them detailed treatment.[1] He offers a detailed exegesis of the passages in Acts where Paul's persecution activity is described. He notes, correctly, that Luke is at pains to paint a vivid and detailed picture of Paul's persecution activity: in 8:1 Paul is a bystander, but has some responsibility for Stephen's death;[2] in 8:3, 9:1-2, 13-14, 21 and 22:4 his activity is more direct, putting his victims in dire straits, both men and women;[3] in 22:4-5 and 26:11 the picture grows in intensity, revealing a man whose ferocity knew no bounds in its attempt to stamp out the Church.[4] In contrast to this, as an individual Paul is levelled off and portrayed as a typical Jew (Acts 22:2). This picture, Klein thinks, contrasts strikingly with Paul's epistles. For here Paul's persecution activity is merely mentioned and not described and there is no hint of the vivid, progressive sketch we find in Acts. Thus the verbs used are commonplace and 'neutral' (πορθέω, διώκω especially Gal. 1:13f) and most of the references are incidental and unemphatic (I Cor. 15:9; II Cor. 11:22; Phil. 3:5f). Moreover, he does not see his position in Judaism as typical; rather he sees himself as an exceptional and eminent Jew (Gal. 1:14; Phil. 3:4 ἐγὼ μᾶλλον, II Cor. 11:22 ὑπὲρ ἐγώ). Thus Klein concludes: 'That one [Luke] levels off the ἀναστροφὴ ἐν τῷ Ἰουδαϊσμῷ and accentuates the persecution

suggests that the Church's claim to possess the Messiah was to the pre-Christian Paul 'an insult to God and a subversion of the Law', because they stood on the fringe of Judaism and included many of the poor of the land in their midst. After his conversion Paul learns that salvation is intended for the outcast and even for those outside the Law.

[1] Klein, *Apostel*, pp. 114-44.
[2] Klein, *Apostel*, pp. 116f, thinks that συνευδοκῶ (8:1, 22:20) is connected with Luke's idea of witness, which involves both a recognition of the significance of something and an involvement in it.
[3] Klein, *Apostel*, pp. 118-19, thinks that λυμαίνομαι (8:3) has 'undertones of wanton, foolish and unrestrained activity', whereas πορθῶ (9:21; Gal. 1:13, 23) has no moral undertones. However, as the lexicons show, one cannot draw such a sharp distinction between the two words.
[4] Klein, *Apostel*, pp. 123-5.

activity of Paul; this one [Paul] levels off his persecution activity and accentuates his ἀναστροφὴ ἐν τῷ 'Ιουδαϊσμῷ.'[1] Concentrating on Acts for a moment, let us try to follow Klein's logic a little more closely. Luke, he argues, emphasises that Paul is a violent and extreme persecutor of the Church, while at the same time he portrays him as a typical Pharisaic Jew. This may be so, but Klein tries both to have his cake and eat it; for, taken together, his two assertions exclude precisely those conclusions he wishes to draw. If Paul is characterised both as an extreme persecutor and as a typical Jew then, logically, we can only conclude that Luke saw all Pharisaic Jews as violent and extreme persecutors of the Church. In turn, this tells us nothing about Luke's view of Paul in particular, but only about his view of the Jews in general. Yet clearly this is not the conclusion Klein wishes to draw; in fact, he explicitly denies it. Commenting on Acts 26: 11, where it is said that Paul forced Christians to blaspheme, Klein asks whether this is because Luke, thinking of Paul as a typical Pharisee, wishes to characterise all Pharisees as persecutors so ruthless that they forced Christians to blaspheme. He concludes correctly that this is not Luke's purpose, for in vv. 5–8 he emphasises the close affinity between Pharisees and Christians. Luke is interested in spotlighting not the Pharisees but Paul, to show 'that he does to his victims the worst that one man can do to another'.[2] The whole point of Klein's analysis, as he makes abundantly clear, is to characterise Paul's activity as violent and his person as typically Pharisaic. But unless he intends an over-subtle distinction between Act and Being, Klein fails to see that while in Acts Paul is seen as a Pharisee, the one thing which singled him out from his fellow Pharisees was precisely his excessive zeal for persecution. He was not, therefore, a typical Pharisee in every way. Thus apart from details of exegesis, in purely logical terms Klein is arguing in a circle.

While Klein is correct when he says that Paul never equals Luke's detailed description of his persecution activity, nevertheless Paul does give us a hint in Gal. 1: 13 that Luke's picture is not wholly unwarranted. The phrase καθ' ὑπερβολήν (which means 'utterly', 'excessively', 'to an extraordinary degree') gives us a description of the intensity and ferocity of Paul the

---

[1] Klein, *Apostel*, p. 132.   [2] Klein, *Apostel*, p. 126.

persecutor.[1] One cannot, with Klein, pass off this as a formal emphasis on the reality of the persecution; it is also a description of it, even if a brief one. Further, we must enquire more closely into Paul's eminent position in Judaism to which he refers in Gal. 1: 14: Paul says that he was advanced over and above the Jews of his own age group (συνηλικιώτας); he is not comparing himself with Pharisaic Judaism as a whole. And when Paul says 'so extremely zealous was I for the traditions of my fathers' (v. 14b) is it not possible that he is making a veiled reference to his persecution activity (cf. Phil. 3: 6; Acts 22: 3)? If not, then at least we can say that the immediate and most tangible result of Paul's zeal for the Law was his persecution of the Church. Either way, we are not far from the picture Luke gives in Acts. To this we must add that the reference in Acts 22: 3, on which Klein places so much weight, is surely no more than a parallel to Phil. 3: 4f. In both places Paul emphasises what he has in common with other Jews, since that is what the situation demands. In Philippians Paul is using himself as an example of how a man could, but should not, 'boast in the flesh'. In Acts Paul is faced with a hostile crowd of Jews and Luke, therefore, portrays him as opening his speech with an astute emphasis on his Jewishness and orthodoxy, both past and present. Luke, with sensitive artistry, convincingly portrays Paul as opening with a *captatio benevolentiae*. Luke's emphasis here on Paul's orthodoxy does not preclude him (or Paul, in places other than Phil. 3) from showing how at other times Paul's activity was exceptional.

The origin of Luke's picture of Paul's pre-Christian existence is obscure, but not too difficult to surmise. Klein, for the reasons given above, rejects the suggestion that Luke's view goes back to the historical self-understanding of Paul. Nor, he claims, does it come from the post-Pauline Church: Eph. 3: 8 is a mere rhetorical reference and I Tim. 1: 12–16 is a parenetic picture which contrasts the two phases of Paul's life as a typical example of conversion. Later references, when one omits those that merely deny Paul's apostolic office or those Jewish traditions where accusations are made against the mode of Paul's conversion, are sparse and dependent on Acts (e.g. Ps. Clem. 1. 71). Thus Klein concludes that the Lukan portrait stands as 'an erratic boulder', a result of Luke's own handiwork, into which

[1] Bauer, p. 848.

he has worked specific tendencies. When we ask what is the purpose of Luke's portrait, Klein answers, 'It is clearly set out... that this must..., in point of fact, have the effect of a degradation'.[1]

We have already seen reason to disagree with Klein's exaggerated contrast between Luke and Paul. If we are right, then Paul's remarks are to be seen as the ultimate source of Luke's portrait, for in essentials they are the same. To say, as Klein does, that what Paul only mentions Luke amplifies is true, but insignificant. It really says no more than that Paul was writing an epistle and Luke a narrative. For this is their real difference: Luke is a historian with a story-teller's eye for vivid, colourful tales; Paul uses an autobiographical sketch only occasionally, to illustrate a homiletic or theological point – in Galatians to show that he could not conceivably have been dependent on the Jerusalem Apostles for his own apostleship or gospel, and in Philippians to show the stupidity of 'boasting in the flesh'. In the same way Luke differs from Ephesians and I Timothy. Not that he was blind to rhetoric or to the parenetical use of a narrative, including this one, but his primary aim at this point was to tell a lively and interesting story. Whether all the extra details in Acts are Lukan is impossible to say. The likelihood is that they are not. It is a psychological fact that some men, when converted, tend excessively to blacken their pre-Christian past in order to heighten the contrast with their present transformation. A similar process may have occurred in the account of Paul's pre-Christian life as it developed in tradition. When Luke received it he touched it up for use in his work, but between the time it left Paul and reached Luke it had probably already acquired various accretions.

How then are we to assess Luke's purpose in giving this extended description of Paul's pre-Christian life? We have already both disagreed with Klein and implicitly given the correct explanation. Luke is not intentionally degrading Paul, but is rather concerned to tell a vivid and dramatic story. The blacker Paul's pre-Christian existence is painted, the more striking are both the miracle of his conversion and his eminent position as the leading Gentile missionary. In other words, Luke's purpose is to produce a contrast-effect between Paul the persecutor and

---

[1] Klein, *Apostel*, p. 144.

Paul the Christian.[1] Even this Klein has disputed, on two grounds.[2] First, the unique miracle of Paul's conversion is never specially described apart from Acts 9: 21, and since this reference is omitted in chs. 22 and 26 it is inessential to Luke; with this, Klein contrasts Gal. 1: 23. Secondly, if Luke had intended a contrast-effect he would have portrayed Paul as the Jew *par excellence* and not as a run-of-the-mill Pharisee, since this would have produced a more dramatic contrast. We have already disputed and can, therefore, safely ignore the second point. Exactly what Klein means by his first objection is not clear. By referring to Acts 9: 21 and Gal. 1: 23, he appears to equate 'the unique miracle of Paul's conversion' with the reaction to it of other Christians. If this is so, then the single reference in Gal. 1: 23 is not significantly different from Acts 9: 21. Besides, one can scarcely claim that Luke does not emphasise Paul's miraculous conversion, for he relates it three times, each time with a theophany. The very fact that he does this shows that, in view of the dominance of Paul in the second part of Acts, for Luke, Paul's conversion was a miraculous event of immense significance.

THE THREE ACCOUNTS

We turn now to the accounts of Paul's conversion. The variations between Luke's three accounts are well known. There are minor variations which are of no real significance: in 9: 27 Paul's companions hear but see nothing, while in 22: 9 they see but hear nothing; in 9: 4 Paul falls to the ground and his companions remain standing, while in 26: 14 they all fall to the ground. These variations are classic examples of Luke's inconsistency in detail; they are odd and untidy, but each assertion has, in its place, a point, without essentially altering the narrative: 'only the means of expression are changed and not the meaning of the statement'.[3] There is no need to resort to source theories at this point[4] and most modern commentators correctly see the three accounts as Lukan variations on a theme.[5]

---

[1] Loisy, *Actes*, p. 357; Reicke, *Glaube*, p. 170.
[2] Klein, *Apostel*, pp. 143-4.   [3] Haenchen, *Apg.*, p. 271.
[4] Haenchen, *Apg.*, pp. 274f, gives a summary of the main views.
[5] Haenchen, *ibid.*; Conzelmann, *Apg.*, p. 59; Klein, *Apostel*, p. 144; Stählin, *Apg.*, pp. 309f; Hanson, *Acts*, pp. 216f. O. Linton, 'The third

There is one major difference between the three versions, namely the gradually diminishing role of Ananias from ch. 9 through ch. 22 to ch. 26. Together with this goes the account of Paul's blindness and his healing and baptism by Ananias. A more important concomitant is the varying account of the time, place and manner of Paul's call. In Acts 9: 6 Paul is told to go to Damascus and there he will be told what to do. This promise is not, at least in ch. 9, fulfilled. For although it is made clear to Ananias in a vision what is God's purpose for Paul in the future (9: 15–16), it is not said that Ananias passed this on to Paul. It is merely said that he laid his hands on Paul, who was immediately both healed and filled with the Holy Spirit. In ch. 22 Ananias does explain to Paul the purpose of his conversion (22: 14–16), but the explicit call to the Gentile mission is reserved for a subsequent vision in the Jerusalem Temple (22: 17–21). Also, in ch. 22 it is not said that Ananias laid hands on Paul, that Paul received the Holy Spirit or that he was baptised. In ch. 26 Ananias disappears altogether, and with him the account of Paul's blindness and healing. This time Paul receives his call directly from the Lord on the road to Damascus, at the time of his conversion (26: 16–18).

It has been claimed on the basis of Gal. 1 that Ananias is a figure who has been imported into the account of Paul's conversion either by Luke or his predecessors. In Gal. 1: 1 (cf. 1: 12) Paul says that he is an Apostle 'not from men nor through man'; it is asserted, therefore, that the Ananias incident is a piece of 'unverifiable legend'.[1] But it is easy to draw excessively narrow conclusions from Gal. 1, for we have to remember that in Galatians Paul is defending his independence from Jerusalem and not from the Church in Damascus. In fact, it is quite possible that in Gal. 1 Paul is referring obliquely to a Jewish-Christian perversion of the Ananias incident which was prevalent in the Jerusalem Church. Exactly what Ananias' real role was is difficult to say. Certainly, in view of Gal. 1: 1, 12, he

aspect. A neglected point of view', *St. Th.*, 3 (1950–1), 79f, makes the interesting, though unprovable, suggestion that the various elements in the narratives Luke uses are old traditions which go back to the kind of thing which was said by Paul's opponents in his lifetime. Luke, he thinks, uses these traditions unwittingly, with no intention of degrading Paul.

[1] E. Hirsch, 'Die drei Berichte der Apg. über die Bekehrung des Paulus', *ZNW*, 28 (1929), 311.

cannot have played a role of major significance. That is, he neither ordained Paul as an Apostle nor taught him his Gospel, otherwise Paul would have been compelled to mention him in Gal. 1 or to have omitted vv. 1 and 12. This is also what we would conclude from Acts, for there Ananias never instructs Paul in any detailed manner; rather, he lays hands on him, as a result of which Paul is healed and receives the Spirit. In only one of the versions is it said that Ananias explained to Paul the purpose of his call (22: 14–16), and here the chief purpose of the call, namely the Gentile mission, is only alluded to and is not made explicit until 22: 17f. One should not read into this that Paul came under the direct influence of Ananias or that the essentials of Paul's later gospel were passed on to him at the beginning.[1] Luke may have overplayed, as Paul has probably underplayed, the true role of Ananias, but in essentials Acts is probably correct. The omission of Ananias in ch. 26 is because Luke is telescoping the narrative either simply for the sake of brevity or because the Ananias incident was not particularly relevant for Paul's defence before Agrippa. On the other hand, by emphasising Ananias' Jewishness in ch. 22, Luke has made good use of the narrative in the immediate context.

It is sometimes said that while Luke, by way of the Ananias incident, separates Paul's conversion and call, Paul himself sees the two as inseparable (Gal. 1: 12).[2] But in Gal. 1: 16 where his call and vision are connected, they are connected in a causal and not a temporal manner (n.b. ἵνα εὐαγγελίζωμαι), which accords closely with the accounts of Acts.

The fact that Luke retains and Paul omits the Ananias incident is of immense significance to some, since it implies that Paul's call was indirect, mediated by a human agent. Ananias is seen as a representative of the Church and its tradition and Paul, consequently, is no longer the independent Apostle he claims to be in Gal. 1.[3] He is subordinated to ecclesiastical tradition and, ultimately, the Twelve:[4] 'The place of Paul in the Church is mediated from its origin onwards.'[5] But Klein is in

---

[1] Nock, *Paul*, pp. 63f.　　　　[2] Klein, *Apostel*, pp. 145f.

[3] Klein, *Apostel*, p. 146 n. 704: 'There can be no doubt that he [Ananias] represents ecclesiastical tradition in this narrative.'

[4] Haenchen, *Apg.*, p. 277.

[5] Klein, *Apostel*, p. 146. Klein becomes very obscure when he claims that the 'objectification' of Paul's conversion means that the mediatorial element is

danger here of falling foul of the same perversion that some of Paul's contemporaries were guilty of, namely grossly misinterpreting the role of Ananias. For if Luke's overriding purpose had been to subordinate Paul to the Church's tradition, it becomes difficult to explain why he is so vague about it: why does he not say that Ananias mediates Paul's call in ch. 9? Why does he allow ch. 26 to stand, where Paul's call comes directly from the Lord? Why in the one place where Ananias unambiguously sets out to announce the purpose of Paul's vision (ch. 22: 14–16), is the reference to the Gentile mission allusive and made explicit only in a later, private, unmediated vision in the Temple? The answer to these questions is surely that it was not Luke's overriding purpose to emphasise the mediatorial role of Ananias in Paul's call. If it had been, he would not have hesitated to make his view clear with each opportunity.

To this we must add that if the point of ch. 9 was primarily to show how Paul was absorbed into the Church's tradition or, as Haenchen would have it, legitimised by the Twelve through their representative, then one might have expected Luke to have made a clearer line of contact between the Twelve or the Jerusalem Church and Ananias in Damascus. It is an oft-noted fact that Ananias, a Christian who apparently permanently resides in Damascus, suddenly appears in Acts 9 without any clue being offered how Christianity had spread from Jerusalem to Damascus. We are not told that the Twelve preached or legitimised preaching there as, for example, they did in Antioch and Samaria.

Luke portrays Ananias as he does primarily because he believed this really was his historical role. There is no anti-Pauline tendency here; Luke is far removed from the disputes which gave rise to Gal. 1–2. Certainly there is a difference between Luke and Paul insofar as Paul claims that his own meeting with the Risen Lord was equivalent to that of the other Apostles in the immediate post-Resurrection period (I Cor. 9: 1, 15: 8; Gal. 1: 11f), whereas in the scheme of Luke this is not so (Acts 1: 21–2). But this is not done for polemical purposes, for

a matter of principle and not only applicable at the beginning (*Apostel*, p. 148). He appears to be trying to explain away the disappearance of Ananias in the later accounts. There is no evidence, however, that Luke would have drawn the same conclusion as Klein.

by the time Luke wrote the disputes of the apostolic era were scarcely known and, if known, scarcely understood. Luke is, at this point, more concerned with historical truth than with theological polemic. He may not have got the truth, but this was his aim. For Luke it was natural and inevitable that at some stage Paul should be accepted into the fellowship of the Church like all new converts (cf. Acts 8, 10–11, 18–19). On the basis of tradition he received, Luke believed that with Paul this event took place in Damascus, primarily through Ananias. As a human figure or as a representative of the Church Ananias is unimportant for Luke in Paul's call, though more important in his healing and baptism. The use of the double vision makes it clear that Ananias' significance is not as a representative of the Church, but of God (9: 10–16, 22: 12–16). To Luke, whether Paul's call came directly or through Ananias its source was the same and it was still essentially the call of God. In 22: 14–16, where Ananias relates Paul's call to the Gentiles, God is the subject of Paul's election and sending. It is not Ananias or the Church who elects, converts, or commissions Paul, but God. Ananias is God's instrument, not his substitute.

We turn now to the second account and, in particular, the vision in the Temple 22: 17f. Klein attempts to show that ch. 22 strengthens rather than weakens the principle of mediation he finds in ch. 9. He considers the important element of vv. 17–21 to be the location of Paul's vision, namely the JerusalemTemple, which is an important centre of Luke's *heilsgeschichtlich* scheme: 'The call first comes into force by this means, namely when it is confirmed in a place which was distinguished in salvation-history. The mediation is, as it were, doubled.'[1] It is probable that the location of Paul's vision is important for Luke, but it is not so clear why, nor is it clear what is the main theme of vv. 17–21. Where Luke found the narrative is impossible to say, and he may simply have constructed it. He does not date the incident, but it seems most probable that he thought it occurred during Paul's visit to Jerusalem, soon after his conversion.[2]

It seems that the point of placing this vision in the Temple is, like the whole of 22: 6f, an attempt to show Paul's Jewishness.

[1] Klein, *Apostel*, p. 155.
[2] Acts 9: 27f differs considerably from the parallel account in Gal. 1: 17f. See below on the Apostolic Council.

This is the reason for Acts 22: 3f, which we have already discussed; it is also the reason why Ananias is portrayed here as a devout Jew (cf. 22: 12, and the language of v. 14).[1] This is a master-stroke of Luke's who, recounting Paul's self-defence before the Jews, places all the weight on his Jewishness. It captures the audience's attention and also helps to appease their anger.[2] This has to be seen also within the wider context of Luke's attempt to show an element of continuity between Christianity and Judaism. But this is not all, for more important than the location is the content of the vision. It is partially to be seen as a defence of the legitimacy of the Gentile mission and, in particular, of Paul's unique role in this.[3] But it also has to be seen in the wider context of Luke's scheme of the relationship between Judaism and Christianity. For while one element in this is the emphasis on the continuity of the two, yet another, more important, element is that the Gentile mission develops as a direct result of the Jews' rejection of the Gospel. Luke expresses this schematically in 13: 46, 18: 6 and 28: 28, and the same theme obtrudes in 22: 17–21. Paul wishes to stay in Jerusalem, thinking that the Jews will be bound to listen to him after his miraculous conversion from persecutor to preacher of the gospel. But the Lord commands him to leave Jerusalem, because he knows that they will not listen to Paul. Paul's task lies farther afield among the Gentiles (22: 21). It is emphasised that Paul was reluctant to go on the Gentile mission, but could not disobey a direct command of God. Ironically, it is in the Temple itself, the heart of Judaism, that God prophesies the Jews' rejection of the gospel and the consequent turning to the

---

[1] In ch. 22 the only hint that Ananias is a Christian is the appellation 'brother' (v. 13). Ch. 9 portrays him as a full-blown Christian (9: 10).

[2] Haenchen, *Apg.*, pp. 555f; Conzelmann, *Apg.*, pp. 125–7. It is no argument against this to ask, 'Why then does Luke mention the vision of Christ, which would be repellent to the Jews?' (Klein, *Apostel*, p. 154). It is precisely this vision and the ensuing command which Paul is justifying to the Jews by claiming that it occurred in the Jerusalem Temple.

[3] Haenchen, *Apg.*, pp. 555f; Knox, *Acts*, p. 27. Klein objects that the problem of the Gentile mission is not limited to Paul in Acts – but surely this does not exclude a reaffirmation of its legitimacy to its chief herald, Paul? Klein, *Apostel*, p. 153, also asks, 'Why should a vision to a Jew in Jerusalem be any more legitimising than a vision on the Damascus road?' But at this point Paul is talking to Jews, for whom a vision in the Temple would carry more weight.

Gentiles. Thus the location plays a role in 22: 17f., but it is not the only or the most important one, nor is it the role of limiting Paul's call spatially.

Before going further we must take a look at the last point in Klein's thesis. Having argued for a strong element of human mediation in ch. 9 and spatial mediation in ch. 22, he turns his attention to ch. 26. Here, as Klein admits, the account is telescoped and very close to Paul's account in Gal. 1. But, on the basis of the use of the word ὑπηρέτης, which is used of Paul in 26: 16, Klein argues that despite the disappearance of Ananias there yet remains a 'limitation' – this time a 'temporal limitation'.[1] For, he argues, there are only two other comparable uses of ὑπηρέτης or the verb ὑπηρετῶ in Luke–Acts, namely in Lk. 1: 2 and Acts 13: 36. Klein proceeds: the one, Lk. 1: 2, is not a relevant parallel, since it is qualified by its connection with αὐτόπται; the other, Acts 13: 36, has another meaning, since it is used of David, who was a bearer of the word of God 'for his generation only'. Klein's conclusion is simple; in Acts 26: 16 ὑπηρέτης implies that Paul was a witness, but only 'to his own generation'; that is, there is still a limitation. Thus, regardless of semantic context, Klein extracts all the connotations of ὑπηρετῶ gained from the context of Acts 13: 36 and, without a moment's hesitation, adds them to ὑπηρέτης in 26: 16. He thus underpins his theological conclusions by illegitimate semantic analysis. For Acts 13: 36 is no more a parallel to Acts 26: 16 than Lk. 1: 2, since the phrase ἰδίᾳ γενεᾷ (Acts 13: 36) qualifies ὑπηρετῶ as much as αὐτόπται qualified ὑπηρέτης in Lk. 1: 2.[2] In fact, the context of both occurrences (Acts 13: 36 and Lk. 1: 2) disqualifies them from use as close parallels to Acts 26: 16. The words ὑπηρέτης and ὑπηρετῶ (= servant, to serve) are 'neutral'; they gain 'extra' meaning only as a result of their individual semantic contexts. We cannot agree with Klein, therefore, when he says in conclusion that, 'In the first account he mediates the position of Paul through a man; in the second, moreover, through a place; and in the third, through a time.'[3]

The purpose of Paul's conversion is, as we have noted in

[1] Klein, *Apostel*, pp. 157–8.
[2] In some ways the connection with 'witness' in Acts 26: 16 makes the use in Lk. 1: 2 a closer parallel than Acts 13: 36.
[3] Klein, *Apostel*, p. 159.

passing, primarily to spread the gospel to the Gentiles. This is clear from all three accounts which, in their varied, though essentially similar ways, recount the Gentile mission as Paul's major task for the future (Acts 9: 15, 22: 15, 21, 26: 16–18). The language used here is unremarkable and of no great significance except for the echoes of the calls of some Old Testament prophets, in particular Jeremiah and the Servant figure of II Isaiah. This is particularly so in Acts 26: 16–18; v. 16 echoes Is. 42: 7, v. 17 echoes Jer. 1: 7–8, v. 18 recalls Is. 42: 6–7 (cf. Is. 61: 1); the phrase σκεῦος ἐκλογῆς (Acts 9: 15) has no direct Old Testament parallel, but it recalls Jer. 27: 25 (cf. 50: 25).[1] The echoing of Old Testament prophecies is also a feature of Paul's accounts of his conversion, especially in Gal. 1: 14f, where it is also said that the prime purpose of Paul's vision is his call to the Gentile mission. As in Acts, Paul meets with the Risen Lord and is immediately commissioned to his apostleship to the Gentiles (Gal. 1: 11f, 16). The prophecies alluded to in Gal. 1: 15f are the same as in Acts 26: 16f, only the reference is more clearly to Jer. 1: 4f and Is. 49: 1–6. Thus both Luke and Paul see Paul's call as parallel to, though more than, the prophetic call in the Old Testament.

Intimately connected with Paul's call in Acts is the foreshadowing of his suffering. This is made explicit in Acts 9: 16 (πάσχω is used of a Christian's, as distinct from Christ's, suffering only here in Luke–Acts). There is more emphasis in Acts on the suffering of Paul than on the suffering of the Apostles (Acts 1: 8, 8: 1; though cf. Acts 3–5, and 12: 1f).[2] This close connection between Paul's call to the Gentiles and his suffering is paralleled by Paul, since he also connects apostleship and suffering intimately (I Cor. 4: 9, 15: 30; II Cor. 11: 23f, 6: 3f; and cf. Col. 1: 24, which forms a close parallel to the use of πάσχω in Acts 9: 16).[3] Thus in both Acts and Paul a necessary concomitant of apostleship is suffering, which is 'the same as the suffering of Christ and of equal value to it'.[4]

---

[1] Munck, *Paul*, pp. 27f, refers to the similarities between the accounts in Acts and Ez. 1–2; I En. 14: 18 – 16: 4. Others think that the Heliodore legend (II Macc. 3) has influenced Luke. See H. Windisch, 'Die Christophanie von Damaskus (Act. 9; 22; 26) und ihre religionsgeschichtlichen Parallelen', *ZNW*, 31 (1932), 1f.

[2] Klein, *Apostel*, pp. 148f.   [3] Schmithals, *Apostelamt*, pp. 38–9.

[4] Schmithals, *Apostelamt*, p. 39.

There are a few more conclusions we can draw for our study of the Gentile mission in Acts. The unexplained presence of a Church in Damascus is one of the frequent lacunae in Luke's work. It is improbable – if we can place any value on the incidental remark of Ananias in Acts 9: 13 – that we can assume that the Church in Damascus was founded as a result of the flight mentioned in 8: 1f, though it is not improbable that it received a new influx after that event. Nor do we need to resort to the theory of a Galilean origin of the Damascus Church. More probable is that it was begun by tradesmen and merchants who frequently travelled between Jerusalem and Damascus, or possibly by some of those Jews who had been present at Pentecost. Whichever is correct, this Christian community is yet another witness to the idealism of Luke's plan of the development of the Church's mission. For here we have a community founded by unknown Christians who, as far as we know, worked with no set plans or official authorisation.

Further, the primary narrative of Paul's conversion is astutely placed within the total structure of Acts. The call of the Gentile missionary *par excellence* is slotted between the brief account of the beginnings of the Samaritan mission (Acts 8) and the twice-repeated account of the first symbolic step in the Gentile mission. The threefold account of Paul's conversion, like the twofold account of Cornelius' conversion, shows that both events were of great significance for Luke, to whom the most obvious way of impressing this on his readers was the simple, but effective, method of repetition.

Another important fact, which is particularly clear in 22: 17f, is Luke's penchant for finding the impetus for the Gentile mission in two main factors: first and most important, it is a result of a direct, unequivocal command of God, which even the reluctant Paul cannot disobey; second, on the human level, so to speak, the Gentile mission is a direct result of the rejection of the gospel by the Jews. In both of these points, as in much else, Luke has a similar view to Paul himself – though not in every respect (cf. Gal. 1: 14; Phil. 3: 4f; Rom. 9–11). We might also note in passing one more connection between the Gentile mission and the work of the Spirit, for Paul receives the Spirit almost simultaneously with his call. However, this connection is only implicit and we cannot make much of it.

In conclusion, it will be valuable to draw together our results with regard to the similarities and differences between the accounts of Luke and Paul:

1. On Paul's pre-Christian life they are essentially in agreement. There were two important things to be known about Paul, namely that he was both a Jew and a persecutor of the Church. The major difference, namely that Luke is far more effusive in his descriptions than the reticent Paul, is explained by the different genre of writing each was employing. In neither case is there any evidence for saying that Paul was a budding schizophrenic or a dissatisfied legalist.

2. On the road to Damascus Paul saw the Risen Lord (Gal. 1: 16).

3. There was no mediation by any human agent of Paul's apostleship or gospel. This is clear from both Gal. 1: 1, 12, 16 and Acts 9, 22, 26. The role of Ananias is ambiguous, perhaps as a result of Luke's expanding and Paul's telescoping his true role.

4. At the time of his conversion Paul received his call to be 'Apostle to the Gentiles'. The language used to describe this call echoes the call of Jeremiah and the mission of the Servant-figure, both of whom were called to go to the 'nations'. A concomitant of this call is the necessity of suffering.

5. A major difference between Luke and Paul is that the latter equates his vision of the Risen Lord with the post-Resurrection appearances, whereas Luke does not.

6. A further difference is that we miss in Luke the profound reflection on the meaning of his conversion which Paul himself gives in his doctrines of righteousness, justification and predestination. This suggests a difference between the two writers, a difference which will become clearer as we study the rest of Acts, namely that while Paul is a 'theologian', Luke is not.

CHAPTER 7

CORNELIUS AND THE APOSTOLIC COUNCIL

THE CONVERSION OF CORNELIUS

Before discussing the Cornelius incident, we must first consider the story of the conversion of the Ethiopian eunuch (Acts 8: 26–40). The word εὐνοῦχος can mean a 'treasurer' or a 'castrated man'.[1] In the LXX it can, like the Hebrew סָרִיס,[2] refer to a castrated man or to a man who holds high political or military office. If by εὐνοῦχος Luke means a castrated man,[3] then it is said that he cannot have been a Jew, for according to Dt. 23: 1–2 no castrated man can become a Jew or part of the Jewish community. Thus it is said that Luke must have understood the man to be a God-fearing Gentile.[4] However, it is not clear that Dt. 23: 1–2 does refer to eunuchs, though this is often assumed. Moreover, if it does and Luke was aware of it, then it may be that he thought that its restrictions have been overstepped by the fulfilment of Is. 56: 3f in Christ, so that eunuchs could now become Jews as well as members of the Church. A more probable suggestion is that Luke took the title to refer to the man's high office in the Ethiopian court and not to his castration. For Luke, the man was a proselyte[5] rather than a God-fearer, a Jew rather than a Gentile, for Acts 10–11 make it clear that he saw Cornelius as the first Gentile convert.

Conzelmann and Haenchen think that the original narrative

---

[1] *B.C.*, IV, 96.

[2] It is not clear what is the primary reference of סָרִיס – to a man's castration or to his courtly office. Most of the texts do not specifically refer to castration (Is. 56: 3–4 is the clearest) and could simply mean 'courtier' or 'chamberlain' – though both meanings may be intended in some passages.

[3] Conzelmann, *Apg.*, p. 56.

[4] Stählin, *Apg.*, p. 126; Wikenhauser, *Apg.*, p. 106.

[5] The fact that he is an Ethiopian probably implies that he is a proselyte rather than a Jew by birth, though the fact that he reads Isaiah and is returning from worship in Jerusalem could be used to argue either way.

came from Hellenistic-Christian circles and that it was their equivalent to the Cornelius narrative, namely the story of the conversion of the first Gentile.[1] Luke, therefore, intentionally leaves the man's religious status obscure: he could not call him a proselyte, because his source said he was a Gentile; and he could not call him a Gentile without anticipating the theme of Acts 10–11. Also, in this way Luke could give the impression that the Church's mission had taken a step beyond the Jews and Samaritans, but not quite to the Gentiles, with all the problems which that involves. It may well be that Haenchen and Conzelmann are right in thinking that the original version made it clear that the eunuch was a Gentile.[2] But it is unlikely that Luke knew this and deliberately covered it up, for it would have been a simple enough matter to position this narrative at a later point, after chs. 10–11, as he has done with 11: 19f. It is more likely that Luke did not realise that the eunuch was a Gentile, maybe because the tradition he received did not make this clear. If the eunuch was a Gentile, then this narrative affords yet one more example of the way in which Luke's idealistic picture of the extension of the Church's mission is betrayed by stories which he himself relates. For Luke the narrative has significance as the story of the conversion of a semi-Jew, a conversion in which God is the main actor.

M. Dibelius has done more than any other scholar to draw our attention to the problems and significance of the Cornelius episode.[3] He attempts to isolate the narrative underlying Luke's stylised version, and concludes that Luke used a simple, straightforward legend of the conversion of a godly Gentile, Cornelius. He likens this legend to that of the conversion of the Ethiopian eunuch and thinks that both were originally simple conversion legends, unconcerned with matters of principle. He argues that they both reflect the actual conditions in the Church before the Antioch dispute (Gal. 2: 11f), when individual Gentiles were occasionally accepted into the Church without its raising any

---

[1] Conzelmann, *Apg.*, p. 26; Haenchen, *Apg.*, pp. 264–5.

[2] Hahn, *Mission*, p. 51 n. 2, thinks this story came from the Antioch source and was an account of the conversion of a Jew, since according to the Antioch source the first Gentiles were reached in 11: 19f. This argument has force only if one accepts that it was part of the Antioch source and that this source has not misplaced or misinterpreted it.

[3] Dibelius, *Acts*, pp. 109–22.

difficulties.[1] Haenchen has challenged his conclusion.[2] He argues that a community expecting an imminent End would not preserve such traditions and that all the evidence we have points to the reluctance or indifference of the early Church when faced with Gentile converts. Moreover, if Peter had won a Gentile convert, Paul would have known of this and used it in his arguments with the Judaisers. But none of these are strong objections to Dibelius' case. Expectation of an imminent End was prevalent throughout the first century A.D., and the fact is that we know, if only from the Gospels, that the communities did preserve legends and stories which they believed to be significant. Nor is it necessary to believe that Paul must have known about this incident or, if he had known about it, that he would have used it. The original story was probably more obscure and less important than Luke makes it out to be and it may be that Peter's involvement in Cornelius' conversion is a Lukan addition.[3] Certainly, the early Church was reluctant to accept Gentile converts, but this does not mean that there were no Gentile converts before the more organised mission of Paul. A few isolated cases of pious Gentiles becoming Christians would not have aroused the same opposition as the wholesale, Law-free Gentile mission of Paul. There is no reason, therefore, to suppose that Dibelius has not given us a valuable clue to the nature of the pre-Lukan version of Cornelius' conversion.

We must ask, therefore, what Luke has added to this simple legend. The criterion which Dibelius and later Conzelmann use, is that all the parts which make the story a matter of principle are Lukan.[4] For this reason the whole of ch. 11 is seen as Luke's construction. It is a repetition, with minor variations,[5] of ch. 10 and makes a universal example out of a single case. The principle of the acceptance of Gentiles is applied to the whole Church, as represented by the leaders of the Church in Jerusalem. Moreover, the problem of table-fellowship, which sparks

---

[1] Dibelius, *Acts*, pp. 120f; Conzelmann, *Apg.*, pp. 61–2.

[2] Haenchen, *Apg.*, pp. 306f.

[3] On the other hand Peter may have been involved in Cornelius' conversion and this may be what lies behind Paul's comment in Gal. 2: 18.

[4] Dibelius, *Acts*, pp. 109f; Conzelmann, *Apg.*, p. 61.

[5] Ch. 11 is less dramatic and tense and the main difference in details is that while in ch. 10 the Spirit comes after Peter's speech, in ch. 11 it comes at the beginning of it.

off the speech of justification in 11: 3f, is only a minor detail of the narrative in ch. 10. Therefore ch. 11 is probably Luke's repetition of ch. 10 by which he both emphasises the immense significance of the event and uses it to express a principle, thus preparing the way for the use he will make of it in Acts 15.

Peter's vision (Acts 10: 9–16) may be an addition of Luke though, as Dibelius says, it could reflect a true experience of Peter in some other context, perhaps the Antioch controversy.[1] Luke found it and, not knowing the original context, uses it here. However, we cannot exclude the possibility that this vision came to Luke as an original part of the narrative. The most obvious reference of the vision is to the question of foods, whereas Luke clearly means it to be understood as a reference to the problem of clean and unclean men (10: 28). This has led some to think that the original reference was only to foods and that Luke has used it to refer to the problem of unclean men.[2] But apart from the fact that the problems of unclean foods and men are closely related, this notion ignores the nature of visions. A vision which is aimed at teaching something does not necessarily have the same content as the problem to which it refers. That is, visions can have parabolic significance. The vision of foods and the twofold command and refusal may originally have been intended to teach Peter something about clean and unclean men. Because Peter's vision is to do with eating, this does not narrow its terms of reference to the problem of foods. It may be a parable whose terms of reference are much wider. Thus it is possible that the vision is in the right context and does not need to be repositioned to the Antioch controversy.

Peter's speech is the other main part of ch. 10 which is usually

---

[1] Dibelius, *Acts*, pp. 111–12; Conzelmann, *Apg.*, p. 61. Haenchen (*Apg.*, p. 306) argues against this because: (a) Peter's objection is to eating unclean animals, but he could have eaten a clean one. But if both clean and unclean animals are implied (Peter mentions only unclean ones), their mixing may have caused all to become unclean. (b) If one applies the meaning of the vision to foods, it means that all foods are clean – and we have no evidence that Peter or the early Church abandoned the Jewish food laws. But if the vision is a parable referring to men this problem does not arise.

[2] Dibelius, *Acts*, pp. 111–12; Conzelmann, *Apg.*, p. 61; Wikenhauser, *Apg.*, p. 120. Cf. 11: 3f, where the vision is used as a defence against the charge that Peter ate with the uncircumcised.

ascribed to Luke.[1] Like the other speeches in Acts it betrays Lukan features and is too long to have been passed on as part of a legend.[2] There are certain odd features, such as the phrase 'you know the word which he sent to Israel' (10: 36) and the fact that it does not resemble the other speeches to the Gentiles in Acts 14 and 17. But these do not show that the speech is largely pre-Lukan;[3] rather they show that Luke was writing the speech on the basis of a stereotyped pattern and consequently some parts of it are not well suited to the particular situation. Some scholars think that the whole speech is irrelevant to the situation into which it is inserted,[4] though U. Wilckens has argued that both the framework and the context of the speech are entirely appropriate to their context.[5] The truth lies between these two extremes: some parts are ill-fitting, as we have seen, but there are points at which Peter's words bear directly on the question of the Gentiles' admission to the Church. Acts 10: 35, the reference to Jesus as πάντων Κύριος (10: 36), and the phrase πάντα τὸν πιστεύοντα εἰς αὐτόν (10: 43) all refer to the universality of the gospel, though these hints are not prominent and they are counterbalanced by more particularist references in 10: 36f, 42. The most likely explanation of these two factors – appropriateness and yet irrelevance – is that Luke has constructed the speech with one eye on the context and the other on the stereotyped pattern of the speeches in the early part of Acts.

It is often asserted that there are two distinct problems underlying the Cornelius narrative: first, the problem of table-fellowship between Jewish and Gentile Christians; second, the question of Gentile circumcision. Luke, it is argued, has superimposed the one upon the other and got them both hopelessly muddled.[6] Peter's vision and the Jerusalem leaders' objections

---

[1] Dibelius, *Acts*, p. 113; Conzelmann, *Apg.*, p. 61. They also think that vv. 27–9 and the reference to Peter's companions are Lukan.

[2] Haenchen, *Apg.*, p. 304; Wilckens, *Missionsreden*, pp. 49f.

[3] *Contra* Hanson, *Acts*, p. 124.

[4] Dibelius, *Acts*, pp. 110–11.

[5] Wilckens, *Missionsreden*, pp. 49f. He explains the phrase 'you know' (10: 36) in two ways: first, it may include Peter's companions; second, one has to assume that the hearers are already proleptically believers before the first word is spoken.

[6] Wikenhauser, *Apg.*, p. 125; Williams, *Acts*, p. 134; Haenchen, *Apg.*, p. 306; Dibelius, *Acts*, p. 112; Conzelmann, *Apg.*, p. 61.

are concerned with table-fellowship, whereas the central point of ch. 10 is that Cornelius was an uncircumcised Gentile who became a Christian. It is true that these were two distinct problems, but false to treat them as if they were wholly unrelated. Both are closely connected with the problem of admitting Gentiles into the Church and it is quite conceivable that not only were the two themes fused when Luke wrote,[1] but that they also arose simultaneously when the Church first faced the problem of Gentile converts. As Hanson says: 'The subject of table-fellowship was involved with the subject of food regulations and both with the subject of circumcision. When therefore Luke introduces into his story of the acceptance into the Church of an uncircumcised Gentile a sub-plot describing a vision about clean and unclean food, it may well be that he is combining two different traditions, two different pieces of material, but they are not incompatible. Ultimately they are both concerned with the same subject, and Luke knows this.'[2]

The narrative of Cornelius' conversion is important for Luke in a number of ways. One of the striking themes of these chapters is the emphasis placed on the piety of Cornelius. He is portrayed as the classic example of the godly and devout Gentile, a fact which Luke highlights in his usual manner, by repetition (Acts 10: 2, 4, 22, 30; and cf. Lk. 7: 1–10). Luke may have thought of Cornelius as a God-fearer, but his description is not only to show this. Haenchen thinks that Cornelius is seen as the representative of all God-fearers and that the emphasis on his piety is to show that the Church did not accept all Gentiles, but only the devout ones whom the Jews would accept too.[3] This may be so, or it may be that Luke has another motive in mind, namely to show that the Gentiles were not such a bad crowd after all. By making Cornelius a typical example of a Gentile, Luke may be trying to say that, all things considered, there is not much to choose between a Jew and a Gentile. There is no need for Jews to look down their noses at Gentiles as if they were an inferior breed, for God has shown that the pious centurion is subject to his guidance and blessing as much as any thoroughbred Jew. As in Lk. 7: 1–10, Luke seems to be introducing a thoroughly pragmatic justification of the Gentile mission alongside the

[1] Conzelmann, *ibid.*   [2] Hanson, *Acts*, p. 120.
[3] Haenchen, *Apg.*, pp. 302–3.

more 'theological' justifications found both here and elsewhere.

No other narrative in Acts is given quite such epic treatment as the Cornelius episode. Not only is it dealt with in chs. 10–11, but ch. 15 repeats the whole narrative again in a shortened form. Sheer length and repetition are Luke's way of impressing upon his readers the immense significance which this event had for him. It is for Luke the test-case *par excellence* for the admission of the Gentiles into the Church. God has made it clear that the Gentiles need no circumcision before entering the Church, since he has poured out his Spirit on them freely, as at Pentecost (Acts 10: 44, 11: 15f). Nor is there need for food regulations in the common meals of Jews and Gentiles (Acts 11: 3f). Henceforth there can be no doubt that it is God's will that the Gentiles should become equal members of the Church.

This leads us to note the dominant role which God plays in chs. 10–11, as contrasted with the relatively passive role of men. The references to angels (10: 22, 30, 11: 13), Peter's vision (10: 9–16) with its threefold command, the vision of Cornelius (10: 3f), and Peter's ignorance of the meaning of and blind obedience to God's commands all emphasise the dominant role of God. The Gentile mission is from the beginning seen not as the work of men, even if they are Apostles, but of God. In fact, both Peter and the Jerusalem leaders are suspicious of and reluctant to obey God's command, but despite this his will is fulfilled. Yet although Peter and the Apostles resisted the will of God temporarily, it is important for Luke to emphasise that the first Gentile convert was won through Peter who, up to this point, has been seen as the leader of the Twelve. Thus the Gentile mission is not only authorised, but actually begun, by one of the Apostles, and at last we have at least a partial fulfilment of Acts 1: 8. Luke has done his best to connect the Apostles with the Gentile mission, and thereby he makes it clear how important this was for him – as we shall see in ch. 15. Finally we note one other main theme which here, as elsewhere in Acts, is connected with the Gentile mission, namely the Holy Spirit (Acts 10: 44f, 11: 15f). There is no reference to the guidance of the Spirit, but it is the fact that God creates a new, Gentile Pentecost – an unforeseen fulfilment of Jesus' promise (Acts 1: 5) – which convinces Peter, his companions and the

Jerusalem leaders that God really was at work in the conversion of Cornelius.

THE APOSTOLIC COUNCIL

Acts 15 is of central importance both for Luke's attitude to the Gentiles and for assessing his reliability as a historian. For here, Luke says, the problem of the Gentiles and the Gentile mission is once and for all decided at a meeting in Jerusalem of all the main figures in the early Church.

The first question we must ask is whether Acts 15 = Gal. 2: 1–10; that is, can we use Gal. 2 as a means of checking the reliability of Luke's account? Any attempt to harmonise the chronologies of Luke and Paul is beset with notorious difficulties. All but the most absurd computations have been seriously defended, with varying degrees of success.[1] We shall take a brief look at the main theories, but without becoming involved in detailed discussion which would go beyond the scope of our primary theme.

The two accounts of the relevant visits of Paul to Jerusalem are as follows: Acts 9: 26–30, 11: 27–30, 15: 1–30, 18: 22; Gal. 1: 18–24, and 2: 1–10. Although it has been disputed,[2] there is little reason to doubt that the complex of events described in Acts 9: 19–30 is the same as those described in Gal. 1: 15–25. Despite marked differences in the dating and details of the two versions,[3] they seem to refer to the same events.

The problem now is to fix the correct parallel to Gal. 2. According to the chronology of Acts it should be Acts 11: 27–30 (12: 25),[4] but this raises serious problems, the most important of which is that there are so few essential points of contact between the two versions. The initial impetus for the journey and the

---

[1] For summaries of the main views see Caird, *Apostolic Age*, pp. 200f; Haenchen, *Apg.*, pp. 396f; K. Nickle, *The Collection* (London, 1966), pp. 51f.

[2] Schlier, *Galater*, pp. 66–78; P. Parker, 'Once more, Acts and Galatians', *JBL*, 86 (1967), 175f.

[3] Luke dates Paul's visit 'several days', and Paul himself three years, after his conversion (Acts 9: 19, 23; Gal. 1: 18). According to Acts Paul is introduced to the Twelve by Barnabas, whereas in Galatians there is no mention of Barnabas and Paul sees only Peter and James.

[4] Bruce, *Acts*, pp. 214f; Knox, *Acts*, pp. 49f; Williams, *Acts*, pp. 22–30; A. Geyser, 'Paul, the Apostolic decree and the liberals at Corinth', *SP*, pp. 124f.

reference to the Collection are the only links, and even these have been disputed.[1] There is a chronological inconsistency in the time-span between Paul's conversion and this visit;[2] and it is odd that a public session (Acts 15) was later needed to ratify what had already been decided in private. Further, unless one dates Galatians before the Council,[3] some explanation must be found for Paul's silence about this later trip.[4] Taken together, these difficulties militate decisively against a straightforward identification of Gal. 2 and Acts 11.

Apart from the rather eccentric equation of Gal. 2 with Acts 18: 22,[5] we are left with the conclusion that Acts 15 is the true parallel to Gal. 2.[6] There is a sufficient number of parallels between the two to confirm this view, although it does raise almost as many problems as it solves. Acts 15: 2 mentions companions of Paul and Barnabas, which could include Titus (Gal. 2: 4–5); in both Acts 15 and Gal. 2 the problem of circumcision of Gentiles is raised and the decision reached that circumcision is not to be forced on Gentiles who become Christians.[7]

---

[1] The reference to 'revelation' (Gal. 2: 2) is often seen as a close parallel to Agabus' prophecy, but Nickle (*Collection*, p. 42) argues that Paul never uses the word of communication through another person. Gal. 2: 10 could be translated 'go on remembering the poor' and could be seen as a reference to Acts 11: 27f; but it could also simply mean 'remember the poor' and refer forward to the great collection of the third journey.

[2] It is unlikely that Luke thought that 13–16 years (Gal. 1: 18, 2: 1) elapsed between Acts 9 and 11.

[3] W. M. Ramsay, *St Paul the Traveller and Roman Citizen* (London, 1903), pp. 54f. But it is more likely that Galatians was a late epistle: see C. H. Buck, 'The date of Galatians', *JBL*, 70 (1951), 113f.

[4] Caird, *Apostolic Age*, p. 204, suggests that it is because Paul wanted to defend only the gospel he preached in Galatia; he therefore includes only those events prior to the Galatian trip.

[5] D. F. Robinson, 'A note on Acts 11: 27–30', *JBL*, 63 (1944), 179f.

[6] Dibelius, *Acts*, pp. 93f; Burton, *Galatians*, pp. 115f; Wikenhauser, *Apg.*, pp. 178f. See also notes p. 180, nn. 3 and 4, below.

[7] Gal. 2: 3 makes it clear that Titus was not compelled to be circumcised. In Gal. 2: 5 the MSS which omit οἷς οὐδέ are secondary, since it is difficult to think that a scribe would add it, thereby making an incomplete and ungrammatical sentence. Even so, 2: 5 could still mean 'we did yield in fact, but not abjectly'. O'Neill, *Acts*, p. 103, thinks that whereas in Acts it is always clear that circumcision of the Gentiles is out of the question, Paul has to use negative arguments in Gal. 2. Moreover, circumcision is a live issue in Paul's later letters and it is unlikely, therefore, that an authoritative statement was made, otherwise Paul would have used

Finally, in both instances Paul's mission to the Gentiles is recognised and agreement is reached (Acts 15: 25–6; Gal. 2: 7–9).

The major problem which the above equation poses is the visit of Acts 11, since according to Galatians the visit of 2: 1f is Paul's second visit to Jerusalem, whereas Acts 15 is his third. Paul could scarcely have omitted to mention a visit to Jerusalem,[1] since this would have imperilled his whole argument in Gal. 1–2, where he tries to show that his apostleship and gospel did not originate in Jerusalem. The most common solution is to conclude that Acts 11 and 15 are duplicate accounts from two different sources of the one event described in Gal. 2.[2] Luke, not realising that they referred to the same visit, made two separate journeys of them. Some who accept this explanation date the council to coincide with Acts 11[3] and others to coincide with Acts 15.[4] More recently it has been argued that Acts 11: 27f is not a parallel to Acts 15, but a creation of Luke's for specifically theological purposes, though containing a residue of historical material.[5] G. Strecker bases his argument on the consistently Lukan language of this section, on Luke's distinctive view of the Collection, and on the noticeable Lukan motifs, such as the leading of the community by the Spirit, the mention of elders and the centrality of Jerusalem. He thinks there is a historical kernel, namely Agabus' prophecy, Paul and Barnabas' visit to

it. However, assuming that Titus was not circumcised, as seems most probable, then this is an authoritative decision which Paul quotes. Whoever they were, it is clear that the Judaisers were not commissioned by the Twelve (though they may have made spurious claims to this effect), so that even after such a decision the Judaisers would not automatically cease to function.

[1] Lightfoot, *Galatians*, pp. 123f., thinks Paul omitted to mention his second visit (Acts 11) since on that occasion he saw only 'elders' and not 'Apostles'.

[2] P. Benoit, 'La deuxième visite de St. Paul à Jérusalem', *Bib.*, 40 (1959), 778f, thinks Acts 11 and 15 are both from an Antioch source and that the former was originally the introduction to the latter (15: 1–2 being redactional).

[3] H. Lietzmann, *An die Galater* (Tübingen, 1932), p. 9; Stählin, *Apg.*, p. 209.

[4] Haenchen, *Apg.*, pp. 396f; Conzelmann, *Apg.*, p. 87; Wikenhauser, *Apg.*, pp. 178f; O'Neill, *Acts*, pp. 94f; K. Lake, *B.C.*, v, 195f; A. Oepke, *Der Brief des Paulus an die Galater* (Berlin, 1957), pp. 51–5.

[5] G. Strecker, 'Die sogenannte zweite Jerusalemreise des Paulus, Apg. 11: 27–30', *ZNW*, 53 (1962), 67–77.

Jerusalem and the Collection, but he thinks that Luke has got them all hopelessly muddled.[1] He thinks that although Acts 11 : 27f is a mistake of Luke's, it is a meaningful one, since it fulfils a theological purpose. In his overall attempt to preserve the continuity of *Heilsgeschichte* between Jerusalem and Antioch, Luke gives expression to two theological motifs: first, the unity of the Church, as expressed in the Collection; second, the legitimacy of the Gentile mission, effected by the connection of the journey (Acts 11 : 27f) with the events in Jerusalem (Acts 12) and, through Acts 12 : 25, the further link with the mission in Asia Minor (Acts 13 : 1f), which shows that the latter was authorised by Jerusalem!

Strecker has highlighted the major problem of the traditional assertion that Acts 11 and 15 are duplicate versions of the same event, namely that apart from the reference to Paul and Barnabas going to Jerusalem there is no connection at all between the two accounts. This, in turn, makes it clear that if Luke was using sources at this point, as seems most probable, he can hardly be blamed for failing to realise that they were duplicate accounts. No one, lacking the knowledge of Paul's epistles, would have guessed that they were even remotely connected. Luke has made a mistake, but it is an understandable and excusable one. Further, it does seem more likely that Luke was misled by his sources than that he deliberately constructed an extra journey in order to demonstrate the continuity of the *Heilsgeschichte*. Many of the so-called Lukan motifs and much of the so-called Lukan language are overemphasised by Strecker;[2] at the most this evidence shows that Luke has rewritten and

---

[1] Strecker summarises the historical elements in Acts 11 as follows: Agabus' prophecy – though not the account of its fulfilment; Paul and Barnabas' visit to Jerusalem – though it is misplaced, having been transferred from Acts 15 to Acts 11; the idea of the Collection as διακονία – though the motivation for and date of the Collection differ in Luke and Paul.

[2] For example, ὀνόματι, σημαίνω, οἰκουμένη, διακονία, κατοικῶ, ἀδελφοί, and ἀποστέλλω, are not exclusively or even specially Lukan terms. The localisation in Antioch and the backward look to Jerusalem are not particularly significant. The inspiration of prophecy by the Spirit is not exclusive to Luke. Common charity is mentioned in the early chapters of Acts, but it is not a true parallel to the Collection, for the one is an internal arrangement of the Jerusalem community and the other a gift of the predominantly Gentile Churches outside Jerusalem to the poor in Jerusalem. Thus there is little evidence for a specifically Lukan origin of the narrative, even though Luke has clearly got confused.

reconstructed his sources. As Strecker makes clear, the traditional material Luke did have was probably confused and obscure and Luke, as usual, tried to rationalise and clarify it. The theological motives which Strecker ascribes to Luke are ambiguous. The rather tortuous attempt to show that the mission in 13: 1f is, by a series of connections, legitimised by Jerusalem is highly improbable. Nothing in 11: 27 – 13: 4 suggests that this is the case; the only legitimiser is the Spirit, not the Jerusalem Church. The second motive, Church unity, probably was in the forefront of Luke's mind, but this may simply reflect the historical facts, since Paul himself sees the Collection in this way. At the least, it does not exclude the theory of dual sources, which Luke has justifiably got muddled.

Having reached tentative conclusions on the chief problem of the chronology and identification of Paul's visits to Jerusalem, we turn now to the details of Luke's narrative. There are a few obvious points of contrast between Acts 15 and Gal. 2 that are not of decisive significance. Titus plays an important role in Paul's version, whereas he is not mentioned by Luke; but the problem of Gentile circumcision, for which Titus is the test-case, is quite clearly dealt with in Acts 15. It is often claimed that Luke portrays the Council as a public meeting of the whole Church, whereas Paul describes it as a private consultation between himself and the Pillars.[1] However, it may be that Luke implies that there were two meetings: the first (15: 4) was a general gathering of the Church to welcome the Antioch delegation, and the second was the Council meeting with the Apostles and elders alone (15: 6f), when the real business was decided.[2] This certainly implies more than the small Jerusalem delegation in Paul's account (Gal. 2: 2), but both emphasise that the discussions took place with the leaders of the Jerusalem Church. Being ignorant of Galatians and knowing only that it was with the leaders that Paul met, Luke uses the stylised phrase 'Apostles and elders' to describe them.[3] But this does not amount to a serious contradiction.

---

[1] Haenchen, *Apg.*, pp. 384–5; Nickle, *Collection*, pp. 51f.

[2] Wikenhauser, *Apg.*, p. 178; Stählin, *Apg.*, p. 102. Contrast Haenchen, *Apg.*, pp. 384. Gal. 2: 2 is also ambiguous on this point: it may imply two meetings rather than one (Burton, *Galatians*, p. 71).

[3] This phrase (15: 2, 4, 6, 22, 23, 16: 4) may have been in Luke's source.

However, there are more serious problems, the first of which is the motivation for Paul's journey to the Council. In Gal. 2: 2 Paul claims that it was a result of 'revelation'. It is probable that Agabus' prophecy is to be seen as a parallel to this,[1] but many find it difficult to square up with Luke's view that Paul was sent by the Church in Antioch. This is because many see Gal. 2: 2 as part of Paul's defence of his independence from the Jerusalem Church, so that it implies that Paul was not delegated by any Church, either Jerusalem or Antioch. But while Paul's intention probably is to exclude the notion of constraint from Jerusalem, there is no reason why his revelation should not have coincided with the decision of the Antioch Church; indeed, the decision itself may have been a result of this revelation. Nor does Gal. 2: 2 exclude the notion that the factor which necessitated this decision or revelation was a disturbance in Antioch caused by Judaisers,[2] even though Antioch is not mentioned in Gal. 2: 1f and Paul clearly 'does not intend to give a historical lecture on the reasons which led to the meeting in Jerusalem being arranged'.[3]

When in Jerusalem, Paul meets with opposition from an extremist faction. Luke describes them as Christian Pharisees (Acts 15: 5), whereas Paul simply refers to them as 'false

[1] Hahn, *Mission*, p. 78 n. 3.

[2] Schmithals, *James*, pp. 39f, argues against this view. He thinks that Gal. 2: 2 shows that it was the Jerusalem Church in particular who were eager for this discussion and that the cause did not lie in the circumstances of Paul's work. If it had, then even Paul's opponents would not have thought that the Jerusalem Church had summoned him, and his need for a discussion would have been so urgent that Gal. 2: 2 would be quite incomprehensible. However, this last point is simply not true and further, if the trouble was in Paul's Churches, it is perfectly possible that the Jerusalem leaders could have summoned him or that his opponents could have claimed that this was so. Schmithals argues further that it is improbable that after fifteen years of successful missionary work Paul would have met with opposition on matters of principle from Jerusalem. This is true, but then Schmithals asks, 'If the Judaisers were a separatist group, why the need for an agreement with the Jerusalem leaders?' But if, as some think, the Judaisers claimed authorisation from Jerusalem, then it would be natural for Paul to consult with Jerusalem to clear the matter up. In the face of strenuous opposition Paul would at any rate feel the need to retain and confirm the link with the original disciples of Jesus, who were the prime witnesses of the Resurrection, lest he should 'run in vain' (Gal. 2: 2b).

[3] Schmithals, *James*, p. 42.

brethren'. In both cases they appear to be a different group from the Judaisers in Antioch,[1] arriving unexpectedly to complicate the business of the Council; but it is possible that both Luke and Paul thought that the two groups were connected in some way.[2] The only difference is that whereas Luke sees them as Christians (15:5 πεπιστευκότες), however misguided, Paul's description (Gal. 2:4 ψευδαδέλφους) implies that they were 'counterfeit Christians'. That is, in Paul's view they were not simply Christians in error, but in reality not Christians at all.[3]

A more obvious discrepancy between the two versions is that Luke minimises the role of Paul and Barnabas in the discussion while emphasising the decisive influence of Peter and James. The minor role of Paul and Barnabas is evident from Acts 15: 12 – their sole contribution to the discussion – which merely recounts the successes of their previous missionary journey, but without any detail. While Dibelius is correct in saying that the brevity of 15:12 is explicable on literary grounds,[4] since Luke's readers already know the facts from chs. 13–14, this does not lessen the contradiction by much. The extensive speeches by Peter and James are almost certainly Luke's construction. The reference back to Cornelius by both speakers is intelligible only on literary grounds.[5] The readers of Acts alone would catch the allusion; the speakers' audience would not have understood a reference to an obscure and distant event which achieved prominence only under the hand of Luke. At least we can only assume that this was so, because if the Cornelius episode had had the importance which Luke attaches to it, the Apostolic Council should not have been necessary, since such a momentous decision could scarcely have been forgotten so quickly. The quotation from Am. 9: 11–13 (Acts 15: 16–18) is taken from the LXX; the Hebrew cannot bear the interpretation which James

---

[1] Munck, *Paul*, p. 232, makes the improbable suggestion that the Judaisers were Gentile Christians from Pauline Churches, whom Luke has misplaced in Jerusalem.

[2] Acts 15: 1, 5 seem to distinguish the two groups. There is no evidence that the false brethren of Gal. 2 were active in Antioch or other Gentile communities, but it is possible that Paul did connect them with the Judaisers in Antioch.

[3] Nickle, *Collection*, pp. 47f.

[4] Dibelius, *Acts*, pp. 95–7; Haenchen, *Apg.*, p. 388.

[5] Dibelius, *Acts*, p. 95.

gives to it. This would scarcely have been James' way of using the Old Testament and must be ascribed to Luke.[1] Further, in neither speech is reference made to the missionary work of Paul and Barnabas which, according to Gal. 2, was the main factor in persuading the Jerusalem leaders of the legitimacy of Paul's apostleship and gospel. We must conclude, therefore, that the minor role assigned to Paul and Barnabas and the speeches of Peter and James are the work of Luke. In reality, the Antioch delegation took a much more active part in the Council's deliberations. Luke wants to show that the Gentile mission was affirmed and actively supported by the Jerusalem Church, in particular by the leading figures Peter and James, and in the process of showing this he underplays the role of Paul and Barnabas, though without intentionally degrading them.[2]

The agreement reached and formularised in Gal. 2: 9, that Paul should preach to the Gentiles and Peter to the Jews, has no parallel in Acts. Moreover, while Paul certainly is the Gentile missionary *par excellence* after ch. 15, he also preaches to the Jews. And although there is in Acts a Jewish mission after the Council, neither Peter nor the other Apostles take part in it. The agreement in Gal. 2: 9 is itself a problem, because whether it is understood geographically or ethnographically it seems to be impractical and unrealistic.[3] Haenchen, therefore, thinks it must be taken to mean simply that Jerusalem recognised the Law-free Gentile mission of Paul, and Hahn thinks it 'indicates the main emphasis and purpose of the missionary activity'.[4] More recently it has been argued that Gal. 2: 9 must be taken at its face value and not watered down in this way.[5] Schmithals, in particular, has insisted on an ethnographical interpretation of this verse and believes that it was an agreement which both Paul and the Jerusalem leaders upheld for the rest of their

---

[1] So most commentators. Attempts to deny this are unconvincing. Thus Bruce, *Acts*, p. 298, thinks James had learned Greek and, because of the presence of Paul and Barnabas, used the LXX. F. V. Filson, *Three Crucial Decades* (London, 1964), p. 79, makes the dubious suggestion that the Hebrew text mentions the inclusion of the Gentiles and that it was natural for Luke to write up James' speech in Greek, using the LXX.

[2] Conzelmann, *Apg.*, p. 87: 'The intention behind Paul's passive role in Acts is certainly not to degrade him.'

[3] Haenchen, *Apg.*, pp. 408–9.   [4] Hahn, *Mission*, p. 81.

[5] O'Neill, *Acts*, p. 104; Schmithals, *James*, pp. 45f.

careers.[1] Paul's antinomian gospel could easily have become an embarrassment to the Jerusalem Church. As the Law was the basis of Jewish national existence, any connection with antinomianism would, in a time of increasing national fanaticism,[2] endanger the existence of the Jerusalem Church. Thus it is for this practical, political reason that Paul and the Jerusalem leaders agree to a strict ethnographical division of labour. According to Schmithals, this agreement did not create any essentially fresh situations, but merely clarified and confirmed what had already been found to be practicable. However, throughout his argument Schmithals simplifies things far too much. For example, Paul's attitude to the Law is far more complex than Schmithals would have us believe. There is no evidence that Paul ever encouraged Jews to abandon the Law; in fact, all the evidence points in the opposite direction (I Cor. 7: 17f; Gal. 5: 6, 6: 15). Further, there is evidence which probably implies that after the Council Peter worked among Gentiles in Corinth (I Cor. 1: 12, 9: 5)[3] and at least a hint that Paul continued to work with Jews (I Cor. 9: 19f; Gal. 5: 11).[4] Nor can we abandon out of hand the evidence of Acts, which says that Paul continued to approach Jews as well as Gentiles after the Council.[5] Moreover, if Gal. 2: 9 was merely a formal confirmation of an already

[1] Munck, *Paul*, pp. 275f, argues that the difference between Paul and the Jerusalem leaders was in their assessment of the place of the Gentile mission: Paul believed that it was only through the success of the Gentile mission that the Jews would eventually be saved, whereas the Jerusalem leaders believed the opposite.

[2] B. Reicke, 'Der geschichtliche Hintergrund des Apostelkonzils und der Antiochia-Episode', *SP*, pp. 172f.

[3] It could, of course, be argued that Peter worked only among the Jews in Corinth.

[4] I Cor. 9: 19f does not say that Paul preached to the Jews, though this might seem a natural implication. Gal. 5: 11f, where Paul seems to be defending himself against a charge of inconsistency over circumcision, may be a result of his preaching that Jews may keep the Law, whereas Gentiles need not.

[5] Schmithals, *James*, p. 60, argues that the synagogues would, for the antinomian Paul, be the last places he would preach in, for he would meet immediate opposition. However, this objection is valid only if Paul preached a wholly antinomian gospel indiscriminately to Jews and Gentiles, for which there is no evidence. Paul's 'antinomianism' did not consist of a wholesale rejection of the Law; rather, it was a denial of the efficacy of the Law as a way of salvation.

existing agreement, what made this confirmation necessary? Schmithals suggests that the cause was Paul's extension of his mission from the coastal lands of the eastern Mediterranean to the lands further west. But this does not really explain the sudden need for a formal agreement to confirm the Church's existing practice. The mere fact of Paul's extension of his mission would scarcely have given rise to suspicions that Paul would suddenly change the missionary strategy which had served him so well for fifteen years. It seems, therefore, that the evidence of Acts and the epistles combines to show that whatever the original meaning and intention of the agreement in Gal. 2: 9, it soon fell by the wayside. A few years later Peter and Paul were probably acting in contradiction to the terms of the agreement. From this we must conclude either that Paul has made the agreement sound much more precise than it really was, or that the agreement was overtaken by events and soon forgotten. This in turn makes it not at all surprising that Luke does not mention it. Taking into account his ignorance of Galatians and the date at which he was writing, we should be astounded if the reverse had been true and Luke had included it.

The letter which accompanies the decree (Acts 15: 23–9) has some odd features which suggest that it may be pre-Lukan.[1] It is addressed to a limited number of Gentile Churches – Antioch, Syria and Cilicia (15: 23) and up to this point in Acts Luke has not related a mission in Cilicia.[2] If it were Lukan, we would expect a wider destination, such as Luke adds in 16: 4. Also, the mention of Judas and Silas is odd, for Judas is not mentioned elsewhere in Acts. One might have expected Luke to have made more of the role of Paul and Barnabas. Haenchen has argued that the letter is a literary construction of Luke's.[3] Certain features, such as the 'ecclestiastical' style, 15: 28 which reveals Luke's concept of the Church and the Spirit, and the phrase 'apostles and brethren', which Haenchen thinks Luke copied from the similar phrase 'men and brethren', betray

[1] Hanson, *Acts*, pp. 156–7.
[2] Conzelmann, *Apg.*, p. 86, points to 15: 41 where Cilicia is mentioned in such a way that it is clear that although he has not related it, Luke believed there had been a mission there. But this verse may have been constructed under the influence of 15: 23. In Acts 9: 30 Paul returns to Tarsus, but it is not said that he preached there.
[3] Haenchen, *Apg.*, pp. 401–2.

Luke's hand at work. But this evidence is not strong, for an ecclesiastical style is not entirely unexpected in an ecclesiastical letter and other Lukan features show only that Luke has at points written up the letter in his own language. Lukan features here, as elsewhere in Acts, do not exclude pre-Lukan sources.[1] Thus we can conclude that a pre-Lukan version of the letter is probable, though this cannot be proved.

We turn our attention finally to the problems which surround the apostolic decree (Acts 15: 20, 29, 21: 25). Despite manuscript variations, modern scholars are unanimous in their acceptance of the so-called 'neutral' text of the decree.[2] The omission of πορνείας in 𝔓45 is an accidental error rather than a deliberate variant. The Western text substitutes the negative form of the 'golden rule' for πνικτόν, which in turn makes possible an ethical interpretation of the other three demands. It is agreed[3] that the cultic version of the neutral text is the more original: first, a development from the cultic to the ethical is easier to understand than the reverse process; and second, the Western version consists of such widely accepted ethical norms that a decree to this effect would be superfluous. The four demands of the decree are based on the Pentateuchal laws for non-Israelites living amongst Jews (Lev. 17–18).[4] They were the minimum demands made on non-Jews to enable them to mix with Jews, and they are a partial parallel to the better known Noachian precepts which fulfilled a similar purpose.[5] They remained valid in Palestine until the Rabbinic period and were probably kept by God-fearers in the Diaspora.[6]

Some see the decree as an attempt to regulate table-fellowship between Jews and Gentiles.[7] However, this is improbable:[8]

---

[1] As Conzelmann notes (Apg., p. 87 – contra Dibelius and Haenchen), when one has proved Luke's hand at work in ch. 15 one has not automatically excluded the notion of pre-Lukan sources.

[2] See the list in Haenchen, Apg., pp. 390–1.

[3] Contrast A. C. Clark, The Acts of the Apostles (Oxford, 1933), pp. 360f.

[4] H. Waitz, 'Das Problem des sogenannten Aposteldekrets', ZKG, 55 (1936), 227f.

[5] S.B., II, 722f; G. F. Moore, Judaism in the First Centuries of the Christian Era (Cambridge, 1927), I, 274–5, 339.

[6] S.B., II, 722f; H. J. Schoeps, Paul (London, 1961), pp. 232f.

[7] Conzelmann, Apg., pp. 84–6; Stählin, Apg., pp. 206f.

[8] Schmithals, James, pp. 100–1; Haenchen, Apg., p. 411; O'Neill, Acts, pp. 102f; Wikenhauser, Apg., p. 175.

first, the rules are too limited for table-fellowship, for they do not even guarantee that no forbidden meat or wine (for example, pork, or wine from libations) is used; and second, Lev. 17f does not play any part in Rabbinic rules for table-fellowship. Rather, they appear to be minimal rules which made contact possible between Jews and Gentiles, perhaps for common worship in the synagogue or Church.

The origin of the decree is as disputed as its meaning. Several factors point to a date after the Apostolic Council. Most important is Paul's statement in Gal. 2: 6 that the Pillars added nothing to him, which contradicts the very notion of a decree.[1] Nor does the decree bear on the main business of the Council, namely the problem of Gentile circumcision. Further, Peter's behaviour in Gal. 2: 11f becomes inexplicable if the decree was promulgated at the Council.[2] Also, Paul does not mention the decree in any of his epistles, and its absence from I Corinthians[3] and Galatians[4] is particularly striking. Also, in Acts 21: 25 Paul is told of the decree as if he had not heard of it before, which is a further hint that the decree was not promulgated at the Apostolic Council.

When we abandon the view that the decree originated at the Council, several other theories become possible. One of the most common is to date the decree at a second Council which met, in the absence of Paul, after the Antioch dispute. Thus the decree

---

[1] Filson, *Decades*, p. 110, argues that the majority of Gentiles kept these rules long before the Council, in deference to Jewish scruples. The decree was merely a diplomatic arrangement, confirming an already accepted practice. Since Paul had already encouraged the practice, Gal. 2: 6 does not contradict Acts 15. However, this view makes the decree redundant; and why formularise an accepted practice in this way? Also, even if the decree was not new, Paul would have had to mention it in Galatians, if only to show that it was not new, otherwise he would have endangered the whole argument of Gal. 1–2.

[2] Unless with Stählin (*Apg.*, p. 210) we date Gal. 2: 11f before 2: 1f.

[3] Though J. C. Hurd, *The Origin of I Corinthians* (London, 1965), thinks Paul did encourage the Corinthian Church to keep the requirements of the decree.

[4] T. W. Manson, 'St Paul in Ephesus: 2. The problem of the epistle to the Galatians', *BJRL*, 24 (1940), 69f, thinks Paul dropped the decree after a while because his opponents used it as a sign of his dependence on Jerusalem. But in Galatians Paul would need specifically to refute this false interpretation, so Manson's view would at any rate only cover the silence of I Corinthians.

is seen to have arisen directly out of the Antioch controversy.[1] This would account for all the objections raised to dating it at the Acts 15 – Gal. 2 Council. Often this theory is based on Acts 21 : 25 which, it is claimed, gives an indirect hint of the real origin of the decree. However, it has been argued that we cannot imagine that Luke would allow Paul to be told of the decree twice for the first time, so that Acts 21 : 25 should be read as a conscious repetition by Luke, addressed primarily to his readers,[2] emphasising the importance of the decree. Yet when we consider the frequent internal inconsistencies in Acts, the notion that 21 : 25 may be yet another becomes quite feasible. Therefore, this evidence is ambiguous and there is no other evidence which conclusively shows that the decree is early or pre-A.D. 70,[3] though we cannot exclude this possibility.

If we do not take the latter view, then various theories of a later origin are possible. The second-century evidence for similar prohibitions is not, as Schmithals notes, to be directly related to the decree. They are incidental parallels to the decree and the motives for following the various prohibitions do not elucidate the decree in its present context.[4] Schmithals thinks the decree may have originated outside the Christian Church, in the Jewish Diaspora. Luke, noticing that the behaviour of the post-apostolic Church coincided with Lev. 17f, declared the rules to be apostolic, thus affording an example of the Jewishness of the apostolic Church.[5] More probable is the suggestion

---

[1] Hanson, *Acts*, pp. 157f; Wikenhauser, *Apg.*, pp. 179f; *B.C.*, v, 204f.

[2] Haenchen, *Apg.*, p. 412; Schmithals, *James*, pp. 98f.

[3] Hanson, *Acts*, p. 155, argues for a pre-A.D. 70 date because: first, at least two of the prohibitions were still being observed much later (Rev. 2: 14, 20); second, the decree is based on the Old Testament and, therefore, the substance is not Lukan; third, the decree is clearly a concession made by Christians and, therefore, presupposes a Jewish-dominated Church where the Jews were in a position to lay down the law. However, the first point proves nothing about an early origin of the decree (see above); the second point may be true, but it shows only a pre-Lukan and not a pre-A.D. 70 date of origin. With regard to the third point, it may be that the decree originated in a Jewish-dominated synagogue, which does not help much in dating it. Moreover, it may be that the decree presupposes a Jewish-Christian minority who were eager to get guarantees for the preservation of their own practices from a Gentile-dominated Church (O'Neill, *Acts*, pp. 108f).

[4] Schmithals, *James*, pp. 99–100.   [5] Schmithals, *James*, pp. 101f.

that Luke took the decree from a Christian source. O'Neill, for example, thinks Luke found the decree in an 'old source',[1] which represented a specific Jewish-Christian proposal that Gentiles should observe the Levitical requirements for 'strangers within the gates'. Luke uses the decree because it seemed to justify the customs prevalent in the Church and because it buttressed the tolerant relationship which he wished to see between Jewish and Gentile Christians. Haenchen thinks the source of the decree was the Church of Luke's day. Luke, therefore, reflects a living tradition, which probably already projected the decree back into the apostolic period. Luke used the decree in the hope of securing Jew–Gentile harmony in the Church: 'The prohibitions will have become important in a strongly mixed Diaspora community, where Jewish requirements were more moderate and where one rested content with those four commandments which Moses himself gave to the Gentiles.'[2]

To conclude: it seems clear that both the decree and the accompanying letter were not promulgated at the Apostolic Council. It is possible, though not certain, that both were given at a later Council at which Paul was not present. If we think the letter shows signs of a pre-Lukan origin and take it closely together with the decree – since without the decree the letter is a torso – then the theory of a later Council is probably the most satisfactory explanation. In view of the facts we have discussed, this is still the best overall explanation. However, if we think the letter is Lukan then it is open to us to date the decree much later, though one cannot be more precise than to say that it was probably pre-Lukan and that it was probably lifted from a Christian source. Whatever this source was, Luke understood it to imply that the decree was early and had apostolic sanction and, accordingly, he worked it into the rest of his knowledge about the Apostolic Council.

We turn now to a discussion of the significance of this chapter and its relationship to the rest of Acts. Our first problem is to discover if and how Luke saw ch. 15 in relation to chs. 10–11. Luke does not appear to be reopening the question of table-fellowship which is implicit in Acts 10: 17f and 11: 3f, since this is a topic which does not arise in ch. 15, unless one interprets

---

[1] O'Neill, *Acts*, pp. 109, 115; cf. Dibelius, *Acts*, pp. 99–100
[2] Haenchen, *Apg.*, p. 413.

the decree in this way. But in chs. 10–11 the problem of the entry of Gentiles into the Church is apparently settled in principle once and for all. God has shown that the Gentiles are to be part of the Church as Gentiles, that is, they need not become Jews first. Yet in ch. 15 this problem arises once again both in Antioch and Jerusalem, despite the previous agreement between Peter and the other Jerusalem leaders. This problem is heightened by Luke's insisting that Peter and James justified Paul's mission by reference to the Cornelius episode at the Council, a mere mention of which was enough to silence all opposition! Perhaps the reference to Christian Pharisees (Acts 15: 5) is important and we must assume that, owing to their increasing influence, they began to make their demands felt more strongly.[1] This does not necessarily explain the trouble at Antioch, but it is possible that Luke saw this as a partial explanation of the change of attitude in Jerusalem. Or maybe Haenchen is right when he suggests that Luke intends us to think that the Church had simply forgotten about the Cornelius incident.[2] The phrase 'God has, in olden days...' (15: 7) is not only a rather exaggerated way of saying that the event was long ago, but may also be partially an explanation of why the Church had forgotten – precisely because it was so long ago! Clearly, as Haenchen sees, if the Cornelius episode had been as epoch-making as Luke makes out, the Church could not have forgotten it so quickly. Perhaps we must assume that Luke did not notice the contradiction and therefore did not try to explain it at all. Either way, it is the reliability of Luke's account of the Cornelius episode, rather than his account of the Council, which is thrown into doubt. This is not to say that the whole incident was a myth, but that 'it is wholly unlikely that this obscure and isolated episode would have had the prominence and the publicity which Luke attributes to it'.[3] Apart from the historical question, Luke clearly sees the Apostolic Council as a confirmation of the momentous turning point in chs. 10–11, when Gentiles are accepted as equal members of the Church. The use of the Cornelius episode in ch. 15 confirms the immense significance, already evident from chs. 10–11, which Luke attached to it.

Ch. 15 forms a watershed in the book of Acts. It is a, if not the,

---

[1] Stählin, *Apg.*, p. 199.
[2] Haenchen, *Apg.*, pp. 404f.　　　　[3] Hanson, *Acts*, p. 160.

turning point of the whole narrative.[1] It concludes and justifies past events and makes possible all future developments. Before ch. 15 Jerusalem dominates the scene and all Churches are under her influence and direction (Acts 8: 14f, 9: 31f, 10–11, 11: 27f). After ch. 15 the Jerusalem Church fades in importance, though it does not disappear; the Church moves out and heads for Rome. Together with Jerusalem go Peter and the Twelve, who dominate most of the events up to the Council. After Acts 16: 4 they are no longer mentioned; James and the elders take their place in Jerusalem and Paul and his Gentile mission becomes the dominant theme. From this point on the question of Gentile circumcision does not arise, since it has been settled once and for all. Paul gains official approval over against the Judaisers and this recognition becomes 'the foundation of the European Gentile Church'.[2]

At various points we meet familiar themes connected with the Gentile mission. Emphasis is placed on the work of God in planning and provoking the Law-free Gentile mission. This is done in many ways: Peter's speech is dominated by references to God's activity in the Cornelius episode (15: 7–10); God chose to speak first through Peter to the Gentiles (15: 7, 14f); God has 'cleansed the hearts' of the Gentiles (15: 9); Paul and Barnabas justify their work by reference to the 'signs and wonders' God has wrought (15: 12); and finally, God's word in the Old Testament confirms his action with Cornelius (15: 16–18).[3] This use of Scriptural proof to justify the Gentile mission is a theme we have met before and will meet again. It emphasises that it was part of God's eternal will and plan that Gentiles should be accepted as equal members of the Church. That the Gentiles need not keep the whole Law is justified negatively by reference to the inability of the Jews themselves to keep it (15: 10), but it is made clear that the Law-free Gentile mission stands in full harmony with the Mosaic Law (15: 21).[4] As well as the references to Old Testament promises, there is also the passing reference to Jesus' promise (15: 8), as in the Cornelius episode.

---

[1] Haenchen, *Apg.*, pp. 402f; Conzelmann, *Apg.*, p. 87; P. H. Menoud, 'Le Plan des Actes des Apôtres', *NTS*, 1 (1954–5), 44f.

[2] Haenchen, *Apg.*, p. 404.　　　[3] See below, ch. 9.

[4] For a variety of interpretations of this obscure verse see Dibelius, *Acts*, p. 97; Munck, *Paul*, p. 235; Haenchen, *Apg.*, p. 391; O'Neill, *Acts*, p. 102; Hanson, *Acts*, p. 163.

Yet another theme occasionally peeps through, namely the connection between the Gentile mission and the Spirit – by way of reference back to Cornelius (15: 8) and through the phrase 'It seemed good to the Holy Spirit and to us' (15: 28). The authorisation of Paul's mission by the Twelve is yet another familiar theme. Despite Acts 1: 8, Luke finds it difficult to make them actively participate in the Gentile mission; but it is Peter who makes the first and all-important move, and here in ch. 15 the Apostles are solidly united behind Paul. They finally authorise and set their seal on Paul's work. In this way too, Luke makes it clear that the Church was united; it is only a minority which causes the trouble, and they are utterly repudiated by the Jerusalem leaders.

Finally, we can draw a few tentative conclusions about Luke the historian in ch. 15. Are we to regard the whole of Acts 15 as Luke's imaginative construction, devoid of both sources and historical worth?[1] Or, when we take into account the different motives of Luke and Paul, can we say, 'the two accounts can be brought naturally into harmony with each other, for they coincide in essentials and the differences are not such that they either endanger the historical value of Acts or necessitate an earlier dating of Galatians'?[2] There is, of course, no simple answer to this question. We have rejected several attempts to defend the total reliability of Acts 15 and we have found that in parts Luke was mistaken. He got the number of Paul's journeys to Jerusalem muddled; he has added the decree and letter where they do not belong; and he has ascribed to Peter and James speeches which, at least in their Lukan form, they did not make. These differences are considerable and they show that the early controversies have been to some extent glossed over. But there is nothing to suggest that Luke is being deliberately polemical. There is no room for the Tübingen School view that Acts 15 is the *locus classicus* for Luke's cold-blooded perversion of the facts as he knew them. Rather, they have the appearance of genuine mistakes, which Luke made as a result of his ignorance of Gala-

[1] Haenchen, *Apg.*, pp. 404f; Dibelius, *Acts*, pp. 99f; O'Neill, *Acts*, pp. 94f; Schmithals, *James*, p. 28. Dibelius sums this view up: 'Luke's treatment of the event is only literary-theological and can make no claim to historical worth.'

[2] Wikenhauser, *Apg.*, p. 178.

tians and of the details of the Council, and because of the vagueness of his sources. Writing a considerable time after the event, Luke inevitably had a different perspective from Paul, whose version was written passionately, in the heat of controversy. Also, Gal. 2 is not straight history: it is at times a simplification and it mixes historical report with references to the contemporary situation in Galatia.[1] When Luke wrote many of the original controversies were forgotten. He knew of the controversy over circumcision and he knew that, despite strong pressure, the Jerusalem leaders accepted the Gentiles without circumcision; and, looking back, this was the significant result of the Council. Therefore, the fact that he relates this, together with some other correct details, shows that Luke's account cannot be abandoned altogether as historically worthless. Certainly, Luke has written up the event and used it to express some of his main themes, and to this extent Haenchen and Dibelius are justified in emphasising Luke's role. But this does not exclude *a priori* that Luke had access to sources which, in some points, were reliable. Nor does it mean that he attempted to alter the facts as he knew them. When his facts ran out, Luke sometimes guessed; but his guesswork was aimed at producing a reliable, rounded and intelligible account and not a tendentious perversion of history.

[1] Haenchen, *Apg.*, pp. 406f; Hahn, *Mission*, p. 80 n. 1.

CHAPTER 8

PAUL'S SPEECH ON THE AREOPAGUS

In this chapter we shall concentrate on the famous speech to the Gentiles at Athens (Acts 17: 22f). The speech at Lystra (Acts 14: 15–17), like the Areopagus speech, is addressed to 'pure' Gentiles, that is, those who have had no previous contact with Judaism. The speech at Lystra is considerably shorter than the Areopagus speech. Also, it raises fewer exegetical problems and its language is more clearly dependent on the LXX. Consequently, it will be dealt with mainly insofar as it throws light on Acts 17: 22f. As well as a detailed discussion of Acts 17: 22f, we shall try to discover clues both to Luke's understanding of the religious status of Gentiles over against Jews and Christians, and to his views on the methods to be used by Christian missionaries to the Gentiles.

THE CONTEXT OF THE SPEECH

It appears that for Luke Athens was the symbol of Greek culture.[1] He is not concerned simply with the mission at Athens, but also with the way in which this signifies the overall approach of the Church to the pagan world. Similarly, though he singles out the Stoics and Epicureans for special mention, this does not mean that the speech's appeal is limited to them; rather they represent the two main views held in Greece at that time. Luke is not concentrating solely on the propagation of the gospel to the intellectual aristocracy of the pagan world; rather, he is addressing himself to the popular philosophies, the *Volksglaube* of the average Greek. The philosophers, like Athens itself, are used as symbols of a wider reality.

In the first century A.D. Athens was the centre of Greek life and piety. Luke's description of the city is vivid and realistic, but whether it is the result of a visit there or whether it is based

[1] Haenchen, *Apg.*, p. 466.

on literature and popular belief, is difficult to say.[1] Paul's immediate reaction on seeing the various idols is one of perplexity; but however distasteful they appeared to him, when he begins to speak with the philosophers his rebuke of their idolatry and polytheism is relatively mild (cf. vv. 16, 22). This is chiefly because the preamble to the main speech (vv. 22-3) is a *captatio benevolentiae*,[2] an attempt to establish some rapport with his audience rather than antagonise them at the outset with a violent attack on the falsity of their religious faith and practices.

His audience at first misconstrue Paul's reference to Jesus and his Resurrection, possibly imagining that he was the envoy of a new pair of deities.[3] Paul responds to the Athenians' legendary curiosity and takes as his starting point an altar 'to an unknown god'. Examination of both literary and archaeological evidence has brought to light no parallel to this inscription.[4] The closest we get to it are inscriptions to 'unknown gods',[5] which were probably made through fear that, in ignorance, a deity might be denied the homage due to him; such inscriptions would placate the wrath which might otherwise be inflicted on men. There are three possible explanations open to us: first, it may be that there was such an altar, which has not yet been unearthed, and that Luke's reference to it is correct; second, Luke may have made a genuine mistake, that is, knowing there were altars to 'unknown gods' in Athens, he assumed that individual altars were to single deities; or third, Luke may have made a deliberate alteration in order to create a convenient starting point for Paul's rebuke of pagan idolatry and pantheism.[6]

---

[1] Haenchen, *Apg.*, p. 457, quotes A. D. Nock's review of Dibelius, *Acts*, (*Gnomon*, 25 (1953), 506): 'Brilliant as is the picture of Athens, it makes on me the impression of being based on literature, which was easy to find, rather than on personal observation.'

[2] Conzelmann, *Apg.*, p. 97, and 'The address of Paul on the Areopagus', *SLA*, pp. 217f, here p. 220; H. Hommel, 'Neue Forschungen zur Areopagrede', *ZNW*, 46 (1955), 145f, here 159.

[3] They may have taken 'Anastasis' to be a female deity, the consort of Jesus.

[4] Dibelius, *Acts*, pp. 39f; Conzelmann, *Apg.*, p. 98; Gärtner, *Areopagus*, pp. 242-7.

[5] E.g. Pausanias, I. 1. 4f; Philostratus, *Apoll.* VI. 3.

[6] It is unclear where Paul gave the speech and whether Luke was thinking of a trial before the Athens court. See Haenchen, *Apg.*, p. 456; Gärtner, *Areopagus*, p. 64.

THE CONTENT OF THE SPEECH

Studies of Acts 17: 22f fall broadly into two camps. For some, the whole speech is foreign to both Old and New Testaments, an isolated outcrop of Stoic philosophy in a Jewish-Christian landscape. M. Dibelius is the most consistent advocate of this view, though his views, in a modified form, have been accepted by many since.[1] The other main stream of scholars have rejected Dibelius' philosophical interpretation and insisted that, although the language of Acts 17 may have a Stoic-philosophical ring, the ideas behind it are wholly based on the Old Testament and Judaism. B. Gärtner has argued this view at the greatest length and many have since followed his interpretation.[2] Before either of these extreme views was propagated, E. Norden proposed that the speech was predominantly based on Jewish-Christian thought, but has a secondary Stoic element. He was thus the precursor of those recent scholars who avoid the extreme views of Dibelius and Gärtner and point to the parallel ideas in both Jewish and Greek thought.[3] This mediating position will be confirmed in the following study, but the question will be raised again after a look at the details of the speech.

Vv. 24–5 God the Creator. The phrase ὁ θεὸς ὁ ποιήσας τὸν κόσμον καὶ πάντα τὰ ἐν αὐτῷ, οὗτος οὐρανοῦ καὶ γῆς ὑπάρχων Κύριος is a mixture of Jewish and Greek thought. The language used takes advantage of the convergence of Jewish and Greek thought and language, particularly in Hellenistic Judaism. ποιέω is used by both Greek and Jewish writers about creation.[4] κόσμος is not a typically Old Testament word, but it was used by Philo and Josephus and here it is clarified by the use of the typically Old Testament phrase οὐρανοῦ καὶ γῆς.[5] The funda-

---

[1] Dibelius, *Acts*, pp. 26f; Vielhauer, 'Paulinism', pp. 36–7; W. Eltester, 'Gott und die Natur in der Areopagrede', *NS*, pp. 202f; M. Pohlenz, 'Paulus und die Stoa', *ZNW*, 42 (1949), 66f.

[2] Gärtner, *Areopagus*, pp. 146f; Williams, *Acts*, pp. 200f; Hanson, *Acts*, pp. 176f.

[3] E. Norden, *Agnostos Theos* (Leipzig–Berlin, 1913), pp. 3–83; Haenchen, *Apg.*, pp. 454f; Conzelmann, *Apg.*, pp. 96f; W. Nauck, 'Die Tradition und Komposition der Areopagrede', *ZTK*, 53 (1956), 11f.

[4] Gen. 1: 1, 3: 14; Is. 42: 5; II Macc. 7: 28; Plato, *Tim.* 28c, 76c; Epictetus, IV. 7. 6.

[5] Gärtner, *Areopagus*, pp. 171f. 'Cosmos' is not used pejoratively here (contrast Jn 12: 31, 14: 30, 16: 11). The use of 'cosmos' and 'heaven and

mental ideas behind v. 24 are Jewish, possibly based on Is. 42:
5, with echoes of Gen. 1: 1f, but the language seems deliberately
chosen to be intelligible also to Greeks. The opening phrase of
the speech at Lystra (θεὸν ζῶντα) also has a biblical ring to it,
and on the whole the language and style follow those of the LXX
more closely than Acts 17. The opening phrase of the Areopagus
speech sets the pattern for what follows. The language is sometimes typically Jewish and sometimes typically Greek; frequently
it is ambiguous and open to both interpretations. Also, we shall
find that the Greek elements in Acts 17 often appear not to be
directly dependent on Greek thought, but to have been
mediated through the usage of Hellenistic Judaism.

Three conclusions are drawn from the assertion about God in
v. 24a. First, he οὐκ ἐν χειροποιήτοις ναοῖς κατοικεῖ, οὐδὲ ὑπὸ
χειρῶν ἀνθρωπίνων θεραπεύεται. The general tenor of this statement is Jewish: the false localisation of God in the Temple
(Is. 66: 1–2; Sib. Or. 4. 8; cf. Acts 7: 48); and the attack on
idols as things made by men's hands (Dt. 4: 28; Is. 2: 8, 31: 7,
37: 19; II Chron. 32: 19; Philo, *Dec.* 51, *Post. Cain.* 166,
Spec. Leg. 1. 22). But such attacks on false religion were common among the Greeks too and, in particular, the application
of χειροποίητος to the Temple is more characteristic of Greek
than of Jewish and Christian thought.[1] Luke is using ideas
familiar to both Jews and Greeks, though the grounds for the
condemnation of v. 24b are Jewish rather than Greek, namely
that as Lord and Creator of the universe God cannot be confined to one building or represented by idols.

Secondly, God is self-sufficient – οὐδὲ . . . προσδεόμενός τινος.
Dibelius claims that this is part of the Greek attempt to describe

earth' is probably only a linguistic variation (of which Luke is fond),
using language familiar to both Jews and Greeks. Gärtner thinks the
phrase πάντα τὰ ἐν αὐτῷ is an 'explanatory rider' to stop the audience
from misinterpreting the familiar terminology with an alien mode of
thought.

[1] Gärtner, *Areopagus*, p. 211, claims that χειροποίητος used of the Temple
is an Old Testament idea. But he can point to only one example (Is. 16:
12 LXX) and that is not applied to the Temple but to Moab's sanctuary.
He also thinks Mk 14: 58 is the source of both Stephen and Paul's attacks
on the Temple; this may be so, but it is also likely that the pair χειροποίητος and ἀχειροποίητος were added to the original saying at a later
date.

God in a series of negative statements.[1] Certainly, straightforward claims of God's αὐτάρκεια are typical of Greek literature.[2] But there is also a Jewish tradition which speaks of the self-sufficiency of God, from which it is concluded that God needs neither sacrifice nor prayer.[3] Probably there are echoes of both notions in Acts 17: 25, since it is not an exact replica of either: it is not an independent, straightforward statement of God's self-sufficiency and, although the general context is one of worship, it is not concluded, as it is in the Jewish parallels, that God does not require sacrifice and prayer.

Finally, in contrast to God's self-sufficiency, it is said that he gives to all ζωὴν καὶ πνοὴν καὶ τὰ πάντα. The phrase ζωὴν καὶ πνοήν recalls Gen. 2: 7; Wisd. 1: 7, 14, but again it is language which would be familiar to Greeks.

Vv. 26–27a. God and the nations or natural revelation? Of all the verses in the Areopagus speech none is more important or more obscure, or provokes more diverse interpretations than v. 26. The syntax is obscure and the vocabulary ambiguous: nor is it clear how the verse should be related to what precedes and follows it. It is the crux for both the 'Jewish' and 'Greek' interpretations of the whole speech.

The relationship between ἐποίησεν, κατοικεῖν and ζητεῖν is unclear. Dibelius translates, 'he created . . . both to dwell and to seek', that is, both infinitives are infinitives of purpose standing parallel to each other.[4] Pohlenz objects that it is extremely harsh to have two parallel, final infinitives standing side by side and that as parallels they have no inner connection; also, God did not create man to live *and* seek, but to seek and therefore to dwell.[5] He prefers, therefore, to translate ἐποίησεν in a 'neutral' manner ('he caused to dwell'), ζητεῖν being the sole infinitive of purpose. But although Dibelius' interpretation is harsh, it is still possible Greek and, since ποιήσας in v. 24 means 'created', it is probable that ἐποίησεν in v. 26 also means 'create'. And if there is a reference to Adam in the phrase ἐξ ἑνός, this would

---

[1] Dibelius, *Acts*, pp. 43f; Hommel, 'Areopagrede', p. 160; Norden, *Agnostos*, pp. 13f.

[2] Plutarch, *Moral.* 1052d; Plato, *Tim.* 33d, 34b; Seneca, *Epist.* 95. 47.

[3] Ps. 50: 8–13; II Macc. 14: 35; III Macc. 2: 9f; Jos. *Ant.* VII. 111; Philo, *Spec. Leg.* I. 271.

[4] Dibelius, *Acts*, pp. 28f; Conzelmann, *Apg.*, p. 99; Gärtner, *Areopagus*, p. 153.

[5] Pohlenz, 'Paulus', pp. 84f; Eltester, 'Areopagrede', p. 211 n. 13.

further confirm Dibelius' interpretation by giving another link with the Genesis narratives. Thus we can read κατοικεῖν and 3ητεῖν as both being dependent on ἐποίησεν, expressing a dual purpose in the creation of men.[1] The phrase ἐξ ἑνὸς πᾶν ἔθνος ἀνθρώπων is equally ambiguous. There may be a reference to Adam in ἐξ ἑνός,[2] but the Jews were not alone in possessing theories of an *Urmensch* and Luke has probably deliberately left the phrase vague to allow for Greek ideas as well. Some take πᾶν ἔθνος ἀνθρώπων to mean 'all nations of men',[3] while others translate it 'mankind', 'the whole human race'.[4] The end result of both translations is the same, but the former is said to have a more biblical ring, whereas the latter is neutral and therefore more suited to the philosophical interpretation of the whole verse. If the difference is real, which is doubtful, it is too slight to help prove one or the other interpretation; rather, it is itself dependent on this interpretation.

The two most difficult words in v. 26 are καιρούς and ὁροθεσίας in the phrase ὁρίσας προστεταγμένους καιρούς καὶ τὰς ὁροθεσίας τῆς κατοικίας αὐτῶν. Several interpretations have been proposed:

(a) Gärtner argues in detail that καιρούς means 'epochs of history' and ὁροθεσίας 'national boundaries'.[5] God is Lord not only of creation, but also of history, and not just the history of the Jews, but the history of all men. This idea of God is based on the Old Testament and can best be illustrated from Daniel (cf. Dt. 32: 8; I Enoch 89–90; Lk. 21: 24), where the history of nations is seen as divided into divinely ordained epochs. This view emphasised that v. 26 is a proclamation of God's character

---

[1] Gärtner, *Areopagus*, p. 154, calls them the 'material' and 'spiritual' sides of creation.

[2] Gärtner, *Areopagus*, pp. 151f, 230f, makes much of the implied Adam–Christ parallel in Acts 17. But if Luke had intended this he would surely have made the reference to Adam less ambiguous. Gärtner compares Acts 17 with Rom. 5, but in Acts 17 no mention is made of the connection between Adam and sin, which is the basis of the treatment of Adam in Rom. 5.

[3] Nock, *Gnomon*, 25 (1953), 507f.

[4] Dibelius, *Acts*, p. 28; Nauck, 'Areopagrede', p. 21; Haenchen, *Apg.*, p. 462; Pohlenz, 'Paulus', pp. 86f.

[5] Gärtner, *Areopagus*, pp. 147f; K. Lake, *B.C.*, IV, 216; Williams, *Acts*, p. 204; Hanson, *Acts*, pp. 179f; Wikenhauser, *Apg.*, p. 204.

and not a proof of his existence; it is about the relation of God to history and not about his control of nature. Pohlenz argues for this interpretation also, but he believes that there is a proof of God's existence here, which uses the familiar Greek argument *e consensu gentium*.[1] This was, briefly, that despite the variety of nationality, culture and religion in the human race, they all shared in a common belief, namely that God exists, and that this consensus of opinion constituted a proof of God's existence.[2]

(b) Dibelius challenges this historical interpretation and offers in its place a philosophical one, which he believes amounts to a proof of God's existence from nature.[3] He translates καιροί as 'the seasons of the year' and ὁροθεσίαι as 'zones'. By the latter he means the notion that the universe consists of five zones, only two of which were fit for human habitation. By some this fact was observed gratefully, since the Deity had made these two zones differ favourably from the others (Vergil, *Georg.* I. 237f; Cicero, *Tusc. Disp.* I. 28. 68f).

(c) Eltester, finding neither of these views satisfactory, offers yet another explanation of the two words.[4] He agrees with Dibelius that καιροί refers to the seasons of the year and produces evidence which he thinks shows that, in the Koine, καιροί could be a synonym for ὧραι, the more usual word for 'seasons'. He rejects Dibelius' interpretation of ὁροθεσία, however, and argues that the reference is to the boundaries between the sea and the dry land which God has clearly fixed. This idea ultimately reaches back to the ancient creation myth, where God struggles with and overcomes the watery chaos. Thus God has made a habitable earth, which he has separated by boundaries from the watery chaos. By giving fruitful seasons (Acts 14: 16) and dry land God has given all that is essential for men to live. For proof, Eltester points to Old Testament material (Ps. 73: 12–14, 88: 9–11; Prov. 8: 28–9; Jer. 5: 22; and especially Ps. 73: 16–17 and Jer. 38: 36, where the two motifs are combined), and

---

[1] Pohlenz, 'Paulus', pp. 86f.

[2] H. J. Cadbury, 'Lexical notes on Luke–Acts', *JBL*, 44 (1925), 219f, argues for a temporal translation for the whole phrase under discussion, rather than one category being interpreted spatially and the other temporally.   [3] Dibelius, *Acts*, pp. 28f.

[4] Eltester, 'Areopagrede', pp. 206f; followed by Stählin, *Apg.*, pp. 234–5; Hommel, 'Areopagrede', p. 162; Haenchen, *Apg.*, p. 461; Nauck, 'Areopagrede', pp. 15f.

to similar ideas in post-apostolic literature (*I Clem.* 20. 1–12, 33. 3; *Ap. Const.* VII. 34, VIII. 12). He also points to Lk. 21 : 25 where, in the picture of the End-time, chaos has a brief return to power.

(d) Conzelmann rejects all these views and argues that the 'historical'–'philosophical' alternative has been overplayed. On the basis of some Qumran texts collected by F. Mussner, he argues that Acts 17 : 26 presents an abstract view which is neither popular-Greek nor Jewish, but is based on a tradition where the events of both the natural universe and history are fused.[1]

After this brief summary of the main interpretations of v 26 we must now consider the evidence. καιροί is the crucial word, since ὁροθεσία is so rare that it is difficult to pin it down to a specific meaning. καιροί clearly is ambiguous and needs further definition. The attachment to προστεταγμένους is not much help, for the idea of fixation would fit with the translation 'seasons' or with the idea of epochs. The strongest support for the translation 'seasons' is the parallel in Acts 14 : 17, where καιροὺς καρποφόρους clearly refers to the seasons of the year. None of the other uses of the plural of καιρός in Luke–Acts is of much help in elucidating Acts 17 : 26. Lk. 21 : 24; Acts 1 : 7, 3 : 19 are all used in an eschatological context, which does not seem relevant to Acts 17 : 26. The objection to using Acts 14 : 17 as a parallel is that it is only the καρποφόρους which clarifies the meaning of καιροί; on its own, καιροί would not necessarily mean 'seasons'. Similar objections have been raised to the evidence which Dibelius adduces:[2] where καιροί means 'seasons' this is made clear either by an adjective or by the general context; on its own, no one without the help of Dibelius would take it to mean 'seasons'. Moreover, some of Dibelius' examples have ὧραι and not καιροί. Can we assume, with Eltester, that the two are synonymous? The evidence he produces is far from convincing.[3] Philo, *Op. Mund.* 59 is the clearest example, where in his comments on Gen. 1 : 14 Philo interprets καιροί to mean

[1] Conzelmann, *Apg.*, pp. 99–100, and *Areopagus*, pp. 222–3; F. Mussner, 'Einige Parallelen aus den Qumran-texten zur Areopagrede', *BZ*, 1 (1957), 125–50. Cf. IQH 1: 13f; IQM 12: 7; IQP Hab. 7: 12.

[2] Pohlenz, 'Paulus', pp. 86f; Gärtner, *Areopagus*, pp. 149f.

[3] Bauer, p. 395, Liddell and Scott, p. 859, and Moulton and Milligan, p. 315, give 'seasons' as only a minor meaning of καιροί, and the evidence they produce is slight. At all times the immediate or general context makes the meaning 'seasons' clear.

ὧραι, which is his usual word for 'seasons' (cf. *Spec. Leg.* I. 210). The LXX of Gen. I: 14 and Wisd. 7: 18 are both ambiguous; they may not mean 'seasons', but simply 'periods of time'. In *Ep. Diogn.* 4: 5 and *Apost. Const.* VII. 34. 2, 4 καιροί is used of 'seasons', but it is the context in both cases which makes this clear. It is true that καιροί is used for divisions of the natural (Ps. 103: 19) and cultic (Ex. 23: 14, 17; Lev. 23: 4; Gal. 4: 10; and *I Clem.* 40: 4) year and it is but a small step to use it for the 'seasons'. But the question is, was this step ever taken in popular usage? On the evidence available, the answer must be that it was a rare usage, always made clear by the context, and that it was not the meaning that would spring most readily to mind when the word was used without clarifying circumstances. Thus we must conclude that καιροί means 'periods of time' or 'epochs of history'.

As we have already noted, ὁροθεσία occurs so rarely that it is difficult to define it from extant parallels. Dibelius' interpretation of 'zones' has correctly been criticised. The fact that two of the zones were made habitable is a dubious proof of God's existence, for it could be used equally well to argue the opposite case. Moreover, Dibelius' view is contradicted by v. 26 itself, which says that God created men 'to live on all the face of the earth'. Eltester's view has much to recommend it, since he can point to a complex of Old Testament ideas which are widely evidenced.[1] Particularly striking are the LXX of Ps. 73: 16–17 and Jer. 38: 36, where the ideas of 'seasons' and 'boundaries' are linked. But apart from Lk. 21: 25, which is in an apocalyptic context, Luke does not elsewhere see the sea as an element of chaos, but simply as a part of God's creation (Acts 4: 24, 14: 15). Also, the Old Testament parallels, when they mention the notion of 'boundaries', generally speak of the 'boundaries of the land' or the 'bounds of the sea' and not, as in Acts 17: 26, the 'boundaries of their habitations'. Moreover, what little evidence we have shows that ὁροθεσία most naturally refers to the boundaries that divide nations.[2] Finally, the translation 'national

---

[1] It is insufficient for Gärtner to dismiss Eltester's view as meaningless in the context of 17: 24f, for by 'context' he seems to mean his own interpretation of the speech (*Areopagus*, p. 148).

[2] The one inscription we have seems to mean this – δικαίαν εἶναι ἔκριναν τὴν Ῥωδίων κρίσιν τε καὶ ὁροθεσίαν (*Inschr. v. Priene*, 42, 11, 8). Eusebius also

boundaries' fits better with our conclusions with regard to καιροί. What then is v. 26 saying? A proof of God's existence from nature is ruled out by our translation of καιροί and ὁροθεσίαι. This is also seen by Haenchen and Conzelmann even though they favour, as a whole or in part, the views of Eltester. The use of καταγγέλλω in 17: 23 also gives the speech a tone of pronouncement rather than proof.[1] There is considerable truth in Stählin's assertion that Paul 'stands not as a philosopher among philosophers, but as a prophet'.[2] Pohlenz's idea of an argument *e consensu gentium* reads into the text something that is not there. It implies that God implanted searching in all men in spite of their differentiation, and the text does not say that.[3] The parallels drawn from Qumran, while interesting, give one no reason to suppose that they have influenced the language or content of Acts 17: 26. Conzelmann is uncharacteristically vague when he concludes that v. 26 expresses an 'abstract idea' equivalent to neither Jewish nor popular-Greek thought and maybe combining 'historical' and 'natural' elements. 'Abstract idea' is too vague to be of use, and presumably Luke did not mean both 'seasons–land/sea boundaries' and 'epoch–national boundaries' when he wrote καιροί and ὁροθεσίαι. Therefore, we take the reference to be a historical one, expressing the ideas of the creation and control of men and nations by God. This idea of a God who is active in the events of history is fundamentally, though not exclusively, a biblical idea. The Greeks also thought of history as occurring in a series of epochs (Dionysius of Hal. I. 2; cf. preface to Appian's *Roman History*), but the basis for and style of their pronouncements are very different from the biblical notion of a God who actively participates in and plans the course of history.

The purpose of God's creation of men and nations is that they are 'to seek God'. This phrase has also sparked off very different interpretations. Dibelius claims that in the context of Acts 17 ζητεῖν does not have its typical Old Testament meaning of an

---

uses ὁροθεσία of national boundaries (*Demonstr. Evan.* IV. 9). Hippolytus uses it to mean 'river-bank', i.e. the boundary between the water and the land (*De Theoph.* 2).

[1] Gärtner, *Areopagus*, p. 152.   [2] Stählin, *Apg.*, p. 232.
[3] Conzelmann, *Areopagus*, p. 222.

act of will, trusting and obeying God, but rather its characteristic Greek meaning of seeking-out and examining what is
true.[1] It is difficult to choose between these two interpretations.
Luke may have been thinking of both views or, more probably,
he did not think about the matter systematically at all, but
simply used a word familiar to both Jewish and Greek religious
speculations.[2] Two factors give marginal support for the view
that the Old Testament-Jewish idea dominates here. First, the
object τὸν θεόν is more often connected with ζητεῖν in the LXX
than elsewhere, and means 'to turn to', 'to cleave to', or even
'to enquire about' God (which comes close to the Greek idea).
Second, since the Stoics believed that God could easily be in-
ferred from nature, the phrase εἰ ἄρα γε ψηλαφήσειαν αὐτὸν καὶ
εὕροιεν, which expresses an uncertainty about the end result of
the seeking, would be foreign to Stoic thinking. Thus while God
may have left clues in his Creation, it does not follow that men
will automatically recognise and correctly interpret them. The
rare εἰ + optative which hints at uncertainty, is strengthened if
we interpret ψηλαφῶ to mean 'grope' or 'fumble', for which
there is some evidence.[3] However, the word may have its more
usual meaning of 'grasp with the hands' or 'touch', which
Norden takes to be a Stoic term.[4]

Vv. 27b–28. The proximity of God and man. We come now to the
section which Norden thought to be the Stoic core of the Areopagus speech. Before analysing the individual statements it is
worth nothing that, in contrast to the material we have already
discussed, the total atmosphere and *Weltanschauung* of vv. 27b–
28 is that of Greek (Stoic) philosophy rather than of the Old
Testament and Judaism. This is made clear by the quotation of
Aratus, but is also true of the rest of the material. οὐ μακρὰν
ἀπὸ ἑνὸς ἑκάστου ἡμῶν ὑπάρχοντα has close parallels in Greek

[1] Dibelius, *Acts*, pp. 32f. Cf. Plato, *Apol.* 19b, 23b, *Rep.* 449a. For the Old
Testament view see Gärtner, *Areopagus*, pp. 155f, and cf. Dt. 4: 29; II Sam.
21: 1; Hos. 5: 15.
[2] H. P. Owen, 'The Scope of Natural Revelation in Rom. 1 and Acts 17',
NTS, 5 (1958–9), 135, thinks Luke means an intellectual search culminat-
ing in a living encounter. Haenchen, *Apg.*, pp. 461–2, thinks neither the
Old Testament nor the Greek idea lies behind 17: 26, but rather a vague
idea of 'intuition'.
[3] Gärtner, *Areopagus*, pp. 160f.
[4] Norden, *Agnostos*, pp. 15–17.

writings,[1] the closest being in Dio Chrysostom's Olympic Oration (*Discourses*, XII. 27–8; cf. Seneca, *Ep.* 41. 1, 120. 14; Jos. *Ant.* VIII. 108f). There is an overlapping idea found in the Old Testament (Dt. 4: 7, 30: 11; Ps. 139: 7f),[2] but there the emphasis is on God's readiness to help. Conzelmann may be right when he interprets the emphasis on God's nearness to man to mean that man's groping, fumbling and lack of faith cannot be blamed on God's distance from man.[3] He has left clues in his creation and those that follow them find that God is near.

The phrase ἐν αὐτῷ γὰρ ζῶμεν καὶ κινούμεθα καὶ ἐσμέν, is unparalleled in the New Testament. ζῶμεν, ἐσμέν and, in particular, κινούμεθα recall Stoic ideas.[4] Many interpret the phrase as an expression of the well-known cosmological concept of the close relation between God, man and the world.[5] Most of the examples from Greek literature speak of the Deity as permeating all things and not of men living ἐν αὐτῷ. But since they believed that God and man were virtually identical, one cannot make much of this distinction. The phrase as a whole is open to a monotheistic as well as a pantheistic interpretation, and any Jew hearing it would interpret it monotheistically, along the lines of Ps. 139.[6] But the Old Testament and Jewish notion of God's omnipresence is not the real background to this phrase. The closest parallels to ἐν αὐτῷ are found in the Hermetic literature (e.g. 5. 11), in Paul's phrase ἐν χριστῷ, and above all in I Jn 4: 13, 15, though it must be said that Paul's phrase is regularly ἐν χριστῷ and not ἐν θεῷ. The language of this phrase is basically Stoic, but it is improbable that Luke intended it to be understood pantheistically. The beginning of the speech (vv. 23f), which is monotheistic in tone, excludes this, but it is clearly an accommodation to the language of the audience. The language was

---

[1] Dibelius, *Acts*, pp. 47f; Haenchen, *Apg.*, p. 462; Conzelmann, *Apg.*, p. 100; Pohlenz, 'Paulus', p. 89.

[2] Gärtner, *Areopagus*, pp. 162–3; Hanson, *Acts*, p. 180.

[3] Conzelmann, *Apg.*, p. 104.

[4] H. Hommel, 'Platonisches bei Lukas. Zu Acta 17: 27a', *ZNW*, 48 (1957), 193f, has shown that it is unlikely that this phrase is a quotation from a Greek poet (*contra* Dibelius, *Acts*, p. 48).

[5] Norden, *Agnostos*, pp. 21f; Gärtner, *Areopagus*, pp. 105f, 177f.

[6] Gärtner's attempt to see the three verbs as synonymous and based on the Old Testament is not convincing.

probably so familiar to Luke that he did not give it systematic thought.

Similar conclusions arise from a consideration of the quotation from Aratus: τοῦ γὰρ καὶ γένος ἐσμέν (*Phaenomena* 5). Of all the statements in Acts 17 this is the one which is most readily interpreted pantheistically, not least because it is a direct quotation from a Stoic poet. The 'philosophical' element, if only linguistic, cannot be denied at this point. Strictly speaking, the notion that men are God's γένος contradicts the biblical creation narratives. But the fact that Aristobulus (Eusebius, *Praep. Ev.* XII. 12. 3f) uses the same quotation from Aratus to expound and maintain the biblical creation narrative shows that the phrase was open to a more Jewish, monotheistic interpretation. On hearing this quotation, a Christian or Jew would immediately associate the idea of the *imago Dei* in Genesis with the idea of relatedness to God in Aratus' γένος, though strictly speaking the two do not converge.[1] It is probable that Luke understood the phrase biblically, though how far he was aware of its pantheistic connotations is difficult to say. Certainly, it was not uncommon to quote an author out of context and use the quotation to support a view different from or even opposed to its original meaning.[2]

The point of the quotation from Aratus is to decry the representation of God by man-made idols; the οὖν of v. 29 makes this clear. Thus the quotation from Aratus is not used primarily, if at all, to reproduce Aratus' ideas on the relationship between God and man, but to attack idolatry and the false conception of God which underlies it.[3] Exactly how the quotation proves its point is unclear: the argument may be that because we are related to God we ought to know better than to think him adequately represented in stone or wood; or it may be that the common factor between God and man is that both have 'life', a quality conspicuously lacking in idols, and that it is therefore as absurd to portray God, as it is to portray man, in images.[4]

---

[1] Nauck, 'Areopagrede', pp. 22f.

[2] Gärtner, *Areopagus*, p. 193 n. 1.

[3] Thus Conzelmann is correct when he says that Luke is not interested in ontology in vv. 28–9, but in the origin of true service of God (*Apg.*, p. 101).

[4] Gärtner, *Areopagus*, pp. 166f. Conzelmann suggests that there is a confusion between Greek and Jewish thought in v. 29; the Jewish idea that the

The attack on images is, as we saw earlier, both a Jewish and a Greek phenomenon; and here, as in vv. 24–5, the basis for this attack on idolatry is a mixture of both elements. The difference is that in vv. 24–5 the Old Testament notion of the one God, Lord and Creator, is the chief motivation of the attack, whereas here the Greek idea of the relatedness of God and man dominates the scene. In this context it is also worth noting the impersonal designation for God in v. 29 (τὸ θεῖον) and the neuter locution in v. 23, both of which are more Greek than Jewish, though both Philo and Josephus use τὸ θεῖον.

Vv. 30–1. Resurrection and judgement. We come finally to the only 'Christian' part of the Areopagus speech, and even here Christ is mentioned only indirectly in v. 31 (ἐν ἀνδρί). The mention of the ignorance (τῆς ἀγνοίας) of the Gentiles, which God has overlooked (ὑπεριδών), recalls other passages in Acts where the same motif is used with reference to both Jews and Gentiles (3: 17, 13: 27, 14: 16). The significance of τῆς ἀγνοίας is unclear: for Dibelius the word means primarily intellectual ignorance and involves a positive assessment of the Greek's religiosity;[1] but for Gärtner the word is loaded with Old Testament connotations, making it almost equivalent to the word 'sin' and implies not tolerance, but positive condemnation of Greek idolatry and religion.[2] Moreover, on the one view μετανοεῖν means primarily a turning from ignorance to knowledge and on the other view it means a turning from sin to grace. Gärtner is justified in noting the implied condemnation of the Greek's previous existence in μετανοεῖν and κρίνειν, but this does not mean that we can interpret 'ignorance' as equivalent to 'sin'. One cannot off-load on to Acts 17: 30 the total connotations of the Old Testament idea of ignorance; if Luke had meant 'sin', there is a perfectly good Greek word he could have used. Moreover, v. 30 (and v. 23) lacks both a catalogue and condemnation of the vices of the Gentiles such as we find in parallel passages (cf. Rom. 1: 18f); to this extent v. 30 is mild and conciliatory. Even so, the very use of ἄγνοια, whichever interpretation we

Creator should not be portrayed by his creatures and the Greek critique of images on the grounds that living things cannot be represented by the non-living (*Areopagus*, pp. 224f).

[1] Dibelius, *Acts*, pp. 53f, 60f; Pohlenz, 'Paulus', pp. 95–6; Nauck, 'Areopagrede', pp. 33–4.
[2] Gärtner, *Areopagus*, pp. 233f.

give to it, implies some form of condemnation. The clue seems to lie in v. 23: here it is said that the Greeks worship God but do not know him, while in the following verses the expression of their worship – the idols and images – are shown to be false. There is both a positive assessment of their religiosity and worship and a positive condemnation of their idolatry. There is a mixture of both tolerance and reproof, conciliation and rebuke. The Gentiles have been misguided, but their ignorance is an excuse. But now (τὰ νῦν), after the coming of Christ, a new era has dawned, at the close of which God will judge the world. The world and mankind are no longer regarded as to their being, but as to their end. The course of world history is now seen to be heading for the final Resurrection and judgement, which have been confirmed by Jesus' Resurrection. Judgement is indisputably on its way though, as in the rest of Acts, it is not said to be near. Although the transition from vv. 24f to vv. 30–1 is abrupt, this does not mean that vv. 28–9 form the climax of the speech and that vv. 30–1 are an anticlimactic addition. The reference to judgement is the motif which underlies the Gentiles' urgent need to turn from ignorance to worship of the one true God. And while the earlier parts of the speech do have independent value, they also serve to underline and explain the parenetic ending.[1]

THE ORIGIN OF THE SPEECH

It is clear from what has been said above and from most modern studies that Acts 17 (and to some extent Acts 14: 15–17) is closely connected with, if not directly dependent on, the amalgam of Jewish and Greek thought found in Hellenistic Judaism. Almost all the more Greek elements in Acts 17 are paralleled in the writings of Hellenistic Judaism and in other Christian writers dependent on Hellenistic Judaism.[2] It is likely, therefore, that Acts 17 is dependent not directly on Greek thought, but on that thought as mediated through Hellenistic Judaism.

---

[1] Nauck, 'Areopagrede', p. 31: 'The statements about creation and the universal authority of God have an ancillary function and are aimed at the paranetical conclusion of the speech, where the way of deliverance is indicated in the exhortation to repentance.'

[2] Nauck, 'Areopagrede', pp. 11f. Conzelmann notes (*Apg.*, p. 103) that many of the central Stoic themes are missing from Acts 17, which makes direct dependence less likely.

Norden compared Acts 17 with a broad type of literary mission-speech (cf. Ps. Clem. 1. 7; Sib. Or. 1. 150f; *Corp. Herm.* 1. 27f, 8. 1f) and believed it to be a literary imitation of a speech of Apollonius of Tyana, which originated in the second century A.D. and was interpolated into Acts. The latter notion has rightly found no general assent, but his comparison with some of the Jewish and early Christian writings was the first step towards later, more detailed studies. Many of Norden's parallels are too vague and he does not allow sufficiently for the differences between Acts 17 and the parallel literature; also, it has become clear that Acts 17 must be treated as a whole unit and not as a jumble of individual ideas. This approach has been worked out most exhaustively by W. Nauck. He sees a basic threefold structure underlying both early post-apostolic literature (*I Clem.*, *Epist. Apost.*, and *Apost. Const.*) and Jewish missionary literature (Sib. Or. and Aristobulus). This threefold pattern of God's *creatio*, *conservatio* and *salvatio*, is thought by Nauck to be the basic structure of Acts 17: 22f. Thus he believes that 'Luke has concentrated into the smallest possible space the most important motifs which were employed in Jewish and Christian missionary sermons to Gentiles and has given, in this way, an "illustrative excerpt"[1] of a typical Gentile sermon'.[2] But the threefold pattern which Nauck sees in Jewish and Christian propaganda is not a consistent pattern which thoroughly pervades these writings. Often it seems that the pattern does not emerge naturally from the text itself, but is imposed on it by Nauck. Moreover, as Conzelmann notes, the analogy breaks down at the middle point, for none of the parallel texts have the theme of the proximity of God and man (Acts 17: 27–9) as their central section.[3] The placing of this anthropological section in the centre is an innovation; the ideas are not new, but nowhere else is this viewpoint bracketed between two other basic themes as in Acts 17.

However, Nauck's valuable study has shown that the ideas and literature current in Hellenistic Judaism and post-apostolic Christianity give the closest parallels we have to the structure and ideas of Acts 17. This is what we would expect from our study of the details of the speech For it became clear that the

---

[1] H. J. Cadbury, *B.C.*, v, 407.   [2] Nauck, 'Areopagrede', p. 36.
[3] Conzelmann, *Areopagus*, pp. 226–7.

fundamental motif of the speech is Jewish-Christian, whereas the Stoic element is secondary.[1] The beginning and end of the speech is basically Jewish-Christian, but the language used would have been intelligible to Greeks as well. The middle section (vv. 27b–29a) is basically Stoic, but the language used is sufficiently ambiguous for a Jew or Christian to give it a monotheistic, biblical interpretation. Moreover, the bracketing of these Stoic motifs within a monotheistic pattern of belief means that these motifs undergo a shift of meaning, since they cannot be interpreted in isolation.

However, this view is largely dependent on the acceptance of Acts 17 as a literary work of Luke's rather than as a speech of Paul. For if we consider Acts 17 to be a genuine record of a speech by Paul to pagans, the question is further complicated by our having to imagine the response of his audience. Although we can analyse Acts 17 for its Jewish and Greek elements, arguing for the primacy of one or the other, if the language is often capable of a Stoic interpretation, then presumably that is the way Paul's audience would have understood it (until they got to v. 31), and Paul would know this. It is to this problem of the Pauline origins of Acts 17 that we must now turn.

Between them, Gärtner and Nauck have made the best possible case for the Pauline origins of Acts 17.[2] Gärtner lists the reasons why he thinks that a speech very much like Acts 17: 22f was spoken by Paul at Athens: our knowledge of Paul is limited and Acts 17 does not contradict what we do know of Paul's teaching; Acts 17 has pre-Lukan elements – the setting, context and altar inscription; the theme of natural revelation is the same in Acts 17 and Rom. 1, that is, it is shown to be untrustworthy and often leads to ignorance and idolatry; the critique of idolatry is the same as in the Old Testament, Judaism and Romans 1; and finally, the universalism of Acts 17, with its parallelism between Adam and Christ, is thoroughly Pauline. Most defenders of the Pauline origin of Acts 17 admit that the language is not Pauline, but they explain this as a result par-

---

[1] Norden, *Agnostos*, pp. 3f; Haenchen, *Apg.*, pp. 460f; Conzelmann, *Apg.*, p. 103; Nauck, 'Areopagrede', pp. 31–2.

[2] Gärtner, *Areopagus*, pp. 248f; Nauck, 'Areopagrede', pp. 36f; Hanson, *Acts*, p. 182; Williams, *Acts*, p. 201; Wikenhauser, *Apg.*, p. 211. Stählin (*Apg.*, pp. 239f) and Eltester ('Areopagrede', p. 227) are less sure, but do not exclude the possibility of a Pauline origin.

tially of Paul's accommodation to the language of his audience and partially of Luke's influence. Also, those who recognise that the polemic against idolatry in Acts 17 is milder than Rom. 1 explain it as the result of a missionary situation, where the aim is not to antagonise, but to establish rapport with, the audience. Nauck adds to these arguments a further interesting suggestion, namely that where in details and emphasis Luke differs from Paul, this is because he was influenced more by 'liberal' Jewish missionary propaganda, whereas Paul was more in line with the 'conservative' element. The 'liberal' view is found in Aristobulus and the 'conservative' view in the Sibylline Oracles.[1]

Most of the arguments which Gärtner offers are convincing only to those who accept his overall interpretation of the speech. As we shall see, it is debatable whether Acts 17 does not contradict Rom. 1, or whether the assessment of Gentiles' pre-Christian religion is the same. And although the setting of the speech may be pre-Lukan, this is no argument for the pre-Lukan, even less the Pauline, origin of the speech itself. Frequently Luke seems to have had reliable tradition about the setting of events, but has constructed a speech which he thinks fits the situation. Also, Gärtner's emphasis on an Adam–Christ parallel in Acts 17 is unwarranted; if Luke had intended this he would presumably have made an unambiguous reference to Adam.

Moreover, there are several differences between Acts 17 and Paul's writings which suggest that Paul was not the author of the Areopagus speech.[2] First, the use of the knowledge of God implied in nature is used differently in Luke and Paul. Paul does not expound this knowledge as if to construct a natural theology. It has no independent value for him, but is merely one stage in his total argument. It is adduced to justify God's condemnation of all men: the Jews are without excuse, since they have the Law; the Gentiles are equally culpable, as they have had the revelation of God in nature. Paul can conclude, therefore, that 'all who have sinned without the Law will also perish without the Law, and all who have sinned under the Law will be judged by the Law' (Rom. 2: 12). The Gentiles could have responded to this revelation, but they did not respond; they worshipped the creature rather than the Creator. As a result, παρέδωκεν αὐτοὺς ὁ θεὸς . . . (Rom. 1: 24, 26, 28); and Paul

---

[1] Nauck, 'Areopagrede', pp. 41f.   [2] Dibelius, *Acts*, pp. 58f.

underscores his point with a lengthy catalogue of Gentile vices. Luke also concludes that the Gentiles have not correctly interpreted this natural revelation, but the tone and emphasis are completely different. There is no castigation of Gentile immorality in Acts 17 and the interpretation of the Gentiles' response to the natural revelation is different from Paul's. For whereas Paul claims that the Gentiles knew God but did not honour him, Luke claims that they worship God but do not know him. The one view emphasises the Gentiles' culpability, while the other interprets their basic response as correct but misguided. Paul's is a passionate condemnation, while Luke's is a combination of magnanimity and admonition. Nor does Luke have any notion of God 'handing over' the Gentiles, which recurs like a refrain in Rom. 1: 18f; and the tone of the rebuke of idolatry is not, as it is in Rom. 1, indignant, but mild and conciliatory.

Second, the relationship between God and man, their proximity and relatedness, described in Acts 17: 27–9, is not typical of Paul. He can speak of Christians being 'in Christ', but when speaking of pagans he is deeply concerned to emphasise their estrangement from God (Rom. 1–3, 5: 10; II Cor. 5: 20–1).

Third, the two epochs, before and after Jesus, are characterised in Acts 17 as 'ignorance–knowledge', whereas for Paul they are characteristically described as 'sin–grace'. Nor does Acts 17 show any traces of the characteristic Pauline themes of justification, the wrath of God, Law, faith and works,[1] and a *theologia crucis*. Further, while Rom. 3: 25 is a parallel idea to Acts 17: 30, in Paul it is a passing reference, whereas Luke emphasises it by repeating it elsewhere.[2]

What then can we say about the question of the Pauline nature of Acts 17? The question is complicated by unknown factors. We are limited in our knowledge of Paul; in particular, his epistles are written mainly for Christians and it may be that he spoke differently when addressing pagans. Also, our assessment of the Pauline nature of Acts 17 will depend on the amount

---

[1] In Acts 17: 31 πίστις means 'proof' or 'assurance', which is not a Pauline usage.
[2] So Dibelius, *Acts*, pp. 58f; Haenchen, *Apg.*, pp. 466f; Pohlenz, 'Paulus', pp. 95–6; Hommel, 'Areopagrede', pp. 160f; Vielhauer, 'Paulinism', pp. 36–7.

of Greek influence we find in the speech, for on the whole those who defend the Pauline origin of Acts 17 interpret it along Jewish-Christian rather than Stoic lines. But even when allowance is made for these factors, it does seem improbable that Paul would have spoken in the way Luke says he did. The differences between Acts 17 and Rom. 1–3 are too great, and there is a limit to which the missionary situation can be used as an explanation of this. The language and style of Acts 17 are, not surprisingly, Lukan; but the divergence between the ideas of Acts 17 and Rom. 1–3 and the absence of Pauline themes militates against a specifically Pauline origin. This is not to say that there are no common ideas in the two sections. Luke and Paul stand in a common Christian tradition and share the same basic creed, so that we would expect some similarities. It is also true, as Nauck shows, that Luke and Paul stand in a common tradition influenced by Hellenistic-Jewish missionary practice. But this does not mean that Luke and Paul say the same things, for tradition develops and changes. And when Nauck, probably correctly, claims that Luke and Paul were influenced by different schools of thought in Hellenistic-Jewish missionary propaganda, it is not enough simply to call this a difference of emphasis, for there is also a difference of facts and ideas. Thus it seems that we must conclude that the Areopagus speech is a Lukan and not a Pauline product and that when he composed the speech, Luke was considerably influenced by the ideas and missionary methods of Hellenistic Judaism and the post-apostolic Church.

THE SPEECH AND THE GENTILE MISSION

Acts 14: 15–17 and 17: 22f are of immense value in assessing how Luke believed the preaching to the Gentiles should take place. Certainly, the Areopagus speech was for Luke an account of a unique historical occasion, when Paul took the gospel to the heart of Greek culture, Athens. It shows how, at one time, Paul dealt with Greek philosophers.[1] But the significance of the

---

[1] Conzelmann, *Areopagus*, p. 227, thinks Luke is addressing his readers: If Greek intellectuals were not converted by a sermon of Paul, they will not respond today. Thus the Church finds its own experience substantiated for they also found that intellectuals would not accept the gospel.

speech does not end there; the event has a broader implication too. It is more than an individual event, for it also gives an example of missionary preaching to the Gentiles. It is as much an answer to the question 'how is one to speak?' as to the question 'how did Paul speak on that occasion?'[1] As Stählin says, 'he wishes with this to give the classic example of a speech in which the attempt is made to bring the biblical message of God close to men to whom it is completely foreign and unintelligible'.[2] The fact that Paul's success at Athens was small does not stop Luke from using a golden opportunity to give the classic pattern for a Gentile mission sermon.[3] When Luke was writing, the Church was no longer recruiting steadily from Gentiles already connected with the synagogues, as in Paul's day, but from thoroughbred Gentiles. The starting point for missionary preaching, therefore, could not be that Gentile hearers have the same monotheistic presuppositions as the Jews, and Old Testament proof-texts would be irrelevant. Thus the speech begins at the point of natural revelation and, instead of quoting the Old Testament, uses a quotation from a Greek poet. Luke saw that Greek wisdom was open to a Christian interpretation, but he does not go to extremes. For the harmony of Old Testament and Stoic ideas does not extend as far as the centre of the Christian faith, namely the Resurrection, which is the contradiction of Greek wisdom.

'The view of revelation expressed in the Areopagus speech bears a pronounced universalistic stamp. No limits to the universal revelation are mentioned. God is presented as the God of the whole world.'[4] This is made clear from the start, when the natural revelation of God is seen to be based on the act of creation. God is Creator of the whole world and exerts his rule over both nature and history (vv. 24-6). The purpose of God's creation, that men should seek him, is universal, because it is based on creation (v. 26). Corresponding to this is the emphasis

---

[1] Dibelius, *Acts*, pp. 70-1; Haenchen, *Apg.*, pp. 467-8; Nauck, 'Areopagrede', p. 36.

[2] Stählin, *Apg.*, p. 241.

[3] The fact that the response to Paul's sermon was small does not mean Luke saw it as a failure. It is not so much a failure of Paul as a refusal of the Greeks. If Luke had thought it a failure, he would not have described it in such detail.

[4] Gärtner, *Areopagus*, p. 229.

on the revelation through Christ as being of universal validity. This is made abundantly clear in v. 30, τοῖς ἀνθρώποις πάντας πανταχοῦ, which corresponds to πᾶν ἔθνος ἀνθρώπων in v. 26. The revelation of Christ is as universal as the act of creation. This universalism is expressed in the frequent use of πᾶς and related ideas: God made the world and all that is in it – πάντα τὰ ἐν αὐτῷ (v. 24); he gives τὰ πάντα to all men – πᾶσι (v. 25); he creates from one all men (πᾶν ἔθνος ἀνθρώπων) to dwell on the whole earth (ἐπὶ παντὸς προσώπου τῆς γῆς) v. 26; he is never far from each one of us – ἑνὸς ἑκάστου ἡμῶν (v. 27); the gospel is proclaimed to all men everywhere – τοῖς ἀνθρώποις πάντας πανταχοῦ (v. 30), because Christ will judge the whole world – τὴν οἰκουμένην (v. 31). In contrast to this pronounced universalism there is no mention at all of the Old Testament *Heilsgeschichte* or of Israel as the chosen people of God – themes which are prominent in the speeches to the Jews. Instead, the past history of the Gentiles is evaluated as a pre-history of Christianity, and although it is made clear that the Gentiles have been ignorant and misguided, as is seen in their idolatry, this is no worse than the frequent lapses of the Jews in the Old Testament and at the time of Jesus and the early Church.

Luke's liberal and magnanimous assessment of the Gentiles' pre-Christian religiosity can be connected with his pragmatic justification of the Gentile mission which we have found elsewhere, particularly in the healing of the centurion's servant (Lk. 7: 1–10) and the conversion of Cornelius (Acts 10–11). While the Gentiles have been misguided and ignorant in their idolatry, this is no different from the comparable blindness and disobedience of the Jews. The Gentiles, although they lack the Law and the advantages of being part of the chosen people of God, have a religious attitude which can be positively evaluated. The average Gentile's response to God is no worse, though neither is it any better, than that of the average Jew. Also, Luke's generous assessment of the Gentiles' worship of God is very different from Paul's use of natural revelation in his total theological framework, where the themes of the righteousness of God and the justification of man predominate. While both have a theory of natural revelation, they use it in very different ways: Luke treats it as a theme of independent value and approaches it in a liberal, almost non-theological way; Paul uses it, in passing, as one point in the total argument of his massive and complex theological structure. Luke's assessment is positive and Paul's is negative: for Luke, the Gentiles' religiosity is the first stage on the way to salvation; for Paul, it is the basis for their condemnation by God.

CHAPTER 9

JEWISH AND GENTILE MISSIONS

In this section[1] we shall look in detail at a number of passages: Acts 2: 39, 3: 25–6, 13: 46–7, 15: 14–17, 18: 6, 28: 26–8. In all of these the problem of the relationship between the Jewish and Gentile missions is raised. At this stage we are concerned in particular with Luke's view, although a comparison with Paul at a later stage will attempt to show how near to or far from the historical facts Luke is. In dealing with these programmatic statements in Acts, in particular 28: 26–8, we shall also need to discuss the various theories concerning the ending of Acts.

PROGRAMMATIC STATEMENTS

Acts 2: 39

The phrase πᾶσιν τοῖς εἰς μακράν is ambiguous: it could refer to the Gentiles,[2] but in the context of Acts 2 probably refers to the Jews.[3] εἰς μακράν is best understood spatially (cf. Acts 22: 21; Is. 57: 19; Sir. 24: 32),[4] as a reference to Diaspora Jews contemporary with those being addressed, rather than as a reference to the future descendants of Peter's audience.[5]

Acts 3: 25–6

This is one of the most important verses for understanding Luke's view of the relationship between the Jewish and Gentile missions; unfortunately, its exact meaning is obscure. It is generally agreed that there is a reference to the future Gentile mission in the phrase πᾶσαι αἱ πατριαὶ τῆς γῆς and an allusion

---

[1] We shall not discuss all the journeys of Paul where he preaches to Gentiles, since this would involve a full-scale study of the whole of Acts 13–28. Apart from the sections already discussed, therefore, we shall limit ourselves to the programmatic statements about the Gentile mission and the general picture of Paul as a missionary to Jews and Gentiles.
[2] Wikenhauser, *Apg.*, p. 49.
[3] Williams, *Acts*, pp. 70f.
[4] Conzelmann, *Apg.*, p. 31; Haenchen, *Apg.*, p. 147.
[5] Stählin, *Apg.*, p. 54.

219

to it implied in the use of ὑμῖν πρῶτον (v. 26).[1] The problem is to discover the exact meaning of ἐν τῷ σπέρματί σου. The reference could be to Israel.[2] J. Jervell takes it in this way, interprets αἱ πατριαί τῆς γῆς to mean the Gentiles, and argues that the meaning of the verse is that through Israel, or at least the repentant part of Israel, blessing will come to the Gentiles: 'The addition of the Gentiles belongs to the re-establishment of Israel.'[3] This view, he claims, fits best both with the immediate context and with Luke's other uses of σπέρμα, all of which refer to Israel (Lk. 1: 55; Acts 7: 5–6, 13: 23).[4] This latter point has some validity, but apart from this he offers no compelling evidence for his view. Moreover, two things, in particular, give support to the view that σπέρμα refers to Christ and not Israel.[5] First, Luke's version of the blessing-of-Abraham saying does not accord exactly with any of those in the LXX. Gen. 22: 18, 26: 4 are the closest parallels, but in place of their πάντα τὰ ἔθνη τῆς

---

[1] Wilckens, *Missionsreden*, p. 43 n. 1, like most commentators, takes πρῶτον together with ὑμῖν and sees a hint of the future Gentile mission. πρῶτον presumably includes Jesus' ministry as well as the early mission of the Church (cf. Haenchen, *Apg.*, p. 169, who takes ἀναστήσας in v. 26 to refer to the Incarnation and not the Resurrection).

[2] Wikenhauser, *Apg.*, p. 62.

[3] J. Jervell, 'Das gespaltene Israel und die Heidenvölker', *St. Th.*, 19 (1965), 68f, here p. 87.

[4] Jervell, *ibid.*, argues that to take σπέρμα to mean 'Christ' does not fit the immediate context because then (a) v. 26a has no proper relation to v. 25b, (b) the Gentiles apppear suddenly, and only by implication, in πρῶτον (v. 26a), (c) αἱ πατριαί τῆς γῆς has an artificial effect, and (d) it is odd to find Christ called a descendant of Abraham when shortly before the Jews are called the descendants of the Patriarchs. However, point (d) is not compelling and the other points have force only if, with Jervell, we assume that if σπέρμα means 'Christ' then αἱ πατριαί means 'the Jews'. But there is no reason why σπέρμα should not mean 'Christ' and αἱ πατριαί τῆς γῆς 'all peoples', including Jews and Gentiles. Verse 26a then has a definite point, singling out the Jews as the first to receive universal blessing effected by Christ; also, αἱ πατριαί τῆς γῆς is no longer artificial and includes a reference to the Gentiles which prepares for the πρῶτον (v. 26a). Jervell himself is not wholly consistent, for having argued that σπέρμα means 'Israel' and that αἱ πατριαί refers exclusively to the Gentiles, he then goes on to suggest that in effect σπέρμα refers only to the repentant part of Israel, i.e. Jewish Christians, while the ambiguous αἱ πατριαί in reality includes unrepentant Jews as well as Gentiles.

[5] Hanson, *Acts*, p. 75; Haenchen, *Apg.*, p. 169; Stählin, *Apg.*, pp. 68–9; Dahl, 'Abraham', p. 149.

γῆς Luke has πᾶσαι αἱ πατριαὶ τῆς γῆς. Exactly where Luke's version originated is difficult to say,[1] but if he had wanted to show that by σπέρμα he meant Israel, then the use of πάντα τὰ ἔθνη, as in Gen. 22: 18 LXX, would have made his point clear. By using the ambiguous αἱ πατριαὶ τῆς γῆς he has merely obscured the point. In fact, Haenchen thinks that the use of αἱ πατριαὶ τῆς γῆς is deliberate, since the use of the LXX of Gen. 22: 18 would have anticipated the themes of chs. 10–11.[2] On the assumption that Luke knew the LXX of Gen. 22: 18, therefore, his alteration of it appears to emphasise that both the Gentiles and the Jews will be recipients of the blessing which will come in Abraham's 'seed'. That is, αἱ πατριαὶ τῆς γῆς refers to both Jews and Gentiles and σπέρμα to someone else – presumably Christ. The second point in support of this view is the close connection between vv. 25 and 26, in particular the echo of ἐνευλογηθήσονται (v. 25) in the εὐλογοῦντα of v. 26. Since the 'blessing' of v. 26 clearly comes through Christ, one could argue that the same is true of v. 25.[3] Thus on the assumption that Luke did consider the exact meaning of every word he wrote, it seems probable that he saw σπέρμα as a reference to Christ and αἱ πατριαὶ τῆς γῆς as including both Jews and Gentiles. On the other hand, if Luke was ignorant of the exact wording of the LXX versions of the saying, then Jervell's interpretation cannot be ruled out. Yet we may be building on a false assumption altogether, namely that Luke did consider the exact meaning of each word of the quotation. For Luke may have used it solely because it was a universalistic promise. He may have been interested only in the phrase πᾶσαι αἱ πατριαὶ τῆς γῆς and, consequently, may not have stopped to consider the precise meaning of σπέρμα. He may simply have wanted to ascribe to

---

[1] The use of πατριαί may be influenced by the LXX, cf. Ps. 21: 28, 95: 7, where πατριαὶ τῶν ἐθνῶν is used. Gen. 12: 3, 28: 14 use πᾶσαι αἱ φυλαί rather than Luke's πᾶσαι αἱ πατριαί. T. Holtz, *Untersuchungen über die Alttestamentlichen Zitate bei Lukas*, *TU*, 104 (Berlin, 1968), pp. 74–6, thinks Luke received the saying from the oral tradition of the Church and made his version up without knowing the exact wording of the LXX. He thinks Luke's version says the same as Gen. 22: 18 LXX, but this is partly because he does not consider the possibility of taking 'seed' to mean Christ.

[2] Haenchen, *Apg.*, p. 169.

[3] Cf. Dahl, 'Abraham', p. 150, commenting on Lk. 13: 16, 19: 9: 'Both stories illustrate how God's promise to Abraham was fulfilled to his children through the ministry of Jesus.'

Peter an allusion to the future Gentile mission, which he then qualifies by making it clear that the order is to be Jews first and then Gentiles (cf. Acts 1: 8, 13: 46; Rom. 1: 16).

Acts 13: 46–8

It is almost universally agreed among commentators[1] that these verses state that because the Jews rejected the gospel, the Church turned to the Gentiles. While the prior claim of the Jews had been recognised, their refusal of the gospel became a contributory, though not the primary (cf. chs. 10–11), cause of the Gentile mission. Verses 46–7, therefore, give the principle which forms the basis of the following scenes in Acts.[2] Against this view Jervell raises two objections:[3]

(a) Since in v. 47 the Gentile mission is justified from Old Testament prophecy, the Church must have known of the need for a Gentile mission long before the events of Acts 13; therefore the motivation for the Gentile mission was not the rejection of the gospel by the Jews. In v. 47 Is. 49: 6 is applied to the work of Paul and Barnabas; the σέ, Jervell argues, means 'Israel' – as represented by the Apostles, Paul and Barnabas.

(b) After the pronouncement of 13: 46–7 Paul and his fellow missionaries still go to the Jews (14: 1, 17: 1, 10, 17, 18: 4, 19: 8, 26, 28: 28). The response of the Jews is typically divided (vv. 43, 46), since not all of them reject the gospel. Only the unrepentant part of Israel are shut out; those who believe the gospel are gathered in. Luke is not saying that the Gentiles have been chosen to take the place of the unrepentant part of Israel, but that the influx of the Gentiles will occur because the promises to Israel are being fulfilled in the gathering-in of repentant Jews. Moreover, the judgement of 13: 46–7 refers only to Pisidian Antioch and is not universally applicable.

However, neither of these objections carries much conviction. The fact that the Gentile mission could be justified from the Old Testament does not exclude either the prior proclamation of the gospel to the Jews or the possibility that Jewish obduracy could

---

[1] Williams, *Acts*, p. 167; Hanson, *Acts*, p. 146; Wikenhauser, *Apg.*, p. 158; Haenchen, *Apg.*, pp. 356, 359–60; Stählin, *Apg.*, p. 186; Conzelmann, *Apg.*, p. 78.

[2] Dupont, 'Gentils', pp. 140–1.

[3] Jervell, 'Israel', pp. 88–90.

become an immediate cause of the Gentile mission. Both Luke and Paul see the order 'Jew first, then Greek' as fundamental in the practice of the early Church; but equally, they both see an organic connection between the Jews' refusal and the influx of the Gentiles. That Luke saw no contradiction between the idea that the Gentile mission was foretold in the Old Testament and that in practical terms the turning to the Gentiles was frequently a result of Jewish obduracy, is made clear by the fact that both themes are prominent throughout Acts and not just in ch. 13. Luke himself makes it clear that the Jews' refusal was not the primary motive of the Gentile mission (chs. 10–11), but it was nevertheless a major factor in later developments. Thinking back to the historical situation it might seem odd that the Church, aware of these Old Testament prophecies of a Gentile mission, should wait for the Jews' refusal before obeying them. But for the early Church and for Luke these prophecies were not causes of the Gentile mission so much as a justification of this mission after it had begun.

Jervell's second point is even less convincing. While he is correct in noting both that the Jews show a divided response and that after ch. 13 the missionaries still go to the Jews, neither of these observations justifies his interpretation of the passage as a whole. In effect, his interpretation is that Paul and Barnabas turn to the Gentiles as a result not of the Jew's rejection, but of their acceptance, of the gospel, whereas the plain meaning of vv. 46–7 is the exact opposite of this! Even if his forced interpretation of σέ in v. 47 were valid – which is improbable, since Luke surely sees Paul and Barnabas as representatives of Christ and the Church (13: 1f) and not of Israel – it would scarcely justify reversing the plain meaning of vv. 46–7.

There is a partial truth in Jervell's assertion that 13: 46–7 is limited to Pisidian Antioch, for this is its primary reference, as the subsequent narrative shows. But this does not exhaust the significance of the passage, for as Haenchen notes, it is also an ideal, typical scene which sums up the whole of the Pauline mission. It is a proleptic statement of the end result of Paul's missionary endeavours (28: 26–8). This helps to explain the apparent contradiction between v. 46 and the later mission to the Jews: 'The Jews in Antioch who become jealous of the Christians are, at the same time, the Jews in general; and the

ἔθνη who come to the synagogue in Antioch . . . are τά ἔθνη . . .
all those Gentile multitudes who flock into the Christian Church
and arouse the jealous resentment of the Jews.'[1]

Acts 15: 14–17

The quotation from Am. 9: 11f in Acts 15: 16–17 may give
another clue to Luke's understanding of the relationship
between the Jewish and Gentile missions. The main problem is
the interpretation of the phrase καὶ ἀνοικοδομήσω τὴν σκηνὴν
Δαυεὶδ τὴν πεπτωκυῖαν (v. 16). Some take the reference to be
to the Resurrection, the event which causes Gentiles to seek the
Lord.[2] However, it is equally possible, and perhaps more
natural, to take the phrase as a reference to the reconstitution
or salvation of Israel which will precede the influx of the Gentiles
(v. 17).[3] The Gentiles are grafted on to the root which is Israel:
the presupposition of the salvation of the Gentiles is the salvation of the Jews. This latter interpretation would be strengthened
if we accepted Dahl's interpretation of 15: 14.[4] He takes the
phrase ἐξ ἐθνῶν λαὸν τῷ ὀνόματι αὐτοῦ to mean that the new,
Gentile λαός are not a new people of God, but are grafted on to
the old people of God, namely Israel. That is, the Church,
which includes the Gentiles, is not thought of as a new Israel.
This notion that the conversion of the Gentiles is a fulfilment of
God's promises to Israel may be paralleled elsewhere in Acts,
for example in Acts 3: 25–6. It could be that at this point Luke
reflects the early Jewish-Christian view of the Church and
mission, for we have seen that at other points Luke's material
betrays primitive Christian views – even if he misunderstood
them. Certainly, Haenchen's interpretation of v. 16 as a reference to the Resurrection is scarcely warranted either by the

---

[1] Haenchen, *Apg.*, p. 360.
[2] Haenchen, *Apg.*, p. 389.
[3] Munck, *Paul*, p. 235; Wikenhauser, *Apg.*, p. 172; Jervell, 'Israel', pp. 79–
82. Stählin, *Apg.*, p. 204, says this verse shows 'that Israel forms the basis
of the new people of God and that the election of the Gentiles is meant in
the sense of a co-election'.
[4] Dahl, *NTS*, 4 (1957–8), 319–27. Cf. Dupont, *NTS*, 3 (1956–7), 47f, who
thinks ἐξ ἐθνῶν λαόν is a conscious paradox, a deliberate expansion of a
term normally restricted to the Jews to include the whole world. The
basis of both views is the apparently exceptional use of λαός in Acts 15:
14, 18: 10 to include the Gentiles, whereas normally in Luke it refers to
the Jews.

content or context of the verse.[1] However, one has to beware of ascribing to Luke views which may not have occurred to him. The two unusual uses of λαός may simply be due to Luke's carelessness. At other points Luke uses terms loosely and with no obvious theological subtleties in mind.[2] What for us may seem to be a conscious paradox may for Luke simply have been linguistic imprecision. It would be dangerous to build on Luke's use of λαός, whether we are claiming deliberate or unconscious motives to be at work. Moreover, the use of Am. 9: 11f may not be as significant as the above interpretation supposes. Luke may have seen the fulfilment of 15: 16 in the coming of the Messiah or in the role of the Twelve. Or, what is more probable, Luke may have used Am. 9: 11f solely because it contains a reference to the inclusion of the Gentiles.[3] He may want to show only that the Gentile mission is grounded in the Old Testament and therefore in the will of God; the reference to the relationship between Jews and Gentiles in this scheme may have been purely incidental and may have escaped Luke's notice. For this reason one has reservations about building much on this verse.

Acts 18: 6

This verse repeats the judgement pronounced in 13: 46–7. Paul leaves the Jews of Corinth with a symbolic act (cf. II Sam. 1: 16; Matt. 27: 25), which makes it clear that the Jews are themselves responsible for the judgement which will follow on their unbelief, and that Paul considers that he can now turn to the

---

[1] Haenchen, *Apg.*, p. 389, argues against the Jew–Gentile interpretation because it contradicts Luke's pattern of salvation-history. But Luke may unwittingly reflect the viewpoint of an earlier period and, furthermore, it is not certain that he had a clear or consistent view of the relation between the Church and Israel.

[2] Cf. the earlier treatment of the kingdom of God and Apostles in Acts.

[3] Holtz, *Lukas*, pp. 25–6, notes that whereas 15: 17 reproduces the LXX exactly, 15: 16 does not. He suggests that Am. 9: 11 (Acts 15: 16) circulated without v. 12 among those who believed in a restitution of Israel in a Davidic form. Luke got it from Jewish Christians, placed it appropriately in James' speech, but adds something which he himself had observed about it, namely that its continuation in Am. 9: 12 LXX contains a universal promise. Thus Luke uses a familiar Jewish prophecy to legitimise the Gentile mission simply by continuing the quotation. The basis for Holtz's view is that apart from 15: 16 all Luke's quotations from the Twelve prophets follow the LXX exactly.

Gentiles with a clear conscience. Here, as in 13: 46f, 28: 26f, the language is vivid and the tone severe.

Acts 28: 26–8

First in Asia Minor (13: 46), then in Greece (18: 6) and now finally in Italy we meet the same solemn judgement that, as a result of the Jews' refusal, Paul turns to the Gentiles. Thus in each of the main areas where, according to Luke, Paul carried out his missionary work, the same sombre pronouncement is made. Here Is. 6: 9–10 is used; it was probably one of the best-known testimonia for the Jews' rejection of the gospel (cf. Mk 4: 12f pars.; Jn 12: 39f; Just. *Dial.* 12. 2, 33. 1, 69. 4). Here, as in ch. 13, not all the Jews reject the gospel; ἐπείθοντο (v. 24) shows that some were persuaded.[1] But the accent does not lie here, as the subsequent verses show. This third explanation of the turning from the Jews to the Gentiles is final;[2] it is Luke's over-all assessment of the Jew's position. Its appearance at the end of the book gives it, and the parallel passages in 13: 46–7, 18: 6, a certain prominence, which emphasises their importance for Luke.[3] The threefold repetition does not mean that each has a purely local reference; such an interpretation misunderstands Luke's technique. For when Luke wishes to impress on his readers something he considers of prime importance he uses the simple but effective method of repetition, as we have already seen in the accounts of the conversions of Cornelius and Paul. Haenchen's summary cannot be bettered: 'With Acts 28: 28 the original situation before 13: 46 is not repeated, as if the gospel must first be announced to the Jews from now on. Much

---

[1] Jervell, 'Israel', p. 77 n. 21, is right to criticise Haenchen at this point. There is no warrant for Haenchen's statement (*Apg.*, p. 646) that 'with ἐπείθοντο Luke does not think of a real conversion, any more than in the analogous scene in 23: 9. Theoretically the Jews are not united; neverthe-less, in practice neither of the two groups make a decision for Christianity.' Conzelmann, *Apg.*, p. 149, is nearer the mark when he says that v. 24 gives the usual picture of a divided Israel, but that 'the accent does not lie on the fact that, nevertheless, one part has been converted. The scene is sketched in order precisely to give the impression that the situation of the Jews is hopeless.' Jervell's own view, that Luke's tradition at this point spoke of a total rejection by the Jews and that Luke has deliberately weakened this by the insertion of v. 24, is pure speculation.

[2] Commentaries *ad loc.* and Jervell, 'Israel', pp. 91f.

[3] Dupont, 'Gentils', pp. 136–8.

rather, this refusal at the end of the book – with the reference to Is. 6: 9f, which gives scriptural proof – makes it clear that Luke wishes to describe a final rejection of Israel and the substitution of the Gentiles.'[1]

Having studied the details of these verses we now turn to the overall picture which they convey. The usual, almost universal, view is that to a greater or lesser extent Luke saw the reception of the Gentiles and the Gentile mission as being a result of the Jews' rejection of the gospel.[2] It is this view in particular which Jervell sets out to disprove, for he believes it is a fundamental misunderstanding of Luke's view: 'Normally one understands the situation in the following manner: the way to the Gentiles is only opened when the Jews have refused the gospel. It is more correct to say: the way to the Gentiles can only be trodden when Israel has accepted the gospel.'[3] That is to say, it is not the Jews' rejection, but their acceptance, of the gospel which is the pre-supposition of the Gentile mission. Jervell's evidence can be summarised as follows:

1. There are frequent references in Acts to the success of the mission to the Jews (2: 41, 47, 4: 4, 5: 14, 6: 1, 7, 9: 42, 12: 24, 13: 43, 14: 1, 17: 10f, 21: 20), while there are few parallel references to mass conversions of the Gentiles (only 11: 21, 24, 14: 1, 17: 4, 18: 8, and often these are 'God-fearing' Gentiles). The references to Jewish conversions before Cornelius' conversion show a steady increase (2: 41, 4: 4, 5: 15, 6: 7) and all the references to mass conversions of the Jews show them as having occurred in Jerusalem. Whereas in Acts 1–12 opposition to the Church comes mainly from the Jewish leaders (4: 1f, 5: 17f, 6: 8f) and the ordinary folk are receptive (2: 47, 4: 21, 5: 14, 6: 17), in chs. 13f a larger proportion of the Jews is portrayed as opponents of the Church. On the basis of these observations Jervell asserts that Luke is at pains to show that the mission to the Jews was successful, particularly in Jerusalem and before Cornelius' conversion. Luke does not think that the vast majority of the Jews rejected the gospel or that this was a primary cause of the Gentile mission: 'Luke does not sketch a

---

[1] Haenchen, 'Judentum', p. 185.
[2] See commentaries on 13: 46, 18: 6, 28: 28; O'Neill, *Acts*, pp. 81–2; Cadbury, *Making*, p. 255; Wilckens, *Missionsreden*, pp. 50f.
[3] Jervell, 'Israel', p. 83.

picture of a Jewish race who *en bloc*, as a race, reject the gospel, which for its part will bring about the Gentile mission... Israel does not reject the gospel but, by reason of the message, is divided within herself.'[1]

2. Luke thought of the Church, including the Gentiles, as an integral part of the old, empirical Israel: 'The post-apostolic, early-Catholic understanding of the Church as a *tertium genus* in relation to Jews and Gentiles, perhaps as the New Israel which is composed of Jews and Gentiles, is not to be found in Acts.'[2] Thus Acts emphasises the Jewishness of the early Church and makes it clear that God's promises were fulfilled in the old and not in the new Israel. The Gentiles share in salvation by participating in the promises given to and now being fulfilled in empirical Israel (15: 16–17). The presupposition of the Gentiles' participation in Israel's salvation is that the promises should first have been fulfilled in Israel herself (3: 25–6, 13: 16f, 28: 26f). In fact, it is only through Israel that salvation reaches the whole world. This explains why the Apostles are so slow to obey Jesus' commission in 1: 8, for by preaching to the Jews they are, in effect, reaching out to the Gentiles. It also explains why in their mission to the Jews the Apostles mention their mission to the Gentiles (2: 39, 3: 25–6) and in their mission to the Gentiles speak of salvation coming to the Jews (10: 34–43).

3. One problem which Jervell notes is the Cornelius episode. If the Twelve acknowledged that salvation would come to the Gentiles (2: 39, 3: 25–6) why then the need for so much prompting from God in the Cornelius episode? Jervell solves the problem by arguing that in Acts 10–11, 15, the question at stake is not the Gentile mission as such, but a Gentile mission free from circumcision. A special divine revelation was needed, not to decide whether or not the Gentile mission should take place, but to clarify what form it should take.

Insofar as he has highlighted the extent and success of the Jewish mission in Acts, Jervell has provided a useful corrective to those who tend to emphasise only Luke's interest in the Gentiles. He has also drawn attention to the tension between the programmatic statements in 13: 46, 18: 6 and 28: 28 which, despite Jervell, seem to imply a rejection of the Jews as a whole, and those passages which speak of Jews believing (cf. especially

[1] Jervell, 'Israel', p. 76.　　　[2] Jervell, 'Israel', p. 77.

13: 43, 46, 28: 24, 28). Novel and stimulating as his argument is, and despite the fact that he has broken some new ground, Jervell's overall conclusions must remain in doubt, because:

1. Luke's portrayal of the Jewishness of the early Church does not necessarily have the theological implications which Jervell gives it. Various theological tendencies have been ascribed to Luke, but in essentials he is merely expressing a historical fact, namely that the early Christians were Jews and remained Jews after accepting the gospel. There was conflict with the Jewish authorities, but the Church did not at first form a breakaway movement. Luke is more concerned to relate this historical fact than the theological theme of the priority of Israel.

2. Likewise, the success of the Jewish mission in Jerusalem does not imply, as Jervell supposes, that this success was a presupposition of the Gentile mission. The temporally prior claim to the gospel of the Jews is a presupposition of the Gentile mission, but its success or failure is incidental – although both in reality and according to Luke, the failure of the Jewish mission gave an immediate impetus to the Gentile mission. The prior claim of Israel is recognised by Luke from the start (Lk. 24: 47; Acts 1: 8, 3: 25–6) and due respect is paid to this up to the end of Acts. In this respect, too, Luke reflects the actual course of events, even though his account is schematised. Moreover, when due weight is given to the repeated statements that it was the failure of the Jewish mission which was an important immediate cause of the Gentile mission (13: 46, 18: 6, 28: 28), Jervell's thesis becomes even less credible; and it must be said that throughout, Jervell undervalues the importance of these three passages.

3. Jervell's argument that Luke believed that salvation would come to the Gentiles only through the Jews is based ultimately on two passages, 3: 25–6 and 15: 16–17. Certainly, we cannot avoid these verses by claiming that they reflect the views of the speakers, Peter and James, and not the view of Luke, for it is almost certain that Luke composed the speeches himself. On the other hand, both passages are Old Testament quotations and, as we argued above, it is not certain how far Luke considered the exact meaning of either verse, except insofar as they both contained a clear universalistic reference. This alone may

have been why Luke used them. If Acts 3: 25 means that the Gentiles will receive salvation only through the efforts of the Jews, then it stands alone in Acts. Acts 15: 16–17 does not imply any outreach of the Jews to the Gentiles, though it may mean that the conversion of the Gentiles is a fulfilment of a promise to Israel.

A decisive objection to Jervell's interpretation of 3: 25 and 15: 16 is that at other points Luke seems to betray a very different view. Acts 13: 46, 18: 6 and 28: 28 are obvious examples, but they do not stand alone. J. C. O'Neill has argued a view diametrically opposed to that of Jervell, namely that a, if not the, main theme of Acts is the picture of Christianity's progressive disentanglement from Judaism. Acts does not simply tell how the gospel went from Jerusalem to Rome, but how the Church increasingly discovered its identity as a unit distinct from Judaism. 'Luke's thesis is that the gospel is free to travel to the ends of the earth only when it is freed from the false form which the Jewish religion has taken.'[1] Thus Luke is telling his educated Roman readers that it is the Church which is the only true Israel; she alone can interpret the Old Testament correctly and is the true representative of Judaism. O'Neill's view is based, a little precariously, chiefly on Acts 19: 8–10 (cf. 18: 6–7), where Paul begins separatist activities. Because of opposition from the Jews, he takes the Christians of Ephesus out of the synagogue and sets them up as an independent Church. As an interpretation of the whole of Acts, O'Neill's view is based on surprisingly little evidence; like Jervell's view, it suffers from trying to force on Luke a uniform overall viewpoint which is precisely and logically thought out, and it ignores part of the evidence. Nevertheless, it is not wholly unfounded, and Acts 19: 8–10 is an important strand of evidence against Jervell's view. Another important passage is Acts 10: 34–5 to which, as one of the bases of Luke's justification of the Gentile mission, Haenchen gives special emphasis.[2] The fundamental idea is that God is not partisan (προσωπολήμπτης); he has no special love for one race over against another. This implies a radical challenge to and even denial of the idea that Israel has a privileged relationship with God. Certainly, Luke does not expand and develop

---

[1] O'Neill, *Acts*, pp. 81–2, 170f, here p. 82.
[2] Haenchen, *Apg.*, p. 90, and 'Judentum', p. 168.

the full implications of this idea as he might have done, but then the same can be said for 3: 25 and 15: 16–17.

When scholars such as these come to such different conclusions, it is frequently the case that each has selected his evidence to suit his conclusions, albeit unintentionally. The evidence used by Haenchen and O'Neill is quite valid, and the same can be said for Jervell, particularly if one can go the whole way with his interpretation of 3: 25–6 and 15: 16–17. Both strands of evidence are important and it is false to isolate one and make it the basis of an interpretation of the whole of Acts. This is not to say that we are dealing here with subtle paradox, simple confusion, or uncertain oscillation between two viewpoints; rather, the evidence reveals that Luke did not consider the question at all, at least not in our modern terms with our fondness for nice definitions. Certainly, Luke considered the general question of the relationship between Christianity and Judaism, in particular from a practical viewpoint, but not in the theological terms of whether the Church is a 'new' or a 'renewed' Israel, or to what extent it formed a *tertium genus*. Luke looked at the question more pragmatically: from a historical angle, in answer to the question of how the Gentiles became part of the Church and how the Jews reacted; and, from a pastoral angle, to see how far these historical events contained a message for the Churches of his own day.[1]

4. The Cornelius narrative is not so easily dispensed with as Jervell imagines. He thinks that Luke says that Peter and the Apostles were quite prepared to participate in a Gentile mission, provided that the Gentiles were first circumcised. They did not object to a Gentile mission on principle, but only to a Gentile mission without circumcision. Yet surely this means that they were prepared to approach not Gentiles, but only those Gentiles who, as proselytes, were prepared to become Jews. The Gentiles were to be saved not as Gentiles but as Jews. In other words, they were prepared to participate in a Jewish-Christian proselyte mission, but not in a Gentile mission. Circumcision was not a minor factor; it meant the difference between a man being a Jew and a pagan. The Church's objection, on the basis of the Gentiles' lack of circumcision, was fundamental and not simply a detail of missionary tactics.

[1] For a similar conclusion see now P. Richardson, *Israel and the Apostolic Church* (Cambridge, 1969), pp. 159–65.

5. Jervell is right to point out the tension between 13: 46, 18: 6 and 28: 28 and the continuing mission to the Jews. The reaction to Paul's preaching makes it quite clear that the gospel was a divisive force; not all Jews rejected the gospel and not all Gentiles accepted it. One problem is that Luke seems to use the word 'Jews' loosely: the implication of 13: 46, 18: 6 and 28: 28 is that all Jews are meant, whereas 13: 43 and 28: 24 show that this cannot be so. Yet the answer to this difficulty is not to de-value 13: 46, 18: 6 and 28: 28, and overemphasise the references to the conversion of the Jews. It is generally agreed that the programmatic statements in 13: 46, 18: 6 and 28: 28 are Luke's own summary of the events in the Church's mission. If they represent Luke's own interpretation of the Jew–Gentile question, then they cannot be so lightly dismissed as Jervell supposes.

It seems that the most satisfactory explanation of this tension lies in taking full account of the situation of the Church in Luke's day. It was almost certainly a predominantly Gentile Church. The influx of Jews had ceased long before, and the enmity between the Church and Judaism had grown more bitter and the gulf wider after A.D. 70. It was the experience of the Church in Luke's day that, almost without exception, the Jews were totally unresponsive to the gospel. This rift between Christians and Jews and the Jews' obduracy in face of the gospel probably influenced Luke's interpretation and summaries of the events in the apostolic era (13: 46, 18: 6, 28: 28). On the other hand, Luke knew full well that the gospel had been proclaimed to the Jews first and that many had accepted it; it is this which accounts for his references to the conversion of the Jews.[1] As a historian Luke is not always successful, but he has good intentions. He would not, therefore, suppress the historical fact of Jewish conversions, however convenient that may have been for a neat, straightforward theory of the Jews' response to the gospel. Thus Luke was torn between historical and parenetic motives: he wished to be true to the historical facts as far as they could be surmised, but he also wished to interpret these facts for the Church of his day, a Church whose circumstances and experiences were not the same as those of the apostolic age. Here

---

[1] The numbers are, of course, exaggerated (2: 41, 4: 4, 5: 15, 6: 7) – a simple technique of Luke's to emphasise God's blessing of the Church.

as at other points, Luke's view of history is influenced by the beliefs and experiences of the Church at the end of the first century A.D. If this is the correct explanation of the tension between 13: 46, 18: 6, 28: 28 and the rest of Acts, then the significant fact and the one which for Luke is most important in the Jews' response to the gospel is not that some accepted, but that many rejected it. And if this is so, then Jervell, in his attempt to characterise Luke's attitude, has got hold of the wrong end of the stick.

THE CONCLUSION OF ACTS

The above discussion of the programmatic statements about the Gentile mission, in particular 28: 26f, leads us immediately to the problem of the ending of Acts. The abrupt and uninformative way in which Luke ends his narrative has always been a puzzle for scholars. Paul is pictured as living under a very lenient form of house arrest in Rome, preaching the gospel μετὰ πάσης παρρησίας ἀκωλύτως. Why Luke ends his narrative here is a mystery to which there is no fully satisfactory answer. In particular, after the detailed and lengthy accounts of Paul's earlier trials (chs. 21f), it is odd that we hear nothing about either his trial in Rome or his ultimate fate. This uncertainty has opened the way for a myriad of explanations:

1. It could be argued that Luke's knowledge of events ceased with Paul's arrival in Rome. If Luke was writing towards the end of the first century A.D. this is scarcely conceivable, so the usual form this argument takes is to assert that he was writing much earlier (*circa* A.D. 65) and that the narrative has caught up with the events.[1] Some would go on to argue that Acts was specifically written to influence the outcome of Paul's trial,[2] although on this view one has difficulty explaining the purpose of Acts 1–12. But Luke's use of Mark and the dating of Lk. 19: 41–4, 21: 20–4 after A.D. 70 are a stumbling-block to this view. Also, Acts 20: 25, 28 imply that Luke was aware of the outcome of Paul's trial, rather than that the result was still in the balance.

[1] Clark, *Acts*, p. 389.
[2] D. Plooij, 'The work of St Luke: a historical apology for Pauline preaching before the Roman court', *Expos.*, VIII/8 (1914), 511–23.

2. Some argue that Luke planned or even began to write a third volume, which picked up the narrative from Acts 28: 31. Thus Ramsay interprets Acts 28: 31 as a magna charta of religious freedom and suggests that the third volume was planned to include the use Paul made of this freedom, his second trial and eventual martyrdom.[1] There is no positive evidence for this view, it ignores what roundness and completeness there is in the total structure of Acts, and it does not explain why, if Paul was acquitted at his first trial, Luke does not mention his acquittal, for it would have formed a grand climax to the narrative of Acts.

3. A. Ehrhardt suggests that we have no account of a conversation between Paul and Nero in Acts, because in the Acts of the pagan martyrs much buffoonery was written at this point, and Luke wishes to avoid this.[2] He also suggests that we have no account of Paul's martyrdom because Luke wanted to avoid too close an analogy with Jesus' death. But other writers' buffoonery would not stop Luke giving a sober, serious account, and, if Luke was avoiding a parallel with Jesus' death, how does one explain his account of Stephen's martyrdom?

4. O'Neill suggests that the primary interest of Luke and his readers was not biographical, but theological.[3] We may desire to know Paul's fate, but Luke's readers would not have shared this desire. They would have been interested in more theological questions, such as the relationship between Christianity and Judaism. This would explain why Acts contains nothing about Peter's death and only a brief mention of James' (12: 2). Also, Cadbury has found some parallels to the uninformative ending of Acts in Philostratus and II Maccabees.[4] But Hanson is surely right to reject this view.[5] Biographical interest is seen in the Gospels, Pastoral epistles and apocryphal Gospels and Acts from the end of the first century A.D. onwards, and in classical literature the biography was a popular and recognised literary genre. It is likely, therefore, that Luke's readers would have been as curious to know the outcome of Paul's stay in Rome as we are.

5. It has been suggested that Acts 28: 31 implies that at the

---

[1] Ramsay, *Paul*, pp. 308f; Knox, *Acts*, p. 59.
[2] Ehrhardt, *Framework*, pp. 80–1.   [3] O'Neill, *Acts*, pp. 69f.
[4] Cadbury, *Making*, pp. 29–30, 33.   [5] Hanson, *Acts*, pp. 33–4.

end of two years in prison Paul was automatically released.[1] It is argued that the Romans had a custom whereby a prisoner was automatically freed after two years if his accusers failed to turn up within eighteen months. However, there is no evidence that such a law was in force at this time. The two parallels usually quoted – Pliny, *Ep*. x. 56; Philo, *In Flacc*. 128f – do not demand this interpretation and Jos. *Vit*. 13f speaks against it.[2] Moreover, it is not clear why Paul's accusers should have defaulted. The cost of a journey to Rome was great, but the Jerusalem Jews were not poor and Paul was their implacable enemy. It is never hinted in Acts or elsewhere that the case against Paul was dropped, and Acts 28: 30–1 emphasises only Paul's freedom to preach, not his freedom from a trial.

It could be argued that Paul was freed, on the basis of information in the Pastorals and I Clement, which seems to imply that Paul underwent two trials in Rome. At the first he was acquitted and at the second condemned and executed (cf. II Tim. 4: 6, 11, 16–18). Often it is assumed that between these two trials Paul fulfilled his intention to visit Spain (Rom. 15: 24, *I Clem*. 1: 5) and also paid a return visit to the Aegean littoral. The problem with this view is the uncertainty of the evidence: *I Clem*. 1: 5 is ambiguous and may not refer to a visit to Spain; Rom. 15: 24, 28 speak only of Paul's intentions; and the evidence of the Pastorals is late and not easy to evaluate historically. Moreover, if this view were true, it is odd that Luke omits to mention Paul's acquittal after the first trial. It would have been a golden opportunity to illustrate and summarise his overall view of the impartiality and friendliness of the Romans towards Christianity, and would have been a good formal ending to the book.

6. Haenchen thinks Luke implies that Paul was executed at the end of his two years under arrest. Luke never implies that Paul's trial will have a happy end; in fact, he implies the exact opposite (20: 25, 28). He does say that Paul deserves neither death nor imprisonment, but that is a different thing from saying he got what he deserved. Thus Luke presupposes the martyrdom of Paul, but does not describe it for fear of reviving 'martyr-piety': 'He does not wish to prepare Christians for

---

[1] *B.C.*, v, 326f.
[2] Conzelmann, *Apg.*, p. 150; Haenchen, *Apg.*, p. 647 n. 2.

martyrdom like the Revelation of John, but to spare the Church the possibility of martyrdom.'[1] But if this were so, it is odd that Luke gives such a detailed description of Stephen's martyrdom, which is a close parallel to Jesus' death and seems to be Luke's ideal picture of the pattern of Christian martyrdom. It might also be objected to Haenchen's view that if Paul was killed by the Romans and this was well-known, it would destroy Luke's case for Rome's friendliness and impartiality. But as Haenchen points out, if Paul was executed on the orders of Nero this would not be the case. For Nero was an aberration, a man whose memory was rapidly disgraced after his death even by his fellow Romans. Death at Nero's hands, therefore, would not have seemed a disgrace and would not have been considered incompatible with Luke's account of the impartiality and fairness of Rome.[2]

7. The explanation which comes closest to solving this perplexing riddle is twofold: First we must assume that Luke's silence about Paul's trial and its outcome is because his readers were already well acquainted with the facts. Whether he was executed after two years or acquitted and later martyred in Rome is difficult to say, since the evidence is so scanty. But whichever is true, Luke's readers must have known what had happened. They needed to be told not what happened to Paul in Rome, but how he got there.[3] This is not a wholly satisfactory answer, but it is the best we can offer.[4]

Secondly, it is also necessary to realise that for Luke Acts 28 summarises and rounds off the rest of his narrative. The theme of Jewish obduracy (vv. 26–8) pervades the previous narrative, despite the fact that some Jews were converted. Moreover, the picture of Paul actively preaching in Rome, presumably chiefly

---

[1] Haenchen, *Apg.*, p. 655.

[2] Both Hanson (*Acts*, pp. 31f) and Haenchen (*Apg.*, p. 655) think Paul was executed under Nero.

[3] Cf. Hanson, *Acts*, p. 35, who thinks Acts was written for readers in Rome. This may also explain why Luke's interest in personal and geographical details decreases in the last few chapters (Cadbury, *Making*, pp. 241–2), i.e. Luke did not think it necessary to give details which were already well known to his readers.

[4] On this view it is perhaps more likely that Haenchen is right in thinking that Paul was killed after two years in Rome. Had there been an acquittal and further activity of Paul, unless it was all confined to Rome, one would expect Luke to have included it.

to Gentiles, fulfils Jesus' commission in Acts 1:8; the gospel has now reached the 'ends of the earth'. While Acts may be incomplete biographically, in its main theme of the triumphant and irresistible progress of the gospel it is complete. In principle, the gospel had been preached to all the Gentiles. Paul's arrival in Rome and unhindered preaching there probably seemed to Luke not only 'to fulfil the scope of Jesus' commission, but also to make a true, triumphant and effective conclusion to his own narrative'.[1] As in his Gospel, Luke brings the narrative to a triumphant close and, from a literary-artistic viewpoint, Acts 28 must have seemed to him to be a fine conclusion to the preceding story.

As well as this retrospective reference, in fulfilment of 1:8, these last few verses of Acts may well have a prospective purpose.[2] Because the gospel has reached Rome and Jesus' commission has in principle been fulfilled, this does not mean that the Church can sit back and relax. The emphasis on the open and unhindered proclamation of the gospel to the Gentiles, the finality of the rejection of the Jews, and the ending of the story in Rome all point in the same direction: the future of the Church lies among the Gentiles; Christianity is to be a universal religion. Luke looks forward to the time when Christianity will be the religion of the Empire and wants to prepare the Church for this role.

In concluding his narrative in this way Luke has to pay a price: he has virtually to ignore the presence of a Christian community in Rome before Paul's arrival. It is mentioned briefly in 28:15, but not again. Paul's dealings in Rome are chiefly with the Jews, although the implication of vv. 30–1 is that afterwards he preached mainly to Gentiles. Clearly, Paul's arrival in Rome is not that of the first Christian missionary. The origins of the Church in Rome remain a mystery; it is one of the many Christian communities whose existence Luke assumes but does not explain (Damascus 9:10f, Lydda and Joppa 9:32, 36, Ephesus 18:19, 26, and Puteoli 28:13). These

---

[1] Cadbury, *Making*, p. 323; cf. Haenchen, *Apg.*, p. 654; Stählin, *Apg.*, p. 9; Conzelmann, *Apg.*, p. 150.

[2] This point is particularly well made by O'Neill (*Acts*, pp. 175–7) and Jervell ('Israel', pp. 71–2), though they both tend to neglect the element of fulfilment of Acts 1:8.

237

references form one of the many lacunae in Luke's account. But if Paul's arrival in Rome is not the first, it is the definitive one,[1] since he was in full fellowship with the Twelve and was personally commissioned by Christ to preach to the Gentiles. And it is Paul in Rome who, in pronouncing the final judgement on the Jews, at the same time points to the future direction of the Church.

[1] Menoud, 'Plan', p. 50. O'Neill's objections to this view (*Acts*, p. 69), that the arrival of Paul in Rome is not enough to fulfil Acts 1 : 8 and that Acts is based on a geographical movement which depends on others besides Paul, do not seem to be decisive. The first point is a matter of opinion, and while the second point is true, one can nevertheless scarcely overemphasise the centrality of Paul's role in Luke's account.

CHAPTER 10

SUMMARY AND CONCLUSIONS

In this final section two major tasks will be undertaken, namely a consideration of the Gentile mission in Luke–Acts from both a theological and a historical viewpoint. The first section will be a summary of the 'theology' of the Gentiles in Luke–Acts, including a comparison with Paul's epistles. The second will consist of a drawing-together of the varied results which, on the question of historical reliability, have been reached in the detailed study of those sections of Acts which concerned us, and the use of these to guide us in our assessment of Luke as a historian.

THE THEOLOGY OF THE GENTILES

The word 'theology' is used here as the most convenient way of distinguishing this section from the next, which is concerned chiefly with the historical question. As will become apparent, the description of Luke's approach to the Gentiles as 'theological' is misleading, for the most striking characteristic of Luke–Acts is precisely the lack of any consistent theology of the Gentiles.

Associated themes

At various points in earlier chapters we have noted how certain themes are frequently associated with the Gentile mission, either directly or by implication. They are not always related to it in a systematic way, but the fact that they arise in related contexts shows that there is some connection between them in Luke's mind.

The first is the connection, albeit indirect, with Jerusalem. As we have noted earlier, several writers have worked out the role which Jerusalem plays in Luke–Acts. It acts as one of the essential links which bind together the two volumes. It is the goal of the Gospel narrative; all events point to and find their climax in the events in Jerusalem. There is no room for Galilean traditions of the Resurrection; Jerusalem dominates. But as well as being the goal of the first volume it is the starting point of the second. Jerusalem is the home of the Apostles and the base for the Church's mission, which eventually reaches the Gentiles. The gospel has first to be preached in Jerusalem (Lk. 24: 47; Acts 1: 8, 2–8) and even Paul begins his work by preaching in Damascus and Jerusalem (Acts 9: 20f, 26: 20). Moreover, as the mission widens its scope, reaching out to Samaritans and Gentiles, the Jerusalem Church is always close on its heels, enquiring after and checking each new development (Acts 8: 14f, 11: 1f, 22f). And it is in Jerusalem that the Apostolic Council convenes (Acts 15) to decide once and for all the exact requirements to be made of Gentile converts.

There is no doubt that Luke's account of Jerusalem's role is to some extent schematised, in particular the way in which the Jerusalem Church regularly checks each new development of the mission. Luke himself has left hints which show that Jerusalem did not enjoy such a ubiquitous role as overseer of all missionary developments as his overall scheme implies (Acts 9: 10f, 9: 32, 36, 18: 19, 26, 28: 13). It is not easy to know how to label Luke's presentation of Jerusalem. To many it is best described as theological, since they see Jerusalem's role as essential to Luke's concept of *Heilsgeschichte*. However, true as that may be, one should not overlook the purely historical-geographical element in Luke's account. It is a historical fact that Jerusalem was the home of the early post-Resurrection Church and that the gospel was preached there first, so that all later developments could ultimately be traced back there. It is also highly probable that the Twelve and the Jerusalem Church were inquisitive and a little suspicious when large numbers of non-Jews were converted and, as far as possible, they probably checked what was going on. So that while it may be claimed, with some justice, that Jerusalem has a special role in Luke's writings, one should not 'theologise' it unduly to the neglect of purely historical and geographical factors.

Closely intertwined with Jerusalem as a missionary centre is the role of the Twelve (Lk. 24: 47; Acts 1: 8, chs. 10–11, 15). While there is no real fulfilment of Acts 1: 8 in the later work of the Apostles, Luke does the best he can by making Peter's dealings with Cornelius the first and decisive approach to the Gentiles. And even if they do not, as a group, fulfil Jesus' commission, after an initial hesitation (11: 1f) they take their stand firmly

beside Paul and Barnabas (15), who do fulfil the commission of
1: 8. Thus Luke makes it abundantly clear that the Gentile
mission was in no way an illegitimate offshoot of renegade
Christians. The Apostles not only gave full support to Paul and
Barnabas, but one of their number, Peter, was the man whom
God chose to initiate the Gentile mission. Paul is portrayed as
being in full harmony with the Apostles and the Jerusalem
Church; he is not the leader of a breakaway group in conflict
with the early leaders. In this way Luke legitimises the Gentile
mission, though he does this not from ecclesiastical, but from
historical motives. It is not so much a theology of the Church
or a theory of apostolic succession which inspires Luke's account; rather it is a desire to trace the Gentile mission back to
the primary witnesses of Jesus' life, death and resurrection,
namely the Apostles, and ultimately therefore to Jesus himself.

Luke's treatment of the Gentiles is frequently connected with
the theme of the Holy Spirit (Lk. 2: 27f, 4: 16f, 24: 47f; Acts 1:
4–8, 2: 1–10, 17, 21, 8: 26, 39, 10: 44f, 11: 15f, 13: 2, 15: 8, 28,
16: 6, 28: 25). We have already, in an earlier chapter, discussed
the relationship between the Spirit, eschatology and the Gentile
mission. We suggested there that Luke's treatment of these
themes is more an attempt to reconstruct and make intelligible
the experience of the early Church, at the same time reflecting
the experience of the Church of his day, than it is an attempt to
produce a systematic and logical theology of the Spirit. His
presentation of the theme of the Spirit in Acts confirms this
suggestion.

The work of the Spirit permeates the story of the Gentile
mission, guiding and prompting the Church at every stage and
confirming the most important turning points, in particular,
Cornelius' conversion (10: 44, 11: 15, 15: 8). According to
Jesus' commands in Lk. 24: 47f and Acts 1: 4–8 the Spirit is a
necessary presupposition for all the missionary preaching, both
to Jews and Gentile alike, for the Apostles are commanded to
stay in Jerusalem until they have received the Spirit and they
do not begin their work until this happens. The point of all these
references is clear; they show that the extension of the Church's
mission was at every point both inspired and confirmed by
manifestations of the Spirit. By implication, therefore, it was not
solely or even chiefly the work of men, however important or

revered they were or had become by Luke's day. Closely associated with this theme is the role which God or the Risen Christ plays at the crucial turning points of the narrative, frequently through the medium of angels and visions. This is particularly evident in the accounts of the conversion of Paul and Cornelius (9: 1f, 22: 17f, 10–11). In both, the chief actors are not men but God. Peter and Paul are both reluctant, but have no choice but to obey the clear and irresistible will of God. The Apostles and Paul did not naturally abandon their Jewish past and set out on a Gentile mission; they clung to the Temple and Jewish food laws, but God forced them out to the Gentile mission. As Haenchen says, 'That these men embark on the Gentile mission is only possible insofar as God compels them to it against their will'.[1]

Closely connected with the themes of divine intervention and the Spirit is the role which miracles play (10: 41f, 15: 12), for miracles and signs are only another way of talking about the direct intervention of God in events. They show that God favours a particular turn of events and that the Church, therefore, is on the right road. The regular appearances of God, Christ, the Spirit, angels and visions all point in the same direction: Luke's understanding of history is theocentric. Indeed it could be claimed, with some justification, that Luke has gone too far and that in his eagerness to emphasise the role of God he has reduced the human participants to mere puppets – a problem which is probably more noticeable to men of the twentieth century than it was to those of the first century A.D. Divine intervention nevertheless makes clear that the development of the Church's mission, in particular the switch from a Jewish- to a Gentile-dominated Church, is not only the will, but also the work of God. But because Luke's understanding of history is theocentric it is not necessarily theological. Rather, it is a simple and, in first-century terms, effective justification of the Gentile mission in terms of divine intervention. What to us may seem a naive approach to theology and history was probably to Luke and, more importantly, to his readers a far more effective means of emphasising the essential motivation of the Gentile mission than an intricate theological system such as we find in Paul.

Historically, Luke places the origins of the Gentile mission in

---

[1] Haenchen, *Apg.*, p. 90.

the words and actions of Jesus. In his lifetime Jesus did, in exceptional cases, deal favourably with Gentiles (Lk. 7: 1f), but more importantly, after the Resurrection he commissioned his Apostles to embark on a mission that would be universal in scope (Lk. 24: 47f; Acts 1: 8). However dubious this may be historically and however much it may create tensions with the later narrative of Acts, this commission was fundamental to Luke's way of thinking. It was the necessary continuation and fulfilment of Jesus' own ministry. And not only the Apostles, but also Paul – the man who proved to be the Gentile missionary *par excellence* – was commissioned directly by the Risen Christ (Acts 9: 1f, 22: 6f, 17f, 26: 12f). The Gentile mission did not originate as a bright idea of the early Church, nor did it occur unexpectedly or by accident; it was rooted in the words of Jesus, as a promise in his earthly ministry and as a command after the Resurrection.

The idea that God is not partisan (10: 34, 15: 9) is yet another motif which underlies Luke's justification of the Gentile mission. As we suggested in an earlier section, this notion could have formed the basis for a far-reaching and radical theological justification for the Gentile mission, especially when allied to Luke's liberal assessment of the pre-Christian history of the Gentiles (Acts 14: 15–17, 17: 22f). Yet Luke never makes full use of it by drawing out all its implications. It is momentarily picked up and then immediately dropped. Here, where there was the potential for developing a theology of the Gentile mission, he was content merely to mention it in passing.

The proof-from-prophecy theme is one of the most widespread phenomena in Luke's version of the Gentile mission. Throughout the Gospel and Acts quotations from (Lk. 3: 6; Acts 2: 17, 3: 25, 13: 47, 15: 17) and allusions to (Lk. 2: 32, 4: 25–7, 24: 46; Acts 1: 8, 2: 39, 10: 34, 15: 14, 26: 17, 28: 26f) the Old Testament are used to prophesy, explain and justify the proclamation to the Gentiles. It is significant too, that Luke is careful to use passages which actually do refer to Gentiles. It is improbable that the Gentile mission was, in the first instance, inspired by these passages; rather, as Luke himself implies, they were used to justify it *post eventum*. The purpose of these frequent references is undoubtedly to legitimise both the original Gentile mission and the subsequent Gentile Churches, to show that this major turning point in the Church's development was, from the beginning, part of the will of God. God did not have a sudden change of mind, nor was he caught unawares by an unexpected turn of events, for he had planned and willed it from the beginning. The Gentile mission was not a novel element in the teaching of Jesus, nor did it occur simply as a result of the obduracy of the chosen people; its roots went back far deeper – to the eternal will of God. Of all the various methods Luke uses to justify the turning to the Gentiles, this appeal to the Old Testament and, by implication, to the eternal will of God, is the most profound and fundamental. It is the closest Luke gets to constructing a 'theology' of the Gentiles and the Gentile mission. It reaches beyond the simple reference to miracles, visions and other modes of divine intervention, the work of the Apostles, and even the command of Jesus – although he himself claims the same Old Testament precedent for his commission. Together with the notion mentioned in 10: 34 it could have been worked into an overall theological structure, but Luke fails to do this.

Closely allied to this use of the Old Testament is the appeal to Scripture in explaining the obduracy of the Jews which, in an immediate and practical way, was an important impetus to the Gentile mission. Luke makes it clear that the prior claim of Israel to the gospel has been respected. Despite their rejection of Jesus, the gospel was proclaimed to them first in no uncertain terms, giving them a second chance to repent. The responsibility for their refusal and the consequent loss of salvation rested not on God, who had given them repeated chances, nor on the Church, who had made continual efforts to break through their obduracy; rather, the responsibility was their own. The fact that so many Jews reject the gospel may seem at first to jeopardise the idea of proof-from-prophecy, but even this rejection was foretold in the Old Testament. The Jews' refusal to hear and obey God's will was no new phenomenon; rather, it conformed to the regular pattern of Old Testament history (Lk. 1: 34, 4: 25–7, 6: 22–3, 26, 8: 10, 11: 47–51, 13: 23–30, 34, 14: 24, 19: 41–6, 20: 19f, 21: 20f; Acts 3: 23, 4: 25f, 7: 35f, 13: 40f, 28: 25f). Whether the Jews refuse or accept the gospel, the Old Testament, including God's promise to the Gentiles, is fulfilled. The Jew's rejection of the gospel is not a fundamental motivation of the Gentile mission, for the decisive move was taken not as a result of the Jews' refusal, but as a result of God's prompting (10–11). Yet in a practical way the Jews' obduracy influenced Paul's decisions at several points. The impression Luke leaves is that Paul's whole ministry was characterised by Jewish opposition and that it was only after his attempts to persuade the Jews were frustrated that he turned his attention to the Gentiles.

Finally, we recall one more theme which crops up in Luke's narrative in connection with the Gentiles, namely that which we have called his pragmatic approach to the Gentiles (Lk. 7: 1–10; Acts 10: 1f, 14: 15–17, 17: 22f). That is, the way in which Luke, by his description of the centurion and Cornelius and by his assessment of the religious status of the Gentiles in the Areopagus speech, tries to show that the Gentiles are, in their own way, as devout and as likeable as the Jews. The Jews have no cause to be arrogant, thinking that their position as God's chosen people gives them a monopoly of religious devotion or an exclusive claim on God. The Gentiles may not belong to the chosen race and they may lack the religious insight of the Jews, but within the limits set for them they prove to be neither more nor less responsive to God's revelation of his character and will. The Jews may mock the Gentiles for the primitive conception of God expressed in their idolatry, but then the Jews' own past is chequered with lapses into a similar degradation of true worship. In fact, with their less ambiguous revelation, they could well be considered more culpable. The Gentiles may be ignorant, but the only result of a full revelation to the Jews seems to have been a more deliberate disobedience. Luke seems to be saying that an unbiased look at the past and the present shows the Gentiles to be in every way as good as the Jews. And if this is so, then there is no good reason why the gospel should not be preached to them and the Church welcome them. Apart from the Jew's temporal priority, the Gentile has as great a claim on the gospel as the Jew; the response of the one is as valid as that of the other.

How then are we to assess Luke's varied approach? At the beginning of his article, Jervell mentions a number of the points made above and notes that if taken together they are not always logical. For example, if the Church or Luke thought that the motivation for the Gentile mission lay in the Old Testament prophecies and in the non-partisan character of God, why the hesitation and reluctance as regards this mission? Why was it necessary to wait for the intervention of God or the refusal of the Jews? Jervell's answer is to deny that all these motives lie behind the Gentile mission in Acts and to find an overall pattern into which all the parts logically fit. And this is precisely where he goes wrong. For a characteristic of Luke's writings at this and at other points is that Luke has no apparent logic. His account of the motivations for the Gentile mission is neither logical nor theological. There is no single underlying theme, but rather a jumble of miscellaneous themes, none of which is fully developed in itself or in relation to the others. Sometimes ideas are used which have the potential for forming the basis of a systematic and more logical justification, but their potential is never realised.

In his overall account of the Gentiles and the Gentile mission Luke clearly has a historical and practical rather than a theological interest at heart. From the historical angle, he was genuinely concerned to show how the Church expanded to allow for a Gentile influx. The fact that his attempt may be judged historically worthless does not destroy the intention. The primary inspiration lay far back in the Old Testament promises, which Jesus takes up in his commission to the Apostles; here lay the historical roots of the Gentile mission. But in practical terms the Church needed a lot of persuading and this was done, according to Luke, by a combination of the direct intervention of God and the refusal of the Jews to accept the gospel. On both these scores there is no doubt that Luke's account contains a considerable amount of truth: the Church was, or believed it was, prompted by God, though Luke may have underplayed the role of men; likewise, Jewish obduracy probably was an important cause of the Gentile mission, and although Luke has probably over-schematised this pattern, the essential idea is not in doubt.

However, there is more than a straightforward historical interest in Luke's approach; he was also addressing the Church of his day. At the time Luke wrote, it is generally agreed that Jewish Christianity was largely a spent force. There were still Jews who were also Christians, but the enmity between the Church and Judaism was so great that there was scarcely a Jewish mission at all. As we saw in our study of 13: 46, 18: 6 and 28: 28, Luke gives the impression that these passages reflect the situation of his own time rather than that of the apostolic era. In Luke's day the Jews, almost without exception, refused the gospel, and consequently the Church was dominated by the Gentile element.[1] Yet Luke's contemporaries knew that this state of affairs had not always been so. Both they and Luke knew that the early Church had sprung up from Jewish roots and that the Jews had not always rejected the gospel *en bloc*. Thus to some extent Luke may be explaining and justifying how the Church had become both an independent entity separate from Judaism and dominated by the Gentiles. This turn of events, Luke says, was not the result of a deliberate, uninstigated separatist movement in the early Church led by the Apostles or Paul. The fault lay not with the Church but with the Jews, for they had openly and persistently refused the gospel. Paul did not reject the Jews; rather, they rejected him. Unremitting efforts had been made to convert the Jews, but after an initial success they met with increasing opposition. At the end, in Rome, Paul gives a final summary of the Church's Jewish mission of the past and, by implication, points to the hopelessness of continuing this mission in the future: the Jews will no longer hear the gospel, but the Gentiles will. As Jervell says, the ending of Acts shows that, 'throughout the world, from Jerusalem to Rome, where the Jews live, the gospel was preached and the destruction of unrepentant Israel proclaimed. Jews throughout the world know the gospel, and with the conclusion of Acts comes also the conclusion of the Jewish mission. Actually, Luke has removed the possibility of a further Jewish mission in the Church of his day, because the decision by and about the Jews has been irrevocably made.'[2]

Exactly what circumstances Luke's account presupposes and how far they have influenced his narrative is not easy to say. It is unlikely that the Church spontaneously became conscience-stricken over the lack of any Jewish mission in their time,[3] for

---

[1] Dahl, 'Abraham', p. 151: 'The priority of Israel is regarded as a matter of history; it is no longer a present reality for Luke and for the churches like those in Corinth and Rome.' Haenchen, *Apg.*, p. 91: 'The Christian mission of his time was directed only to the Gentiles.'

[2] Jervell, 'Israel', pp. 91–2.

[3] Jervell, 'Israel', p. 95; Haenchen, *Apg.*, pp. 478, 68of, has a similar view, but never makes it clear why the Church should be wrestling with the problem of the Jews' rejection.

there would have been no reason for this problem to arise at such a distance from the apostolic age. To some, the important fact in Luke's account is the continued efforts of the Church to convert the Jews and the emphasis on the Jew's own responsibility for their rejection, for this is part of Luke's attempt to show that Christianity was a Jewish αἵρεσις and, therefore, a *religio licita*.[1] But as has often been said, this view neglects much of the evidence of Acts and it is unlikely that Roman readers would have been either capable of or interested in drawing such conclusions from a narrative which is largely irrelevant to this theme.[2] Eltester suggests that the Church of Luke's day had begun to have doubts about its rights to use the Old Testament, the book of the Jews, as the basis of their faith.[3] But again, he does not explain why the Church suddenly began to have such doubts.

The most likely explanation is that Luke's Church was involved in disputes with their Jewish contemporaries and that it was these which sparked off the Church's interest in and defence of her historical roots.[4] It is possible that the Jews accused the Church of being an illegitimate offspring of Judaism, an aberration in the true course of the history of God's people. This kind of accusation was probably accompanied by personal attacks on Paul, the founder of so many Gentile Churches. It was probably said that Paul was an apostate Jew and that this stigma remained on all the Churches which had descended from him. This would explain why Luke's defence of the Gentile mission is bound up with his more personal defence of Paul. The way in which Luke emphasises the faithfulness of the Apostles and Paul to their Jewish origins and their continued efforts to convert the Jews, may be in part a defence of the legitimacy of the Gentile Churches in the form of a defence of their co-founders. The emphasis Luke places both on the Old Testament

---

[1] Haenchen, *Apg.*, p. 560.

[2] Schmithals, *James*, pp. 57–60, rejects all the usual explanations for Luke's account, but fails to offer any alternative.

[3] W. Eltester, 'Lukas und Paulus', in *Eranion*, Festschrift for H. Hommel (Tübingen, 1961), pp. 1f.

[4] J. Jervell, 'Paulus – der Lehrer Israel. Zu der apologetischen Paulusrede in der Apostelgeschichte', *Nov. Test.*, 10 (1968), 164f. On pp. 187–90 Jervell gives a description of the circumstances in which Luke's Church existed, a description to which the above paragraph is much indebted.

prophecies of the Gentile mission and on the Jews' wilful rejection of the gospel may be his response to Jewish calumny. Such a defence may imply that while Luke's Church was predominantly Gentile, it lived in a predominantly Jewish milieu.

In emphasising this apologetic motive in Luke's account of the Gentile mission, the element of simple historical curiosity should not be overlooked. Apart from Jewish accusations, it would be natural for a Gentile, or for that matter a Jewish, Church to be inquisitive about its origins, the men involved in them, and how it had reached its present form. How far this, and the attempt to prove the legitimacy of the Gentile Churches, can be described as Luke's desire to preserve the continuity of *Heilsgeschichte* is uncertain. Such a description may be too grand and a little misleading for describing Luke's practical and historical purpose. As we have seen, the word *Heilsgeschichte* is often used with pejorative undertones; also, although it may seem to us satisfactorily to describe what Luke is doing, it is unlikely that he was thinking in such theological terms as its modern usage implies, so that if we do use it, it must be carefully defined.

A comparison with Paul

Our investigation of Luke's approach to the Gentiles and the Gentile mission is complete. A brief comparison with Paul will serve to emphasise some of the distinctive elements in Luke:

1. One of the most noticeable characteristics of Luke's portrait of Paul is that he spends as much, if not more, of his time preaching to the Jews as to the Gentiles. At each point in his itineraries Paul begins his work in the synagogues (9: 20, 13: 5, 14, 14: 1, 17: 1–2, 10, 17, 18: 4, 19, 19: 8) and, though frequently frustrated, his efforts continue up to the very end of Acts (28: 23f). While he is the Gentile missionary *par excellence*, he also does more than any other figure in the early Church to promote the mission to the Jews. The historical reliability of this portrait has been radically questioned by Schmithals,[1] while others stoutly defend it.[2] Schmithals' view is based on a total mistrust of the historical reliability of Acts, the evidence of

[1] Schmithals, *James*, pp. 54–62.
[2] Haenchen, *Apg.*, p. 445; G. Bornkamm, 'The missionary stance of Paul in I Cor. 9 and in Acts', *SLA*, pp. 194–207, here p. 200.

Paul's epistles, and practical considerations as to Paul's most 'natural' missionary methods. However, while Acts must be handled with care, we cannot reject its evidence out of hand. It is true that many of Paul's extant epistles are addressed to predominantly Gentile Churches and that Paul designates himself as the Apostle to the Gentiles (Rom. 11: 13, 15: 16, 18; Gal. 1: 16, 2: 2, 9; I Thess. 2: 16), but one cannot ignore passages like I Cor. 9: 20 and II Cor. 11: 24, which imply that Paul did, at least early in his ministry, preach to Jews as well as Gentiles. It is nowhere said in the epistles that he did not approach Jews, for although Rom. 9–11 says that Paul's method of reaching the Jews was through the Gentiles, these are the ideas of a man reflecting on something like twenty-five years of missionary experience and not the notions which inspired him when he set out on his endeavours. Schmithals rejects as 'unthinkable' Haenchen's claim that the synagogues were the natural starting places for Paul's work. But it is only 'unthinkable' when one believes, with Schmithals, that Paul preached a radically antinomian gospel to both Jews and Gentiles. But since there is no evidence that Paul did encourage Jews to abandon the Law, Schmithals' objection has little force. The synagogues, with their numbers of God-fearing Gentiles who accepted the basic tenets of the Jewish faith, would have been the ideal place for Paul to begin his missionary work. Certainly, Luke's account is stylised and follows a rigid pattern which does not always do justice to the complexity of the actual events, but its essential reliability is not to be doubted.

2. Bornkamm argues that whereas Paul views the Jewish and Gentile missions as occurring simultaneously, Luke sees them as occurring in succession – first the Jewish and then the Gentile mission.[1] But such a bald statement does not do justice either to Luke or to Paul. For while we have argued that Paul did participate in a Jewish and a Gentile mission, presumably simultaneously, when he gives his bird's-eye view of the pattern of history in Rom. 9–11, he sees the pattern as Jews first, then the Gentiles, and finally once again the Jews. The first approach to the Jews met with refusal, therefore Paul suggests that when the next stage – the Gentile mission – reaches its climax, the Jews will be moved by jealousy to accept the gospel. Also, while Luke

[1] Bornkamm, 'Missionary stance', p. 201.

makes it clear that the gospel went to the Jews first, and while the end of Acts seems to indicate the end of the Jewish mission and usher in the era of Gentile Christianity, throughout the narrative of Acts from ch. 10 onwards the missions to the Jews and the Gentiles are carried on simultaneously (14: 1, 17: 4, 18: 6, 19: 10, 26: 20). Thus it seems that Bornkamm has created a false contrast. In essentials Luke and Paul agree: the gospel went first to the Jews; then the Gentile mission began and for a while ran concurrently with the Jewish mission; finally, the Jewish mission ground to a halt and the Church turned its attention exclusively to Gentiles.[1]

More to the point in contrasting Luke and Paul is the fact that Luke appears to lack Paul's final stage in the development. For whereas Paul clearly hopes for the ultimate salvation of Israel,[2] the overall impression left by Luke is that the Jews are lost for ever.[3] If this was not Luke's view, he has left no clear indication to this effect.[4] Here then is one point of contrast between Luke and Paul, which probably results from the fact that Luke was writing at a much later time than Paul, when the Jew's rejection had been accepted as a matter of course, and because unlike Paul, Luke was not personally and emotionally involved in the fate of the Jews.

3. Haenchen has noted three aspects in which Luke has misrepresented Paul.[5] First, Luke sees Paul as a great miracle-worker (13: 6f, 14: 8f, 19: 12f, 20: 7f, 28: 3f) and, although the real Paul did perform miracles (II Cor. 12: 12), they did not play a central role either in his work or in his concept of apostleship. But Haenchen exaggerates the difference: one

---

[1] On the general question of *Heilsgeschichte* in Luke and Paul see P. Borgen, 'Von Lukas zu Paulus. Beobachtungen zur Erhellung der Theologie der Lukasschriften', *St. Th.*, 20 (1966), 140f.

[2] I Thess. 2: 14–16 may seem to belie this, but O'Neill (*Acts*, p. 91) is correct in saying that they are either (a) not Paul's words, (b) one side of a paradox which is explained more fully in Rom. 9–11, or (c) a momentary outburst of anger with no serious theological implications – the last perhaps being the most likely explanation.

[3] Haenchen, *Apg.*, p. 91; Jervell, 'Israel', p. 92; Conzelmann, *Apg.*, p. 149.

[4] O'Neill, *Acts*, p. 82, thinks Luke does believe in the future salvation of the Jews; but Acts 1: 6f, 3: 20–1, which he quotes, do not seem clear or sufficient evidence for this view.

[5] Haenchen, *Apg.*, pp. 99–103.

should not underestimate the reference in II Cor. 12: 12,[1] especially in the light of Rom. 15: 18–19 – which Haenchen ignores – from which it appears that miracles are a regular feature of Paul's missionary work. Paul, according to both the epistles and Acts, sees miracles not as a ground for boasting, but as signs of the work of God (Acts 15: 9; Rom. 15: 18). Luke's penchant for the miraculous may have led him to exaggerate a little, but his account is based on sound historical fact, even if influenced by the heroic proportions which the figure of Paul had reached in some post-apostolic Church traditions.

Second, whereas Paul saw himself as an Apostle of equal standing with Peter and the other Apostles and as having a direct commission from God, Luke does not portray Paul as an Apostle and emphasises his dependence on the Twelve in Jerusalem. There is certainly an element of truth in what Haenchen says here, but again he has to exaggerate to make his point. We have already suggested in an earlier section that Acts 14: 4, 14 cannot be lightly dismissed and that they reveal that Luke did not deliberately deny Paul the title 'Apostle'. He uses it more frequently of the Twelve because it is a convenient nomenclature, which saves him from listing them all each time they appear. Also, in the section on Paul's conversion, we have suggested that Luke's account is closely parallel to Paul's own versions, at least on the question of his direct commission from God and his dealings with the Jerusalem Church.

Finally, Haenchen notes that Luke portrays Paul as a persuasive orator (24: 1f, 40f, 22: 1f) before Jews (13: 16f, 23: 1f), Gentiles (17: 22f) and magistrates (13: 9–11, 24: 10f), whereas the real Paul was a weak and unimpressive speaker (II Cor. 10: 10). Haenchen is correct in emphasising at this point how Luke's picture is affected by the ideas of a later generation than that of Paul, when the legendary figure of Paul had been idealised and the memory of the real man blurred.

4. The most striking and important difference between Luke and Paul is that whereas Paul has a theology of the Gentiles, Luke has not. Even allowing for the fact that Acts and the epistles belong to different literary genres, the contrast is still

---

[1] Schmithals, *Apostelamt*, pp. 26–7, thinks that in II Cor. 12: 12 Paul is either using a well-known formula without thinking what is really meant, or he is thinking of speaking in the Spirit and power.

marked. Paul explains and justifies the turning to the Gentiles within the total structure of his theological ideas.[1] To give a full explication of Paul's theology of the Gentiles would be impossible, since 'his view of the mission is inseparable from his entire theological thought; it therefore leads us into almost all the problems of his theology'.[2] Also, that Paul has a theology of the Gentiles and that it is an integral part of his total theological outlook is not in dispute; and, for the purposes of this book, this is enough to allow for a comparison with Luke. A few brief comparisons will serve to confirm our conclusions. First, we can refer back to the chapter on the Areopagus speech and the contrast drawn there between Luke and Paul. Luke's assessment of the Gentiles' pre-Christian religiosity is positive, magnanimous and non-theological compared with the way Paul handles the same theme in Rom. 1–3. In accord with this is their treatment of the question of the Law.[3] Paul's doctrine of Law and grace, that is, his theology of justification, is the basis of his total theological outlook, including his attitude to the Gentiles. For Paul, the Law leads not to salvation but to sin (Gal. 3: 19; Rom. 4: 13–16; II Cor. 3: 6), and in this way serves God's purpose by preparing men for the revelation of his righteousness in Christ, which puts an end to the Law as a way of salvation (Rom. 10: 4). For Gentiles to turn to the Law as a means of salvation would be equivalent to returning to their previous slavery to the elemental cosmic powers (Gal. 4: 8–10). This new revelation in Christ is universal; it both condemns and reaches out to all men (Rom. 1: 14), for as all men were condemned in Adam so all are saved in Christ (Rom. 5: 12f). Thus on the basis of the work of Christ alone, Paul can claim that there is no distinction between Jew and Greek (Rom. 3: 22f, 10: 12; Gal. 3: 28; I Cor. 12: 13). Jews and Gentiles are united in the one epochal event of salvation, which is rooted in Christ's death and resurrection.

In Luke's account, justification plays no part at all. It is alluded to in Acts 13: 38–9, but it is differently understood; it is

---

[1] This is not meant to imply that Paul's theology can be forced into a systematic framework, but simply that it comes a lot closer to being systematic than Luke's.

[2] Hahn, *Mission*, p. 97.

[3] Haenchen, *Apg.*, pp. 102–3; Vielhauer, 'Paulinism', pp. 37f; Bornkamm, 'Missionary stance', pp. 194f.

equated with the idea of forgiveness and it is not expressly based on Christ's death. Also, there is but a faint echo (Acts 15: 10) of Paul's account of the insufficiency of the Law and nothing of his contrast between Law and grace. Luke does not see the Law as a way of salvation; it is insufficient, but it is not brought to an end in Christ: 'Luke speaks of the inadequacy of the Law, whereas Paul speaks of the end of the Law, which is Christ.'[1] Moreover, Luke repeatedly refers to the Law in a positive way: the Gentiles are encouraged to follow the requirements applicable to them (15: 21, 28) and Paul is portrayed as one who does not speak against the Law (21: 21, 28), but positively fulfils its requirements (16: 3, 18: 18, 21: 20f). For Luke, the Law is no longer a burning issue concerning the fundamentals of belief; rather, it is an ecclesiastical-historical problem. Even in his account of Paul's conflict with the Jews, he suggests that the cause of these was belief in the Resurrection (4: 2, 28: 23; cf. 23: 6, 24: 5, 21, 26: 6f, 27, 28: 20), while one of the real reasons, his teaching on the Law, lies obscurely in the background (15: 5, 21: 21, 28).[2] Luke has lost Paul's insight into the solidarity of the human race expressed in the Law–grace, Adam–Christ contrasts, and in place of Paul's understanding of the equality of all men in Christ, he resorts to a pragmatic understanding of the equality of Jews and Gentiles.

Luke has lost completely Paul's logical and theological justification of the Gentiles and the Gentile mission; in its place he offers a collection of unconnected, miscellaneous themes. Certainly, the problem and the right of the Gentile mission is as important to Luke as to Paul, but in their approach to the problem they could not be more different. Paul's approach is that of the theologian, Luke's that of the pragmatist; and while the end result in Paul is logical and integrated – the result of profound theological reflection, in Luke it is varied, at times confused, and altogether more naive.

In recent years we have been offered several attempts to portray Luke as a theologian in his own right; he is no longer seen as a man who simply passed on tradition as he received it and as a writer of dramatic stories, but as a man who has a theological axe to grind. He is said to have produced a *heilsgeschichtlich* theology which is both broad in outline and precise in

---

[1] Vielhauer, 'Paulinism', p. 42.　　[2] Haenchen, *Apg.*, pp. 102–3.

detail. The various individual theological themes are thought to fit logically into the overall pattern. Scholars differ in their assessment of which particular theme dominates Luke's theology, but they all agree that he is a theologian. However, our studies have led us to precisely the opposite conclusion. We have found that the one thing Luke is not, is a theologian. Insofar as he writes about God, Luke can properly be called a theologian. But this is probably better expressed by saying that Luke's writings are theocentric, rather than by calling him a theologian. For in comparison with the profound, logical and complex theology of Paul, Luke cannot be said to have produced a theology at all. His main interests were historical and practical. He was far more concerned to produce an intelligible history, which at the same time spoke to the practical, pastoral problems of the Church of his day, than he was to produce what we would call a theology. We found this to be true at several points, in particular in his treatment of eschatology and in his presentation of the Gentile mission. It would perhaps be more exciting to offer a new and original presentation of the theology of Luke, but the facts force us to conclude that he was a pastor and a historian rather than a theologian.

HISTORICAL RELIABILITY

Opinions on the reliability of Acts range from those who see it as a bundle of legends, an uninterrupted fiction, to those who claim that it is a history whose trustworthiness is unsurpassed. Between these two extremes there are endless variations. Before summarising our own results on this question, we shall give a few examples of the various shades of opinion.

It has been claimed, for example, that not only is Acts totally unreliable, but that this unreliability is a result not of Luke's lack of reliable sources or critical acumen, but of his deliberate perversion of the facts as he knew them. If he is accurate at some points, this is not because he was genuinely concerned with historical truth, but because the truth at that point happened to fit in with the particular axe he was grinding. This view is most frequently associated with the name of F. C. Baur, who argues that Acts was written in A.D. 110–25 with an irenic purpose, namely to mediate between the Petrine and Pauline parties which had divided the Church from the earliest days.[1] The result was a deliberate perversion of history. Few scholars nowadays would accept Baur's analysis of first- and second-century Christianity, but scholars like G. Klein and S. G. F. Brandon have a very similar view of the reliability of Acts.[2]

The opposite school of thought claims that apart from a few excusable errors of fact the narrative Luke relates is substantially reliable. Luke was certainly an artist who selected and arranged his facts, but he did not therefore distort them. He did not have a 'tendency', nor did he pervert facts which he knew to be true; rather, he aimed at recounting the historical movement of the Church from Jerusalem to Rome. Such views came to the fore as a reaction to the radicalism of Baur in the writings of men like M. Baumgarten and G. V. Lechler.[3] W. M. Ramsay, on the basis of his archaeological research, also argues for the acceptance of Luke as a historian of the first rank, reliable both in general and in detail.[4] Not many recent authors credit Luke with such a high rating as these scholars, but many of them hold opinions which come close to this view – C. S. C. Williams, A. Wikenhauser, B. Gärtner, F. V. Filson, F. F. Bruce, W. L. Knox, J. Munck, A. Ehrhardt.[5]

The third approach to Acts which we shall mention is distinguished by its relative lack of concern about the question of reliability. These scholars are more concerned to understand Luke's theology than to assess his reliability. While most of them agree that at times Luke is reliable, they argue that the important thing is what Luke means by a narrative and not how reliable it is. Even so there is a wide variety of opinion within this theological approach to Luke: thus E. Haenchen, H. Conzelmann, M. Dibelius, J. C. O'Neill, U. Wilckens and Ph. Vielhauer are sceptical about Luke's reliability,[6] whereas

[1] F. C. Baur, *Paul, the Apostle of Jesus Christ*, i (London, 1873).
[2] Klein, *Apostel*; S. G. F. Brandon, *The Fall of Jerusalem and the Christian Church* (London, 1951).
[3] M. Baumgarten, *The Acts of the Apostles; on the History of the Church in the Apostolic Age*, vols. I, II (Edinburgh, 1854); G. V. Lechler, *The Apostolic and post-Apostolic Times* (Edinburgh, 1866). [4] Ramsay, *Paul*.
[5] Williams, *Acts*; Wikenhauser, *Apg.*; Gärtner, *Areopagus*; Filson, *Decades*; Knox, *Acts*; Bruce, *Acts*; Munck, *Paul*; Erhardt, *Framework*.
[6] Haenchen, *Apg.*; Dibelius, *Acts*; Conzelmann, *Apg.*; O'Neill, *Acts*; Wilckens, *Missionsreden*; Vielhauer, 'Paulinism'.

R. P. C. Hanson and G. Stählin think Luke is frequently close to the truth.[1] Clearly there are many variations within the broad categories we have outlined and most of the views are more complex than we have described them. Nevertheless, this summary is sufficient to show the wide range of opinion in modern studies of Acts and to serve as a background to our own conclusions. We must now draw together the various strands of evidence we have studied and, while being aware that only select passages have been considered, propose some tentative conclusions of our own on this broad and complex issue.

In the section on Luke's Gospel it was concluded that while Luke had mistakenly placed the command for a Gentile mission on the lips of Jesus in the immediate post-Resurrection period, he did not anachronistically place the origins of this mission within the ministry of Jesus. While Jesus prophesied the future inclusion of the Gentiles in the kingdom of God and responded positively on the rare occasions he met a Gentile, he does not begin the Gentile mission itself. In view of Luke's interest in the Gentiles, it might have been tempting for him to make Jesus into the first Gentile missionary, but instead he follows in all essentials the pattern laid down in Mark's Gospel. With his knowledge both of Mark and of the fact that the Gentile mission had taken place, it would have been virtually impossible for Luke to probe behind the Gospel traditions and discover that Jesus did not authorise a historical Gentile mission.

In our studies of the first few chapters of Acts, we examined the origins of the mission in the earliest years of the Church. Luke's view, that the Gentile mission was commissioned by Jesus, was found to be historically unreliable. If it were true, then it makes inexplicable the fact both that the mission was so slow in starting and that the Apostles raised objections when this mission first came to their notice – not to mention Peter's reluctance to approach Cornelius until God had directly intervened. Moreover, in the midst of the intense eschatological expectation of the earliest Christians, which is still detectable beneath the early chapters of Acts, it is improbable that the Church expected to complete a gradual, planned mission such as is envisaged in Acts 1 : 8. Also, if the conclusions of the first

---

[1] Hanson, *Acts*; Stählin, *Apg.*

part of this thesis are correct, and Jesus did not foresee a historical Gentile mission, then it is unlikely that the Church would have suddenly and spontaneously discovered that such a mission was to be a precondition of the End. The tension between Luke's view and the historical facts is still discernible in the narrative of Acts, despite Luke's attempt to impose on it his own interpretation of events. The confinement of the Apostles to Jerusalem, their suspicion when the mission moves out of this locale (8: 1, 14f, 11: 1f), and Peter's reluctance to approach Cornelius (10: 9f), are all inconsistent with the explicit command given to them by Jesus in 1: 8.

The reluctance of the early Christians to embark on a Gentile mission is to be explained not simply by reference to their disobedience or their Jewish scruples, but by acknowledging a far more fundamental factor, namely that in all probability they shared the same view as Jesus. He did not expect a historical, but an apocalyptic, proclamation to the Gentiles. Therefore, the early Christians, like Jesus, believed that the Gentiles would participate in the future kingdom, but they did not expect this participation to begin before the End and did not, therefore, see the Gentile mission as a task they had to fulfil. It was not that they were disobeying God's will; rather, as far as they knew, it was not part of his will for the present. But as their hope for an imminent End was regularly disappointed, and as the Church increasingly broke free from the bounds of Judaism and found sympathetic Gentile hearers, it gradually dawned on the early Christians that history had taken a new turn, a turn which was then justified and firmly grounded by placing a universal missionary command on the lips of Jesus. This in no way implies that Luke was deliberately perverting the facts as he knew them. Long before he wrote, Jesus' teaching on the Gentiles had been either altered, forgotten or misunderstood, so that already in Mk 13: 10 the universal mission is seen as a precondition rather than as a result of the End. And although the critical eye may detect the eschatological fervour of the primitive Church beneath the first few chapters of Acts, this does not mean that Luke was aware of it and sought deliberately to cover it up. Writing at a time when the Gentile mission was a well-established fact, some of the early traditions of the primitive Church would have been extremely difficult for Luke to comprehend, apart from the fact that they were probably obscure and fragmentary when they reached him. In the light of events in the intervening years, Luke attempts to unravel and make intelligible the minds of the early Christians. The intention is laudable even if the result is not.

The next main problem we encountered was the origin and influence of Stephen and the Hellenists. Here, too, it was discovered that Luke's own analysis of the events often misses the historical truth. This is a result partly of the confusion of the material he was dealing with and partly of his own view of the development of the Gentile mission. Luke believed it was a planned, schematic advance, begun by the leading Apostle and followed up above all in the work of Paul. According to Luke, Cornelius was the first and decisive convert from the Gentile world. As a result of his conversion, the question of the admission of Gentiles into the Church was, in principle, settled. Before this the problem had not arisen, since no Gentiles were converted before Cornelius. Not only is this ideal, schematic account intrinsically improbable, but also Luke himself uses material which suggests a rather different picture. It is improbable that the problem of the Gentile mission was introduced and solved in and around the person of the first Gentile convert. It is more probable that Gentiles were converted simultaneously, a few in one Church centre and a few in another, rather than that the expansion of the Church followed the concentric pattern envisaged in 1 : 8. Jerusalem held a pre-eminent position in the early Church, but Luke has exaggerated this fact. The early Church was never focused on Jerusalem to the extent which Luke implies, except perhaps in the first few months. Luke may have left a hint of this in the Pentecost narrative. He does not interpret it as a miracle directly affecting the Gentiles; they have their own 'pentecost' in ch. 10. But if there was some exceptional event witnessed on that first Christian Pentecost by numerous visitors to the city from the Diaspora, then one would presume that, on returning to their own country, those who had been impressed or even converted by this event and its aftermath would pass on the message as they went. This would imply a sort of *Wandermission*, unplanned and unauthorised, where the message was passed spontaneously from one to another, both Jews and Gentiles alike. Presumably this is how the otherwise unexplained Christian community at Damascus arose. A further hint that this was so we found in Acts 11: 19f, which is very significant – the more so if we link it together with Acts 8: 4 as part of a common source. In the latter case, if the source reached Luke in one piece, he has split it up and inserted Acts 8: 5 – 11: 18 between the persecution of the Hellenists and their flight to distant lands which resulted in preaching to the Gentiles. The corollary of this would be that Luke has consciously imposed his own understanding on the material, reserving the Hellenists' Gentile mission for the period after the test-case, Cornelius, has been approved. Apart from any source theory, the natural time-reference of Acts 11: 19f is to events which occur either before or simultaneously with those of Acts 8: 5 – 11: 18, so that a succession of events different from that which Luke offers seems to be implied. The Hellenists' mission also has an air of spontaneity about it; it is unplanned and unauthorised, and results not from a conscious decision of the Church to embark on a Gentile mission, but from ferocious persecution of the Hellenists by the Jews.

This leads us immediately to the narrative in Acts 10–11. As we have already implied, Luke has magnified and schematised the account of Cornelius' conversion. What was originally a simple, straightforward legend about the conversion of a godly Gentile, has been transformed into a type or pattern for all Gentile converts. Cornelius is singled out as the test case around which all the problems of Gentile converts are settled once and for all. That Luke has magnified it out of all proportion is clear from the fact that a few years later a council convenes in Jerusalem to settle these problems once again, when ostensibly they had already been settled earlier. Since the main elements of Acts 15 are supported by Paul's account (Gal. 2: 1f), the narrative in Acts 10–11 is not, as it stands, the historical truth. Certainly, it has a historical core, but this core has been embellished, probably both in pre-Lukan tradition and by Luke himself.

Much the same can be said about Luke's account of the Apostolic Council. The outline of the narrative accords with what we find in Galatians, but at several points Luke betrays the presuppositions of a later age. The conflict between Paul and the Jerusalem Church is treated lightly and it is the

Apostles Peter and James who, rather idealistically, are the chief defenders of the right of the Gentile mission. The Apostles and Paul are in perfect harmony over the question of the Gentiles. Luke has also misplaced the apostolic decree, and he assumes wrongly that Paul assented to it. Clearly, Luke is not aware of the depth or the extent of the conflict over the Law in Paul's teaching. It might appear that the extent of the harmonising and idealising process in Acts 15 is so great that it betrays more than a simple understanding, namely a deliberate distortion of the facts. If this is so, then we cannot impute the whole of this process to Luke, for he rarely, if ever, gives the impression that he distorts facts which he knows to be true; rather, it is the facts which were available to him and his own understanding of them which are deficient. In the tradition which Luke uses in Acts 15, it is possible that at one or more stages the account was deliberately recast. Or it may be that Luke or his tradition were unwittingly influenced by traditions which stemmed from Paul's opponents. In either case, being both ignorant of Paul's epistles and influenced by the ideal picture of Paul in Christian tradition, and living at a time when the heated disputes of the apostolic era had faded in importance, it was almost inevitable that Luke would accept the tradition as he found it. Even if he was not the man to perpetrate deliberate falsehoods, neither was he exactly looking for evidence of disharmony in the primitive Church.

In general, Luke's account of the origins and early development of the Gentile mission follows a broad and ideal pattern. Haenchen's comment is both judicious and fully justified: 'Luke the historian does not sketch the frequently broken line of the real development of the Gentile mission, but its ideal curve.'[1] Whereas in reality it was spontaneous, unplanned, unauthorised and unorganised, the result of a *Wandermission* which was not based on a single geographical or ecclesiastical centre, in Acts it is a planned, gradual progression which follows a strict pattern. Where in reality there was, after this ragged start, a series of sharp disputes between various factions in the Church, Luke gives a picture of almost complete harmony. The details of historical reality are lost in the broad sweep and schematic lines of Luke's own interpretation.

[1] Haenchen, *Apg.*, p. 93.

How then are we to assess Luke's presentation of Paul? In general, a rather different judgement from that on the first part of Acts is required, for Luke is closer to historical actuality more frequently than in the earlier chapters. There is similar evidence for idealisation and schematisation, but its role is less important than before. Luke's account of Paul's conversion is, as we have seen, essentially in accord with Paul's own evidence in the epistles. Luke lacks Paul's profound theological reflection on the event and has a different evaluation of the Resurrection appearances, but apart from this his threefold account is a close parallel, and at times an additional source of material, to the facts which Paul himself gives. The overall picture of Paul in the second part of Acts as a missionary to Jews and Gentiles, a miracle worker, and as an Apostle seems to be a reasonably reliable guide to the real Paul. There are, of course, differences of emphasis and sometimes of fact: the rigid scheme of Paul's prior mission to the Jews in each new area, the lack of any emphatic application of the title 'Apostle' to Paul, and the frequent references to Paul's miracles are all differences of emphasis; the picture of Paul as a persuasive orator and the lack of any ultimate hope for the Jews in his preaching are differences of fact. But despite this, the main outlines of Luke's sketch are reliable.

In his account of Paul's preaching to the Gentiles, Luke goes a little more astray (Acts 14, 17). He is correct in supposing that Paul did use arguments from nature and more general philosophical notions, but the use Paul makes of these arguments and the conclusions he draws from them are very different in Acts and Romans. In Acts 17, Gentile religiosity is assessed positively and independently of any overall theological framework; it is seen as the first stage on the way to salvation. In Romans, it is used negatively and is integrated into Paul's total theological complex; it is seen as the basis of the Gentiles' condemnation. Luke seems to have allowed his picture of Paul's preaching to be influenced by the sort of Gentile missionary sermon common in his own day.

One final fact to be noted is the unexpected and unexplained appearance of Christian communities in the narrative of Acts, about whose origins Luke is either ignorant or deliberately silent. The appearance of these communities (9: 10f, 32–6, 18:

19, 26, 28: 13, 15) makes it clear that Luke's concentration on the figure of Paul can easily lead to misconceptions. Undoubtedly, Paul was the most important and active Gentile missionary in the early Church – a fact witnessed by himself and others – but he was not the only one involved in this work, as he himself is aware (Rom. 15: 20). Were it not for the occasional lacunae noted above, one might suppose from Acts that, apart from Barnabas, virtually all the missionary preaching to the Gentiles was the work of Paul (though cf. 11: 19). The fact that Luke includes these occasional lacunae is a mark in favour of his honesty. That he uses here, as at other points, material which is not homogeneous, shows that even though he had his own view of how events developed, this did not lead to the suppression of material which contradicted his own interpretation.

Luke's portrait of Paul betrays no elements of a deliberate degrading of Paul, as Klein supposes. In fact, if anything it is the opposite which is true: Luke magnifies and idealises Paul, making him into a heroic figure. When the facts may seem to be wide of the mark there is no reason to suppose that this is Luke's own work, but rather that he used traditions whose historical worth he could not easily assess. Luke's account of Paul has been influenced by a variety of factors: the historical facts; the Church's traditions about Paul; his ignorance of Paul's epistles; and finally, both his ignorance of the disputes in the early Church and the consequent tendency to reflect the settled opinions of his day and to project these back into what were originally burning and divisive issues.

On the basis of the material we have examined we can now draw some tentative conclusions about the reliability of Acts. They must remain tentative, since there are so many major fields we have left untouched, such as the speeches in the early parts of Acts, the 'we' source, and both the general outline and the minor details of the missionary journeys of Paul.

First, our conclusions exclude any simple answers to this problem; one-word definitions of Luke's reliability will not cover the whole of Acts. Sometimes Luke is very close to the truth, at other times far from it; but most of the time he is somewhere between the two. For the same reason any extreme conclusions are out of the question. It would be as false to claim that

Acts is reliable down to the smallest detail in every case as it would be to claim that it is a wholly tendentious work and utterly lacking in historical worth. Each extreme can account for but a few of the facts. As Cadbury wisely says, 'Our alternatives are not to take it or to leave it, to accept it "from cover to cover" or to reject it *in toto*. We shall prefer to form our verdict about its contents piece by piece.'[1]

Second, we have found no evidence to suppose that Luke cold-bloodedly perverted the facts as he knew them. As we have seen, the frequent tensions and contradictions in his account militate against such a view. A man who was intent on imposing a strict and uniform view on his material would have suppressed far more of the material than Luke has. As Sanders says, 'It is a kind of tribute to his fundamental honesty that he leaves so many loose ends and so many clues for the ingenious critic who wants to unpick and refashion the complicated patchwork of his narrative'.[2] This does not mean that Luke did not have his own interpretation of events and that at times this led him to reshuffle the material he had. But this is a very different picture of Luke the writer from that which the Tübingen School, Brandon and Klein would have us accept.

Third, when Luke goes wrong and gets things a bit muddled, this is normally due to a combination of several factors. In many parts of Acts, particularly the early chapters, Luke seems to have been faced with the task of unravelling incomplete and obscure tradition. The fact that his attempt to sort it out and present a readable, continuous narrative is at times historically unreliable is, therefore, hardly surprising. Not only were the traditions he built on obscure, but at times the tradition itself had developed over the decades to give a picture, for example of Paul, which did not always conform to sober historical reality. Moreover, the importance of Luke's ignorance of Paul's writings can scarcely be overemphasised, for much of our modern criticism of Acts is based on our knowledge of Paul's extant writings. This lack was a serious handicap to Luke in his attempt to reconstruct the events of the apostolic age. A further factor is the way in which Luke allows the conditions of his own time to influence

[1] Cadbury, *Making*, p. 365.
[2] J. N. Sanders, 'Peter and Paul in Acts', *NTS*, 2 (1955–6), 133f, here p. 143.

his description of events which occurred some sixty years before. Lacking some of the knowledge we have and not possessing our modern, overriding desire for 'the facts as they actually happened', it may not have seemed so naive to Luke – when he drew a blank in his historical enquiries or was left with a vague and obscure impression – to assume that the conditions in the Church of his day were also those of the apostolic age. This is not the place to enter into a discussion of the limits of the historian, but it is worth observing that even the modern, historiographically conscious historian frequently reveals the presuppositions of his own time. A man can look at the past only through the spectacles of his own environment. This cannot be used as an excuse for rank mishandling of known facts, but it goes part of the way towards explaining what Luke has done. And although Luke reflects the conditions and attitudes of his day, one does not get the impression that this was the result of an irresponsible imposition of these views on material which would not bear them. This, in turn, leads us to another motivating force in Luke, namely his desire to show that the events of the apostolic age had a direct, relevant message for his contemporaries. This led him to look for and emphasise those facts which were most pertinent to the problems which his fellow Christians faced. Luke's history is not a bare chronicle of the facts; it is history with a message. In order to find such a message he does not normally create new facts or falsify known ones; rather, he takes as his starting point a relevant fact or event in the apostolic era and then isolates it for special attention. Thus we saw that his account of the Jews' refusal of the gospel, while reflecting an indisputable experience of the early Church, is also influenced by the experience of his contemporaries and his desire to address himself to them.

This last point raises a major issue in Acts, namely the purpose of Luke's composition and the extent to which this purpose has influenced the end-result. It would be impossible and inappropriate to launch into a full discussion of the diverse theories on the purpose of Acts. Our main task is to summarise our own findings in this sphere and compare them with other theories.

Recent studies of Acts have shown that it is almost always unsatisfactory to isolate any one theme as representing Luke's total purpose, because to do so fails to do justice to the whole book. To claim that Acts is aimed solely at providing a defence[1] or a degrading[2] of Paul, a defence of Christianity as a *religio licita*,[3] an answer to the problem of disillusioned expectation of the Parousia,[4] an anti-Gnostic tract,[5] or a manifesto of the centrality and power of the Holy Spirit,[6] is to neglect in each case a considerable amount of the material. Each of these claims may contain some, but none contains all, of the truth. Nor does the claim that Luke's purpose was wholly historical or wholly theological fit the facts as we have interpreted them.[7] The need is for some sort of 'umbrella' term or terms which at the same time correctly characterise the motivating force behind the composition of Acts and leaves room for a variety of main themes. O'Neill has, with a certain amount of credibility, tried to do this under the general description of Luke's purpose as 'evangelical', that is, at all points Luke is trying to convince and convert educated Roman readers.[8] But from our studies a different description is required. The most convenient is to say that Luke's purpose was a combination of historical and practical elements. He wanted to write history, but history that had a message for his contemporaries. Such an emphasis on the practical, pastoral motivation of Luke's writing leaves ample room for distinguishing various themes within this general description and, at the same time, shows where the centre of gravity of Luke's interests lies. He was interested primarily in

1 Either at his trial (Plooij, 'Pauline preaching') or against Jewish calumnies (Harnack, *Acts*, pp. 41–3, 129).
2 Klein, *Apostel*, pp. 213f.
3 Haenchen, *Apg.*, pp. 89f; B. S. Easton, *Early Christianity* (London, 1955), pp. 33f.
4 Conzelmann, *Luke*, pp. 95f and *Apg.*, pp. 9f; Grässer, *Parusieverzögerung*, pp. 204f.
5 Klein, *Apostel*, who thinks Luke is reclaiming Paul for the Church from the Gnostics. C. H. Talbert, *Luke*, thinks the whole of Acts is an anti-Gnostic tract.
6 Ehrhardt, *Framework*, pp. 64f; cf. U. Luck, 'Kerygma, Tradition und Geschichte bei Lukas', *ZTK*, 57 (1960), 51f.
7 For the former view see Ramsay, *Paul*, pp. 309f. The main drift of the commentaries by Haenchen and Conzelmann is in the direction of the latter view, although it would be unfair to restrict them to this one line of interpretation.
8 O'Neill, *Acts*, pp. 166f.

practical and not in 'theological' problems.[1] Of course, these problems and their answers had theological implications, and one might justifiably claim that the man who deals with practical issues from a Christian viewpoint is as much a theologian as the man whose interests lie in the more systematic and philosophical fields. But if this is done, then it must be made clear that they are theologians of a very different type, both in the motivation and in the focusing of their interests. The contrast between Luke and Paul is sufficiently sharp to make this differentiation clear.

To conclude: Luke is neither totally reliable nor is he a wholly tendentious writer. He intends to write good history even if he is not always successful. When he fails it is due to a variety of reasons and not simply because he uses his history to speak to his own generation. Luke has undoubtedly made clear his own interpretation of events, but he has also left a sufficient number of lacunae and loose ends for us to be able to construct our own interpretation – and this says a lot for his basic honesty. While it would be naive to accept uncritically everything Luke says, it remains true that for the careful and critical reader Acts contains an immense amount that is of great historical value.

[1] Some writers have emphasised Luke's attempt to speak to the Church of his day on practical issues – see Haenchen, *Apg.*, pp. 93f; Dibelius, *Acts*, pp. 165f; Braumann, 'Mittel', pp. 117f; Bartsch, *Wachet*, pp. 1f – but on the whole this has been a neglected factor in recent studies of Luke. O'Neill, *Acts*, thinks Luke's pastoral interest is secondary to his evangelistic aim and Cadbury (*Making*, p. 302) suggests that Luke was not concerned with the problems of his contemporaries at all.

BIBLIOGRAPHY

Alt, A. *Kleine Schriften zur Geschichte Israels*, II, Munich, 1953, pp. 436f.
'Die Deutung der Weltgeschichte im Alten Testament', *ZTK*, 56 (1959), 129f.
Althaus, P. *Die kleineren Briefe des Apostels Paulus* (NTD 8), Göttingen, 1955.
Argyle, A. W. 'The Ascension', *ET*, 66 (1955), 240f.
Baer, H. von *Der Heilige Geist in den Lukasschriften*, Stuttgart, 1926.
Bammel, E. 'Matthäus 10: 23', *St. Th.*, 15 (1961), 79f.
Barrett, C. K. *The Holy Spirit and the Gospel Tradition*, London, 1954.
'The background of Mark 10: 45', *NTE*, pp. 2f.
Luke the Historian in Recent Study, London, 1961.
'Stephen and the Son of Man', in *Apophoreta*, Festschrift for E. Haenchen, Berlin, 1964, pp. 32f.
'Paul and the "Pillar" Apostles', *SP*, pp. 1f.
Barth, G. 'Matthew's understanding of the Law', in *Tradition and Interpretation in Matthew*, London, 1963, pp. 58f.
Bartsch, H. W. *Wachet aber zu jeder Zeit! Entwurf einer Auslegung des Lukasevangeliums*, Hamburg–Bergstedt, 1963.
Bauernfeind, O. *Die Apostelgeschichte* (THNT 5), Leipzig, 1939.
Baumgarten, M. *The Acts of the Apostles; on the History of the Church in the Apostolic Age*, vols. I and II, Edinburgh, 1854.
Baur, F. C. *Paul, the Apostle of Jesus Christ*, I, London, 1873.
Beardslee, W. A. 'The casting of lots at Qumran and in the book of Acts', *St. Th.*, 14 (1960), 245f.
Beasley-Murray, G. R. *Jesus and the Future*, London, 1954.
Benoit, P. 'La deuxième visite de St. Paul à Jérusalem', *Bib.*, 40 (1959), 778f.
Black, M. *An Aramaic Approach to the Gospels and Acts*, Oxford, 1967.
'The kingdom of God has come', *ET*, 63 (1951), 289f.
Blackmann, E. C. 'The Hellenists of Acts 6: 1', *ET*, 48 (1937), 524f.
Blinzler, J. 'Die literarische Eigenart des sog. Reiseberichtes im Lukasevangelium', in *Synoptische Studien*, Festschrift for A. Wikenhauser, Munich, 1953, pp. 45f.
Boobyer, G. H. 'The miracle of the loaves and the Gentiles in St Mark's Gospel', *SJT*, 6 (1953), 80f.
'Galilee and the Galileans in St Mark', *BJRL*, 25 (1952–3), 340f.
Borgen, P. 'Von Lukas zu Paulus. Beobachtungen zur Erhellung der Theologie der Lukasschriften', *St. Th.*, 20 (1966), 140f.

Bornkamm, G. *Jesus of Nazareth*, London, 1960.
'End-expectation and the Church in Matthew', in *Tradition and Interpretation in Matthew*, London, 1963, pp. 15f.
'The missionary stance of Paul in I Cor. 9 and in Acts', *SLA*, pp. 194f.
'Die Verzögerung der Parusie', *IM*, pp. 116f.
'Herrenmahl und Kirche bei Paulus', *ZTK*, 53 (1956), 327f.
Bosch, D. *Die Heidenmission in der Zukunftschau Jesu*, Zürich, 1959.
Brandon, S. G. F. *The Fall of Jerusalem and the Christian Church*, London, 1951.
Braumann, G. 'Das Mittel der Zeit', *ZNW*, 54 (1963), 117f.
Bruce, F. F. *The Acts of the Apostles*, London, 1962.
Buck, C. H. 'The date of Galatians', *JBL*, 70 (1951), 113f.
Bultmann, R. *The History of the Synoptic Tradition*, Oxford, 1963.
Theology of the New Testament, I (1952), II (1955), London.
Burton, E. D. *The Epistle to the Galatians* (ICC), Edinburgh, 1921.
Cadbury, H. J. *The Making of Luke–Acts*, London, 1961.
'The eschatology of Acts', in *The Background of the New Testament and its Eschatology*, in honour of C. H. Dodd, Cambridge, 1956, pp. 300f.
'Lexical notes on Luke–Acts', *JBL*, 44 (1925), 219f.
Cadoux, C. J. *The Historic Mission of Jesus*, London, 1943.
Caird, G. B. *St Luke* (Pelican Gospel Commentaries), London, 1963.
The Apostolic Age, London, 1955.
Campenhausen, H. von. 'Der urchristliche Apostelbegriff', *St. Th.*, 1 (1948), 96f.
Chadwick, H. 'The shorter text of Lk. 22: 15–20', *HTR*, 50 (1957), 249f.
Clark, A. C. *The Acts of the Apostles*, Oxford, 1933.
Clark, K. W. 'Realised eschatology', *JBL*, 59 (1940), 367f.
Conzelmann, H. *The Theology of St Luke*, London, 1961.
Die Apostelgeschichte (HNT 7), Tübingen, 1963.
'The address of Paul on the Areopagus', *SLA*, pp. 217f.
'Geschichte und Eschaton nach Mk 13', *ZNW*, 50 (1959), 210f.
Cranfield, C. E. B. *St Mark*, Cambridge, 1959.
'The parable of the unjust judge and the eschatology of Luke–Acts', *SJT*, 16 (1963), 297f.
Dahl, N. A. 'The story of Abraham in Luke–Acts', *SLA*, pp. 139f.
'A People for His Name', *NTS*, 4 (1957–8), 319f.
Daube, D. *The New Testament and Rabbinic Judaism*, London, 1956.
Davidson, R. 'Universalism in Second Isaiah', *SJT*, 16 (1963), 166f.
Davies, J. G. 'The Prefigurement of the Ascension in the Third Gospel', *JTS*, n.s. 6 (1955), 229f.

Deissmann, A. *Paul*, London, 1926.
Delling, G. 'Das Gleichnis vom gottlosen Richter', *ZNW*, 53 (1962), 1f.
Delling, G. 'βάπτισμα, βαπτισθῆναι', *Nov. Test.*, 2 (1958), 92f.
Dibelius, M. *Studies in the Acts of the Apostles*, London, 1956.
Paul, London, 1962 (revised by W. G. Kümmel).
Dodd, C. H. *The Parables of the Kingdom*, London, 1961.
According to the Scriptures, London, 1953.
'The fall of Jerusalem and the "Abomination of Desolation"', *Journal of Roman Studies*, 37 (1947), 47f.
Dupont, J. *The Sources of Acts*, London, 1964.
'Le salut des Gentils et le livre des Actes', *NTS*, 6 (1959–60), 132f.
'ΛΑΟΙ 'ΕΘΝΩΝ Acts 15: 14', *NTS*, 3 (1956–7), 47f.
Easton, B. S. *Early Christianity*, London, 1955.
Ehrhardt, A. *The Framework of the New Testament Stories*, Manchester, 1964.
The Apostolic Succession, London, 1953.
Eissfeldt, O. 'Kreter und Araber', *TLZ*, 12 (1947), 207f.
Ellis, E. Earle. *St Luke* (The Century Bible), London, 1966.
Eltester, W. 'Lukas und Paulus', in *Eranion*, Festschrift for H. Hommel, Tübingen, 1961, pp. 1f.
'Gott und die Natur in der Areopagrede', *NS*, pp. 202f.
Evans, C. F. 'I will go before you into Galilee', *JTS*, n.s. 5 (1954), 3f.
'The central section of St Luke's Gospel', *SG*, pp. 37f.
Farrer, A. *The Apostolic Ministry* (ed. K. B. Kirk), London, 1946, pp. 138f.
Feuillet, A. 'Les origines et la signification de Matt. 10: 23. Contribution à l'étude du problème Eschatologique', *CBQ*, 23 (1961), 182f.
Filson, F. V. *The Gospel according to St Matthew* (BNTC), London, 1960.
Three Crucial Decades, London, 1964.
Flender, H. *Heil und Geschichte in der Theologie des Lukas*, Munich, 1965.
Fridrichsen, A. *The Apostle and his Message*, Uppsala, 1947.
Gärtner, B. *The Areopagus Speech and Natural Revelation*, Uppsala, 1955.
Gasse, W. 'Zum Reisebericht des Lukas', *ZNW*, 34 (1935), 293f.
Geldenhuys, N. *Commentary on the Gospel of St Luke*, London, 1950.
Geyser, A. 'Paul, the Apostolic decree and the liberals at Corinth', *SP*, pp. 124f.
Glasson, T. F. *The Second Advent. The Origin of the New Testament Doctrine*, London, 1947.
Goppelt, L. *Die apostolische und nachapostolische Zeit*, Göttingen, 1962.
Gore, C. *The Church and the Ministry*, London, 1921.

Grässer, E. *Das Problem der Parusieverzögerung in den synoptischen Evangelien und in der Apostelgeschichte* (BZNW 22), Berlin, 1959.

Grundmann, W. *Das Evangelium nach Lukas* (THNT 3), Berlin, 1966.

'Fragen der Komposition des lukanischen Reiseberichtes', *ZNW*, 50 (1959), 252f.

'Die Apostel zwischen Jerusalem und Antiochia', *ZNW*, 38 (1939), 110f.

Guy, H. A. *The New Testament Doctrine of the 'Last Things'*, London, 1948.

Haenchen, E. *Die Apostelgeschichte* (KEK 5, rev. ed.), Göttingen, 1965.

Der Weg Jesu, Berlin, 1966.

'Judentum und Christentum in der Apostelgeschichte', *ZNW*, 54 (1963), 155f.

Hahn, F. *Mission in the New Testament*, London, 1965.

Hanson, R. P. C., *The Acts of the Apostles* (New Clarendon Bible), Oxford, 1967.

Harder, G. 'Das eschatologische Geschichtsbild der sogenannten kleinen Apokalypse Mk 13', *Th. Viat.*, 4 (1952), 78f.

Harnack, A. *The Mission and Expansion of Christianity*, vols. i and ii, London, 1908.

The Acts of the Apostles, London, 1909.

Held, H. J. 'Matthew as interpreter of the miracle stories', in *Tradition and Interpretation in Matthew*, London, 1963, pp. 165f.

Higgins, A. J. B. *Jesus and the Son of Man*. London, 1964.

Hirsch, E. 'Die drei Berichte der Apg. über die Bekehrung des Paulus', *ZNW*, 28 (1929), 305f.

Holtz, T. *Untersuchungen über die Alttestamentlichen Zitate bei Lukas* (TU, 104), Berlin, 1968.

Hommel, H. 'Neue Forschungen zur Areopagrede', *ZNW*, 46 (1955), 145f.

'Platonisches bei Lukas. Zu Acta 17: 27a', *ZNW*, 48 (1957), 193f.

Hurd, J. C. *The Origin of I Corinthians*, London, 1965.

Jeremias, J. *Jesus' Promise to the Nations*, London, 1958.

The Eucharistic Words of Jesus, London, 1966.

The Parables of Jesus, London, 1963.

Jerusalem zur Zeit Jesu, i, Göttingen, 1937.

Abba. Studien zur neutestamentlichen Theologie und Zeitgeschichte, Göttingen, 1966.

Jervell, J. 'Das gespaltene Israel und die Heidenvölker', *St. Th.*, 19 (1965), 68f.

'Paulus – der Lehrer Israel. Zu der apologetischen Paulusrede in der Apostelgeschichte', *Nov. Test.*, 10 (1968), 164f.

Jüngel, E. *Paulus und Jesus*, Tübingen, 1964.

Käsemann, E. *Essays on New Testament Themes*, London, 1964.
'Die Legitimität des Apostels', *ZNW*, 41 (1942), 33f.
Kiddle, M. 'The death of Jesus and the admission of the Gentiles in St Mark', *JTS*, 35 (1934), 45f.
Kilpatrick, G. D. 'The Gentiles and the Gentile mission in Mark: Mk 13: 10', *SG*, pp. 145f.
' ΛΑΟΙ at Lk. 2: 31 and Acts 4: 25, 27', *JTS*, n.s. 16 (1965), 127.
King, N. Q. 'Universalism in the Third Gospel', *TU*, 73 (1959), 199f.
Klein, G. *Die Zwölf Apostel* (FRLANT 77), Göttingen, 1961.
'Besprechung von E. Haenchen, "Die Apostelgeschichte"', *ZKG*, 68 (1957), 362f.
'Die Prüfung der Zeit. Lukas 12: 54–6', *ZTK*, 61 (1964), 374f.
Klostermann, E. *Das Markusevangelium* (HNT 3), Tübingen, 1926.
Das Matthäusevangelium (HNT 4), Tübingen, 1927.
Knox, W. L. *The Acts of the Apostles*, Cambridge, 1948.
St Paul and the Church of Jerusalem, Cambridge, 1925.
Kretschmar, G. 'Himmelfahrt und Pfingsten', *ZKG*, 66 (1954), 217f.
Kümmel, W. G. *Promise and Fulfilment*, London, 1961.
'Das Urchristentum', *Th. Rund.*, 22 (1954), 208f.
'Kirchenbegriffe und Geschichtsbewusstein in der Urgemeinde und bei Jesus', *SBU*, 1943, pp. 1f.
Kuhn, K. G. 'Das Problem der Mission in der Urchristenheit', *EMZ*, 11 (1954), 163f.
Lampe, G. W. H. 'The Lucan portrait of Christ', *NTS*, 2 (1955–6), 160f.
'The Holy Spirit in the Lucan writings', *SG*, pp. 159f.
Leaney, A. R. C. *The Gospel according to St Luke* (BNTC), London, 1958.
Lechler, G. V. *The Apostolic and post-Apostolic Times*, Edinburgh, 1886.
Liechtenhahn, R. *Die urchristliche Mission. Voraussetzungen, Motive und Methoden*, Zürich, 1946.
Lietzmann, H. *An die Galater* (HNT 10), Tübingen, 1932.
Lightfoot, J. B. *The Epistle to the Galatians*, London, 1892.
Linton, O. 'The third aspect. A neglected point of view', *St. Th.*, 3 (1950–1), 79f.
Lohmeyer, E. *Kultus und Evangelium*, Göttingen, 1942.
Das Evangelium des Markus (KEK 1/2), Göttingen, 1951.
'Mir ist gegeben alle Gewalt', *IM*, pp. 22f.
Lohse, E. 'Lukas als Theologe der Heilsgeschichte', *Ev. Th.*, 14 (1954), 256f.
'Die Bedeutung des Pfingstberichtes im Rahmen des Luk. Geschichtwerkes', *Ev. Th.*, 13 (1953), 422f.
'Ursprung und Prägung des christlichen Apostolates', *TZ*, 9 (1953), 259f.

'Missionarisches Handeln Jesu nach dem Evangelium Lukas', *TZ*, 10 (1954), 1f.

Loisy, A. *Les Actes des Apôtres*, Paris, 1920.

Luck, U. 'Kerygma, Tradition und Geschichte bei Lukas', *ZTK*, 57 (1960), 51f.

Manson, T. W. *The Sayings of Jesus*, London, 1950.

Jesus and the non-Jews, London, 1955.

'St Paul in Ephesus: 2. The problem of the epistle to the Galatians', *BJRL*, 24 (1940), 59f.

Manson, W. *The Gospel of Luke*, London, 1930.

Martin-Achard, R. *A Light to the Nations*, London, 1962.

Marxsen, W. *Der Evangelist Markus. Studien zur Redaktionsgeschichte des Evangeliums* (FRLANT 67), Göttingen, 1959.

Meinertz, M. *Jesus und die Heidenmission*, Münster, 1925.

Menoud, P. H. 'Pendant quarante jours (Acts 1: 3)', in *Neotestamentica et Patristica*, Festschrift for O. Cullmann, Leiden, 1962, pp. 148f.

'Le Plan des Actes des Apôtres', *NTS*, 1 (1954–5), 44f.

Metzger, B. 'Seventy or seventy-two disciples?', *NTS*, 5 (1958–9), 299f.

Michaelis, W. *Der Herr verzieht nicht die Verheissung. Die Aussagen Jesu über die Nähe des Jüngsten Tages*, Bern, 1942.

Michel, O. 'Der Abschluss des Matthäusevangeliums', *Ev. Th.*, 10 (1950–1), 16f.

Minear, P. S. 'A note on Lk. 22: 36', *Nov. Test.*, 7 (1964), 128f.

'Luke's use of the birth-stories', *SLA*, pp. 111f.

Moltmann, J. *Theology of Hope*, London, 1967.

Moore, A. L. *The Parousia in the New Testament*, Leiden, 1966.

Moore, G. F. *Judaism in the First Centuries of the Christian Era*, vols. I–III, Cambridge, 1927–30.

Mosbech, H. '"Apostolos" in the New Testament', *St. Th.*, 2 (1949–50), 166f.

Moule, C. F. D. 'The Ascension', *ET*, 68 (1957), 205f.

'Once more, who were the Hellenists?', *ET*, 70 (1959), 100f.

Munck, J. *Paul and the Salvation of Mankind*, London, 1959.

'Paul, the Apostles and the Twelve', *St. Th.*, 3 (1950–1), 96f.

Mussner, F. 'Einige Parallelen aus den Qumrantexten zur Areopagrede', *BZ*, 1 (1957), 125f.

Nauck, W. 'Die Tradition und Komposition der Areopagrede', *ZTK*, 53 (1956), 11f.

Nickle, K. *The Collection*, London, 1966.

Nock, A. D. *St Paul*, Oxford, 1955.

Review of Haenchen, *Apg.*, *Gnomon*, 25 (1953), 506.

Norden, E. *Agnostos Theos*, Leipzig–Berlin, 1913.

Oepke, A. *Der Brief des Paulus an die Galater* (THNT 10), Berlin, 1957.

Oliver, H. H. 'The Lukan birth-stories and the purpose of Luke–Acts', *NTS*, 10 (1963–4), 202f.

O'Neill, J. C. *The Theology of Acts in its Historical Setting*, London, 1961.

Ott, W. *Gebet und Heil. Die Bedeutung der Gebetsparänese in der lukanischen Theologie*, Munich, 1965.

Owen, H. P. 'The scope of Natural Revelation in Rom. 1 and Acts 17', *NTS*, 5 (1958–9), 133f.

Parker, P. 'Once more, Acts and Galatians', *JBL*, 86 (1967), 175f.

Pieper, J. *Über die Hoffnung*, 1949, quoted in Moltmann, *Hope*, p. 23.

Plooij, D. 'The work of St Luke: a historical apology for Pauline preaching before the Roman court', *Expos.*, vii/8 (1914), 511f.

Pohlenz, M. 'Paulus und die Stoa', *ZNW*, 42 (1949), 66f.

Preiss, T. *Life in Christ*, London, 1954.

Ramsay, W. M. *St Paul the Traveller and Roman Citizen*, London, 1903.

Ramsey, A. M. 'The Ascension', *SNTS*, 2 (1951), 49f.

Reicke, B. *Glaube und Leben der Urgemeinde*, Zurich, 1957.

'Die Verfassung der Urgemeinde im Lichte jüdischen Dokumente', *TZ*, 10 (1954), 95f.

'Instruction and discussion in the travel narrative', *SE*, 1 (1959), 206f.

'Der geschichtliche Hintergrund des Apostelkonzils und der Antiochia-Episode', *SP*, pp. 172f.

Rengstorf, K. H. *Das Evangelium nach Lukas* (NTD 3), Göttingen, 1966.

'The election of Matthias', in *Current Issues in New Testament Interpretation*, ed. W. Klassen and G. F. Snyder, London, 1962, pp. 178f (cf. *St. Th.* 11 (1962), 35f).

Richardson, P. *Israel and the Apostolic Church* (Cambridge, 1969), pp. 159–65.

Robinson, D. F. 'A note on Acts 11: 27–30', *JBL*, 63 (1944), 179f.

Robinson, J. A. T. *Jesus and His Coming*, London, 1957.

Robinson, Jnr., W. C. *Der Weg des Herrn. Studien zur Geschichte und Eschatologie im Lukasevangelium*, Hamburg, 1964.

Rössler, D. *Gesetz und Geschichte. Eine Untersuchung zur Theologie der jüdischen Apokalyptik und die pharisäischen Orthodoxie* (WMANT 3), Neukirchen, 1960.

Sahlin, H. *Der Messias und das Gottesvolk*, Uppsala, 1945.

Sanders, J. N. 'Peter and Paul in Acts', *NTS*, 2 (1955–6), 133f.

Sass, G. 'Die Apostel in der Didache', *IM*, pp. 233f.

Schille, G. 'Die Himmelfahrt', *ZNW*, 57 (1966), 183f.

Schlatter, A. *Das Evangelium des Lukas*, Stuttgart, 1960.

Schlier, H. *Der Brief an die Galater* (KEK 7), Göttingen, 1962.

Schmithals, W. *Paul and James*, London, 1965.

Das kirchliche Apostelamt (FRLANT 79), Göttingen, 1961.

Schneider, J. 'Zur Analyse des lukanischen Reiseberichtes', in *Synoptische Studien*, Festschrift for A. Wikenhauser, Munich, 1953, pp. 207f.

Schniewind, J. *Das Evangelium nach Matthäus* (NTD 2), Göttingen, 1950.

Das Evangelium nach Markus (NTD 1), Göttingen, 1949.

Schoeps, H. J., *Paul*, London, 1961.

Schubert, P. 'The Structure and significance of Lk. 24', *NS*, pp. 165f.

Schurmann, H. 'Zur Traditions- und Redaktionsgeschichte von Matt. 10: 23f', *BZ*, n.F. 3 (1959), 82f.

'Lu. 22: 19–20 als ursprüngliche Textüberlieferung', *Bib.*, 32 (1951), 364f, 522f.

'Matt. 10: 5–6', in *Neutestamentliche Aufsätze*, for J. Schmid, Regensburg, 1963, pp. 270f.

Schweitzer, A. *The Quest of the Historical Jesus*, London, 1954.

Schweizer, E. 'Zu Apg. 1: 16–20', *TZ*, 14 (1958), 46.

The Spirit of God, London, 1961.

Church Order in the New Testament, London, 1961.

Sharman, H. *Son of Man and Kingdom of God*, London, 1944.

Simon, M. *St Stephen and the Hellenists*, London, 1956.

Sleeper, C. 'Pentecost and Resurrection', *JBL*, 84 (1965), 389f.

Spitta, F. *Jesus und die Heidenmission*, Giessen, 1909.

Stählin, G. *Die Apostelgeschichte* (NTD 5), Göttingen, 1966.

Stauffer, E. 'Jüdisches Erbe im urchristlichen Kirchenrecht', *TLZ*, 77 (1952), 210f.

Stempvoort, P. A. van. 'The interpretation of the Ascension in Luke–Acts', *NTS*, 5 (1958–9), 30f.

Strecker, G. 'Die sogenannte zweite Jerusalemreise des Paulus, Apg., 11: 27–30', *ZNW*, 53 (1962), 67f.

Streeter, B. *The Four Gospels. A Study of Origins*, London, 1924.

Stuhlmacher, P. *Das Paulinische Evangelium. I Vorgeschichte* (FRLANT 95), Göttingen, 1968.

Sundkler, B. 'Jésus et les Païens', *RHPhR*, 16 (1936), 491f.

Talbert, C. H. *Luke and the Gnostics*, New York, 1966.

Taylor, V. *The Gospel according to St Mark*, London, 1952.

Tödt, H. *The Son of Man in the Synoptic Tradition*, London, 1965.

Trocmé, E. *Le 'Livre des Actes' et l'Histoire*, Paris, 1957.

Vielhauer, Ph. 'On the "Paulinism" of Acts', *SLA*, pp. 33f.

Waitz, H. 'Das Problem des sogenannten Aposteldekrets', *ZKG*, 55 (1936), 227f.

Wellhausen, J. *Kritische Analyse der Apostelgeschichte*, Berlin, 1914.

Wetter, G. P. 'Das älteste hellenistische Christentum nach der Apostelgeschichte', *ARW*, 21 (1922), 397f.

Wikenhauser, A. *Die Apostelgeschichte* (Regensburger Neues Testament 5), Regensburg, 1961.

Wilckens, U. *Die Missionsreden in der Apostelgeschichte* (WMANT 5), Neukirchen, 1963.

'Interpreting Luke–Acts in a period of existentialist theology', *SLA*, pp. 6of.

'Die Bekehrung des Paulus als religionsgeschichtliches Problem', *ZTK*, 56 (1959), 273f.

Wilder, A. N. *Eschatology and Ethics in the Teaching of Jesus*, New York, 1950.

'Variant traditions of the Resurrection in Luke–Acts', *JBL*, 62 (1943), 307f.

Williams, C. S. C. *A Commentary on the Acts of the Apostles* (BNTC), London, 1964.

Windisch, H. 'Die Christophanie von Damaskus (Act. 9, 22, 26) und ihre religionsgeschichtlichen Parallelen', *ZNW*, 31 (1932), 1f.

Wink, W. *John the Baptist in the Gospel Tradition*, Cambridge, 1968.

Winter, P. *On the Trial of Jesus*, Berlin, 1961.

Wood, H. G. 'The conversion of Paul; its nature, antecedents and consequences', *NTS*, 1 (1954–5), 176f.

I. INDEX OF PASSAGES

NEW TESTAMENT

INDEX OF AUTHORS

INDEX OF SUBJECTS

24313706R00184

Printed in Great Britain
by Amazon